Jews for Sale?

Jews for Sale?

Nazi-Jewish Negotiations, 1933-1945

Yehuda Bauer

Yale University Press New Haven and London

Dedicated to the Max and Rita Haber Research Endowment Fund in
Holocaust Studies, Institute of Contemporary Jewry, Hebrew University

Designed by Sonia L. Scanlon.

Set in Ehrhardt type by Marathon Typography
Service, Inc., Durham, North Carolina.

Printed in the United States of America by Vail-Ballou Press, Binghamton,
New York.

Library of Congress Cataloging-in-Publication Data

Bauer, Yehuda.

Jews for sale? : Nazi-Jewish negotiations, 1933–1945 / Yehuda Bauer.

p.   cm.

Includes bibliographical references and index.

ISBN 0-300-05913-2 (cloth)

0-300-06852-2 (pbk.)

1. Jews—Germany—History—1933–1945.   2. Holocaust, Jewish (1939–1945)—
Germany.   3. World War, 1939–1945—Jews—Rescue—Germany.   4. Germany—
Emigration and immigration.   I. Title.

DS135.G3315B38   1994

940.53'18'0943—dc20   94-27780

CIP

A catalogue record for this book is available from the British Library.

The paper in this book meets the guidelines for permanence and
durability of the Committee on Production Guidelines for Book
Longevity of the Council on Library Resources.

10 9 8 7 6 5 4 3 2

Contents

Acknowledgments vii

List of Abbreviations ix

Note on Names xiii

Prologue 1

1
Deliverance Through Property Transfer 5

2
Failure of a Last-Minute Rescue Attempt 30

3
Enemies with a Common Interest 44

4
The Road to the "Final Solution" 55

5
"Willy" 62

6
What Really Did Happen in Slovakia? 91

7
Himmler's Indecision, 1942–1943 102

8
Dogwood's Chains 120

9
Satan and the Soul—Hungary, 1944 145

10
The Mission to Istanbul 172

11
The Bridge at Saint Margarethen 196

12
The Swiss Talks and the Budapest Tragedy 222

13
The Final Months 239

Epilogue 252

Notes 261
Bibliography 291
Index 297

Acknowledgments

This book is the result of a protracted research effort initiated and supported by the Institute of Jewish Affairs in London under the direction of Steven Roth, whose help and interest kept it going for years. His successors, Michael May and later Antony Lerman, were equally helpful, and I am grateful to the IJA for releasing me from formal obligations to them. I am also grateful to Mary Pasti of Yale University Press for having been such an efficient and kind editor.

I used materials from the National Archives in Washington, D.C., where the help and kindness extended to me by Robert Wolfe and, especially, by John Taylor and other members of the staff of the Military Archives were outstanding. The late Martin Broszat was equally helpful at the Institut für Zeitgeschichte in Munich, as were the archivists at the Bundesarchiv in Koblenz. The late Gyorgy Ranki in Hungary gave me some invaluable materials. I also wish to thank the staff of the British Public Records Office in Kew and the Swiss National Archives in Bern for their kindness.

Of the many friends whose help was essential in this venture, my collaboration with Barry Rubin was very important and enjoyable: we found "Dogwood" (Alfred Schwarz) and worked on his role in the OSS together. I am grateful to Gila Fatran, whose book on Slovakia, based on her Ph.D. dissertation, was of great importance in preparing this book. Shlomo Aronson, who worked on much the same material, reached similar, though not identical, conclusions, and we worked in harmony and mutual friendship; the same is true of Richard Breitman, whose comments were of crucial importance in the last stages of the work. Avraham Barkai prepared much of the material for the Ha'avarah chapter, and I wish to thank him very much for it. Dov Dinur worked on the Hungarian and the Swedish end and helped me a great deal. Rachel Arzt and Miriam Levine were the computer wizards who enabled me, a computer illiterate, to emerge into the present quarter-century. My overworked secretary, Ilana Dana, bore her fate with fortitude and solicitous care for her errant boss. Israel Gutman, my close companion, suffered my evolving theories with the skepticism they deserved. My daughters, Danit and Anat, provided me with the peace of mind that enabled me to write under difficult circumstances. Lastly, with love, I present this book to Ilaniki.

Abbreviations

AA

Auswärtiges Amt (German Foreign Office)

AB

Aliyah Beth ("Illegal" Jewish Immigration to Palestine; B immigration)

AHA

Aussenhandelsamt der AO (Foreign Trade Office of the AO)

AJC

American Jewish Committee

Altreu

Allgemeine Treuhandstelle für die jüdische Auswanderung
(General Trust Organization for Jewish Emigration)

AO

Auslandsorganisation der NSDAP (NSDAP Organization Abroad)

Ast

Aussenstelle der Abwehr (Branch Office of the Abwehr)

CIC

Counterintelligence Corps of the U.S. Army

DDSG

Deutsche Donau–Schiffahrtsgesellschaft
(German Danube Shipping Company)

FS

Freiwillige Schutzstaffel (Voluntary Defense Unit [Slovakia])

GG

Generalgouvernement (General [German] Government in Poland)

HG

Hlinková Garda (Hlinka Guard)

HIJEF

Hilfsverein für jüdische Flüchtlinge im Ausland
(Aid Organization for Jewish Refugees Abroad)

HSSPF

Höherer SS- und Polizeiführer (Higher SS and Police Leader)

Ia

Operations Officer

ICJ

Institute of Contemporary Jewry, Hebrew University

IGCR

Intergovernmental Committee for Refugees

IRC

International Red Cross

JA

Jewish Agency for Palestine

JAE

Jewish Agency Executive

JDC

American Jewish Joint Distribution Committee

KRIPO

Kriminalpolizei (Criminal Police)

NSDAP

Nationalsozialistische deutsche Arbeiter-Partei (Nazi Party)

OSS

Office of Strategic Services

PKR

Podkarpatská Rus (Subcarpathian Russia; Karpatalja in Hungarian)

RDB

Reichsstelle für Devisenbeschaffung (Reich Office for Currency
Acquisition, Foreign Currency Office)

RELICO

Relief Committee (Committee for Relief of the War-Stricken
Jewish Population)

RM

Reichsmark

RSHA

Reichsicherheitshauptamt (Central Reich Security Office)

RV

Reichsvertretung der Juden in Deutschland (Reich Representation of
Jews in Germany)

RVE

Reichsvereinigung der Juden in Deutschland (Reich Union of
Jews in Germany)

RWM

Reichswirtschaftsministerium (Ministry of Economic Affairs)

SD

Sicherheitsdienst der SS (SS Security Service)

SFR

Swiss franc

SI

Special Intelligence of the OSS

SIG

Schweizerischer Israelitischer Gemeindebund (Union of Swiss Jewish
Communities)

SIME

Secret Intelligence Middle East, a branch of the SIS

SIPO

Sicherheitspolizei (Security Police)

SIS

Secret Intelligence Service [British]

SL'S

Slovenská L'udová Strana (Slovak Peoples' Party)

SO

Special Operations of the OSS

SS

Schutzstaffel (Protection Troop)

ÚHÚ
Ústredný Hospodársky Úrad (Central Economic Office)

ÚŽ
Ústredna Židov (Jewish Center)

Vaada
Va'adat Ezrah Vehatzalah (Aid and Rescue Committee [Budapest])

VH
Va'ad Hahatzalah shel haRabonim (Rescue Committee of [Orthodox] Rabbis [in the United States])

WJC
World Jewish Congress

WRB
War Refugee Board [United States]

WVHA
Wirtschaftsverwaltungshauptamt (Central Office of Economic Administration)

ZAV
Zusatzausfuhrverfahren (Arrangement for Additional Exports)

ZO
Zionist Organization

ŽÚÚ
Židovská Ústredná Úradovna (Central Jewish Office)

Note on Names

Many Jews who lived or live in Israel changed their original family name to a Hebrew-sounding one. I have usually employed those names with which the reader may be more familiar or which were or are more commonly used when these individuals are mentioned in the context of the events described in this book. The other names appear in parentheses.

Prologue

Jews attempted to save Jews from the Nazis through negotiations, and for varying motives a few Nazis entered into such discussions. Most of the attempts failed; some succeeded to a very limited degree. But considering them might be of importance, because they raise a host of historical, philosophical, and moral issues.

Up to now the historical literature has dealt with the Jewish side of these contacts, both before and during the war, though not exhaustively so. The aims of the Jews were quite understandable: before the war they wanted to help Jews emigrate from a country ruled by a threateningly antisemitic regime; during the war they wanted to save Jews, either by enabling them to escape from Nazi domination or by protecting them within Nazi Europe or even by stopping the murder machine through massive bribes. Prior to 1939 the Jews had no political clout and no influence to speak of in the West—contrary to popular belief. After 1939 they lacked, in addition, military forces, or a government-in-exile, central command, or united community anywhere, whether in Europe or in the free world, and had no influence in Allied councils. They therefore resorted to bluffing, to offering ransoms, to bribing Nazis, and to persuading and pleading with the Allies for the lives of the people under Nazi domination.

Was there a realistic chance of saving more Jews from the Holocaust? The main problem is, What were the Nazis prepared to do? Their motives, and especially the motives of Heinrich Himmler, the *Reichsführer*, or leader, of the SS—the organization that committed a large proportion of the killing—and his closest advisers, have not been adequately examined. Even had the Nazis been ready to fulfill any promises they might make to the Jews, were the Allies ready to act upon such offers?

Any examination of Nazi policies toward the Jews and of Jewish reactions to these policies will have to start with the Nazi assumption of power in 1933. It was then that the prewar Nazi policy of emigration was established, and we shall have to see what the guiding principles of these policies and their practical applications were. The

1

main purpose of the first chapters that follow is to set the stage for an examination of the later Nazi policies of mass murder during the war and to discover any elements that persisted into the second stage, as well to find out whether, in fact, the policies of extrusion, expulsion, and even emigration were completely abandoned once the mass murder started in 1941 or whether, under certain conditions, the Nazis might have reverted to the less horrific alternatives. We also need to consider whether Jewish leadership groups were aware of the possibility that the Nazis might have reverted to such alternatives, and what the prospects of utilizing such policies were in the light of Allied concerns during the war.

After a brief examination of the processes that led to the decision to murder the Jewish people, we will examine the contacts that Jewish groups established with the SS—in fact, with Himmler. Equally, we will have to see whether Himmler himself attempted to forge such contacts, and when and to what purpose. Both questions will have to be viewed against the background of the internal struggle in Germany between the regime and its conservative opponents, who ultimately tried to assassinate Hitler on July 20, 1944. The conservatives had tried to work for a separate peace with the Western Allies: Did Himmler consider parallel options, and when? What did he do to realize them, and under what conditions? Did he try to use Jewish contacts for such a policy? Was he willing to release Jews if the conditions were right from the SS point of view? Would the Allies have accepted such refugees?

The complex of problems that we will be dealing with forces us to face another, more profound question: Was the "Final Solution" the result of an immutable, final decision by the Nazi murderers? If emigration, extrusion, or exchange of Jews was remotely feasible even *after* 1941, how can we explain this against the somber background of continuous and radical murder? Is it not possible to argue that there was no inherent contradiction between the Nazi design to murder all the Jews everywhere and their willingness to compromise temporarily, to permit the flight of some Jews from their domain in return for real advantages to the Reich? If the Nazis expected to be in control, directly or indirectly, of the whole world, might they not have seen the flight of *some* Jews as purely temporary, because they would catch up with those escapees sooner or later? What may answers to these questions tell us about Nazi psychology? How might such an inquiry affect our understanding of what some of us call radical evil?

These and other issues will be discussed in detail below. The Holocaust was a watershed event in human history. Attempts at rescue from the Holocaust were a sideshow, but their implications are very significant. The discussion may throw light on human motivations, and it finally brings us back to questions of personal and public ethics with which we grapple in the generations after the Holocaust.

In Israel the controversies over the behavior of Jewish leadership groups during the Holocaust have been a decisive factor in the political and intellectual development of the country. In 1954 a trial was held in Tel Aviv. Reszoe (Israel) Kasztner, the man who had negotiated with the Nazis in Hungary in 1944 for the release of Jews (rather, the state prosecutor did in a reluctant Kasztner's name), accused Malkiel Grünwald, a Hungarian Jew—not a Holocaust survivor—of slandering him by saying that Kasztner was a corrupt traitor to the Jewish cause. A brilliant right-wing attorney for the defense, Shmuel Tamir, turned the trial around, and Kasztner had to defend himself against accusations that implicated not just him but the Jewish Agency for Palestine (JA), the central Zionist body, the majority of whose executives had resided in Palestine during the war and had constituted the political leadership of Palestinian Jews. The Jewish Agency, and the Israeli governments that followed after the Israeli war of independence in 1948, was led by a left-center coalition that Tamir opposed. He accused the government parties and especially the left of betraying Jews and collaborating with the Germans; he also implied that they had been guilty of the same collaboration with the British in Palestine prior to Jewish independence there, and he linked the two charges. It was the beginning of the end for center-left governance in Israel. Kasztner was assassinated by right-wing extremists in 1957, after a weak judge had handed down a verdict that exonerated Grünwald on most counts, thereby in effect finding Kasztner guilty. A year later the Supreme Court quashed the sentence and justified most, but not all, of Kasztner's acts. The public reacted differently, however, and the 1977 swing in favor of the rightist Likud party was in some degree due to the Kasztner Affair. It was a moral judgment no less than a political one. The problem that arose then, and that still arises in Jewish, especially Israeli, society is whether Kasztner was justified in negotiating with the Nazis. What were the moral and political implications of such negotiations? Needless to say, the questions about Nazi intentions in these tentative contacts, which are the subject of our inquiry, are different in quality from the charges and countercharges of 1954–55.

Finally, this book departs in a perhaps not unimportant way from accepted historical writing. It deals with might-have-beens, with historical lines of development that did not come to fruition or that were stunted, although their imprints can, I believe, be discerned in available documentation. Such a treatment of historical material is based on the rejection of historical determinism, one of whose most common, if not always admitted, fallacies is the assumption that because something happened, it had to happen. But Hitler might have been stopped by the Western powers had they managed to forge an alliance, albeit a temporary one, with the Soviet Union in the mid or late 1930s, or even had they acted on their own. Nazi Germany might well have

won the war had it postponed the attack on the Soviet Union and instead conquered the Mediterranean Basin and the Middle East; it might have won the
war even without that, had it pursued a different policy toward the conquered
territories in the Soviet Union and had it concentrated on the conquest of
Moscow in 1942; it might have averted defeat had it concentrated its efforts on
developing the jet fighter, which was already in service in the German Air
Force in early 1945—and so on. The art of the historian—history is hardly a
science—is not just to describe and explain what happened and why but also
to discover the beginnings of processes that realistically could have taken
place but did not, or, in other words, to deal with causal chains that failed to
become main directions of development and then to explain why this was so.
Maybe historians are not supposed to do this, but there is hardly a historian
who does not. Here, at least, I am going to do so consciously.

This, then, is the purpose of the book: to find the start of developments
that might have brought about different events, even slightly different, from
the ones that actually occurred.

1

Deliverance Through Property Transfer

The danger had been apparent to many—Jews and non-Jews alike—but the Nazi accession to power was nonetheless a shock to most people: on January 30, 1933, the senile President of Germany, Paul von Hindenburg, asked Adolf Hitler to become Reich Chancellor. Hitler did not—contrary to post-1945 popular belief—come to power by winning an election. Almost the opposite is true: In the last free election in pre-Hitler Germany, in November 1932, the Nazis lost thirty-four seats in the Reichstag (parliament), or some two million votes, and their share of the vote declined from 37.3 percent to 33.1 percent, although they remained the strongest single faction in a Reichstag of 584 seats. The number of Social-Democratic seats declined from 133 to 121, but the Communists' share rose from 89 to 100. The weakening of the Nazi position, combined with the failure of the military-led government to ensure stability and the rising threat of communism, led the right-wing supporters of a more autocratic solution to Germany's problems to persuade Hindenburg to call upon Hitler to be Chancellor. He would not, they thought, be too dangerous a threat to their position. But as we know, by the summer of 1933 the Nazis had abolished all parties and trade unions, although they left in their previous positions some of the old-time conservatives not too strongly identified with their former right-wing parties; Baron Konstantin von Neurath remained Foreign Minister, and Lutz Schwerin von Krosigk, Finance Minister.

Nazi policies toward the Jews were ill defined; the original Nazi Party platform of 1920 promised to deny Jews citizens' rights and expel all Jewish immigrants who had entered Germany after 1914. By implication, large Jewish retail stores were threatened, and all Jews engaged in journalism, including owners of newspapers, would be removed from their positions; generally, the "Jewish materialistic" spirit was decried. As the new administration took hold, a centrally important addition emerged: to get rid of as many Jews as quickly as possible through emigration.

By September 1933, Jews had been removed from all government or government-controlled positions, with a few exceptions for war veterans. An economic boycott took effect for one day, on April 1. Many Jews were arrested and tortured in makeshift interrogation centers established mostly by the Nazi storm troopers (*Sturmabteilung,* or SA); in most cases they were not arrested as Jews but as opponents of the regime, although they were generally treated more harshly than non-Jews. Support for the former democratic parties disintegrated; the churches were silent, and the Nazis made an attempt to capture the majority Protestants by establishing a German Christian church (Deutsche Christen). The opposition within German Protestantism slowly reorganized and established the Confessing Church, the vast majority of whose clergy disagreed with the regime on purely theological grounds, thus tacitly accepting the antisemitic Nazi program. Most Germans entered the Nazi orbit and, it is generally assumed, agreed with what in retrospect would be regarded as the more "moderate" elements of Nazi antisemitism: deprivation of citizenship; removal from the economic, social and cultural life of German society; confiscation of property; and forced emigration.

Here it is important to realize that the Nazi regime was polyarchic—that is, it consisted of partly autonomous, sometimes largely autonomous, fiefdoms that were constantly feuding. Uniformity in affairs of central importance was achieved through the intervention of the dictator, who set down lines of policy and adjudicated disputes. Theories that Hitler was a weak dictator can hardly be defended any longer.[1]

The Jews of Germany numbered about half a million, or less than 1 percent of the population. Of these, about 20 percent were immigrants from Eastern Europe who had arrived after 1900. Most German Jews were religious liberals (corresponding mostly to the contemporary American Conservatives, though there were Reform-like congregations, especially in the cities). A strictly Orthodox minority accounted for some 10 percent. A strong movement toward conversion to Christianity in the nineteenth century had weakened in the twentieth, but there was a growing rate of intermarriage and a clear trend toward an aging and dying-out of the community. The Zionist movement took in a small minority of perhaps 10 percent in the community. Almost all German Jews were devoted German patriots, including the Orthodox and the Zionists. Except for the latter, they believed in a German-Jewish symbiosis, in complete acculturation, where the only difference between Jews and other Germans would be religious. Most German Jews insisted on belonging to a separate religious community, however. Somewhat in contradiction to their ideology, they maintained links with other Jewish centers, chiefly in the West. Germans, on the other hand, overwhelmingly viewed the Jews as non-Germans, except in the formal sense of shared citizenship, and the opinion of many, even the most liberal-minded, was that full acceptance of Jews in German society was conditional on the Jews abandoning their Jewishness altogether.[2] It was a one-sided love affair; and one-sided love affairs are not usually very successful.

German Zionists were an important part of the world Zionist movement, the center of which had moved from Germany to Britain in the wake of World War I and the Balfour Declaration of 1917, in which the British had promised the Jews a National Home in Palestine. By 1933 the World Zionist movement had established a governing body, the Jewish Agency for Palestine (JA), which in theory was to have a 50 percent representation of non-Zionist Jews but was in fact almost wholly Zionist. The non-Zionists, mainly the American Jewish Committee and similar bodies in the United States, the Anglo-Jewish Association in Britain, and important groups of wealthy people in France, Germany, and elsewhere, were committed to supporting the upbuilding of Palestine as a refuge for those Jews who had nowhere to go but shied away from the Zionist political aim of a Jewish political entity—a state or a commonwealth in Palestine. Zionists and non-Zionists who in one way or another supported the settlement of Jews in Palestine were at loggerheads; there were also important Jewish groups who opposed Zionism altogether, such as extreme assimilationist groups in the West, including Germany, and ultraorthodox Jews on the other end of the spectrum, including most of the Orthodox German Jewish community.

A central organization of German Jews never existed. Liberal and Reform communities were organized by German state, and Orthodox communities were organized separately. The Centralverein deutscher Staatsbürger jüdischen Glaubens, or CV (Central Union of German Citizens of the Jewish Faith)—a basically Liberal grouping, though with some Zionist representation—had been organized in 1897 to fight antisemitism, and it did so courageously and consistently; it supported anti-antisemitic German politicians and intellectuals financially and morally, it fought legal battles against antisemites, and it even organized a clandestine information service and supported Jewish street fighters who were part of the social-democratic militia called the Reichsbanner. It failed, of course, as did all Jewish attempts at fighting antisemitism that were not supported by a majority in the general population.

German Zionists saw the rise of Nazism as consistent with their pessimistic view of Gentile society. Nobody foresaw the Holocaust; and although the Zionist dream of emigrating to Palestine remained theoretical before 1933—the number of German Jews who emigrated there was very small—the realization now spread that the revocation of Jewish emancipation in Germany was final and that Jews would have to emigrate—over a fairly long period, it was hoped, enabling the Zionist movement to direct the stream of emigration largely to Palestine. Most (but not all) Liberals, on the other hand, initially saw in Nazism a transitory phenomenon and thought that only those whose livelihood or politics was directly threatened by the Nazis should emigrate. This attitude changed especially after 1935.

What options did Jews have in reacting to the unleashing of what seemed to be the darkest, most backward-looking forces in European society? After all, Jews generally were among the liberal segments of German society, hoping for progress and a developing emancipation from restrictive nationalistic and antisemitic ideologies. Their view of Nazism as a reactionary force disregarded its modernistic elements, which we see more clearly in retrospect.[3] Jews elsewhere in the world tended to share the views of either liberal German Jews or their Zionist protagonists.

German Jews had no allies in Germany under the new, threatening dictatorship, whose aims regarding the Jews were unclear even to itself. They were a tiny minority in the population and could not dream of physical or other active resistance. "World Jewry" was largely a figment of antisemitic imagination; Jews were split politically and religiously and were patriots of their several host countries. Non-Zionist and anti-Zionist Jews outside Germany wanted to defend German Jewish rights in Germany, in part at least to avoid a flood of immigration into their countries, which might give rise to antisemitism there. Zionists in Palestine were afraid of violent dislocations and wanted an orderly, slow exodus that would help them in building up Palestine. The obvious answer for both, but especially for the Zionists, was to negotiate with the Nazis. The Nazis wanted to get rid of the Jews, didn't they? And the Zionists wanted to absorb them gradually in Palestine—as moneyed settlers, not impoverished refugees. Both sides, for opposing reasons, needed to maintain contact with each other, as only real friends and real enemies do. The result was negotiations over the orderly exit of Jews with capital from Germany.

What was the background to Zionist policies in 1933?

The world economic crisis, which triggered the rise of Nazism, created a new situation for the Zionist movement as well. Two trends impacted on it. On the one hand, the impoverished Jewish masses in Eastern Europe could not stay where they were, because of economic antisemitism and poverty, especially in Poland and Romania; and on the other hand, the crisis had caused a dramatic reduction in voluntary contributions to Zionist funds, primarily in the United States. The British government in Palestine was willing in the early 1930s to increase Jewish immigration into the country if employment was found. But providing employment required capital investments, and these were not forthcoming. Now the rise of Nazism in Germany meant that wealthy German Jews might be willing to transfer their money to Palestine if they could thereby save it, although the vast majority of them had no great sympathy for Zionism. In fact, it seemed for a while as if German Jewish capital would be the *only* major source of funds for Jewish Palestine—a fear that was not realized. Zionist leaders saw the "rescue" of Jewish capital from Germany as a way to encourage emigration; German Jews, known for their excellent education and proficiency in technical matters, would be a crucial addition to those limited numbers of poor Polish and Romanian Jews who would come because of the new capital influx. No one foresaw the Holocaust, and the small Jewish Yishuv (the Jewish population in Palestine— 278,000 souls in 1932) was quite incapable of solving the Jewish emigration problems of either Eastern or Central Europe. But the Zionists thought that over some years they could build the capacity to accept larger numbers of immigrants.[4] What was needed was an arrangement with the new German government that would permit Jews, along with their capital, to leave Germany for Palestine.

The Auswärtiges Amt, or AA (German Foreign Office), took up the issue of Jewish capital transfers on the initiative of its Jerusalem consul, Heinrich Wolff (who was married to a Jew and was therefore dismissed at the end of 1935). Sam Cohen, head of a private company in Palestine called Hanotea, became interested in utilizing German Jewish capital to further local citrus-growing. He established contact with the consul and planned to visit Berlin to arrange for a transfer of capital. But even prior to Cohen's journey to Berlin, Wolff argued in a letter (March 24, 1933) that owing to a more or less unofficial Jewish boycott of German goods in the wake of the Nazi rise to power, orders placed by local Jews with German firms had dropped by 90 percent— this was untrue—and that while local trade with Germany was not very important, the central position of Palestine Jewry within World Jewry might lead to a worldwide boycott that would harm Germany no end. It was less important for German propaganda to deny pogroms in Germany, because East European Jews were used to pogroms; it was much more important to point to the possibility of emigrating with some property. He, Wolff, was sending someone to Germany with practical proposals. That somebody was Sam Cohen.[5] In another letter, dated June 15, Wolff returned to the same argument; it was vitally important, he said, to overcome the danger of the boycott, and Sam Cohen was ideally placed to help in this. He had bought into an important Hebrew daily paper (*Doar Hayom*) and promised to turn it into an effective tool of pro-German propaganda. At the time the letter was written, Cohen was already in Germany, and Wolff added that the Jews were investing heavily in the development of Palestine and should be persuaded not to buy basic equipment from Germany's competitors, such as Czechoslovakia (irrigation pipes, for instance). In another letter, on June 23, Wolff said that according to Cohen an international Jewish meeting would soon take place in London, where a boycott of Germany would be discussed, with likely deleterious results for German interests; it was therefore important that a decision be reached soon at the German Foreign Office.[6]

What bothered Wolff and the Foreign Office in 1933 was the economic danger of a Jewish boycott and its political ramifications. Encouragement of Jewish emigration was secondary at this point. What made Wolff such an enthusiastic supporter of Sam Cohen, as opposed to official Zionist bodies, is not clear. One source suspects that Wolff was getting or was hoping to get some material advantage from Cohen, but regardless, Wolff was undoubtedly hoping to impress his superiors with advice that was going to save Germany from the effects of a Jewish anti-Nazi boycott.[7]

Sam Cohen's attempt to approach the Nazi government to permit the export of Jewish capital in a way that would be attractive to the Germans was picked up by the leaders of the Jewish Agency, especially by the head of its political department, the young Labor leader Haim Arlosoroff. Arlosoroff knew Germany very well and in fact had been a very close friend of Magda Quandt—the woman who became Joseph Goebbels's wife. In a series of intensive contacts conducted not only by Arlosoroff but also by other political and economic activists of the Jewish Agency (among them Levi Shkolnik-Eshkol, a future Israeli Prime Minister), an agreement was worked out between the Reichswirtschaftsministerium, or RWM (Ministry of Economic Affairs), and the agency; it was signed in August 1933. The details were rather complicated, but the general idea was that Jews with capital at their disposal would be permitted to buy German industrial goods, mainly tools of production—irrigation pipes, cement mixers, machinery—that were in demand in Palestine. The financial arm of the Jewish Agency in Palestine, the Anglo-Palestine Bank, found buyers interested in infrastructural German goods; the buyers then deposited the requisite sums of money to pay for them. A Jewish financial organization in Germany set up for the purpose, the Palästina Treuhandgesellschaft, or Paltreu (Palestine Trust Company), received money from German Jewish individuals and ordered the required goods from German industrial enterprises after paying what in effect were ransom taxes to the Nazi government. The goods were shipped to Palestine, and when the German Jewish investors arrived there, they received their money back in pounds sterling, minus deductions for Jewish national institutions and the like.

The results of this arrangement were, from the Jewish point of view, that Jewish capital could flee Germany without the Germans receiving any foreign currency in return. About 20,000 wealthy Jews managed to leave Germany with their capital—this was about 37 percent of all German Jewish immigrants to Palestine. Nearly 24,000 "capitalists" immigrated to Palestine from elsewhere, but they were only 15 percent of all immigrants from these other countries. The capitalist immigration made possible capital investments that enabled larger numbers of Jews—Polish, German, and others—to enter Palestine. For the Germans, the arrangement meant that Jews were encouraged to leave Germany and that German exports were boosted; and although no foreign currency accrued to the Reichsbank, spare parts and replacements would have to be ordered from Germany, giving a promise of future gains.

At the same time as Sam Cohen started his initiative with the help of Consul Wolff, Jewish bodies all over the world began organizing to fight the new Nazi government. The main weapon being discussed outside Germany was an economic boycott of the country. The initiators in the United States were the Jewish War Veterans, and they were followed by much of the Yiddish-speaking political and cultural elite of New York City. A big public meeting to protest Nazi policies was held in Madison Square Garden on March 27, 1933, organized mainly by the American Jewish Congress, and it was chaired by the congress president, Rabbi Stephen S. Wise. A number of prominent Jewish and non-Jewish speakers addressed the crowd. Voices there advocated a boycott, but Wise was hesitant. Some members of the German-Jewish New York aristocracy, headed by Louis Untermeyer, sided with the advocates of boycott, and they were encouraged by the spread of the idea in Europe among the small Jewish merchants and the poor Jewish masses generally. Neither in the United States nor in Europe were the bigger Jewish merchants enthusiastic about the idea. In Palestine, too, the popular mood was in favor of the boycott, but the Jewish public bodies did not encourage the idea. By the summer, however, the American Jewish Congress, with Wise now persuaded to support the boycott, had become the major Jewish body organizing the boycott movement, just when the Jewish Agency reached its agreement with the Nazi government, called Ha'avarah (transfer). Wise was a major leader of mainstream Zionists, and so were some other supporters of the boycott; and because Ha'avarah had been arranged by Zionist bodies in Palestine, a very sharp controversy ensued within the ranks of the Zionist leadership. In addition, an especially bitter fight against Ha'avarah was waged by the Revisionist movement, the right-wing opposition within Zionism. Their argument was that Ha'avarah was an agreement with enemies of the Jewish people, that every effort should be made to topple the Nazi government through an economic boycott, and that the masses of the Jewish people were prepared to fight the Nazis even if the official leadership of the Zionist movement was not. This argument was later adopted in some of the literature about Ha'avarah and the boycott movement.

True, the Nazis were wary of the harm that a Jewish-led boycott movement might do to their newly established government. Their own statewide boycott of Jewish businesses, shops, and professional services on April 1, 1933—originally intended to last until the Jews were forced out of the German economy—was in the end limited to one day (a Saturday, to boot) because of the meeting at Madison Square Garden on March 27 and the perceived threat of a worldwide anti-German boycott. The Nazi leadership actually believed their propaganda: they thought that the Jews controlled Western capitalism and Eastern Bolshevism and that the World Jewish conspiracy was immensely powerful and therefore very dangerous to them.

The question has been asked whether the boycott movement had any chance at all of toppling the Nazi regime in its infancy; and the Nazi fear of it seems at first glance to indicate a positive answer to that question. The truth, however, is that the boycott never posed a threat to the Nazi regime. Why?

The origins of the Ha'avarah agreement lay in the economic conditions of Germany in the 1930s. Two main issues are pertinent: the problem of unemployment, which, on the face of it, could have made the Germans wish to expand exports to provide additional work for their unemployed; and the strain on Germany's foreign currency resources due to the economic crisis generally, which could also have made them look for export opportunities. What, then, was the general condition of the German economy in the early years of Nazi rule? For purposes of comparison, let us choose two years: 1933, when the German economy began emerging from the crisis that had brought the Nazis to power, and 1936, a year before full employment was reached. The same year, 1937, was also the first year of the Four-Year Plan, overseen by Hermann Goering, that was intended to prepare Germany for war within four years, on the basis of Hitler's memorandum to him of August 1936.[8] It was also the year in which German hard currency reserves fell to their lowest level between 1931 and 1945.

Nazi policies, not unlike those of the American New Deal, concentrated on public works and priming the pump; they were implemented beginning immediately upon the assumption of power in January 1933. The results were impressive, as table 1 shows. The GNP grew by 43 percent, the national index by 46 percent, the industrial index by 88 percent, and the number of employed by 36 percent. The figure of 1.6 million unemployed meant that full employment had been more or less attained. Although rearmament became an important item after 1935 or so, affecting the free income per person, it is crucial for our analysis to note that economic gains were made without any significant contribution by way of foreign trade. The reason has to be sought primarily in ideology and politics, not in economic factors. During the worst period of the crisis, in 1929–32, most industrial countries tried to rely on themselves and closed their doors to imports as far as possible, but this changed toward the end of 1932. Although a policy of actively encouraging exports would not have sufficed to get Germany out of its predicament, it would have helped in the fight against unemployment and in the hunt for hard currency. Such a policy was opposed by the Nazis on ideological grounds, however. The priority of agriculture, the reliance on the domestic market, and the desire to solve problems by creating a larger domestic market that would be expanded by conquests and war was at the basis of Nazi thinking and influenced their economic policies. A struggle therefore developed between industrial interests concentrating on exports, on the one hand, and agricultural and other industrial interests concentrating on the domestic market, on the other—with both sides trying to persuade Nazi politicians of the importance of their respective arguments. A first decision in principle was set in place with Hitler's speech during the debate on the Empowering Act (Ermächtigungsgesetz) on March 23, 1933. There he spoke of the primary importance of duties and a differential pricing policy to protect agriculture; exports, which Germany could not give up altogether, came relatively low on the list of priorities.

In fact, there was little change between 1932 and 1936 in the total value of either imports or exports, despite rises in the GNP and in industrial production. The slight increase in 1937 is due to the rearmament program, which required imports of essential raw materials for military purposes (see tables 1 and 2).

It would appear, then, that the fight against unemployment by advancing exports through agreements, like the transfer of Jewish capital and resistance to the Jewish boycott, had little if any objective importance—which is not to say that it carried no weight at all with the decisionmakers in 1933. But these data do present the problem in its proper proportions: the whole matter was of very minor importance for the German economy at large. If foreign trade became a marginal issue for the German economy, then the advancement of the even more marginal trade with Palestine by means of transfer of capital there through exports of German goods could hardly be of major significance from the German economic point of view. As the elimination of unemployment proceeded and Germany became even less dependent on exports than at first, the attitudes toward Ha'avarah were bound to undergo a change for the worse. We must therefore ask why the Germans agreed to these transfers in the first place, and why they agreed to them until the outbreak of war in 1939.

In addition to the marginality of exports, the problem of the hard currency reserves gained increasing weight because, as we have seen, Germany gained little if any hard currency from the Ha'avarah agreement. With the rise in the standard of living and the attendant rise in demand, imports would grow. Also, to procure the foreign-made materials in locally produced goods required allocations of hard currency. The acquisition of materials and currency was restrained by the slow rise in real income and the controls on imports exercised by the authorities, but rearmament demanded expenditures of hard currency that could not be avoided. Some of the expenditures, again, were financed by bilateral agreements arranged by Hjalmar Schacht,

Table 1
The German Economy in 1932 and 1936

Key Indicators	1932	1936
GNP, based on current prices (in billions)	RM 58.0	RM 83.0
National income per person, based on current prices	RM 633.0	RM 922.0
Industrial index, including small industry (1913 = 100)	72.8	137.1
Employment (yearly average, in millions of people)	12.6	17.1
Unemployment (yearly average, in millions of people)	5.6	1.6

Sources: Avraham Barkai, *Hakalkalah Hanatzit* (Hebrew), Sifriat Poalim, Tel Aviv, 1986, p. 197; Barkai, *German Interests in the Haavara-Transfer Agreement,* in *Leo Baeck Institute Year Book,* vol. 35, Mohr, Tübingen, 1990, pp. 245–66.

the financial wizard in Nazi employ, but not everything could be paid for this way. Gold and hard currency reserves fell alarmingly (see table 3).

Strict control over foreign currency dealings had been imposed by the Bruening government in 1931, when foreign capital began to flee Germany. A capital flight tax (*Reichsfluchtsteuer*) was imposed on emigrants who took with them sums in excess of 200,000 Reichsmark. The Nazi government introduced stricter measures as the situation deteriorated. In the summer of 1933 interest payments to foreign creditors were suspended, and a unilateral moratorium on both capital and interest payments in foreign currency was declared. Liquid assets of emigrants were impounded in special accounts, and payments out of these accounts could be effected for exports, tourism, and such, only with special permission. Emigrants could, however, sell these Reichsmark accounts to the Reichsbank for half the price in hard currency.

In the summer of 1934 Schacht, who had been the Reichsbank president since March 1933, became Minister of the Economy. An even stricter control system was now introduced to secure a state monopoly on foreign trade. When Schacht refused to devalue the Reichsmark even after the pound and the dollar had been devalued, German exports became noncompetitive. To recoup the position, a system of differential export premiums was intro- duced, and these subsidies were financed by the income from the Reichsbank subsidiary, the Golddiskontbank, which bought the emigrants' accounts at half their value. Special taxes were also imposed on local production. In addi- tion, from May 1934 on, the capital flight tax was levied on all sums exceed- ing RM 50,000; this, of course, was directed primarily against Jewish emi-

Table 2

Foreign Trade in Germany, 1928–1937, Selected Years

Year	Total (in billions of RM)	Food and Other Agricultural Products (%)	Raw Materials (%)	Industrial Products (%)
		Exports		
1928	12.05	6.4	24.4	69.2
1932	5.74	3.8	18.0	78.2
1936	4.78	?	?	?
1937	5.92	1.5	19.0	79.5
		Imports		
1928	13.93	40.9	46.2	12.9
1932	4.65	32.7	51.7	15.6
1936	4.23	?	?	?
1937	5.49	37.4	54.4	7.3

Source: Adapted from Dietmar Petzina et al., *Sozialgeschichtliches Arbeitsbuch III (1914–1945)*, Munich, Beck, 1978, pp. 73–75.

grants.[9] When we add the difficulties facing Nazi Germany in the area of foreign currency to the overall picture of foreign trade, the question posed above—Why did the Germans agree to a transfer of Jewish capital to Palestine?—becomes even more poignant.

The fear of a boycott remained with the Nazis, and especially the Foreign Office, but it diminished when they realized that the power of World Jewry was weaker than they had imagined. As Germany grew stronger, fear of the boycott yielded to the desire to get rid of the Jews, which had been the basis of Nazi policies toward Jews from the beginning. The Jews were slow to realize that the situation had changed. In March 1935, as the Nineteenth Zionist Congress was being planned, Sam Cohen again raised the specter of the boycott in Berlin. The Reichsbank had until that time agreed to pay in foreign currency (cash!) the 1,000 pounds sterling that each capitalist immigrant to Palestine had to have to attain an immigration certificate. Now the Reichsbank decided to limit this privilege to a total of RM 1,000,000 monthly. If, Cohen argued, the limitation was not revoked, the result would be a strengthening of the pro-boycott circles at the Lucerne Zionist Congress in July. The Reichsbank was no longer impressed; and when Leo David of the Jewish Agency tried to threaten Hans Hartenstein of the Reichsstelle für

Table 3

Gold and Hard Currency Reserves of the Reichsbank, 1928–1938,
Selected Years

Yearly Averages in Millions of RM

1928	2,405.4	1935	91.0
1932	974.6	1936	75.2
1933	529.7	1937	74.6
1934	164.7	1938	76.4

Source: Taken from Wolfram Fischer, *Deutsche Wirtschaftspolitik, 1918–1945*, Peters, Lüneburg, 1961, p. 104.

Devisenbeschaffung, or RDB (Foreign Currency Office), with the boycott in March 1935, Hartenstein was no longer impressed, either. The Jews should be more interested in emigration than the Germans, he said.[10]

The Reichsbank's apparent willingness (up to 1936) to pay out hard cash to emigrants to Palestine is quite surprising. These payments were part of a package deal that the Bruening government signed in Basel on August 19, 1931, when the Western powers agreed to put a moratorium on German repayments of the World War I reparations. Part of the deal was that Germany would pay emigrants up to RM 2,000 per head in foreign currency. But this hardly explains why the Nazis not only kept this particular agreement— they were not exactly famous for keeping agreements in general—or why the Reichsbank agreed, albeit unwillingly, to pay out between RM 12,500 and RM 15,000 per family until the end of 1935. The only explanation seems to be that they saw it as an effective way of emigrating Jews. The fear of the boycott played no role at all.

To sum up: given the relatively insignificant part that foreign trade played in the German economy in 1933, even a successful boycott by Jews could have affected the German economy marginally at most. In fact, the anti-German boycott was never very influential; it scarcely harmed the already very small bilateral trade between the United States and Germany, and elsewhere it had very little effect—nor could the effect ever have been different. Given the world economic crisis and the prevalent ambivalence toward Jews—if not outright antisemitism—the chances of having large numbers of non-Jewish business owners join the movement were slim indeed. On the other hand, the Nazis really believed in a powerful World Jewish conspiracy, and totally illusionary though the conspiracy was, it initially affected their behavior.

The argument within the Jewish world was, it seemed, between a principled stand against a violently antisemitic regime and a pragmatic approach looking toward the strengthening of the Zionist enterprise in Palestine. In fact, both pragmatics and principles operated on both sides. The Revisionist leader, Vladimir Ze'ev Jabotinsky, who was struggling for power within the Zionist movement, violently opposed Ha'avarah, although it made for increased immigration of German and other Jews to Palestine, but he, too, negotiated, mainly after 1935, with the antisemitic Polish regime, which supported him to emigrate Jews to Palestine. For Wise there was the increasing pressure of enraged Jews in the United States demanding action against Nazi Germany. For the Palestinian Zionist leaders—fully supported, in this case, by the dominant figure in the Zionist movement, Chaim Weizmann, who was out of office at the time—the problem was how to ensure a future Jewish Palestine that would solve the pressing needs of Jewish emigration not only from Nazi Germany but also, and mainly, from countries like those of Eastern Europe where Jews could not, in their view, remain.

The question arose then and must arise today whether without Ha'avarah there would have been a massive German Jewish immigration into Palestine. After all, only one third of these immigrants were capitalists, and some, or perhaps many of them, would have come without Ha'avarah. On balance, however, the influx of capitalists was apparently a factor in encouraging immigration of other German Jews as well.

The arguments with which the proponents of Ha'avarah supported the project were often a mixture of the logical and the disingenuous. Thus, leading Agency politicians explained that the expansion of Ha'avarah to countries other than Palestine, which the Nazis had agreed to in part, was not controlled by them at all but by another organization, Intria. In fact, Intria was chaired by Siegfried Moses, one of the heads of the Ha'avarah organization. Also, while the leaders of Ha'avarah played down the damage done to the boycott movement by the agreement with Germany, they simultaneously played up their sabotage of the boycott in their negotiations with the Germans. Their campaign started with efforts in 1933 to persuade Consul Wolff in Jerusalem to give up his support of Sam Cohen and side with the Jewish Agency instead; if Wolff wanted to fight the boycott, they argued, Sam Cohen was not the right person to facilitate that fight.[11] The campaign continued in the repeated interviews that agency leaders had in Germany with German officials. Again, with Zionist leaders opposed to Ha'avarah the argument was that according to the decisions of the Lucerne Zionist Congress of 1935 the arrangement would be justified by an emergency. Such an emergency had occurred with the publication of the Nuremberg Laws in September 1935, said Georg Landauer to Louis Lipsky of the United States in 1936 —as though Ha'avarah had not been in existence prior to 1935.[12]

Another Zionist ideological argument was that at last Herzl's prophecy had come true: he had seen all nations as being basically anti-Jewish and had favored a large-scale exodus from the Diaspora. Now, with an extreme anti-

Jewish government in Germany, an opportunity had offered itself for an exodus that could be orderly and well organized, and here were opponents within the Zionist movement who did not dare to take full advantage of the situation. They should have.[13]

The ideology of the leading people in Ha'avarah can be summarized by saying that they were determined to advance the settlement of Palestine and to rescue Jewish capital from Germany for that purpose, though they were aware of their strike-breaking activity against the boycott; I must add, too, that they were aware of the weakness of the boycott movement and its inability to harm the Nazi regime seriously. They used the boycott argument in their talks with the Germans because they knew the Nazis believed in the existence of a world Jewish conspiracy, and hoped to gain concessions by evoking that fear.

Some of the people who gave money for Ha'avarah to save it and escape themselves lost 25 percent of their capital to the Nazis (until the situation got even worse in August 1937) plus another 30 percent or so to the manipulation of the exchange rates by the Nazis, and then some more for the (quite reasonable) administrative costs of Ha'avarah itself. Zionist organs in Palestine then saw to it that the bank in Palestine gave the immigrants some of their money in Jewish National Fund bonds and in the obligations of Nir, the financial instrument of agricultural settlements in Palestine—neither of which was faring too well in the financial markets. In addition, the Zionist institutions tried to preempt Ha'avarah transfers for money that had accumulated in Germany through Jewish donations there, which came at the expense of transfers of private capital. These institutional transfers were considerable, and in April 1936, Paltreu itself suggested to the Reichsbank that they should be limited to 20–25 percent of the transfers. The Reichsbank agreed.[14] Thus, the aims of the Nazis and the Jews began to converge, albeit from opposing points of view.

Let us now try to answer the question about the Nazi motives in originally agreeing to Ha'avarah and their willingness, initially, to pay out hard currency for that purpose.

As early as July 10, 1933, the Minister of Economic Affairs, Kurt Schmidt, decided that the sterling payments should continue, because the Jewish boycott committee under Lord Melchett would be meeting in London on July 15, and the boat should not be rocked. After Schacht's appointment as Minister on July 30, 1934, however, the Germans demanded that the cash payments to prospective emigrants who wished to transfer their sterling to Palestine before they actually left Germany should be reimbursed by Ha'avarah. Ha'avarah intervened, Werner Senator of the Jewish Agency immigration department was sent to Berlin, and after some negotiations, in which Goebbels showed an interest inimical to Ha'avarah, the status quo was confirmed—until it was abolished, as we have seen, in 1936. But the arguments in 1934 show that already one of the motives for the relatively forthcoming attitude on the German side was the hope of pushing more Jews to emigrate.[15]

In 1935, however, the arguments were still connected with the boycott and only partly with emigration. This emerges, for instance, from an article published on May 27, 1935, in the Nazi paper *Westdeutscher Beobachter*, entitled "Palestine: The Gap in the Boycott." The reporter noted that Ha'avarah had in effect stifled the boycott movement in Palestine, with the exception of the Revisionists, who were not very influential. But the boycott remained dangerous, especially outside Palestine, where non-Jews used it to fight their German competitors. Ha'avarah was therefore important not only because it helped to emigrate Jews but also because of its anti-boycott effect.[16]

Within the German Foreign Office there were internal disagreements. Successive heads of the Near Eastern Department, especially Otto von Hentig (1937–40) seemed to be generally friendly toward Ha'avarah.[17] On the other hand, the Referat Deutschland, which dealt with the "Jewish question" in Germany and related German propaganda abroad, as well as with the Nazi Party external propaganda unit within the Foreign Office (the Auslandsorganisation der NSDAP, or AO), was hostile. (Nationalsozialistische deutsche Arbeiter-Partei, or NSDAP, is the name of the Nazi Party.) It may be possible that until 1935 the heads of the Deutschland Department (Vicco von Bülow-Schwandte and Emil Schumburg) were not yet strong enough to oppose the friendlier approach of the Near Eastern Department, but, on the whole, the differences were not that great. Not only the Deutschland Department, but all of the Foreign Office, including its head, Baron von Neurath, accepted the anti-Jewish policy of the Nazis; attempts to see von Hentig and his predecessors as pro-Jewish seem to be misleading. Their apparent pro-Zionism was in effect the practical application of a basic anti-Jewish bias—they wanted the Jews out. The discussions began to revolve around the question of whether permitting Jews to take out some of their property would emigrate more Jews or whether the concession could be safely refused and Jews could still be expelled. On this issue the heads of the Near Eastern Department were probably more moderate. What is decisive, however, is that the Foreign Office supported Ha'avarah from 1934 on, not because of its opposition to the Jewish boycott movement but because of its desire to rid Germany of its Jews.[18]

The economic departments and ministries were divided in their attitudes toward Ha'avarah. The Ministry of Economic Affairs supported Ha'avarah on the grounds that it would increase German exports, even though the advantages would be marginal. The Reichsbank, as might have been expected, opposed Ha'avarah, to which it had to pay sterling for the capitalist emigrants to Palestine. In 1933–35 these payments amounted to RM 31.1

million. During the same period the net yield to the Germans from all kinds of exports within the Ha'avarah agreement was RM 27.3 million (these were payments from the blocked Paltreu accounts of the emigrants). In 1936, as we have seen, the Reichsbank finally put an end to the cash payments in sterling, which from now on had to be covered by Ha'avarah itself from the sale of its transfer goods in Palestine and elsewhere.

Another factor was the Foreign Currency Office (RDB) under Hans Hartenstein. Hartenstein himself has been described by all memoirists as very friendly to Jews and to the agreement. The office was subject to the Ministry of Economic Affairs (RWM), but because of its specific task of administering the foreign currency reserves, it was subject to pressures. In 1933 officials at the Foreign Currency Office, like everyone else, were still afraid of the world Jewish boycott and its dangers regarding the future of German currency reserves. In later years the importance of exports for the office lay in securing essential imports for the rearmament industry. In that sphere, Palestine, with oranges as the only export to Germany of any value, was totally irrelevant. The economic ministries were less and less happy about Ha'avarah's impact on the currency reserves situation, which was increasingly difficult. On the other hand, the effect of the anti-Jewish measures had been felt in the economic field, as had the increasing impoverishment of the Jews. This in turn strengthened the desire to get rid of the Jews by emigration, and Ha'avarah seemed to be one way to do that. Limited though the encouragement of exports was as a means to increase employment in Germany and as a source of hard currency, Schacht introduced a system of differential export premiums. Generally, these premiums enabled German exporters to bring down their prices abroad to world market levels. As far as Palestine was concerned, the German government did not have to pay German exporters, because Ha'avarah in effect paid the premiums through the so-called bonifications—that is, deductions from the payments by the Palestinian importers, who simply paid less in order to equalize German prices with world market prices. As a result, the German Jews received less because Ha'avarah paid the difference to German exporters out of Jewish funds, but at least the Jews had saved part of their property and had escaped from Germany in the process. In addition, 2–3 percent of the money transferred was also deducted from the capital of the German Jews to pay for the administrative costs of Ha'avarah. The two deductions together were called transfer costs; they amounted to about one third of the funds originally deposited by the owners in Germany.

Another expression of the same principle were the so-called transfer losses, also known as the effective exchange rate of the Palestine pound. This came to RM 40 per pound in 1938, or more than three times the official rate (RM 12.50 per pound). When German Jews transferred their money in 1938 (not

before) they lost two thirds of its value before the other deductions and payments were exacted—a heavy penalty, especially for owners of sums above
RM 50,000, who had to pay an additional 25 percent of their money as flight
tax. From a Jewish point of view, Ha'avarah continued regardless because
when transfers to other countries were allowed at all, the losses amounted (in
1939) to 95 percent.[19]

The system was attractive enough for the Germans to hand over to
Ha'avarah all export and import transactions for Palestine, including those
involving German settlers in Palestine and (surprisingly) Palestine Arabs.
Ha'avarah administrators had no choice but to accept all the confiscatory
deductions to ensure the transfer of a maximum percentage of the sums that
had been deposited with Paltreu in Berlin by German Jews anxious to leave.
Although overall German exports were at a low level, exports to Palestine
grew considerably (see table 4).

Before these figures impress us too much, we should remember that
exports to Palestine did not amount to more than 0.5 percent of all German
exports in 1937. And German exports, as we have seen, did not amount to
much in any case. Ha'avarah transferred RM 31.4 million in 1937, with the
rest of the transferred exports going to other countries. While the transfers
advanced German exports, the actual German income in terms of hard currency was minimal—Ha'avarah paid some small sums in sterling, but they
were marginal and their amount is unknown.

The detailed economic picture of Ha'avarah demonstrates a crucial point:
the Germans had no economic reason to continue Ha'avarah in the late
1930s. What motivated them to persevere, contrary to their economic interests, was the furthering of Jewish emigration.

It would appear that the same motivation was behind the German agreement to permit Ha'avarah exports to other countries in the Middle East: they
could further the emigration of those whose capital was thus transferred. As
with Palestine, the desire to expand exports to these countries and thereby
provide some more jobs back in Germany probably existed in the early years.
The first such transaction—the export of £65,000 worth of irrigation pipes
to Syria—was effected in July 1934. Ha'avarah officials tried at first to mask
such transactions by going through Jewish merchants in Beirut and Cairo,
partly because they feared repercussions from the opponents of Ha'avarah,
partly because they feared the displeasure of the British, who were appre-
hensive about German competition. Also, high fees had to be paid to inter-
mediaries with these transactions, and the German Jewish depositors lost a
third of their money this way. Officials therefore decided to try for only very
large orders and to obtain the explicit approval of the German Jewish depositors.[20] In March 1935, through the German consul in Cairo, the Egyptian
government invited Ha'avarah to participate in an open tender for locomo-

Table 4

German Trade with Palestine, 1930–1938, Selected Years

in Thousands of RM

Year	Imports	Exports	Export Surplus
1930	7,584	11,871	4,287
1933	5,648	11,359	6,311
1936	2,065	18,391	16,326
1937	2,885	27,568	25,683
1938	2,168	16,305	14,137

Source: BA/R7/3298, Folder 3.

tives. But here the Foreign Currency Office objected: Ha'avarah was intended for Jewish importers in the Middle East, not for governments, and only such transactions would be approved that produced exports additional to those that brought in hard currency. The AO also became interested in the proceedings, but not in Ha'avarah's favor.[21] At that time, with the currency reserves situation already grim, an arrangement that did not promise sterling for the Reichsbank was a doubtful proposition. Nothing came of the proposal, but the officials of the Economic Ministry told their Jewish interlocutors—but just orally—that they might consider "additional export" opportunities involving countries other than those in the Middle East if brought to their attention.[22] Apparently, only some minor transactions were effectuated.

The pressure for emigration was great, and the approvals for Ha'avarah exports by the German bureaucracy very slow, so that people in Germany who had paid in their money in the hope that it could be speedily transferred had to wait for years. To widen the bottleneck, Ha'avarah tried to persuade German exporters to put pressure on the German authorities to expedite export agreements. Sometimes this was effective, because German exporters liked to work with Ha'avarah: they received their payments when orders were placed, because Ha'avarah considered its money to be safer with German exporters than with either Paltreu or the private Jewish banks of Warburg and Wassermann that were still permitted to function.

From 1936 on, the Germans steadily increased the number of items that Ha'avarah could not export, hoping that the items could be exported in exchange for hard currency.[23] Generally speaking, the conditions for Ha'avarah deteriorated after 1935. The Germans were interested in Jewish emigration, but refused more and more adamantly to make any financial concessions to achieve it.

A meeting took place in November 1935, apparently at the request of Schacht. Helmut Wohlthat, at that point Schacht's man, said that the problem was not whether to aim at the emigration of Jews—such a decision had to be left to the Führer—but how to effect it without harming German economic interests or asking the Führer for a decision. The representative of the Ministry of the Interior declared that there was a directive from the Führer not to put economic pressure on the Jews. The representative of Rudolf Hess, Hitler's deputy, said that Hess had suggested providing economic incentives for emigration by permitting the partial export of capital, which seems to have been in line with Hitler's reported directive. After such ways were found, the Jews should be forced to emigrate. This, he said, had Hitler's approval. The proposal discussed was to establish an institution that would liquidate Jewish property ("aryanize," i.e., confiscate it); Schacht's man said that discussions on such an institution were already taking place. According to the extant document, it seems that such an institution would have permitted the transfer abroad of some of the capital according to the Ha'avarah precedent. Behind the proposal, apparently, were contacts with the Reichsvertretung der Juden in Deutschland (RV), the representative body of German Jewry under the Nazis, which led in January 1936 to an RV memorandum about establishing just such an institution. The point was made that without such an institution only the rich might emigrate, leaving the poor to be looked after by the German state, which would thereby lose income from taxes, especially if the flight tax was abolished—which some also suggested.[24]

By the end of 1935 it had become clear to the leaders of German Jewry that mass emigration was a preferred solution but that it could not take place without some kind of capital transfer, because foreign countries would not take penniless Jews. Different wings of German Jewry approached the problem differently. A decisive influence among the Jews was Max Warburg, the head of the Hamburg-based banking house of Warburg, who had played a very important role in the economic and financial policies of the democratic governments of the Weimar period. He maintained fairly close relations with Schacht, at first through his membership on the board of the Reichsbank, a position he maintained for a number of years. His brother, Felix Warburg, was the head of the American Jewish Joint Distribution Committee (JDC), the main organization of U.S. Jews helping their brothers and sisters abroad, and after 1929, he was in effect the most influential individual in the councils of the American Jewish Committee (AJC), the main, conservatively inclined political body of American Jewry. Brother Felix's position may have helped brother Max. At the end of 1935 Max Warburg suggested the establishment of the institution mentioned by the German bureaucrats, a Liquidationsbank, leaving open the question of whether this was a Nazi idea or Warburg's. Apparently Warburg pressed Otto Hirsch, the director of the RV, to produce a memorandum, which was submitted to the Nazis on January 17, 1936. The idea there, as Warburg explained, apparently with some hesitation, was to emigrate 25,000 German Jews and transfer RM 250,000,000.

The Germans—without Hartenstein, who was on vacation—feigned surprise at the high sum and the low emigration figure. We should remember that in six years of activity Ha'avarah transferred RM 140,000,000, and during the same time 52,000 German Jews emigrated to Palestine legally (1933–39). Georg Landauer, the Zionist representative who had impugned the figures in the memo, and indeed the whole approach to the Germans, saw himself vindicated when, at the meeting, the Jews were forced to ask the Germans to return the memo to them; they would resubmit it by February 15, with emendations.[25] No traces have been found of such an amended memorandum.

This step was undoubtedly part of a series of steps taken by Warburg to advance the idea of mass emigration from Germany. In December 1935 he had been behind the decision of British Jews to suggest to the leaders of American Jewry, led by Felix Warburg, an ambitious plan to emigrate up to 100,000 young German Jews within four years. The emigrants would then call upon their families to join them, and the rest, the older people, would be permitted to stay in Germany without molestation. The large sums that would be required from Anglo-American Jewry to implement such a program became the bone of contention between Zionists and non-Zionists and between British and American Jews; by March 1936, the effort had failed. The German end, in any case, seems to have been left hanging in the air after the abortive meeting of January 17.[26]

Another initiative, apparently also due to Max Warburg, was the establishment of the Allgemeine Treuhandstelle für jüdische Auswanderung (Altreu), in effect run by the same people who ran Ha'avarah. This office arranged for capital transfers to countries other than Palestine, but on conditions that were much worse than Ha'avarah's; as late as 1936–39, then, at least some influential German officials had a preference for emigration to Palestine. When during the Kristallnacht pogrom (November 9–10, 1938) all the Jewish offices in Berlin were ransacked, Paltreu and Altreu—both registered in Britain— were left untouched. The success of Altreu was apparently very limited, but since the files were bombed in London during the blitz, there is little chance of ever filling in the picture.

Despite worsening conditions for Ha'avarah in 1936–37, the size of the capital transfers did not shrink, though by then German economic experts did not understand why Ha'avarah should be given any privileges at all, because the same limited export goals could be achieved with the hard currency accruing to Germany without Ha'avarah.[27] The new consul in Jerusalem, Walter Döhle, asked for reconsideration of the whole program (March 23, 1937). Why, he asked, should German settlers and Arabs be forced to support the Jews whenever they imported something from Germany? The German settlers and the AO supported him, and the settlers' representative, Consul Timotheus Wurst of Jaffa, declared at the Foreign Office in November 1937 that the Jews should stay in Germany, under Nazi control.[28]

The AO, on its part, took an anti-Ha'avarah stand. A letter from the economic division of the AO to Bohle, head of the AO, on May 26, 1937, complained that the Economic Ministry was still in favor of Ha'avarah, because of support from Hitler ("von höchster Seite"). In the Foreign Office the Deutschland Department was against it, but the economic sections were still in favor. Now, with the report of a British Royal Commission on Palestine headed by Lord Peel approaching, the AO people hoped for a revision.[29]

In the Foreign Office, support for Ha'avarah was waning, too. The influence of the pro-Arab ambassador to Baghdad, Fritz Grobba, and the impact of the Arab Rebellion in Palestine (1936–39) on German policy caused the Germans to ask themselves why they should support their enemies, the Jews, as opposed to their friends, the Palestinian Arabs. The Peel commission of 1937 threatened to establish a Jewish State in the Middle East.

The development of these influences was slow. On September 26, 1936, an interministerial conference under Wilhelm Stuckart, the director general of the Ministry of the Interior, still ended with a call to support Jewish emigration to Palestine—despite objections from the representative of the Nazi Party (Walter Blome).[30] Referat Deutschland, however, in memoranda of January 9 and February 17, 1937, expressed deep concern about a possible Jewish State and recommended careful support of the Arabs—careful, to avoid antagonizing the British too much. Ernst von Weizsäcker, director of the Foreign Office, and, indeed, Foreign Minister von Neurath himself supported this new line, and finally, from within the Foreign Office, came a request for reconsideration of the issue and revision of German support for emigration to Palestine altogether.[31] On July 8, 1937, von Hentig wrote a letter to Weizsäcker in which he supported the idea of emigrating poor Jews and opposed the emigration of rich ones, who should be kept in Germany so money could be squeezed out of them. This, he indicated, was the attitude of the Deutschland Department; but *because the idea stood in contradiction to the instructions of the Führer,* nothing much could be done. Ha'avarah, he said, had supported the emigration of younger middle-class Jews to Palestine, whereas the really rich ones had gone to the West and to South Africa. There was a danger that German Jews emigrating to the West would exercise an anti-German influence on public opinion there, whereas if they went to Palestine they would be among themselves, and Germany would not be affected.[32]

The SS, too, began to evince interest in Ha'avarah. Herbert Hagen, who had become the head of Amt (department) II/112 (Jews) of the Sicherheitsdienst, or SD—the intelligence division of the SS security apparatus—wrote a long memo on "the Jewish problem" in January 1937, in which he supported Ha'avarah, proposed to concentrate on emigrating poor Jews, and opposed the efforts of the AO to stir up Arab disturbances in Palestine, because that would lead to a decline in the number of German Jews going to Palestine.[33]

A completely different approach was pioneered in the report submitted by Hagen and Adolf Eichmann after their largely abortive visit to Palestine in September 1937. They opposed the whole Ha'avarah idea, because it was possible to get rid of the Jews by expelling them without giving them any money to transfer. In addition, the transfer of capital could only help in the establishment of a Jewish State.[34]

The Jewish side was well aware of the change in atmosphere. Werner Senator, the non-Zionist member of the JA Executive in Palestine, wrote to Warburg (March 1, 1937) that he should explain to his friends (i.e., Schacht) that Ha'avarah was the way to emigrate Jews without any long-term disadvantages for Germany.[35] Landauer, too, reported (September 18, 1937) that even at the Foreign Currency Office only one official was still supportive and that for 60 percent of the goods that could be transferred as late as 1935, transfer was now prohibited.[36]

At a meeting between Paltreu and the Ministry of Economic Affairs on October 21, 1937, the Germans made some tough demands: the abolition of the Ha'avarah procedures and their change into normal export practices that would bring in hard currency to Germany. The Reichsbank would give Jews cash to enable them to emigrate, but it would determine who received the cash and in what amounts. The Germans were unhappy about transferring funds for Zionist institutions and wanted whatever cash was transferred to go to the emigrants directly. In other words, whereas the Zionist representatives wanted funds for the development of the Jewish infrastructure in Palestine, the Germans wanted simply to get rid of Jews at the lowest possible cost.[37] Oddly enough, the Germans did not translate their threats into action.

We have seen how Ha'avarah's wings were clipped and how, by early 1938, the opposition to Ha'avarah had become almost unanimous. Why, then, did Ha'avarah continue to function at all, in effect until after the November 1938 pogrom and even until the outbreak of war? The reason is, as all our sources indicate, that Hitler himself supported the existing arrangements. That no document signed by him exists is simply because of the way he ruled Germany generally: he preferred to hand down his decisions orally, and only when it was indispensable that he should do so. The documents show clearly that most of the time officials were impatiently waiting for a decision from the Führer, specifically for a revision of his decision to support emigration to Palestine and, therefore, Ha'avarah as well. There is evidence that in early 1938 he repeated that decision—orally, of course. A January 27, 1938, memo from Clodius, director of the Division of Economic Affairs of the Foreign

Office, reports a statement by Alfred Rosenberg: at a consultation Hitler had reiterated his decision to support both emigration to Palestine and Ha'avarah.[38] Again, typically for the decisionmaking process in the Third Reich, this did not mean that attempts to change the decision were not made. In fact, only von Hentig continued, on practical grounds, to support the Führer's policy in a way; all the others tried to alter it. Ha'avarah was kept alive against the wishes of almost all German government economic bureaucrats because Hitler had decided that emigration of Jews was more important than any economic consideration—and that Ha'avarah was one of the ways to achieve that aim.

In early 1938—on May 23, to be exact—when the economic ministries increased their pressure on Ha'avarah by adding more and more goods to the list of forbidden goods, the Jewish Agency officially turned to Brinkman, the director general of the Economic Ministry, and argued that the worsening conditions seriously endangered the orderly emigration of German Jewry.[39] They could not know that the Party bureaucracy was already swiftly moving toward the total expropriation of German Jews and their expulsion as penniless refugees. Either Hitler was finally persuaded by his underlings, or, more likely, he himself instigated this change in policy. That the impetus came from him is reflected in a memorandum by Weizsäcker that was sent to all German diplomatic representatives abroad (July 8, 1938) and in Hitler's talk with a South African Minister (November 18, 1938) in which he argued that Jewish capital in Germany belonged to the German people.[40] Finally, a memo by Schumburg of Referat Deutschland (January 1939) stated that export of Jewish capital would now be forbidden and that the encouragement of Jewish emigration to Palestine would cease, so that the Jews would be distributed all over the world; they would arrive as penniless refugees and thereby increase international antisemitism.[41]

German attitudes toward Ha'avarah changed, we would argue, in three phases: at first they were supportive because of the desire to fight a threatening Jewish boycott (1933–34); then the desire to see the Jews leave Germany was paramount (1934–38), and finally came the dismantling of Ha'avarah (1938–39). While there is no evidence of Hitler's direct involvement in the first stage, his influence becomes more and more apparent in the second stage and in the transition to the third. His impact there is decisive—without his continued support Ha'avarah would not have survived the 1936–37 crisis. The reason for it, clearly, was his overriding desire to rid Germany of its Jews during the Four-Year Plan as executed by Goering on his orders. But Hitler was also behind the Goering policy after the Kristallnacht pogrom to confiscate Jewish property and drive the Jews out of the German economy, which parallels the third stage of the attitude toward Ha'avarah. Despite the apparent contradiction between the confiscatory policies pursued in line with

Hitler's wishes, and the continued existence of the admittedly much circumscribed Ha'avarah policy, also in line with Hitler's directives, no clear decisions were made, purposely it seems: the door was left open, or perhaps not
completely closed, to initiatives that would permit the Jews to take some of
their capital with them, provided they left Germany. Their departure was the
overriding consideration, to which Hitler returned time and again, and that is
the apparent explanation for why Ha'avarah was not totally abolished even in
1938–39. There was in fact no contradiction: the Jews would have to go, one
way or the other ("so oder so," as Goering put it)—by arrangement, preferably with the Western powers, and with some capital, or by brutal force, ter-
rorized into emigration, with their property confiscated.[42]

The more nazified the officials were, the sooner they abandoned the
Ha'avarah arrangement, or so it seems. But almost *all* German officials fully
supported the developing Nazi line from relatively "moderate" forced emigration to brutal expulsion, because expropriation and expulsion were still
within the consensus of moderate traditional German antisemitism, to which,
in Germany, there were few opponents in official positions.

Interestingly enough, it was precisely in 1937, when obstacles were mount-
ing, that Ha'avarah succeeded in transferring more capital than in any other
year: RM 31.4 million; as much as RM 19 million was transferred even in
1938. The reason lay in the better functioning of Jewish efforts to save Jewish
capital and thereby increase emigration. The total amount of Ha'avarah
transfers in 1933–39, including Reichsbank payments of the thousand-
pound sums in the early years, came to £8,101,500, or 14.9 percent of all capital imports (and 18.2 percent of all private capital imports) to Palestine.[43] I
should perhaps mention that this was but a tiny part of the total capital of
German Jews, estimated at RM 10,000,000,000 in 1933.

Several conclusions can be drawn from this analysis. One is that after a
short initial period in which the fear of a Jewish boycott influenced Nazi policies, the desire to see the Jews leave was a paramount consideration. The second is that the personal involvement of Hitler was decisive in keeping
Ha'avarah going to the end of 1938 and in progressively and partially dismantling it in 1938–39. The third is that in 1938–39 no contradiction was
any longer seen between the wish to get rid of the Jews and the desire to
plunder their property: they could be forced to emigrate and leave most or all
of their capital behind. This consideration was not absolute, however; the
Nazis might consider arrangements that got rid of Jews but permitted them
to take some of their capital with them. Ha'avarah did not actually cease until
the outbreak of war. There was a growing tendency to establish rules, but
rules can be changed without changing basic policies. These policies had the
clear aim of extruding the Jews, but the tactics might change as conditions
demanded.

The patterns of Nazi-Jewish negotiations were set during the Ha'avarah years. The initiative came from the Jews, who wanted to save remnants of Jewish property in order to emigrate German Jews who would thus not arrive penniless in Palestine or elsewhere. The Nazis responded because emigration of Jews was their policy. The two sides were quite unequal in strength. From the very beginning the Jews were in a trap: they had no help from third parties, and in Palestine they were struggling with a British administration that was becoming more and more unfriendly. They used the only option they had to save what could be saved—namely, negotiating with the enemy. Their purpose at that stage was not yet to rescue lives. Indeed, the upbuilding of Palestine was their primary goal, because Jewish Palestine was too weak to undertake rescues in Germany or elsewhere. Given enough time, Jewish Palestine would be able to absorb masses of Jews. Except that enough time was not given.

2

Failure of a Last-Minute
Rescue Attempt

The Evian conference on refugees from Germany (July 1938) has been discussed many times before. Here we need to see how the events at Evian and afterward fit with the analysis of Jewish and German policies before and during the Holocaust.

The initiative for convening the conference was American. Roosevelt wanted to do "something" for the people persecuted by the Nazis, without spending any money and without changing the quota system of immigration to the United States. He thought he could do that if he put the United States at the head of an alliance of nations that would negotiate with the Nazis as a group about permitting emigration with some capital, so the refugees could be absorbed outside Germany. He would thereby score with the liberals in his own country, satisfy his Jewish constituents, present a united front against Nazi Germany on a sensitive issue, and have most of the refugees—experience showed that at least 80 percent would be Jews—absorbed in countries other than the United States, thereby satisfying the conservative opposition to his policies at home. To achieve all that, a new international body to deal with refugees would be set up with the express purpose of negotiating with Nazi Germany so that the refugees could leave with capital, which would make them desirable immigrants in many countries.

Roosevelt's invitations went out, on March 22, 1938, to thirty-three nations (in the end, twenty-nine attended). Myron C. Taylor, a Roman Catholic Roosevelt ally and a former chairman of U.S. Steel, was given the task of convening the conference and chairing it. The administration declared that it was uniting the small Austrian quota with the German one, and the resulting quota, 27,370, was to be filled much more than before. Indeed it was: in fiscal 1937–38, the number of immigrants accepted into the United States was 17,199, whereas in the first half of the next fiscal year it was 19,452, and for the whole of fiscal 1938–39 it was close to 38,000 (including visitors' visas and other arrangements that caused the quota to be oversubscribed).

At the Evian conference itself (July 6–15, 1938), the delegates tried very hard to prevent any refugees from being dumped on their respective countries—certainly no Jews. The Latin Americans declared that they did not want any traders or intellectuals, the Australians said they did not have a racial problem and did not wish to import one, the French and the British said that their countries were full and that they could not accept further refugees, and the British also volunteered the statement that Palestine was closed to mass immigration. Some refugees might be accepted in Kenya and other parts of east Africa—possibly. Switzerland could serve as a stopover to other countries but no more.

The only country that was prepared, on the face of it, to be more liberal was the Dominican Republic, whose dictator President, Rafael J. Trujillo, let those at the conference know that he was prepared to allow up to 100,000 immigrants into his country. But the background to this move bears investigating: The Dominicans had inquired of the U.S. State Department whether such an offer would sound good—they had no intention of letting in so many refugees, presumably Jews. The State Department replied that a Dominican offer would be welcome. The result was a pathetic attempt to settle several hundred Jews on government land on the island. A great deal of money was invested there by the American Jewish Joint Distribution Committee (JDC) for that small group, money that might have been used to much greater effect elsewhere.[1]

The main purpose of the Americans, however, was to set up machinery to negotiate with the Nazis, and this was achieved: the conference delegates agreed to establish an Intergovernmental Committee on Refugees (IGCR). The agreement was by no means easy to reach, because the British and the French were reluctant to remove the refugee question from the League of Nations, of which the United States was not a member. The League had a well-meaning but ineffectual high commissioner for refugees, Sir Neil Malcolm; in the end, the new IGCR swallowed the old High Commission. As a sop to the British, a British chair, Lord Winterton, was elected, and an American lawyer, George Rublee, a Roosevelt nominee, became director—in effect, the prospective negotiator with the Germans. The parallelism with Nazi policies is fascinating. At Goering's famous conference, held in his Air Ministry a couple of days after the Kristallnacht pogrom on November 12, 1938, a similar basic idea was proposed in Hitler's name: "The Führer is now at last to make a major move abroad, starting with the Powers that have brought up the Jewish question"; the aim was to "get around to the Madagascar solution"—that is, deport the Jews to that tropical island.[2] At the time these statements were made, the IGCR had been set up, and Rublee was trying to contact the Germans. Though for opposing reasons, the Nazis and the Americans were thinking in partially parallel categories.

An interesting and rather mysterious event occurred at Evian. A famous Viennese Jewish otolaryngologist, Heinrich Neumann von Hethars, came and asked for a hearing with the principals of the Western delegations. He apparently met with Taylor and claimed that he had been sent, or that he had agreed to come, to Evian to bring to the attention of the delegations there an offer by the Nazi authorities to sell Jews for $250 per person. He had been sent, he said, by the then Nazi ruler of Austria, Artur Seyss-Inquart. When Taylor refused to talk about ransom, Neumann was reportedly told by the Gestapo to tell Taylor that 40,000 Austrian Jews would be sent to concentration camps. According to one researcher, Taylor then appointed a special subcommittee under the Colombian delegate to deal with the threat, but nothing practical emerged. These details are not verified, and the memoirs of the participants do not record Neumann's intervention at all, though accounts of his mission appeared in the *New York Times* (July 7) and the *London Daily Express* (July 12). The diplomats at Evian either did not take Neumann seriously or, on the contrary, did take his mission seriously but refused to consider a ransom proposal by the Nazis. It seems clear that he showed up, and there is limited historical evidence that he indeed proposed some ransom scheme, but it appears impossible to ascertain who sent him and for what purpose.[3] But such a mission fits the general picture: the Nazis wanted to get rid of the Jews and thought that the West might be willing to buy them.

Whatever the truth regarding Neumann, it is abundantly clear that concerning the Jews, the West and the Nazis stared at each other, so to speak, quite uncomprehendingly. The Nazis saw in the Jewish "problem" a central world political issue whose solution was the sine qua non for any permanent solution of global problems generally. The West saw in the Jews another persecuted religious minority, not a national group, as many Jews saw themselves, and not a racial group, as the Nazis saw them. This basic difference in approach—one frighteningly rational in its irrationality, the other the result of rational policies derived from the Enlightenment—was the main cause of inaction on the part of the West when Nazi policies were radicalized later on.

The IGCR, upon its establishment, turned to Jewish philanthropic bodies, primarily the JDC, to provide the necessary administrative and financial backup for its forthcoming negotiations. The first meeting of the new body took place in London on August 3, and Nathan Katz of the JDC participated as an observer. A small administrative budget was put up by the member states. All prospective approaches to the Germans were put on hold, however, with the outbreak of the Sudeten crisis in September, and it was not until October 27 that Rublee presented his ideas of how to deal with the refugees. As his plans were almost identical with what Hjalmar Schacht proposed later on the Germans' behalf, there were probably unofficial contacts with the Germans, possibly also with German Jewish representatives like Warburg, prior to that date. Rublee—and Schacht—proposed that 25 percent of German Jewish assets (estimated at RM 6 billion in 1938, or $2.4 billion—down from RM 10 billion when Hitler came to power) be set up as a trust fund in Germany. Jews abroad would make available an equivalent sum (in non-German currencies), which would nominally be a loan to the prospective emigrants, and this fund would pay for travel and settlement. Emigrants would repay the loan and the interest on it in the form of German goods that they would take with them, bought by money from the trust fund, and sell these goods abroad, thus advancing German exports. Schacht spoke of "additional" German exports, that is, over and above the quantities that Germany was exporting in any case.[4]

The plan was apparently conceived by Hans Fischböck, an economic official from Austria, who suggested it to Goering and Schacht. There are hints of it, especially by Reinhard Heydrich of the SS Security Services, in the protocol of the meeting at Goering's office on November 12, 1938.[5] Schacht went to London in November and presented his version of the plan to Winterton and Rublee. The question is, Who was behind these proposals on the German side? There is plenty of evidence that the German Foreign Office was against it—Joachim von Ribbentrop, the Nazi Foreign Minister, wanted to preserve his own turf from incursion by the Goering-Schacht economic alliance, and he was against giving the Jews any capital whatsoever. But it had been made specific at the November 12 meeting that Hitler had empowered Goering to deal with the "Jewish question." All decisive initiatives had therefore to be cleared with Goering, if not with Hitler himself. Schacht did not inform Ribbentrop of his intention to discuss the Jewish matter in London, and Ernst von Weizsäcker, the director general of the German Foreign Office, tried to pull him up in a telephone conversation: First, why had he not informed Ribbentrop? Second, why was he introducing himself into a matter involving Jews and foreign contacts and which the Minister responsible opposed?

Schacht's answer was blunt: "This is a task entrusted [to me] by the Führer [es handle sich um einen Auftrag des Führers], which has been executed in London in the framework that had been decided on. The Führer wishes a report after [my] return. . . . Also . . . [I] was informed by Field Marshal Goering that [I] should conduct the negotiations in London." Goering wanted the negotiations to be conducted on a purely economic basis, and he also had "an explicit order from the Führer [auch vom Führer einen ausdrücklichen Auftrag]." In addition, Schacht said, on his way to Basel and London he stopped over in Munich and talked to Hitler personally for half an hour in order to hear the Führer repeat the order ("unmittelbar in einer halbstündigen Aussprache den Auftrag ausdrücklich wiederholen zu lassen").

Schacht continued these talks in December, after the Jews had rejected the original proposals as in effect bolstering the German economy. Schacht modified his offer substantially by dropping the idea of "additional exports." Now the Jews would simply export German goods bought with their money in Germany to enable them to settle abroad. Transport and freight expenses would also be covered by these funds, insofar as German means of transportation were used. The Jewish counterfund set up abroad would have no necessary connection with the trust fund in Germany, which would be run by a directorate of three: two Germans and one non-German. Schacht, probably in order to be quite sure of Hitler's continued support, turned to the Führer again. On January 2, 1939, he received Hitler's approval for the steps taken. On the fourth he told Weizsäcker that "he had reported [to Hitler] the day before yesterday. The Führer was in agreement with his—Schacht's—conversations in London and entrusted him with their continuation. Schacht now wants to invite Rublee to come here."[6]

The aim of the plan that Schacht and Rublee agreed on was to settle 150,000 Jews of working age abroad, then 250,000 dependents. A further German promise was that the 200,000, presumably elderly, people left behind would not be molested and, according to a newspaper report, even permitted to reopen some businesses, so that "Jews outside would not be called upon to support their coreligionists in the Reich."[7]

When Rublee finally arrived in Berlin, however, he found that Schacht had been fired by Hitler (on January 20)—not because of the Jewish negotiations but because of his conservative policies on financing the rearmament of Germany. Rublee was received by Goering himself and assured that the German government was serious in its negotiations and, further, that a new representative, Helmut Wohlthat, of Goering's ministry of the Four-Year Plan, would now represent Germany.[8] Rublee returned to London, informed his government and the Jewish representatives of the success of his negotiations, and resigned, fully convinced that he had achieved an outstanding success. His place was taken by Sir Herbert Emerson, until then the League of Nations high commissioner for refugees.[9]

Before we return to the Jewish side of the story, let us examine a crucial point: How can we interpret German policy on Jews given clear evidence of Hitler's radicalization just at that time, peaking in his famous speech of January 30, 1939?[10] Is there not a stark contradiction between this evidence and the evidence just presented?

Historians have made abundantly clear the steps of radicalization that the Nazi regime took in regard to Jews in 1937–39. Jews had to register their property in advance of confiscatory measures (March 1938), Austrian Jews were beaten, humiliated, and arrested in droves (March–June 1938), arrests took place in Germany itself in June 1938, synagogues in Munich (June 9) and Nuremberg (August 10) were burnt and demolished, and then came the pogrom known as Kristallnacht. On November 9–10, 1938, hundreds of synagogues were burnt or demolished, thousands of Jewish stores were broken into and plundered, 26,000 male Jews were arrested and taken to concentration camps, and close to one hundred persons were killed. The purpose was mainly to make the Jews emigrate, as quickly as possible, but also to mobilize the masses against the Jewish enemy and thereby boost the popularity of the Party. The primary aim was achieved, but the second was not, for the bulk of the German population evinced a lack of enthusiasm for the pogrom, which they felt to be unpleasant—they did not particularly like Jews, but they did not like disorder, either. Most of all, they did not like the destruction of property. The Jewish population understandably panicked and rushed to escape from Germany. The wives, children, or parents of the arrestees ran to acquire visas for their dear ones, who could be released if proof was forthcoming that emigration had been assured. An estimated 102,200 Jews left Germany, Austria, and Danzig in 1938; an additional 15,000 left Bohemia and Moravia, which were still part of an independent Czechoslovakia, but most of those who left were German Jews who had fled to the Czech lands. Another 144,000 left the German Reich in 1939.[11]

The signs of radicalization multiplied as 1938 drew to a close. On November 24 the SS weekly, *Das Schwarze Korps,* published a violent anti-Jewish article entitled "Juden, Was Nun?" (Jews, what now?) in which a treatment of blood and iron was promised to anyone who would remain behind, be deprived of a means of subsistence, and therefore become a criminal element. Hitler, in his talks with representatives from South Africa and Czechoslovakia, threatened destruction and annihilation. On January 30, as mentioned, he gave a rambling, two-and-a-half-hour speech to the Reichstag on all aspects of his policy, domestic and foreign. A section of the speech was devoted to the Jewish "question." The oft-quoted passage threatening the Jews of Europe with annihilation came at the end of that section: "If the international Jewish financiers in and outside Europe should succeed in plunging the nations once more into a world war, then the result will not be the bolshevization of the earth, and thus the victory of Jewry, but the annihilation of the Jewish race in Europe." This has been widely interpreted to reflect a plan to annihilate the Jews. A more differentiated interpretation must look at the context. Hitler started the section dealing with the Jews by ridiculing the Western concern about the Jews. If they were such a wonderful people, why didn't the Western powers simply take them? Germany, he said, did not want them and was merely repaying them as they deserved; he accused the Jews of being responsible for the inflation of the 1920s, which had impoverished Germany. The Germans were hardened to all "attacks" of sentimentality. The West had caused German mass starvation during the war and after it, including the deaths of German children, deprived Germany of cattle to produce milk for these children, and kept more than one million German POWs in camps for a whole year after the war had ended. Jews had occupied all the important positions in Germany, and Hitler was determined that the positions would be occupied by Germans. German culture should be German and not Jewish.

These were lies, and the rantings of an extreme antisemite, but the upshot of Hitler's arguments was that the West, which had been responsible for so much misery in Germany, had no right to tell the Germans what to do with their Jews. The Jews were Germany's enemies, and not only Germany's. The West should settle the Jews in the huge territories at its disposal. "The world has sufficient space for settlements, but we must once and for all rid ourselves of the opinion that the Jewish race was created by God only for the purpose of being as a certain percentage [of the population living as] a parasite and feeding on the body and productive work of other nations. The Jewish race will have to adapt itself to sound, constructive activity as other nations do, or sooner or later it will succumb to a crisis of inconceivable magnitude." The crucial sentences were his demands that the Jews should be settled elsewhere by international agreement; and he added: "I think that the sooner this problem is solved the better; for European questions cannot be settled until the Jewish question is cleared up. It may very well be possible that sooner or later an agreement on this problem may be reached in Europe, even between those nations that otherwise do not so easily come together."[12]

A comparison between the speech and Goering's statements in the Führer's name during the November 12 meeting is most instructive. Several common themes emerge. First of all is the centrality of the Jewish question for Hitler—it is an international problem on which depends the peace in Europe and which can and should be settled by international agreement. In his instructions to Goering, as reported by the latter in November, Madagascar was mentioned as a desired place of settlement for Europe's Jews. In the speech, Hitler talked more vaguely about huge areas at the West's disposal. But a little-noticed comment by Goering in November is a foretaste of Hitler's remarks: "Then one can make another proposal: the rich Jews can buy a territory in North America, Canada, or someplace else for their coreligionists." Finally, Hitler told Goering: "The Jewish question is to be summed up and coordinated once and for all and solved one way or the other [*So oder so*]." It is this phrase, "one way or the other," that provides the central clue to Hitler's thinking. Indeed, during the November 12 meeting, Goering uttered a threat very similar to that quoted from Hitler's speech: "If the German Reich should in the near future become involved in conflict abroad, then it is obvious that we in Germany will first of all make sure of settling accounts with the Jews."

What links Goering's statements, the *Schwarze Korps* article, the Schacht-Rublee negotiations, and the Führer's own diplomatic and public interventions is the hands-on policy of Hitler. Goering reported, on November 12, no fewer than three separate Hitler interventions on the "Jewish problem" within three days (November 9–12). In the one on November 9 Hitler explained to Goering the general outlines of his anti-Jewish policy: international agreement if possible (preferably on Madagascar as the place of banishment), expulsion, confiscation of property, and dreams for a possible murderous radicalization. Then—Goering does not say when, but it may have been the tenth—Hitler sent a letter of instruction signed by Martin Bormann, his secretary, to Goering, presumably containing the same general ideas (the letter has not surfaced). Finally, on the eleventh, the Führer telephoned his loyal Hermann to make sure he had understood what he, the Führer, wished to be done. We may surmise that the article in *Das Schwarze Korps* was written with at least the knowledge that it fitted in with Hitler's views.

Then the Schacht-Rublee negotiations began. These were initiated—as both Schacht and Goering indicate and as Weizsäcker reports—not by the officials but by Hitler himself, in total disregard of his own Minister of Foreign Affairs. The compromises that Schacht proposed to his Western counterparts were approved by Hitler, and Schacht was told to carry on in that spirit. After Schacht's dismissal, Goering repeated these undertakings to Rublee. Anti-Jewish policy was too important to be left to underlings—Hitler himself initiated it, conducted it, and coordinated it.

The key to understanding Hitler's policy is Goering's phrase "one way or the other" (*so oder so*)—or was he quoting the Führer? The aim was to get rid of the Jews, first of all the European Jews. This could be achieved—*so oder so*—either by arriving at an agreement with the West, which would give the Jews some capital, promote German exports as a side effect, and let the West see to their settlement; or by arriving at an arrangement to emigrate them to a territory such as Madagascar; or by simply expelling them, after confiscating their property, by means of unbridled terror. And if a war broke out, then—*so oder so*, right?

Both Goering and Hitler mention the coming war, and the question arises whether they themselves took their own proposals, as put forward by Schacht and, later, Wohlthat, seriously—whether they were themselves planning a world war in which they would annihilate the Jews. The point seems to be that the war that Hitler wanted was not the one he got in September 1939. Hitler originally wanted to attack the Soviet Union with Polish help; then he wanted to attack Poland after neutralizing the Soviets with the Ribbentrop-Molotov Pact of August 23, 1939. He certainly did not want to fight the British. Until the very end he hoped to keep Britain, possibly even France, out of the conflict with Poland. A two-front war was the last thing he wanted. Had things gone his way, he would have won a war against Poland and then, strengthened in the East, settled accounts with France in order to deal with the East once and for all. He wanted an alliance with Britain based on the anti-Bolshevik attitude of the British government and would offer a division of the world between a germanized European continent, Britain, and presumably Japan and the United States. The extensive research on Hitler's foreign policy and on the moves leading to the war appear to justify such an interpretation. But what Hitler got in fact was very different: a war with a Franco-British alliance, increasingly supported by Roosevelt's United States.

The Schacht-Rublee agreement might have worked with a neutral Britain and a neutral United States, and even more so if France, too, had stayed out of the fray. There was no contradiction there. But Hitler's threats seemed to indicate that if they all banded against him—which could happen only through the devilish machinations of the Jews—then he would be free to translate his innermost cravings into reality.

We find some confirmation of this interpretation in two other documents of that fateful January 1939. On January 24, Goering instructed Heydrich to set up a Central Office for Jewish Emigration. The key sentence in the document is the first: "The emigration of the Jews from Germany is to be furthered by all possible means." Emigration of poor Jews was preferable. The center was to be run by the SS, and, among others, "the committee will include Ambassador Eisenlohr, who is responsible for interstate negotiations, and Ministerial Director Wohlthat, who is responsible for the negotiations in connection with the Rublee plan."[13] Here, too, the *so oder so* approach was maintained. "All possible means" appears in the same document with the Rublee negotiations. The new central office (run in effect by Adolf Eichmann) was to get rid of the Jews in the quickest and most efficient way.

The other document dates from the following day—January 25. It is a German Foreign Office memorandum sent as a circular to all German representatives in foreign countries. It stated that the aim of the German Jewish policy was emigration. The Jews and their influence were a disease. "The cure of this disease of the body politic was probably one of the most important preconditions for the strenuous effort that in 1938 enforced the consolidation of the Greater German Reich against the will of a whole world." The German successes shattered the Jewish positions in Prague, Bucharest, Budapest, and Warsaw. World Jewry, from its headquarters in the United States, saw Munich as a defeat for itself—after all, parliamentary democracy, which was the Jews' way of controlling democratic countries, suffered a serious defeat. The Jews did not want to make a contribution to Jewish settlement outside Europe but left it to Rublee to exert pressure on the German government to part with money to enable the Jews to leave. On top of that, as

Evian has shown, the various countries did not want the Jews. Even the settlement of 100,000 Jews faced great difficulties, and Poland and Romania were clamoring to be rid of their Jews, too, so that even when the last Jew left German soil the problem for Germany would not be over. Palestine was no solution because of its limited absorptive capacity. Owing to the pressure of Arab resistance, the British now limited Jewish immigration. Germany was against the establishment of a Jewish State there, and Ha'avarah was also against German interests. Germany now wanted to splinter Jewish emigration and not concentrate it in Palestine, so that as many countries as possible would receive Jews, thereby increasing antisemitism and also sympathy for Germany.[14]

We must remember Ribbentrop's unhappiness with the Schacht-Rublee negotiations in considering this Foreign Office document, and the opposition of the Foreign Office to Ha'avarah. But the basis of Nazi consensus is laid out here: To prepare for the expansion of a Nazi Reich was impossible while the Jews were still living there. The Jewish question was of central importance, and the Jews would have to go. Spreading them all over the world would be best, so they would arouse antisemitism and thereby increase understanding of Germany's policies. Nothing in the document appears to contradict the approach outlined above.

The conclusion from this analysis seems to be that while the Nazi aim was fixed—no Jews in the expanding Reich—the means could be varied as occasion demanded. Emigration with capital and by agreement with the West, forced emigration without capital, expulsion to a tropical island, and the threat of much more radical measures—all these could be engaged in simultaneously or consecutively. The threats of annihilation may have been meant seriously by Hitler, Goering, and Himmler-Heydrich, but they were not translated into any operative plan in 1939. The "Final Solution" was not being prepared then, though the climate for it was.

When the improved conditions of the final accord between Rublee and the Germans became known in the West, Jewish opinion about it split. Most Zionists opposed the idea, but two leading American personalities, Stephen S. Wise, head of the American Jewish Congress and the World Jewish Congress, and Louis Lipsky, an outstanding leader of American Zionism, approved. The American Jewish Labor movement opposed the agreement, but most of the non-Zionist upper-class Jewish leaders were either in favor or of two minds. Most of the British non-Zionist leadership supported it.

The crucial point was that the proposed agreement had the full support of the U.S. and British governments. After Rublee's resignation, an extraordinary attempt was made by Roosevelt, via the State Department as well as in person, to make the Jews agree to the terms that the Germans had agreed on. This required setting up a Coordinating Foundation to do two things: direct the prospective emigrants, who now would come out with money, to places of immigration; and raise the counterfunds—according to the agreement, a sum of $600 million—in the midst of what still was a bad economic crisis. Roosevelt again called on Myron C. Taylor to be the go-between, and a first meeting between him and a group of prominent Jewish non-Zionist leaders, roughly representing the American Jewish Committee and the JDC, took place on March 28, 1939; a second, broader meeting, in the chambers of Judge Samuel I. Rosenman, a Roosevelt contact, took place on April 15.[15] The Jewish response was still guarded: "We should take no steps that directly or by implication would give recognition by the Jewish community as such to the validity of any expropriation of private property or of the requirement that German citizens who are Jews shall be driven into exile."[16] If Taylor wanted to form an organization to implement the plan, such an organization should be general, not Jewish. Further, private funds would not suffice, and governmental help was essential.

Negotiations with Taylor followed. Taylor brushed aside Jewish reservations and chose to interpret the Jewish attitude to the plan as positive. To the State Department, however, he said that the Jews feared that by establishing the Coordinating Foundation they would set up precisely that "International Jewry" that the Nazis were ranting about. Yet on April 29 forty-one Jewish leaders met and agreed to the plan. On May 4, Paul Baerwald of the JDC, Henry Ittleson, Lewis L. Strauss, Judge Joseph Proskauer, Sol Stroock—all of them leaders of the American Jewish Committee—and Judge Rosenman met with the President. Sumner Welles and Pierrepont Moffat represented the State Department. Roosevelt urged the Jews to set up the foundation as soon as possible. In the wake of that unprecedented pressure, JDC sent two senior representatives to London to negotiate with the British to set up the foundation.

The first problem of the Jewish leaders was money, or rather the lack of it. The total income of the JDC, which presumably would have to raise the major part of the funds, was $8.1 million in 1939. The settlement of the tragedy of 907 refugees from Germany, who had been wandering all over the Atlantic on the SS *St. Louis* in May and June 1939, cost the JDC $1 million out of that sum. The JDC also had to take care of the growing needs of German, Polish, and Romanian Jews, who grew more and more destitute. Where would they be able to raise the huge sums needed for the vast project of emigrating all or most of German Jewry?

The situation was further complicated by the publication of the British White Paper on Palestine on May 17, 1939. The British were under Arab pressure and feared Arab diversionary activities in the Middle East in case of war in Europe. In fact, the British were quite sure a war would break out soon, and they were largely unprepared for it. The Jews would have to pay the price of making sure that the Arabs did not rebel. Jewish immigration to Palestine would be limited to a total of 75,000 over the next five years; all further immigration would depend on Arab consent. To counteract that blow somewhat, the British took two steps: (1) earlier in the year, but after they had decided to cut immigration to Palestine, they decided to take 10,000 unaccompanied Jewish children from Germany, Austria, and the Czech lands into Britain, and (2) they published a "Report on British Guiana" (also on May 17), in which they held out the prospect of Jewish settlement in that tropical South American British colony. The Guiana project was a red herring, of course. The total number of refugees that might be settled, according to a commission that had been sent there, was 3,000–5,000, as an experiment. And, as the British colonial secretary, Malcolm MacDonald, declared on June 22, the experiment would have to be paid for by the Jews.[17]

British Jewry's resources were strained to the limit. They had to support the children coming from Germany and large numbers of adult immigrants as well—the total number of refugees arriving in Britain in 1939 was over 50,000. In short, as the JDC emissaries soon found out, British Jews would not be able to help in the foundation project. On June 6, JDC therefore decided to allocate $1 million—which it really did not have—to the foundation. An important member of the JDC Executive Committee stated the reason: to eliminate uncertainty about its "readiness to carry through a commitment which in effect was desired by Mr. Taylor and the president."[18] Another meeting of Jewish leaders then took place in New York, at which Wise expressed hesitation regarding the step taken by JDC. Joseph Tennenbaum, who represented the American Federation of Polish Jews, opposed it outright. It would, he said, act against the anti-German boycott and further German exports.

Baerwald, in the meantime, met with Wohlthat in London. The Nazi agreed to negotiate with a purely American foundation if the talks between American and British Jews failed because of lack of funds in Britain. In such a case, he said, only 5–10 percent of German Jewish assets would be turned over to the German trust fund.[19] Baerwald soon had two new problems on his hands: the British Jews, pressured by their government, wanted to spend money on settlement schemes, which JDC, rightly, saw as a waste of money; and the American Jewish Congress and Labor leaders in New York demanded an assurance from JDC that no foreign currency and no additional exports would accrue to Germany as a result of the new approach.

The British government now changed its policy: on July 19 the Foreign Office declared in a communiqué that the British government would be prepared to participate in settlement projects, provided other governments were ready to do the same.[20] JDC now agreed to include a reference to possible settlement schemes in the charter of the new foundation. The charter was signed on July 20—six weeks before the outbreak of World War II.

The questions we have to ask now are, Why did the American government, and its President, find it necessary to pressure the Jews to agree to a plan hatched by Rublee and the Nazis? Why did it invite American Jews to spend huge sums of dollars to settle Jewish refugees in remote places on the face of the earth? What interest did Roosevelt have in persuading American Jews to arrive at an agreement with British Jews over this issue? There is no documentary basis for satisfactory answers. Clearly, a humanitarian motivation, while it may well have played a role, is not a sufficient explanation. We may surmise that Roosevelt wanted to register a major humanitarian foreign policy success and gain additional popularity. But that, too, is not really convincing.

The fact remains that American Jews were pressured by a Gentile President of their country to save their European kin, possibly because Roosevelt read the handwriting on the wall better than they did. But the effort did not succeed. Why?

The negotiations with the West on Jewish emigration played no role in Hitler's moves that ended with the outbreak of war. The Jewish question would be solved, *so oder so,* and Germany's major task was to break out from its Central European shell. This stood in no contradiction to Hitler's willingness to have the Jews leave by agreement with the Americans and the British. But the British chose to enter the war, all contact was broken, and that was the end of that.

Finally, we have to ask, particularly in the context of the Schacht-Rublee negotiations, why World War II broke out. The question seems to have no place here, but appearances are misleading.

In the vast literature dealing with the outbreak of war in 1939, very little has been said about the underlying reasons for it. There are, to be sure, any number of studies on Hitler's diplomatic moves, on the policies of the West and the Soviet Union and Poland, on military preparations on both sides, and so on. The steps toward war are fairly evident. But why did the Germans want the war in the first place? The question becomes more puzzling still when one remembers that the German armed forces, in September 1938, almost rebelled against Hitler because they did not want a war and, further, that military enthusiasm for the war a year later was not much greater. The major German industrialists were for the most part very reluctant for a war to start. The population, as we have been told, was apathetic. The German economy had revived, unemployment had been all but wiped out, Germany was strong and not threatened by anyone—on the contrary, it was Germany that was threatening others. Why war, then? The obvious, and trite, answer is that Hitler wanted war. The obvious, and trite, counterquestion is why?

Hitler said explicitly in a number of statements to his military, to his nearest collaborators, and to others why he wanted the war. His statements can be summarized thus: he wanted the expansion of Germany in order to fortify

the power of the Germanic or Nordic peoples of the Aryan race in the struggle for hegemony in Europe; and this was impossible without contending
with the "encirclement" of Germany by its enemies, who were directed by
International Jewry. The main threat came from Soviet Bolshevism, which
was nothing other than the most dangerous expression of the Jewish will to
rule the world. The Soviet Union, the United States, and France were under
Jewish control, and in 1939 only Britain was still independent, or so Hitler
thought. But when Britain joined the war in September 1939, he became convinced that there, too, Jewish power had become dominant. In other words,
for Hitler the war was waged to fortify Germany as the central Nordic-Aryan
power and secure its predominance in Europe and the world.[21] To achieve
that goal, International Jewry had to be fought, because it was behind every
major power opposing Germany. The war was, therefore, not motivated by
pragmatic considerations or interests—not military, not economic, not prac-
tical-political, but by ideology, and ideology alone. A central part of that ideology was antisemitism. The war was, in the last analysis, a war against the
Jews.

This conclusion, probably because of its enormity, was not arrived at
either by contemporaries who understood the Nazi policy well or by historians and other commentators. But it is inescapable: hatred of the Jews was one
of the two major motivations of the Nazis in starting a war that claimed
dozens of millions of victims, among them close to six million Jews. The
other motivation—perhaps the first in importance from a Nazi point of
view—was the "positive" one of creating a Nordic-Germanic empire that
would control Europe and thence the world.

Does this explication stand in stark contradiction to the pragmatic way in
which Hitler approached the Rublee negotiations? Not at all. Jews were
Satan; one could get rid of them *so oder so,* as occasions presented themselves.
There was a moment when it seemed that an arrangement that might have
saved German Jews would be reached. It did not work—the Jews themselves
were hesitant, and they hardly had the resources to ensure success. The
Western governments were willing to press their Jews to agree to the plan but
did not provide them with funds, nor did they open their gates to the
refugees. The proposal might well have failed because of these unsolved
problems, even had there been time. But in the end it was the timing that
proved fatal—the idea came too late, and was destroyed by the roar of air-
planes and tanks and the dying groans of Polish soldiers as Nazi military
might swept through the fields of Poland. The enemy was time.

3

Enemies with a Common Interest

Between 1938 and 1941 a peculiar set of contacts developed between Nazi officials like Adolf Eichmann and Jewish individuals representing either a Zionist organization or only themselves or sometimes both—contacts whose aim it was to further Jewish emigration from the Reich and immigration into Palestine. The background to the contacts, on the Jewish side, was the increasing tendency of the British in Palestine to limit, even choke off, Jewish immigration.

The reasons for the gradual change of policy have been examined and clarified by a number of historians: the imminent threat of Axis powers to disrupt imperial communications in the Middle East by using Arab guerrillas; the military weakness of Britain in 1938–39 (the British had only six infantry divisions at their disposal, all told); and the desire of British politicians to ally themselves with the rising Arab nations, rather than with the Jewish losers—all these contributed to the erosion of British sympathies with Zionism. (This was especially painful for Polish Zionists, who had gained ground among Polish Jews in the 1930s, when it seemed as though Palestine could provide a home for large numbers of Jews who could no longer stay in poverty-stricken, antisemitic, crisis-ridden Poland.)

Activist Zionist youth of both left-wing and right-wing political persuasions began organizing in 1934 to enter Palestine illegally; from their point of view there was no such thing as "illegal" Jewish immigration: all Jewish immigration to the National Homeland was legal. The leftist Hechalutz movement, spearheaded by the Kibbutz Meuchad Federation of kibbutzim (collective settlements) in Palestine, headed by Yitzhak Tabenkin, organized two trips of the Greek ship *Velos*, in July and November 1934, but the ship was caught by the British on the second voyage, and its passengers had to return to Poland. The attempt by the right-wing Betar movement to send the *Union* to Palestine was successful (in August 1934), but the follow-up with the *Wanda* ended in disaster when the ship sank in Danzig harbor. The official Zionist movement was opposed to these efforts: in 1935 the British permitted a legal immigration of 62,000 Jews to

Palestine, and there was no point in angering the British lion when it was being helpful. But from 1936 on, with the development of the Arab rebellion (1936–39) in Palestine, British policy changed, as we have just seen.

In 1938 "illegal" immigration started again, with the Zionist leadership deeply split on the issue. Chaim Weizmann and David Ben Gurion were opposed, because they were hoping for Britain to return to its traditional pro-Zionist policies, and saw no point in sabotaging their own efforts to that end by causing British animosity through illegal immigration. But dissension on this point developed within Mapai, the Jewish Labor Party, which was the main group represented in the JA leadership. The followers of Tabenkin were now joined by Berl Katznelson, the main moral and spiritual authority of the movement, and the editor of the Mapai daily. Hechalutz sent its team to Europe to buy ships, usually in Greece, along with the right to fly a Panamanian or other flag of convenience, to equip the vessel, to hire captain and crew, and to send it to a port of exit. At first, in 1938, Italian, Yugoslav, and later, in one instance (the *Dora*, in July–August 1939), even Dutch and Belgian ports were used. By May 1939 British surveillance and intervention with the countries of exit to prevent sailings made it impossible to use Mediterranean ports. Instead, the Danube became the main route, so the journeys started from Vienna or Bratislava.

By that time, too, internal disagreements had become more bitter. The right-wing Revisionist movement, of which Betar was the youth branch, had left the Zionist Organization (ZO) in 1935. On the other hand, the armed underground of the ZO, the Haganah, which was nominally controlled by the parties represented on the JA but in fact by the Labor movement, had come to control illegal immigration (Aliyah Beth, or AB—"B" immigration). It established the Mossad Le'Aliyah B (Institute for "B" Immigration) in the summer of 1938 and put Shaul Avigur (Meirov) at its head. The European center was established in Paris. Avigur was connected, not only politically but through family ties as well, with Eliyahu Golomb, effectively the commander of the Haganah, and Moshe Sharett (Shertok), the head of the JA political department. Slowly, too, as negotiations between the JA and the British showed no progress from a Zionist point of view, Ben Gurion came round to an appreciation of the political value of B immigration. In November 1938 he proposed a program of mass illegal immigration, executed in the full glare of publicity in order to arouse public sympathy for the Jews, mainly in Britain.[1] This was anathema to the B-immigration activists, whose aims were to save Polish Jewish youth movements from disintegration and to bring youngsters to Palestine both to rescue them from starvation and hopelessness and to contribute to the building up of a Jewish Palestine. B immigration had to be managed surreptitiously, they said: publicity would destroy the whole effort.

Almost all Mossad immigrants came from Poland, so there was little need for contact with German authorities. Even before Kristallnacht, however, German and Austrian Jewish youth became candidates for Mossad transports to Palestine. There were emissaries of Hechalutz in the Reich, in Berlin, and in Vienna; in Vienna, there was a Mossad emissary, Moshe Agami (Averbuch), and there were also local youth leaders who helped contact the Nazi authorities to facilitate the exit of Jews—Ehud Avriel (Überall) and Teddy Kollek. Agami and the others established a link with the Gestapo through Wolfgang Karthaus, a highly placed Austrian Nazi who was willing to help the Jews, partly for ideological reasons—the policy was, after all, to emigrate them—and he undertook to help in overcoming difficulties. With the aid of some shady characters and bribes, Yugoslav transit visas were obtained, obviously through Gestapo intervention. Mossad representatives from Paris were permitted to enter Austria in the same way. With Karthaus's help, the first Mossad ship to transport people from the Reich (the *Colorado,* which transferred its passengers to the *Atràto* at sea) sailed from Susak, Yugoslavia, in March 1939, carrying 400 passengers (including 280 from Germany). After a short while, however, agents of Goebbels's propaganda ministry discovered the illegal transport arrangement in Yugoslavia, and Goebbels published the story in his paper, *Der Angriff.* One agency of the Nazis had sabotaged another.[2] Agami had to leave Vienna, and the passage through Yugoslavia was "burnt." As early as May, Mossad carried on from Constantsa in Romania, and there, too, some Austrian Jews boarded the ship. Constantsa meant not only a geographic but a political redirection, because ships would have to be found to sail down the neutral Danube waterways, where no transit visas would be needed; using the overland route involved complicated visa problems.

Meanwhile, the political struggle within the Zionist movement was being made public. Things came to a head during the Twenty-first Zionist Congress in Geneva, in August 1939. Katznelson came out openly in favor of B immigration, and Weizmann could no longer muster the necessary support to nullify his intervention, though he was supported by Rabbi Abba Hillel Silver, an American Zionist leader. The JA leadership remained split over and unsure about B immigration.

The Revisionist movement also tried to establish a central organization for its B-immigration activities, which became more and more significant during 1938. By early 1939 a center had been established in Paris, but dissension among the various branches of the movement were such that the center made arrangements for very few of the ships (four at most) that sailed prior to the outbreak of war. The other sailings were arranged by Revisionist individuals who became disillusioned with the slowness and inefficiency of the Paris center; they also made money by organizing these trips on their own. Sincerely held ideological convictions, as with Willi Perl of Vienna (originally from Czechoslovakia), were the determining factor with some. With others, ideology and the desire to make money went together. Hermann Flesch and Paul Haller concentrated on helping other Viennese Jews depart, from the spring of 1938 until August 1939. Most of their ships sailed from Romanian ports. Additional efforts were directed from Bulgaria by another private individual, Baruch Confino, who, however, was closer to Mossad than to the Revisionists. His groups need not concern us here, because he was not connected to the Reich and had no contact with SS authorities.

Together, all these initiatives resulted in the immigration to Palestine of 17,240 people up to the outbreak of war, of whom close to 12,000 arrived courtesy of the Revisionists and the private organizers and about 5,500 courtesy of Mossad.[3]

The prewar negotiations on the German side were likewise complicated. Eichmann arrived in Vienna on March 16, 1938, as the Gestapo delegate charged with emigrating Jews. The local chief of the Gestapo's IIb Branch dealing with "opponents," including Jews, was Rudolf Lange, with whom Eichmann had a good relationship. Lange supported Karthaus in the Susak venture of Mossad. At first, Eichmann appears to have been opposed to illegal transports to Palestine.[4] In his memoirs, Perl reports—and there is little reason to doubt his testimony—that he submitted a written proposal to Eichmann to organize such transports; Eichmann, he says, responded after a short time: "Wir brauchen keine Verbrecherzentrale in Palästina, die Juden werden atomisiert" (We don't need a center of criminals in Palestine; we will atomize the Jews [that is, disperse them as isolated individuals]). This statement appears to echo Hitler's decision to oppose the establishment of a Jewish State in Palestine and was in line with the policies of the German Foreign Office. It may well have represented Eichmann's own preferences. But they soon changed.[5]

Eichmann must have coordinated his steps with Lange, because in May he called a meeting of Revisionist representatives and private organizers, like Perl, Haller, and Flesch, and some community leaders. Gestapo pressure was a powerful reason for the private transports that left Vienna between May 1938 and May 1939.[6] The decisive fact was that Jewish emigration was the central pillar of Nazi policies toward the Jews.

Despite internal squabbles among the Revisionists, which led to the expulsion of Haller and Flesch from the Party, the Revisionist leadership tried its best to facilitate the B-immigration ventures. Jabotinsky met with the Romanian King, Carol II, in London in the summer of 1938 and then again, in October, in Bucharest. The Romanians agreed to permit passage of riverboats with immigrants to a Romanian Black Sea port, provided a vessel was there to receive them and provided some Romanian Jews would be extruded as well.[7] But the Revisionists, just like Mossad, were plagued by a lack of funds and by the unavailability of ships and crews just when emigration from the Reich became a more and more pressing need. Mossad, too, had to change its priorities and began organizing B immigration from the Reich.

From early 1938 on, the SS policy, in line with the dictator's wishes, was to pressure Jews to leave in large numbers. Herbert Hagen, at that time the head of the Jewish department of the SD, the internal intelligence organ of the SS, declared that he would promote all plans for emigration, no matter whither. The possible destinations included Palestine, but because of the problems that the SS had with the Foreign Office and because of opposition by the British, the documents of the refugees did not mention Palestine as the destination.[8]

Both before and after Kristallnacht, which was intended to push the Jews into a helter-skelter flight from the Reich, Mossad representatives, Revisionists, and private organizers of B immigration turned to Eichmann and his office in Vienna for help in getting the Jews out. They had to ask the Germans to convert the emigrants' money to foreign currency to pay for ships, they had to obtain transit visas, they had to procure boats to sail down the Danube, and of course they had to obtain exit permits. Without the Gestapo none of that could be done. And the Gestapo was helpful.

The states through which the Danube flowed were pressed very hard by the British to prevent the "traffic"—as they preferred to call it—of "illegal" Jewish migrants to Palestine.[9] To use the Danube pathway to the Black Sea—and the advantage was, as we have seen, that as the river was an international waterway, visas were not necessary for the river voyage—a German shipping company could be utilized. The main, though not the only, such line was the Deutsche Donau-Schiffahrtsgesellschaft (DDSG), now completely nazified. Its owners definitely wanted a share of the Jewish money, however, and while the Gestapo had leverage with them, they were nevertheless a group that acted in its own, separate interest. Occasionally Jews were also helped by friendly individuals; a man like that, Direktor Schätz, worked in the DDSG.

In August 1938 Eichmann established the Zentralstelle für jüdische Auswanderung (Central Office for Jewish Emigration) in Vienna, apparently in response to a Jewish initiative (the Jews wanted to make emigration easier); the Zentralstelle deprived the Jews of their property and in return provided them with exit permits, one major aim being to force the richer people to pay for the emigration of the poorer ones.[10] After Eichmann's initial hesitation, anyone who could suggest to him how to extrude larger numbers of Jews would receive some kind of help. In principle, the help consisted of pressure on the DDSG to steal slightly less money from the Jews than they otherwise would have taken and to release individuals from concentration camps who were promised places on B-immigration transports. It became clear, however, that the Nazi interest in B immigration was greater than these activities would suggest. The more Jews left the Reich, the greater the success the SS could claim in its internal battles for the dictator's favor. B immigration was, in addition, a promising way to extrude Jews to Palestine in the face of British opposition. The policy of the SS in this matter was radically opposed to that of the Foreign Office, which—as mentioned already—objected to immigration to Palestine because it might create a Jewish State there; the Foreign Office, following Hitler, saw this as an undesirable development. The SS disregarded the opposition of the Foreign Office, probably because Hitler made no comment on the merits or otherwise of B immigration. Perhaps it was not important enough in his eyes, or he may have thought that while a Jewish State had to be opposed, the immigration of a few thousand more Jews to Palestine would not make much difference. That he did not stop Ha'avarah explicitly, even in 1939, and that he approved of the Schacht-Rublee plan although it did not preclude emigration to Palestine increase the plausibility of this hypothesis.

SS relations with the Foreign Office could not, of course, be permitted to deteriorate too much, and after the founding of the Zentralstelle, Heydrich declared that although he was in principle against all illegal immigration, the Palestine transports were different because if Germany did not push out its Jews, countries like Poland would monopolize the ships to get rid of *their* Jews.[11]

Eichmann's success in emigrating some 117,000 Austrian Jews in 1938–39, to which the B–immigration contribution was minimal, caused Heydrich to push for the establishment of a Zentralstelle on the Viennese model in Berlin. Goering, the man responsible, under Hitler, for Jewish policies, signed an appropriate order on January 24, 1939, and although Heinrich Müller, the Gestapo chief, was the formal head of the new outfit, Eichmann ultimately became responsible in fact for Jewish emigration in the whole of the Reich.

He now had several irons in the fire: Mossad, the Revisionists, and the private organizers. Mossad utilized two Hechalutz emissaries (Pino Ginsburg and Max Zimmels), who arrived in Berlin in January 1939 and made contact with the Gestapo on the strength of their mandate to organize Jewish emigration. A man who worked with the Gestapo and who the Gestapo probably charged with furthering Jewish emigration, Alexander von Höpfner, approached the Mossad emissaries and offered to help them in a grandiose scheme. The idea, which became part of the German Jewish leadership's policy, was to send 10,000 German Jews to Palestine on vessels supplied by the German Hapag (Hamburg-Amerika) Lines—"illegally"! The Reichsvereinigung der Juden in Deutschland (RVE), the official organization of German Jews—set up in July 1939 to replace the Reichsvertretung, which had operated until the Kristallnacht—offered to pay 10 million Reichsmark for the venture, quite contrary to its previous policies. The details had evidently been worked out by August 1939, but the outbreak of war foiled the plan.[12] Neither Mossad nor the Gestapo gave up. First they tried to revive the scheme by using neutral Holland as a base, and when that did not work, they devised a plan, in November 1939, to emigrate large numbers of German Jews from Italian ports. Correspondence between the Gestapo and the Foreign Office reveals that von Höpfner worked for Kurt Lischka, Eichmann's deputy in the Berlin Zentralstelle, and may have been genuinely more friendly to Jews in general. But personal goodwill did not help in Italy, because the Foreign Office did not want to complicate its relations there, and the Italians had no wish to have thousands of Jewish emigrants crowding their ports in a doubtful venture.[13]

The matter did not end even there. In January 1940 the RVE was involved in a scheme whereby a subsidiary of Hapag, Apala, set up to send Jews illegally to Palestine, was registering potential Jewish emigrants. The RVE undertook to screen the candidates; apparently 30,000 people registered, and a few were chosen, probably as a tryout. Money for the trip would be covered in part by the wealthier passengers and in part by funds from abroad, in hard currency. Clearly, the Gestapo was behind the scheme, through its Jewish representative, Storfer, of whom more below. We do not know where the ships were to sail from, but in any case nothing came of the scheme.[14]

Eichmann apparently did not want to rely solely on independent Jewish groups, such as Mossad or the Revisionists. He was looking for a Jewish agent of his own, a person he could control, and he found him in Berthold Storfer.

Storfer was born in 1882, in Bukovina, and became a respected merchant and banker in Austria. He was not active in Jewish affairs, but after the *Anschluss* he joined the unofficial Austrian Jewish delegation to the Evian conference. He then became a member of the Austrian Jewish leadership and approached Eichmann with requests to facilitate more Jewish emigration— just the kind of requests that Eichmann liked. Eichmann reportedly nominated Storfer to be his coordinator in B-immigration matters before or in March 1939—in other words, after Eichmann had become the effective head of the Zentralstelle.[15] Throughout the spring and summer of 1939, contact with the Gestapo in Vienna and some contacts in Berlin and Prague were via Storfer. Storfer was involved, for instance, with the *Colorado-Atrato* sailing from Susak in the spring of 1939. In March 1940 Eichmann nominated Storfer to be the sole agent in charge of Jewish emigration generally, and B immigration specifically. The JDC, Mossad, the Revisionists, and the private organizers had to work with and through Storfer, which for most of them—and especially Mossad—was a hard pill to swallow: Mossad and the Revisionists considered Storfer a traitor and a Gestapo agent, pure and simple.

The main bone of contention between Mossad and Storfer, apart from his obvious contacts with the Gestapo, was his acceptance of Eichmann's line that rich Jews should pay for the poor ones—in other words, that no selection of emigrants on the basis of suitability for life in Palestine should be permitted. Mossad was wedded to the prevalent Zionist approach, which held that because the number of immigrants was perforce limited in any case, selection should be on the basis of youth, adaptability, and willingness to work at manual labor in Palestine. But this ideology did not work with Mossad, either; pressures that it could not withstand and lack of funds dictated that wealthy people should also be included.[16]

In actuality, selection of passengers on B-immigration ships generally was increasingly controlled by the Gestapo. Storfer was in touch with the JDC from late 1939 on, and it was the JDC that supplied an important part of the funds for his ventures—not by sending foreign currency to Vienna but by paying for ships and provisions in the Balkans. A central Mossad figure, Zvi Yehieli, met with Storfer twice (in February 1940, in Bucharest, and in May, in Geneva) to try and arrive at some mutually satisfactory arrangement, but the differences were too great, and relations remained very strained.[17] With the benefit of hindsight and in consideration of Mossad's major aim—to get Jews out—we might argue that Yehieli should have held his nose, figuratively speaking, and struck a deal.

Let us now turn to one of the more colorful players in this drama, Willi Perl. Perl had left Austria with the help of a ruse in 1938 and was organizing B immigration from the outside. In early September 1939, Perl called Storfer about a major transport he wanted to arrange now that war had broken out and the situation of Jews had become critical. On June 15, 1939, his cousin in Prague, Robert Mandler, had received permission from the Gestapo to exchange Czech crowns for British pounds up to £20 per person. Germany was suffering from a lack of hard currency, and here the Gestapo was offering the Jews British pounds if only they left! Nor was permission revoked even after the outbreak of war. The Revisionists succeeded in "renting" a Turkish ship, the *Sakariya,* but they encountered the usual problems of cheating shipowners, British pressure on Romania, and a chronic lack of funds. Eichmann personally permitted Mandler to leave Prague in order to help settle the problem in Sulina, the Romanian port of exit, in December 1939. Storfer was also involved, directly and through his deputy, Moritz Pappenheim of the ultraorthodox group of Agudas Yisroel. In the end, the *Sakariya* sailed, on February 1, 1940, with 2,228 people aboard; it reached Palestine on February 13.[18]

After the outbreak of war, Mossad and Hechalutz in Vienna came to the realization that the Austrian Hechalutz members and a number of others who were looking to Mossad to escape from Nazi Germany had to be moved out quickly before all the gates closed. Ehud Avriel, the Viennese youth leader who was in charge of the operation, was contacted by another shady character; this one called himself Ferdinand Ceipek and claimed that he hated the

Nazis and wanted to help Jews. He, too, was clearly in touch with the Gestapo and, whatever his personal predilections may have been, was implementing Gestapo policy by helping to emigrate Jews. In this case, 1,000 Jews were transferred, with the help of bribes, to Bratislava, Slovakia, in November, 1939. Eichmann had ordered Avriel to make arrangements through Storfer, but it seems that Ceipek was not connected to Storfer. Mossad failed to provide a ship at the Romanian end, and the DDSG refused to transfer the passengers to Romania unless a ship was there to take them away. In the spring of 1940 Yugoslav riverboats tried to bring the transport to Romania but failed, and the group found temporary refuge, in terrible conditions, in Kladovo, a small Yugoslav river port.[19] Storfer was approached for help, but he refused to provide money to buy a Turkish ship, the *Wetan*, claiming that Mossad had organized the transport without him and that he would not take responsibility for Mossad's failure without seeing the boat first; of course, the owners insisted on a down payment to start with. The money was obtained from the JDC, and a huge sum (for Mossad), $42,000, was sent to Turkey to buy the ship. But a new Turkish law forbidding such sales was suddenly promulgated, and both the money and the ship were lost. In the end, after the refugees had been transferred to another port, Sabac, Mossad failed to find a ship for them; they were all murdered by the Germans some months after the invasion of Yugoslavia in April 1941.[20]

Storfer had a Greek agent to buy ships, and he also used his family members to help organize transports. He managed to send three ships, which reached Palestine in late 1940 after many difficulties. One of the ships contained the pick of German Hechalutz members; the others contained a mix of people who could pay, youths, and families who managed to obtain passage through Mossad or the Revisionist offices in the Reich. The number of refugees on the ships was 3,551, and Storfer encountered the same problems as the other organizers of the transports did. He was, it seems, quite unscrupulous, and cared very little about the fate of his transports once they were beyond the reach of the Germans. Yet he probably saw himself as a rescuer of Jews—which he was, with the Gestapo's help. The refugees who finally reached Palestine on the *Milos,* the *Pacific,* and the *Atlantic* left Vienna and Bratislava on September 3, 1940. They boarded the three ships on the eleventh and reached Palestine in October and November. There, the British decided to deport all of them to the island of Mauritius in the Indian Ocean, declaring that after the war they would not be permitted to immigrate to Palestine. Passengers from two of the ships were transferred to the French freighter *Patria* at Haifa, but the Haganah sabotaged the ship to prevent it from sailing—actually, without the permission of the JA. The amount of explosives, intended to cripple the ship, was miscalculated, and the ship sank on November 25, 1940. Many lives were lost in the disaster—267—and the survivors were permitted to stay in Palestine. The passengers of the third ship, the *Atlantic,* were deported to Mauritius.

Storfer himself, like Mandler and some of the others, was murdered in the end—just as many other Jewish leaders were murdered who had supped with Eichmann.

Nazi policy on the extrusion of Jews was not affected by the fate of Storfer's ships, and Eichmann continued to press for a speedy removal of Jews. After the outbreak of war in September 1939, in light of increasing difficulties in emigrating Jews legally or semilegally, two parallel policies were enforced: deportation of Jews from the Reich and the Czech Protectorate to Poland, and illegal transports to Palestine. Neither worked very well. Transports to Poland, where Jews were sent near the town of Nisko on the southeastern border—the demarcation line between the Germans and the Soviets—could not be continued because of opposition from the newly established administration of the Polish Generalgouvernement (GG). The governor, Hans Frank, objected to large numbers of Jews and Gypsies being foisted on him, and the deportations had to be stopped in the spring of 1940.

Emigration to Palestine got rid of only a few thousand Jews—in fact, between September 1, 1939, and March 1941, the number of B immigrants was 12,863, not all of them from the Reich, nor did all of them reach Palestine. Eichmann wanted much more to be done, which seems to explain the journeys of the *Sakariya* in the winter of 1939–40 and the three Storfer ships in the autumn of 1940. These results of internal pressure must have looked rather meager to Eichmann, and he tried to make the Jews leave by more brutal pressure. On July 3, 1940, he called the leaders of the RVE in the Vienna and the Prague communities and demanded that they submit a plan within forty-eight hours to remove all Jews from the Reich. Needless to say, this ultimatum did not help. In early 1941 all Nazi attempts to push Jews in the direction of Palestine ceased. What took their place was the development of the "Final Solution." Until October 1941, however, Jews from the Reich were still permitted to leave, and many were pushed across the borders, even though mass murder had started in the areas being conquered in the Soviet Union. Indeed, the October date coincides with the preparation for the activation of the first mass murder camp at Chelmno, where gassings started on December 8, 1941, but preparations were under way in October, when Jews could still leave. In Serbia mass killings were already in full swing by then. The two policies, murder and extrusion, were for a short period in operation at the same time.

Can the Gestapo contacts with Jewish underground movements in 1938–40 be considered negotiations? Or did they represent a kind of lopsided cooperation? Willi Perl captured the gist of the paradox inherent in the situation when he said that "on ships of neutral countries, young Jews of many nationalities were traveling with our organization to British-held Palestine, where they would undoubtedly join the British forces to fight the Nazis. The British tried to prevent this. The Germans not only permitted it; they aided the undertaking of providing the British with young soldiers who were doubtlessly well motivated to fight the Nazis. The Germans let the people out who would otherwise have been able to perform slave labor in factories. The Nazis supplied the riverboats, and they even granted the right to exchange local currency into foreign currency so needed by the Reich."[21]

Yet we can hardly talk of Nazi-Jewish negotiations in this context; the cooperation was between a persecutor, who at that stage wanted to rid himself of the victim, and the representatives of groups of the victims, who were trying to escape his clutches. As for Jewish emigration from Germany discussed earlier, the Nazi aims were paralleled by the Jewish desire to escape. But whereas in the Ha'avarah and Rublee-Schacht cases, real negotiations took place involving recognized interests, no such negotiations took place between Eichmann, Storfer, Avriel, Mandler, or Perl. There was, on one side, brutal, direct pressure, along with some help—if that is what it was—that was extended to achieve Nazi aims and, on the other side, the desperate efforts of Jewish groups and their leaders to escape from a trap—they were caught between the Nazis, an inhumane British policy, neutral indifference, and a powerless Jewish-Zionist leadership.

What is significant, however, is the fact that until the fall of 1941 Nazi policy—and, what is even more important, SS policy—was one of expulsion, and that policy blended into one of mass murder. To the Nazis, as Heydrich expressed it so well during the infamous Wannsee conference, it was perfectly logical that "emigration has now been replaced by evacuation to the East, as a further possible solution"—that is, a solution that did not contradict the earlier policy—"with the appropriate prior authorization by the Führer."[22] Total extinction of the Jews became the aim. Did that necessarily and under all circumstances contradict emigration and extrusion in the stages that followed?

4

The Road to the "Final Solution"

There is no evidence that any major Nazi agency was interested in negotiations with Jews or about Jews, except for B immigration, from the invasion of Poland well into 1942—in other words, during the period of the greatest Nazi ascendancy. Nazi policy toward the Jews moved from forcible extrusion to annihilation in a process that is well known and has been described in detail in current literature.[1]

With the invasion of Poland, all contact with the United States regarding the sale of Jews ceased, and Britain became Germany's enemy when it declared war on September 3, 1939. The reason is obvious: an alternative plan for what to do with the Jews was developed, and it was at least sanctioned, but probably initiated, by Hitler himself. On September 21, 1939, a consultation was held by Heydrich with office heads and chiefs of the special SS and Police Einsatzgruppen (Action Groups), as the police murder units spreading terror in occupied Poland were called. Those attending were very high ranking: Gestapo chief Heinrich Müller; Artur Nebe, head of the Kriminalpolizei (KRIPO, or Criminal Police); Adolf Eichmann, and many others. What to do with the newly conquered Polish territories and their inhabitants, including the Jews, was discussed. The problem was by no means simple, because now the Germans had under their control not just the German, Austrian, and Czech Jews, numbering approximately half a million, but some 1.7 million of the 3.3 million Polish Jews as well (the others were in the Soviet-occupied part of prewar Poland).

The crucial sentences in the protocol of the meeting, written on September 27, read as follows: "The Commissar for Settlement in the East will be the Reichsführer SS [Himmler]. The deportation of Jews to the alien province, extrusion beyond the demarcation line, was approved by the Führer. But all this will take a year." Elsewhere in the document the term "alien province" is explained: it was the future Generalgouvernement, or the core of occupied Poland, minus the western provinces annexed by Nazi Germany. The term "demarcation line" indicated the new border between the GG and the Soviet

Union. In other words, the approval of Hitler (at his initiative, most probably, to judge from precedents) had been given to a plan of extruding all Jews
under German rule into the GG and then removing them further, including
the Polish Jews, into the Soviet Union over the course of a year. The policy
was not yet one of total physical annihilation, but it was designed to rid all
German-held territories of Jews by force. At the same time, future hostile
intentions against the Soviets were hinted at: "[A] new East Wall . . . will
enclose all the German areas, and the alien province will be in front of it."
Future hostility toward the Soviet Union would become evident, presumably, *after* a year, during which time the expulsion of the Jews would take
place.[2]

As a result of the conclave of the SS and police chiefs on September 21,
Heydrich issued an order bearing the same date that provided for the establishment of Jewish Councils in Polish Jewish communities to execute Nazi
orders to the Jews. It also provided for the establishment of concentrations of
Jews next to railway lines and referred to "the planned total measures (i.e.,
the final aim [*Endziel*]) [that] are to be kept strictly secret."[3] When comparing
the two documents produced by the conference, we can see that the "final
aim," which the Führer set, was the expulsion of Jews into the Soviet territories. It was final because it would take a year, whereas the other steps—the
concentration of the Jews and the organization of Jewish leadership groups to
execute Nazi directives—were preparatory to that aim.

The Heydrich directive of September 21 also included the intriguing pro-
vision that in the southeast corner of the new GG, bordering on Soviet-con-
trolled territory, a census of the Jews would be taken and Jewish Councils
would be set up, but there would be no concentration of local Jews. Apparently the idea was to deport all the other Jews there prior to their expulsion
into the Soviet Union. Eichmann tried to put the plan into practice.

In the plan to expel the Jews into the Soviet Union we may perhaps dis-
cern an echo of the Hitler idea to "solve" the Jewish "problem" by some kind
of international agreement. Clearly, no war against the Soviets was planned
for the immediate future, and if the Soviets were to accept millions of Jews
into their territory, negotiations must have been envisioned. No such negotiations took place, however, and the idea so explicitly put forward with the
dictator's concurrence was dropped after a time.

If all the Jews could be expelled—without their property— negotiations
were not needed; expulsion would satisfy, temporarily at least (until hostili-
ties with the Soviet Union began), the desire to "cleanse" the German-controlled areas of the Jewish devils. Despite the obvious development toward
brutality and despite the implications of mass suffering and presumably mass
death that would have accompanied the execution of the Hitler plan at that
stage, this is not yet the "Final Solution" of systematic mass murder.

Following these first plans, Eichmann tried to push Jews into the area around the town of Nisko in the southeastern (Lublin) area of Poland. Tens of thousands of Jews, mainly from Vienna, the Czech Protectorate, and western Poland, were deported there. The idea of concentrating all Jews in the Lublin area was pursued then and later—again with the explicit support of Hitler.[4] The opposition of the new Nazi governor of the GG, Hans Frank, to these deportations, mainly for economic reasons, received the support of Goering, and the idea of a Lublin "reservation" for Jews was dropped in March–April 1940.[5]

Himmler, the person responsible for the execution of Hitler's racial reordering of German-controlled territories, was not quite sure where things were going. As late as May 1940 he declared in a memorandum to Hitler that the "Bolshevist Method of physical destruction of a people [was] un-Germanic and impossible." In the margin Hitler wrote "sehr richtig [very correct]."[6] We cannot read Hitler's mind or gauge how seriously he meant this comment or indeed whether he approved of the particular sentence quoted here or the general contents of the memorandum on the treatment of the population of Poland.

In the document Himmler also spelled out, in somewhat inexact language, the new policy toward the Jews: "I hope that the concept of Jews will be completely extinguished through the possibility of a large emigration of all Jews to Africa or some other colony." This was a clear throwback to the 1938 Hitler notion that the Jews should be deported to Madagascar by international agreement. It was put forward by Himmler *before* the end of the campaign in the west and the capitulation of France in June 1940 but presupposed a German victory. He must have thought that a defeated France and Britain would be amenable to a German proposal regarding a French colonial possession. That, perhaps more than the sentence about the annihilation of a people, may have justified the *sehr richtig* comment in Hitler's eyes.

From then until the autumn, or possibly even the end of 1940, the Madagascar "solution" was the preferred one in Nazi planning. As we have already seen, the idea was by no means new; it had been broached from time to time, ever since the late nineteenth century, as a solution for East European emigration problems generally, and in the 1930s the Polish government even briefly considered the possibility of encouraging Poles to go to Madagascar. Then the proposal became a subject of investigations—in which Jewish bodies participated—in connection with Jewish emigration from Poland. The Nazis picked it up in the second half of the 1930s, and Eichmann worked on the prospect of sending Jews there in 1938. Hitler adopted the idea in the autumn of 1938 at the latest, when he made explicit references to it in his instructions to Goering on the solution of the Jewish "problem." Himmler's memorandum of May 1940 was followed up by the German Foreign Office and the SS, the latter making clear that the solution of the Jewish problem belonged in its own bailiwick. In corresponding with the Foreign Office about Madagascar, Heydrich used the term "territorial final solution" (*territoriale Endlösung*). All this happened in July and August of 1940, after the defeat of France, when the Germans fully expected Britain soon to come to a peace agreement with Germany. In that case, the Germans thought, Madagascar would become a German protectorate, the Jews of Europe would be shipped there, the Jews elsewhere would be forced to pay for their passage, and Madagascar would become a forced settlement of Jews. Nobody even mentioned the indigenous population, of course.[7]

The return to the Madagascar plan, like the idea of pushing the Jews into the Soviet Union and the idea of the Lublin reservation, was not—yet—a program of total physical annihilation, but it already went beyond forced emigration. Madagascar is a tropical island, and it was highly unlikely that a vast number of European Jews, deported to the steamy, malaria-ridden place, without any agricultural or industrial preparations, without capital, under SS supervision, could have survived for any length of time. Terrible suffering and death for many, or perhaps most, deportees were likely. If the Madagascar solution resulted in the decimation of the Jews, no negotiations with the Jews or their well-wishers was called for. A German victory in the European war and the agreement, willy-nilly, of Britain and France to Nazi ideas about the deportation of Jews—this was another, typically Nazi form of the "international agreement" that Hitler had spoken about in his January 30, 1939, speech.

In October 1940 the Nazis deported 7,600 German Jews, mainly from the Baden-Pfalz area, not eastward but westward into France. This choice made sense if the plan was to deport the Jews via French ports to a former French colony. Possibly, then, the Nazis were still thinking at this time of Madagascar as the solution of the Jewish "question." But certain problems were insurmountable. First of all, the British refused to give in, and the Royal Navy controlled the seas. The Germans had no way to reach Madagascar. As the months passed and the defeat of the Luftwaffe in its attempt to prepare for the ground invasion of Britain became evident, Nazi enthusiasm for the Madagascar plan waned. At the same time—actually, from July 1940 on— Hitler began to prepare his main core of collaborators for a war against the Soviet Union.

Hitler prepared the ground for the mass murder of the Jews in his speeches to closed Nazi audiences, especially among the military, and in his meetings with his principal henchmen, as some recent scholarship has shown.[8] The radicalization of the anti-Jewish measures is obviously connected to the decision to attack the Soviet Union.[9] The war against the Judeo-Bolshevik regime, as Hitler saw it, was an ideological struggle between two worldviews. Bolshevism was, in his eyes, an expression of the craving of the International Jewish Conspiracy to rule the world. The war was, in effect, a war against the Jews, hidden behind their Bolshevik facade. Whether the decision to murder all the Jews in the German sphere of influence was taken in early 1941, as Richard Breitman suggests,[10] or whether the decision to murder the Jews in the Soviet Union was taken in the spring of that year and then broadened into a mass murder program in the early or late summer or even early fall is immaterial here. The decision was taken as Nazi Germany seemed on the point of victory in Europe, and as I have argued elsewhere, the order to Heydrich, signed by Goering on July 31, 1941, empowering the police chief to prepare an all-European solution (*Gesamtlösung*) to the Jewish "problem" and to prepare the ground for a "Final Solution" (*Endlösung*), is in fact most probably Hitler's order to murder the Jews.[11]

This Nazi decision seemed irreversible—and, in a way, rightly so. If the situation had not changed for the worse from the Nazi point of view, there is every reason to believe that the decision would have stood. The total annihilation of Jews, wherever they were found, became *the* solution to the Jewish problem. The future seemed to promise a German victory over the Soviet Union, a conquest of parts of the British Empire and the acquisition of warm-water ports from which a sustained sea war—with all the European resources marshaled behind the Germans—would have forced the British to yield. The United States, pressed in Asia by the Japanese, would have had to come to an arrangement with the Nazi Empire, and the Jewish "problem" would then have been solved in the United States as well. Providing capital, arranging for an ordered emigration, preserving Jewish lives—none of this was needed. The murder contained in the ideology from the very beginning but of which most Nazis had not been conscious could now surface without any hindrance. The "Final Solution" could become final indeed.

Yet the very process by which the Nazis reached the point of undertaking mass annihilation implicitly included a certain tactical reservation. As we have seen, radicalization paralleled the strengthening of Nazi power and the expansion of Germany at the expense of an independent Austria, Czechoslovakia, and finally Poland, Scandinavia, and the Western countries. Power and conquest made it possible for the murderous potential in the Nazi ideology to become more manifest. The radicalizing factor was Hitler himself and depended on the hold that his dictatorship had over the German intelligentsia and to an increasing degree over the German populace. His hold in turn depended on the success that the regime had in the economic and social sphere, as well as in the more abstract political sphere of German self-estimation—the result of the reestablishment of German might and power in Europe. The decision or decisions that opened the way to the planned total annihilation of the Jews were dependent, so it seems, on essentially two variables and one constant: on the political and military conditions that made it appear feasible to establish German predominance in Europe and, via Europe, in the world; on the identification of the mass of Germans, and especially the intelligentsia, with the regime and its head, from which it followed that anything Hitler would order—or that the regime would order in his name—would be executed; and the persistent delusion, the anti-Jewish ideology that saw in the Jews the major obstacle to German supremacy.

But if this analysis is correct, then the irreversibility of the decision or decisions was contingent on the factors just enumerated. If some of them changed, would the irreversibility of the murder plan remain? Worth examining here is the proposition that the murder plan, once accepted, would never be given up by a regime that was so heavily ideologized but that it could perhaps be subject to tactical pauses or compromises under certain conditions. These conditions, I suggest, would involve the desire ultimately to execute the "Final Solution" to the fullest extent. But if Germany was in trouble militarily, if the prospect of German control over Europe and the world receded, was it not worthwhile to examine options—tactical compromises, perhaps negotiations with one of the two camps fighting against Germany—in order to provide a breathing space in which Germany might recover? If the price paid for such a breathing space was the release of some Jews, was that not worth it? Once German fortunes were revived, the "Final Solution" would catch up with the released Jews in any case, as it would with all the other Jews who were not (yet) under German control. Delays, negotiations, releases of Jews—these did not mean giving up mass murder. They did not mean a change in Nazi ideology but merely a tactical retreat of little importance made to regain the initiative that would enable Nazi Germany ultimately to execute its ideological genocidal program.

This is the way the situation may have looked from the Nazi side. From the Jewish side, tactical zigzags in the "Final Solution" policy could mean saving lives—not all lives, to be sure, not most lives, but some. According to Jewish tradition, a person who saves one life saves a whole world; it is futile to guess how many worlds were at stake in these tactical considerations.

To the Western Allies, all these considerations were completely foreign. They were fighting a war against an existential threat not only to their political existence but to their culture, society, and way of life. The issue of the Jews was completely marginal to these concerns. The Jews were a religious, possibly ethnic, minority in Europe and America—a not very popular one— and for some mysterious reason the Nazis had decided to persecute them. The Nazis persecuted other minorities, too, and the Western politicians never understood what the difference was, if any, between the persecution of Jehovah's Witnesses, for instance, and the persecution of the Jews. The Jews should not try and jump the queue; the only cure to their predicament—the only cure for everyone persecuted by the Nazis—was Allied victory. The Allies were convinced that one could not negotiate with the Nazis or bribe them; one had to defeat them. No other attitude was permissible. The Allies never understood the Nazis, not even when they defeated them. In the end, they uncovered the horrors of the concentration camps, but why these had existed, what their function had been, and why within the concentration camp system the Jews had occupied such a unique position—these things they did not understand even then.

Nazi fortunes did not dim immediately after the summer of 1941. The first serious defeat of the German Army, in Russia, came in the winter of 1941–42. But the Nazi leadership treated that as an unfortunate setback and set out to recoup their position and bring the Soviets to their knees in the spring and summer campaigns of 1942. The war at sea seemed to be going well for Germany, and the Japanese had defeated the Americans and the Western Allies in the Pacific in the early stages of their intervention in the war. There was, at least on the face of it, no reason to waver in the determination to annihilate the Jewish people—no reason for any negotiations, tactical withdrawals, or reconsiderations.

Not until the autumn of 1942 did German fortunes change. The invasion of North Africa, the British victory at El Alamein, and the bogging-down of the German offensive at Stalingrad all signaled the end of the farthest German advance, the turn of the tide. At that point, not surprisingly, came the first hints of a desire by Himmler, the chief executor of the "Final Solution," to keep options open for possible contacts with the West; and because he was convinced that the Jews controlled the Western powers, just as they controlled the Bolsheviks, he may not have excluded Jewish channels.

5

"Willy"

Historians of the Holocaust have long been aware of the peculiar negotiations that took place in Slovakia in 1942–43 between a group of Jewish leaders and the Nazi *Berater* (adviser) on Jewish affairs in Bratislava, Dieter Wisliceny. These negotiations were described by a participant, Rabbi Michael Dov Ber Weissmandel, in a book published posthumously in New York (1960) called *Min Hametzar* (From the depths), in rabbinical Hebrew.[1] Most subsequent authors, including myself, followed Weissmandel's description of what happened in Slovakia for a number of reasons: first, because Weissmandel wrote in the 1950s, when his memory was presumably still fresh; second, because Weissmandel related dates to the proximity of Jewish holidays, and it was deemed unlikely that an ultraorthodox rabbi of his stature would make a mistake about holidays; third, because Weissmandel accumulated an impressive array of documents, some of which were published in his book in the original, some in Hebrew translation, and it was clear that he would never knowingly change or distort a document. Now, to understand what Weissmandel wrote, some background for the Slovak situation is in order.

Slovakia had been part of the Hungarian monarchy for a thousand years before it joined the newly created Czechoslovak Republic in 1918. Czechs and Slovaks, despite their different fates over a very long historical period, have languages so similar that one could be seen as a dialect of the other. But the Czech lands of Bohemia and Moravia were well developed industrially, with a fairly high standard of living. Slovakia was a mountainous country of poor peasants with few natural resources and less industry. A bitter enmity ensued between the disadvantaged Slovaks and their often overweening Czech cousins. Slovakia was largely Catholic, though there were significant Protestant and Orthodox minorities. A Catholic priest, Andrej Hlinka, founded the Slovenská L'udová Strana, or SL'S (Slovak People's Party), a nationalistic, antisemitic, and anti-Czech political body, which slowly gained adherents in interwar Slovakia. A party militia, the Hlinková Garda, or HG (Hlinka Guard), copied the party

militias in fascist states. The SL'S ideology was a mixture of extreme national-
ism, mainly Italian-type fascism, Catholic orthodoxy, and traditionalism. Its
base was the peasantry and the lower middle class in the small Slovak towns,
but it was led by an important part of the incipient Slovak intelligentsia, people who were struggling for positions in a predominantly Czech government
bureaucracy and within a Czech-dominated intellectual life. After Hlinka's
death in 1938, the party was led by another Catholic priest, Jozef Tiso.

As Nazi Germany encircled Czechoslovakia in the 1930s, the SL'S utilized
the increasing difficulties of the central government in Prague and sought to
extract more and more concessions. The ultimate goal, however, was not
independence but autonomy. Slovakia was an undeveloped country, and its
economic survival was doubtful; even more important, faced with a dangerous Hungarian irredenta, it would be unable to defend itself without a
guardian. A weakened Czechoslovakia—and it was weak between the surrender of the Western powers to Hitler in Munich in late September 1938
and the occupation of Prague by the Germans on March 15, 1939—was quite
acceptable to the SL'S. We do not know whether Hitler had any plans for Slovakia prior to the autumn of 1938. When the time came, however, and he
wanted to occupy the Czech lands, he found it more convenient to have an
obedient satellite than to occupy and rule the country. Tiso at first did not
want to declare independence, but faced with a choice between that and German or Hungarian occupation, he chose an "independent" Slovakia; its independence was declared on March 14, 1939.

As the "independent" fascist Slovak State became established, the chief
actors in the SL'S—all other parties were quickly abolished—split into war-
ring factions. There were two main ones—the clerical-fascist faction, led by
Tiso himself, with František D'určanský, the first Foreign Minister; Karol
Sidor, later ambassador to the Vatican, and many others; and the openly pro-
Nazi group of Vojtěch Tuka, the Prime Minister; and Alexander (Šaňo)
Mach, Minister of the Interior and head of the Hlinka Guard, as the main
figures. The antisemitism of the two factions was also slightly different.
Tiso's tended to be more traditional, Catholic, influenced by economic jeal-
ousy of the Jewish middle-class and Jewish intellectuals. It was the Jewish
property that many of the SL'S adherents were after. The openly pro-Nazi
group clothed its economic antisemitism in a badly imitated, primitive
racism, which they copied from their Nazi mentors.

Among the 2,600,000 inhabitants of the new state there were 88,951 Jews
in 1940.[2] The Jewish community was split into different groups and factions,
too. A high proportion of the Jews were small shopkeepers, artisans, and
entrepreneurs, a proportion were intellectuals, and a smattering were farmers
and laborers. In the south, where the larger towns were located, most Jews
spoke Hungarian, which had been the language of culture until 1918; many

others spoke German, some French, and many, but by no means all, had forgotten their original Yiddish culture. In the north and east, Hungarian was less known or not known at all, Yiddish was much more popular, and Slovak was used for talking with neighbors. The majority of Slovak Jews identified with Jewish Orthodoxy, which, as in Hungary, was led by ultrareligious anti-Zionists. There was a more liberal, "Neologue" minority, somewhat akin in their religious habits to present-day American Conservative Jews. There was another minority, but a growing one, of Zionists, largely influenced by Prague and German-language culture.[3] And there was an alliance, sometimes an identification, of Neologues and Zionists. The Orthodox were led by the Landessekretariat (National Secretariat), headed until 1940 by Isidor Pappenheim. But the spiritual and—in accordance with Jewish tradition—ultimately the social authority was the Rabbi of Nitra, Shmuel David Halevi Ungar, a leader of the extreme anti-Zionist wing of the anti-Zionist, international political party of Agudas Yisroel (Agudat Yisrael). Weissmandel was his son-in-law.

In late 1939, faced with ever-increasing antisemitic pressure, Slovak Zionists tried to persuade the Orthodox to join them in an umbrella organization of Slovak Jews called Židovská Ústredná Úradovna pre krajinu Slovenska, or ŽÚÚ.[4] The Orthodox refused, but Zionists and Neologues set up the organization anyway. Its task was to organize social aid for the dispossessed, look after Jewish education, emigrate as many people as possible, and negotiate with the SL'S government to alleviate anti-Jewish policies. In the end, the lack of cooperation by the Orthodox caused the ŽÚÚ to collapse.

On September 26, 1940, in line with Nazi policies in Germany and Poland at the time, the Slovaks forced unification on the Jews by ordering them to establish a Judenrat—the Ústredna Židov, or ÚŽ (Jewish Center). A respected Orthodox community worker, Heinrich Schwarz, was nominated head (starosta, "elder"), and after some hesitation, the Zionists sought to become part of the new body. They received minority status, and Schwarz kept all contacts with the government under his own control.

Anti-Jewish laws and vicious antisemitic propaganda had been introduced, item by item, ever since April 1939. Their introduction was decisively stepped up after a meeting at Salzburg between Hitler and his aides and the Slovak leadership (July 28, 1940). At that meeting Hitler demanded more radical action on the Jewish question. The main drift of new laws and regulations, which on September 9, 1941, culminated in the promulgation of a "Jewish codex," was the expropriation of Jewish property and its division among People's Party members, including those in the Hlinka Guard. Expropriation and reallocation were effected by a special office, the Ústredný Hospodársky Úrad, or ÚHÚ (Central Economic Office), headed by Augustín Morávek. Ultimately, for the Slovaks to secure the position thus won, Jews would be forcibly emigrated or expelled. The main motivation for the Slovak desire to deport the Jews of Slovakia was therefore economic. The expulsion of 10,000 of Bratislava's 15,000 Jews to eastern Slovakia in September 1941 was part of this policy.

In August 1940 the SS—in effect, Eichmann's "Jewish" department at the Gestapo[5]—nominated Dieter Wisliceny to be the adviser on Jewish affairs with the German embassy in Bratislava. His task was to see to the radicalization of anti-Jewish policies. We met Dieter Wisliceny before when discussing Ha'avarah: he was a member of the SS team. Wisliceny was born in Regulowken, in east Prussia, in 1911; he was the son of a Silesian landowner, who died in 1928, leaving the family penniless. Wisliceny wanted to become a physician or historian but settled on becoming a Protestant pastor. He studied theology at the University of Breslau, but left to take a job with a construction company. He joined the Nazi propaganda unit in the German Foreign Office and the storm troopers (SA) in 1931 and the SS in 1934. He was a heavyset young man, weighing 224 pounds in 1944, and wore glasses. As a member of the Jewish department (II/112) of the SD, the SS Security Service, in the late 1930s, he developed very decided views on the "Jewish question." A memorandum (*Vermerk*) of April 7, 1937, signed by Wisliceny presents an argument for the emigration of all German Jews, which could be achieved only by supporting the Zionist enterprise.[6] Overtaken in importance by his friend and colleague Adolf Eichmann, Wisliceny appeared to be a clever, wily character, basically a hedonistic opportunist.

On May 29, 1940, the Slovaks signed an agreement according to which the Germans were to receive 120,000 Slovak workers. On June 17, 1941, Morávek wrote a letter to Tuka in which he reported on a discussion he had had with Wisliceny and another German (Erich Gebert, an economic "expert"), saying that he had offered to the Germans Jews for labor in Poland or Germany.[7] In the late summer of 1941 the Germans demanded 20,000 Slovak workers, and Izidor Koso, head of Tiso's and Mach's chancelleries, again suggested that the Germans should take Jews instead (see below). In the autumn Tiso and Tuka went to see Hitler and Himmler, and Tuka asked Himmler for help in taking the Jews out of Slovakia. There, too, the Slovaks learned of German plans to "liberate" Europe from its Jews—exactly how they were not told, except that the Jews would somehow be "settled in the East."[8] In October they agreed to have Jews with Slovak citizenship living in Germany deported along with German Jews "to the East."[9]

In January 1942 the Slovaks said they could not send Slovak workers;[10] however, they again offered 20,000 Jewish workers—to Sager, the representative of the German Ministry of Labor. Wisliceny, who apparently had not been given the information, was called to Berlin by a furious Eichmann, who wanted Wisliceny to be on top of everything connected with Jews. Returning to Bratislava, Wisliceny reported first to Hanns Ludin, the German ambassador, and then went to Koso, accompanied by Morávek. Koso confirmed that the deportation of 20,000 Jews had been suggested and that he would make the fourteenth department of the Ministry of the Interior, then under Gejza Konka (under Anton Vašek after April 3), responsible for implementation.[11]

Eichmann could use 20,000 Jews. They would build, after proper selection, the death and concentration camps at Auschwitz and Birkenau. Koso demanded that youngsters should be taken from the age of sixteen, not eighteen, as the Germans had demanded, because there were not enough people over eighteen to make up the allotment. Wisliceny then went to Tuka, who told him that he wanted the deportation of *all* the Jews, because if the working people were deported, the remaining families would constitute a burden for Slovakia. In his postwar testimony, Koso generally confirms this; in fact, he says it was he who raised with Tuka the problem of what to do with the families. On February 16 the German Foreign Office informed the Slovaks that "in the course of the measures taken toward a final solution of the European Jewish question [Im Zuge der Massnahmen zur Endlösung der europäischen Judenfrage]," the Germans would take 20,000 young and strong Slovak Jews.

When Eichmann was approached by the Slovaks to take the families as well, he at first refused: he had no place for them yet.[12] Auschwitz was just being prepared for large-scale murder, and none of the death camps was active, with the exception of Chelmno, whose staff were busy murdering the Jews of the Lodz district. Eichmann refused to take Jews at other times, too, because he preferred an orderly procedure, rather than being swamped with Jews: in the summer of 1941 he refused a Romanian demand to take Bessarabian and Bukovina Jews into newly conquered Transnistria (the area between the Dniester and the Bug, in southern Ukraine) because he was not yet ready for them; and in 1942–43, when offered 100,000 Hungarian Jews, he argued for a total, rather than a piecemeal, "solution" to the Jewish "problem" in Hungary.

The context of the negotiations in Slovakia was the infamous Wannsee conference on January 20, 1942, at which Heydrich, the SS police chief, discussed implementing the decision to launch the "Final Solution" on a European basis—a decision made the previous summer—with representatives of a number of German ministries. Eichmann was present, and he looked after the minutes of the meeting. Slovakia was listed among the countries where deportations could start immediately and where no political problems were expected.

Informally, toward the end of February, it became clear that the Germans would relent on the question of also taking Jewish families. On March 3 Tuka declared at a Slovak State Council meeting that "representatives of the German government have declared their willingness to take all the Jews."[13] The next day, at another meeting, he said that the Jews would be sent to the Ukraine and that the Slovaks would pay RM 500 per head to be rid of them.[14] Deportations would start in March and be finished in August. There was some opposition to the government plan, with some delegates arguing that it was against Slovakia's interests to expel *all* the Jews. Tuka answered that if the Slovaks did not do it, the Germans would.

About mid-March, according to Wisliceny, Eichmann finally agreed to take all the Jews. Details were discussed at another meeting in Berlin, attended by Ladislav Ziman from the Central Economic Office, Wisliceny, and Eichmann; no date is given. The Slovaks agreed to pay the Germans for taking their Jews as long as they could lay hands on their property. On May 1, 1942, the Slovaks received an official German note telling them that the Germans would lay no claim to the property of Jews deported to Poland as long as they were paid their RM 500 per Jew.[15]

On March 26, the day the deportations started, another debate took place in the State Council. A prominent delegate, Jan Balko, expressed opposition to the deportations, and the delegates also considered a memorandum from the Jewish Center. In the end, the government won, partly because of the tacit support of the Catholic bishops' representative, Bishop Jan Vojtaššák, who was concerned only that Jewish converts to Christianity should have separate facilities for observing their new religion—a number of Jews tried to escape persecution by converting.[16]

Upon repeated Slovak requests, the German Foreign Ministry advised Ambassador Hanns Ludin in Bratislava on March 27, in writing, that Himmler had decided to accept the Slovak offer and "proposed to deport as well the remainder of the Slovak Jews and thus free Slovakia of Jews."[17] However, he added, political difficulties should be carefully avoided. All Slovak Jews were to be deported in quick stages. Wisliceny was charged with supervising the inefficient Slovak bureaucracy in the task of uprooting the Jews from their homes. At this stage, it is unlikely that the Slovak officials knew of the fate that was awaiting the deportees. Wisliceny claimed after the war that his own knowledge of the murder of the Jews dated from late July or early August 1942. He did visit Auschwitz in May 1942, though he claimed that he only met Rudolf Hoess, the commander, in the SS officers' mess and that he had the impression that the camp was a concentration camp like the prewar ones in Germany. His professions that he was innocent of knowledge may be doubtful, but the possibility exists that they may be true. He himself admits that in late July 1942 he met with an escapee, Ladislav Junger, from the Lublin region in the camp at Žilina, who told him that all the Jews in Poland were being shot (Junger had no knowledge of gassings, for he had not been incarcerated in either Auschwitz or another death camp).[18]

The story on the Slovak side is tangled. According to one German report, Tuka conducted the negotiations with Berlin about the deportation of the Jews without informing Tiso. On the other hand, according to the same report, he informed Giuseppe Burzio, the papal chargé d'affaires (there was no nuntius in Bratislava), knowing full well that that would complicate matters for Tiso, a priest.[19] The result was an attempt by Tiso to fire Tuka, a threat by Tuka to resign, and extreme pressure by the Germans to prevent their ally, Tuka, from doing so. According to another report, Tiso told Mach that he did not wish to receive any reports on the deportations, because he did not want to know anything about them.[20] As the report specifies, however, he did not try to stop the deportations, and on April 4, Ludin reported to Berlin that Tiso was prepared for the deportations to continue despite Vatican protests. Tuka may have conducted the original negotiations without informing Tiso, but it seems highly unlikely that the President did not have his own sources of information about a development that was widely known among Slovak officials. He most certainly knew by March 6.

Representative rabbis of the Jewish Orthodox and Neologue communities submitted a memorandum to the government on March 5, which was followed on March 6 by an appeal of the Slovak rabbis, both Orthodox and Neologue, to Tiso, as a Catholic priest, in which they begged him for mercy. The rabbis said that under the present circumstances, with the separation of families, the deportations would lead to the physical annihilation of Slovak Jewry. Without knowing, at that stage, about the "Final Solution"—both memoranda came before the official announcement of the coming deportations was made to the Jews—they were already using language that would be appropriate very soon. Despite a supporting letter to Tiso from Bishop Pavol Jantausch of Trnava, Tiso refused to respond.[21]

The Vatican made a fairly strong protest against the planned deportations on March 14; the Holy See expressed opposition to the deportation of the Jews as such (converts were not mentioned), emphasizing that they could not believe that a country that was committed to Catholic principles could countenance such an act. The protest was largely a reaction to two memoranda that were sent to the Vatican by the Orthodox group around Rabbi Ungar, who begged for mercy, and one by the Zionist-Neologue group, who mentioned that families would be separated by deportations—a statement that Ungar called it "criminal stupidity" to make. Indeed, the Slovaks and the Germans had no objection to keeping families united on the trains to Auschwitz.[22]

It appears, from Vatican documents, that originally Burzio harbored some not very favorable opinions about Jews. In 1941 he was concerned with converts to Catholicism, whom he did not want to share the fate of the Jews. When the Jewish codex was about to be promulgated in September 1941, Burzio asked the Slovak bishops to take a united stand against it, but the bishops refused. There, too, he was concerned with the converts, not with the Jews who had remained faithful to their traditions. Shortly afterward his attitude changed visibly: he sent a report to the Vatican on October 27, 1941, that was the first accurate description of the mass murder of Jews by the Germans in the Soviet territories.

When he handed the Vatican protest to Tiso, he apparently sent along a letter of his own, of which we have only a report by Nazi intelligence: he warned of the dire consequences of not paying attention to the protest and recalled that the Catholic church still had the power of "interdict" (excommunication)—he apparently did not specify against whom it could be used.[23]

Some of the appeals for intervention addressed to the Vatican reached it; the ÚŽ sent one on March 13, for instance, and the Budapest rabbinate sent another on the twentieth. Sidor, the Slovak ambassador, after he was summoned to Secretary of State Luigi Maglione, went to Bratislava to try and influence his colleagues against the deportations. By March 26, Burzio was calling the Slovak leaders "madmen." Further reports by Burzio, who was becoming more outspoken in his condemnation of the deportations, reached the Pope himself and caused a sharp confrontation between Maglione and Sidor on April 11.

On April 26 the Slovak bishops, apparently unmoved by either Burzio or the Vatican, issued a pastoral letter that repeated the traditional accusations that the Jews were deicides and decried their "pernicious" nature. A minority that opposed the antisemitic tenor of the document was outvoted.[24]

Under Wisliceny's expert management, and despite the corruption and inefficiency of the Slovak fascist organs, deportations began on March 26, 1942, with the transport of girls aged sixteen and up. The first transports were of single young people, but in April, Eichmann declared he was ready to accept families.[25] Eichmann apparently visited Bratislava twice—on April 10 and on May 25. He held talks with Tuka and some of the other officials, though it is not quite clear what he really wanted. According to Wisliceny, he promised Tuka, on the latter's express request, that the Jews would be treated in a humane fashion in Poland. The Jews, he said, would be settled in the Lublin area, where the Germans were building new factories and where the Jews would be able to move about freely.[26]

The deportations were, from the Nazi point of view, going smoothly. Hlinka Guard members and members of the Freiwillige Schutzstaffel (FS), the militia of the German nazified minority in Slovakia, sought out the Jews in their homes and took them to local centers; then they were transported, at first to Žilina, a railway junction near the Slovak-Polish border, and later to a number of centers near railway lines, whence they were sent either to one of the small ghettos near Lublin or to Auschwitz.[27] Those sent to Lublin were left alive for a while in the overcrowded ghettos in the area, until the Majdanek concentration camp, where many of them were ultimately sent, was ready to receive them, in July 1942. Others were sent to be gassed in the Bełżec death camp. In the families sent to Auschwitz, those deemed fit for work were given tattooed numbers, and the others were sent to the gas chambers.

What is clear from this survey is that the deportations in Slovakia were begun at Slovak, not German, initiative, and that the inclusion of families—in other words, the prospective deportation of all of Slovak Jewry—was proposed by the Slovaks and only gradually accepted by the Nazis. The Slovak clero-fascist state thus had the distinction of anticipating and preceding the Germans in their murderous campaign against the Jews.

The initial reaction of the Jewish community to this disaster was panic and despair. The Jewish Center had undergone a change of leadership: Heinrich Schwarz, who had tried to defend his community from corrupt government officials, had been removed from office in April 1941, arrested, and then released, whereupon he fled to Hungary. In his stead the Central Economic Office nominated a nondescript, inefficient, and submissive Orthodox school principal by the name of Arpad Sebestyen. Some heads of departments, Zionists and others who were unhappy with his management of things, consulted on how to deal with a deteriorating situation. Among the Zionists Oskar Neumann occupied a special position: he was in charge of the ÚŽ department for retraining. Under that cover he managed to extend some help to the now-illegal Zionist youth movements. Allied with Neumann was Gizi Fleischmann, a social worker and a member of the local JDC, who, when the official JDC representative, Josef Blum, fled from Slovakia to Hungary, assumed leadership of the committee. Weissmandel was not a member of the ÚŽ, but he had contacts with the Orthodox majority in it.

Less than two weeks before they began, Morávek and Wisliceny came to the Jewish Center and announced that deportations would start soon. The center was charged with collaborating in the effort to handle them smoothly. The key role in this was played by Karel Hochberg, a Jewish engineer, who had become Wisliceny's helper and head of the internal "department for special tasks."[28] Hochberg was in the mold of Jewish traitors during the Nazi period. In Warsaw there was Abraham Gancwajch, head of the Gestapo-supported police, who tried to snatch the leadership of the ghetto from the head of the Judenrat, Adam Czerniakow, and who believed in the final Nazi victory; in Kraków there was the head of the special Jewish police, Szpiro, a Hasidic Jew who became a Gestapo agent—and there were others, not surprisingly, under the impossible pressure of the Nazi murderers.

After the war, the charge was made that the ÚŽ knew the destination of the transports and did nothing to warn the Jewish public. The charge was made especially by one of the survivor heroes of the Holocaust, Rudolf Vrba (Walter Rosenberg), who, together with Alfred Wetzler, escaped from Auschwitz in April 1944 to tell the world about Auschwitz. It has been repeated and analyzed by a foremost historian of the period, John S. Conway of Vancouver, in two articles in a prestigious German quarterly.[29] He argues (1) that the Germans initiated the deportations, not the Slovaks; (2) that Vrba himself was taken from his home in May 1942 and shipped to Majdanek and then to Auschwitz without having any idea of the mortal danger that he and all the others deported with him were facing; (3) that during early spring at least one direct testimony about Majdanek was already in the hands of the ÚŽ ,[30] namely, a letter by one Dionys Lenard, which arrived in April; (4) that the ÚŽ had information from other sources about Auschwitz and had withheld it; and (5) that the ÚŽ actively participated in the deportations and prepared the lists of deportees. The general conclusion is that the members of the ÚŽ were collaborators and that the Jewish "underground" leadership failed to do what it could to save Jewish lives.

These arguments are erroneous. It was the Slovaks, not the Germans, who initiated the deportations, though they did so without knowledge of the mass murder plans of the Germans. Majdanek was not turned into a concentration and death camp before July, and Lenard escaped from Majdanek at the end of June, not in April, and his report was dated July.[31] Lenard could not testify about mass murder in either Majdanek or Auschwitz because he knew nothing about it.

The main point to remember, however, is that not even the Slovak leaders had any definite knowledge in March, April, or perhaps even May or June that all the Jews were indeed destined to die in Poland. Hlinka Guard members who accompanied trains from Žilina were certain that the Jews would be killed in Poland, but the half-civilized officialdom of the "independent" Slovak Republic found this hard to believe. After the war, Ervin Steiner, a ÚŽ activist in Žilina, who had a heroic record of trying to help deportees, claimed that he had heard from acquaintances that according to foreign radio reports the deported Jews were being killed.[32] But we know very well that the first time the "foreign radio"—that is, the BBC—reported on mass Jewish deaths in Poland was in June, in the wake of the May report from the Jewish Socialist Party, the Bund in Poland.[33] Andrej Steiner, the man with whom Wisliceny negotiated in the autumn, says that he interrogated three persons who had escaped from Poland as early as April and who reported shootings of Jews there.[34] He immediately contradicts himself, however, by saying that the contents were smuggled abroad and that Vašek received a copy—in July! We know that Gizi Fleischmann reported to Switzerland about atrocities in Poland in July. Arguably, even Wisliceny learned about them only in the course of the action itself. The ÚŽ had no clear information about death camps. The staff did know that mass pogroms had occurred in Poland, and that being sent to Poland involved immediate and extreme danger. In the summer of 1942, according to Ervin Steiner of Žilina, they learned that Auschwitz was a horrible and life-endangering concentration camp. What exactly went on there they did not know.[35] More testimonies of this kind all point to the conclusion that Slovak Jews learned of the life-threatening conditions in Poland in the summer of 1942—from postcards sent by relatives, from those who escaped from Poland, from Slovak friends with contacts in Poland. The ÚŽ was another source of information for the general public, but the ÚŽ staff could not tell more than they knew themselves. People became aware of the difference between a general threat to life and a massive murder campaign directed against Jews specifically in the fall of 1942, and many even later than that.

We must differentiate between information and its internalization, or "knowledge"; and in this case there is absolutely no proof that information on planned mass murder, as opposed to pogromlike shootings and other persecutions, was received during the early months of deportation.[36] Internalization—that is, acceptance of information as correct and thinking in accordance with that information, and later possibly action—is a complicated process. During the Holocaust countless individuals received information and rejected it, suppressed it, or rationalized about it, were thrown into despair without any possibility of acting on it, or seemingly internalized it and then behaved as though it had never reached them. This is true not only of people who were outside the kingdom of death but also of people within it.

When Vrba was deported in June, the ÚŽ had information about pogroms, suffering, and starvation, not about the "Final Solution." In addition, Vrba claims that five months after he was deported, he still saw, in Auschwitz, transports of Slovak Jews who were unaware of what was awaiting them. If he was deported on June 30, five months thereafter was November. But there were no transports in November. The transport of September 23—most likely before Vrba reached Auschwitz—had to be put together by the security groups chasing and hunting Jews; by that time the Jews knew what was awaiting them in a general way. They were, in fact, explicitly warned by the ÚŽ, which is why the authorities had to fill the transport quota with inmates of the labor camps, who had been promised immunity from deportation.

In the case of the ÚŽ, the knowledge that some of the Zionist and Orthodox leaders had was sufficient for them to try first of all to prevent the deportations by hastily organizing bribes to Slovak officials. Josef Blum, the Orthodox Jew who represented JDC in Hungary and Slovakia and who was in contact with his group in Slovakia, tried to influence the Hungarian Cardinal Justinian Seredi to protest the deportations, but to no avail. Zionists in Hungary contacted the Italian government; they received in return a report in which it was claimed that Foreign Minister Galeazzo Ciano had responded that any intervention with the Germans would be futile.[37] It was through the group of oppositionists within the ÚŽ that Jewish protests reached the Vatican and triggered the Vatican protest against the deportations on March 14, 1942. Members of the group also transmitted letters from the rabbis, via Bishop Pavol Jantausch of Trnava, to Tiso, begging the Slovak President to refrain from the deportations.

Independently of these failed initiatives, Neumann, in March, sent members of his department on train trips throughout Slovakia to warn not only his charges, members of the youth movements, but also the Jewish communities in general to escape to Hungary. We must understand that such information could not be transmitted by phone—all phones were tapped, especially those within reach of Jews—or by letter. Neumann's emissaries informed the youth and the heads of the communities and suggested that they flee to Hungary. A very similar path was followed by the Orthodox. Weissmandel reports—and enough documents support his contention to prove it—that especially within the "Vatican," as the ultraorthodox compound in Nitra where Rabbi Ungar resided was jocularly known, plans were immediately made and implemented to transfer the most endangered people to Hungary—in particular the many Polish refugees who were illegally hiding there.[38]

A further charge made by Vrba is that the ÚŽ participated in the deportations. Again, there is no evidence to support this, unless one identifies Hochberg's special department with the ÚŽ. Sebestyen, head of the ÚŽ, had no control over Hochberg, who was a German agent and who in fact threatened to achieve control over the whole ÚŽ organization. Nor was the official ÚŽ—certainly not the budding opposition within it—able to halt Hochberg's gang, although they and everyone connected with Jewish affairs saw him as a traitor. Hochberg and a group of specially recruited Jewish agents who composed his team were very active in helping the Slovaks and the Germans round up Jews. They provided technical and secretarial help, and they worked on lists supplied to them by Slovak authorities—and because they were supposedly attached to the ÚŽ, many people in the community identified the ÚŽ with them. But the lists of people to deport were put together not by Hochberg's people but by special committees with SL'S and Hlinka Guard members, in many cases with the addition of Freiwillige Schutzstaffel delegates and local officials.[39]

In arguing that members of the ÚŽ were collaborationists, Conway implies that the Slovak Jews would have been better off without the ÚŽ, the Jewish Center.[40] But the impoverishment of Slovak Jewry was such that the establishment of a central Jewish organization to deal with social welfare became an absolute imperative; for example, of the 90,000 Slovak Jews, 15,872 were on the welfare rolls by May 1941. Also, some historians fail to compare the Jewish case with the cases of other groups oppressed by the Nazis. Were, for instance, members of the British prisoner-of-war committees in German POW camps collaborators because they represented British soldiers in captivity to the Germans?

The efforts of Neumann and the Orthodox led to a massive flight of Slovak Jews over the Hungarian border into relative safety. Probably 7,000–8,000

Jews fled this way in the spring of 1942, or 9 percent of the Jewish population. If Vrba says that he had no inkling about Auschwitz, it is undoubtedly true—neither had anyone else—but the Jews had enough knowledge of the dangers of being taken into Poland for every twelfth person to flee. Was Vrba unaware of that, too?

Flight to Hungary could not serve everyone. At first, there were desperate efforts to remove individuals from the transports, and that was just the kind of response that the Nazis and their Slovak pupils had expected and were prepared to deal with. Weissmandel's postwar account seems at first blush to fill in the picture of what happened next.

The individuals in both the Zionist-Neologue and the Orthodox camps seeking a way out of the horror were involved in an informal process of uniting their forces. On the Zionist side unification was undoubtedly aided by the late 1941 visit of Jacob Edelstein, the leader of Prague Jewry and the Elder of the Theresienstadt ghetto, who came to Bratislava and told his Zionist friends there, on the basis of his own bitter experience, not to cooperate with the Nazis. According to Weissmandel and other sources, the central figure in the new grouping was Gizi Fleischmann. Blessed with an even temper, great wisdom, tremendous personal courage, and a very practical bent, Fleischmann was the one person who could unite the disparate individuals into a coherent group. They called themselves the Pracovná skupina (Working Group), or Vedlejší Vláda (Alternative Government), or, in Weissmandel's Hebrew phrase, Hava'ad Hamistater (Hidden Committee). That Fleischmann was a relative of Weissmandel's apparently made it easier for the Rabbi to accept the leadership of a woman and a Zionist.[41] The central figures in the group, apart from Fleischmann and Weissmandel, were Neumann; Tibor Kováč, an assimilationist intellectual far removed from both Zionism and Orthodoxy; the chief Neologue Rabbi, Armin Frieder; and, perhaps more important than these, Andrej E. Steiner, a practical, nonideological person, an engineer who felt a strong feeling of responsibility toward his people. Other individuals were brought in, consulted, or recruited for special activities.

According to Weissmandel, he, too, was in a state of shock, trying to rescue individuals from the disaster. This feeling came to him most strongly on a Friday sometime in Tammuz (June 16–July 14, 1942). Moved by the report that a man had been released by a ransom payment made to Wisliceny, Weissmandel conceived the idea of sending Hochberg to Wisliceny and offering him a major bribe in order to stop the deportations. He says that he went to Hochberg, presenting himself as the representative of the world's rabbis, whose influence was decisive in the policies of the "Joint"—which Nazi mythology considered to be equivalent to a World Jewish government. Hochberg was told that he now had done his share for the Germans and that he should cover himself in case the Allies won the war. Hochberg swallowed

Weissmandel's bait and went to Wisliceny. He came back and said that the price would be $50,000 in dollar bills, in two payments: $25,000 immediately and another $25,000 six weeks later. He also said that the Slovaks should be bribed, and that the Jews should enlarge the three labor camps set up by the ÚŽ to "productivize" the remaining Jews in Slovakia, and thus provide the Slovaks with an economic incentive not to deport them. Weissmandel says that he agreed to the conditions, and then, on Ungar's advice, he sought out the members of what became the Working Group. Weissmandel's account makes it appear as though he took all these steps before consulting with the Working Group;[42] but this is contested by the other available testimonies and does not seem plausible. The continuation of the account in the different testimonies makes the order of events clear.

Fleischmann and the others objected to giving Hochberg, the traitor, such an assignment. He might turn them in to the Slovaks or the Nazis. Weissmandel explained that Hochberg would undertake the job precisely because he felt uneasy about his role in facilitating the deportations; he might undertake it to redeem his name. Weissmandel then said that he invented a representative of World Jewry in Switzerland, a Ferdinand Roth, who supposedly was the source offering the bribe. A bribe from within the country would have no attraction for the Nazi. Weissmandel had traveled extensively before the war, and he possessed some Swiss writing paper with Swiss watermarks on it, as well as an old English typewriter. He wrote letters to himself with Roth's signature and asked Hochberg to present them to Wisliceny. Wisliceny, according to Weissmandel, responded that he would be uninterested in further deportations, but of course he could do nothing if the Slovaks demanded them.

The first $25,000, Weissmandel says, were obtained from Solomon Stern, a wealthy Orthodox businessman in Slovakia, and paid to Wisliceny by Hochberg. We should remember that the only Jew in contact with Wisliceny at this point was Hochberg, who was the source of all that the Working Group knew about Wisliceny's attitude. According to Weissmandel, deportations stopped for six weeks. In the meantime, emboldened by the stop of the deportations, the Working Group tried to obtain the other half of the money from abroad. In tandem with the bribe to Wisliceny, members of the Working Group managed to reach Izidor Koso, head of both Tuka's and Mach's chancelleries, and Anton Vašek, head of the fourteenth department in the Ministry of the Interior—Mach's man, who was instrumental in facilitating the deportations on the Slovak side. These were centrally important individuals, who controlled the deportation.

By the end of July, 52,000 Jews had already been sent to Poland; those who had not been deported were largely people who had letters of protection emanating from Tiso or who had been certified as economically important Jews and exempted, together with their families, from deportation. Bribing the Slovaks facilitated the inclusion of more people on the lists of the exempt and might help stop the deportations altogether.

Fleischmann and Weissmandel did turn to Switzerland—to the representative there of the JDC,[43] Saly Mayer; to Nathan Schwalb, the representative of the Palestinian Jewish pioneering organization Hechalutz; and to Bela Leibowitz, the contact man of the Orthodox group. Schwalb had no money to speak of, and it was Mayer who supplied him with most of the funds that he could use. The JDC, the great American Jewish philanthropic organization, had a conservative inclination and followed the State Department's instructions. The European director, however, Joseph J. Schwartz, was much more independent and did things without necessarily awaiting approval from his New York–based board. It was he who in August 1940 nominated Saly Mayer, the conservative President of the Schweizerischer Israelitischer Gemeindebund (SIG, the Union of Swiss Jewish Communities), to be JDC's representative in Switzerland. Mayer was told to act independently and within his budget and to report back—but even the reporting was not to be done too openly because of wartime censorship. The sums that Mayer received were small. He got $6,370 in 1940 and $3,030 in 1941, plus $5,900 for Hechalutz. His main responsibilities were France, Slovakia, Hungary, Croatia, and Bulgaria, and he sent some money to Bratislava. He could not send money himself, because his funds were controlled by Swiss banks and he could not circumvent their regulations, so he gave money to Schwalb, who smuggled cash via couriers, many of whom were less than trustworthy—but he had no choice.

When the demand came to pay Wisliceny—soon he was given the code name "Willy"—Mayer had no way to transfer a sum like $25,000, not even through Schwalb. There was another problem, which he could not explain to the desperate people in Bratislava: ever since April 1942 the Swiss had stopped the transfer of charitable dollars into Switzerland to be transformed there into Swiss francs (no dollars could be transferred as such). The United States did not allow the Swiss to buy American goods with dollars, and the Swiss had no use for idle dollars in U.S. banks, in return for which they would have had to pay out very real francs in besieged Switzerland. From April 1942 until the summer of 1943, therefore, Mayer received no money from the United States. He could use only the monies that were raised within the Swiss Jewish community, most of which went to support the Jewish refugees then in Switzerland. His total budget for 1942, the year in which most of the Jews who fell victim to the Holocaust died, was $235,000, of which $105,295 had to be spent for the Jewish refugees in Switzerland.[44] What was left over he had to divide between countries and communities where Jewish lives were endangered by the Nazis. What he could offer was an arrangement "après," which meant that local funds would be obtained from wealthy persons—Jews or non-Jews—against a promise that they would be repaid after (après) the war in dollars by the JDC. In extreme cases, he could offer, on behalf of the JDC, to put money into Swiss or American banks to be redeemed when the people to whom it was promised escaped. None of these stratagems worked in the Willy negotiations, because hard cash was needed. In dollars.

Weissmandel, in his book, is extremely bitter about Schwalb and Mayer, because so little money was received from them. He accuses Schwalb of writing a letter to Bratislava in which he stated that the Jews had to make sacrifices just like everyone else in the war and that the main thing was to fight for Palestine as a Jewish country; only the shedding of blood would bring about a Jewish Palestine, and immigration there was essential. If Slovak Jews could, they should escape and go there. Weissmandel says that Mayer wrote a letter to Slovakia in which he disparagingly referred to "Ostjuden" (Eastern Jews); they were panicky by nature, he said, and one should discount their stories about Poland and Nazi atrocities.

Weissmandel's charges that "Zionists" and "nonobservant" Jews like Schwalb and Mayer abandoned the Jews under the Nazi heel and wrote letters that denigrated the sufferers and indicated that Zionism in Palestine was more important than rescue of the Jewish masses—these charges still reverberate in the Jewish world. They have been used by anti-Zionist Orthodox writers and by antiestablishment non-Orthodox Jews to "prove" that the Jewish Agency, the JDC—in fact, the whole leadership of wartime Jewry—not only did not rescue Jews but in effect did not want to rescue them.[45]

Interestingly, while Weissmandel adduces documentation for most of his stories, he recounts these two crucial letters from memory. So far, the letters or their copies have not been found. Regarding Schwalb's letter, Andrej Steiner confirms Weissmandel's story in a general way but adds that when the letter was received—and he cannot recall the date (neither can Weissmandel, and the likelihood is that it was received before the mass murders became known)—nobody thought that its content was extraordinary. Perhaps Schwalb was commiserating in a clumsy way by saying that the blood being spilt—they were all talking of pogroms in Poland, not of Hitler's "Final Solution"—might earn the Jewish people the postwar right to Palestine; and if they could, they should run there. It is perhaps also worth mentioning that Schwalb was a young man of limited outlook, who had remained in Switzerland when war broke out, more or less by accident, and had been approved *post factum* as the representative of one of the Zionist organizations, the Hechalutz. He was in no way a representative of world Zionism, as Weissmandel portrays him.

A meticulous search of Mayer's very full and comprehensive archive has failed to turn up the letter mentioned by Weissmandel. Mayer was himself a traditionally religious Jew, who greatly admired Polish Jewry and who was becoming increasingly aware of the terrible suffering of Jews under the Nazis. It is difficult to say what the basis for Weissmandel's allegation was, but it is highly doubtful that Mayer ever used phrases denigrating Polish Jews to Slovak Jewry. Steiner does not remember anything like Weissmandel's allegations but does recollect that Mayer said, in one of his letters, that he could not send the money requested because it was illegal—which is a different story altogether.[46] We shall see that Weissmandel's account is flawed on a number of other points, which increases the doubts.

Contact with Mayer was maintained, at first through Blum in Hungary or through Schwalb in Switzerland, by Gizi Fleischmann. Leibowitz was approached by Weissmandel for $10,000 and large sums of Swiss francs, which would be placed in Swiss banks and against which the people in Bratislava would borrow money locally (the après method); but there is no record of Leibowitz coming up with the money. Fleischmann's letter to Schwalb of July 27 was more realistic and accurate: she asked for 100,000 Swiss francs (SFR), that is, about $23,000, for Willy, plus a budget of $420,000 yearly for the labor camps. These amounts were far beyond what Mayer had available. On August 28, Mayer decided to give $5,000 in francs to Schwalb for Slovakia and another $5,000 in September. When September came, he committed himself to a monthly payment of $5,000, and Schwalb persuaded the Working Group to arrange for 40,000 francs paid by the après method.

None of these payments were in dollars, and they bear little if any relation to the $25,000 that Weissmandel writes about.

Weissmandel says that when Wisliceny was not paid the second installment on time, a transport was sent to Auschwitz—on Yom Kippur, the Day of Atonement, the holiest day in the Jewish calendar (September 21, 1942). Immediately afterward, he says, he managed to get the money from his Orthodox contacts in Hungary; it was brought to Nitra by one Naftali Treitel, a wealthy merchant from Hungary. The money was paid, and thereafter deportations ceased for two years.

The problems with Weissmandel's account begin when we remember that *after* Yom Kippur two transports went to Auschwitz, on September 23 and October 20—that is, *after* the second installment had been paid to Wisliceny, according to Weissmandel.

We then have to compare Weissmandel's account with those of the other participants. There are several, the most important being Gizi Fleischmann's letters, which are contemporary and must therefore be given precedence over all the other sources, and Steiner's account. Steiner inherited Hochberg as the contact with Wisliceny and was heavily involved in the bribing of Slovak officials. He testified a number of times after the war, and his early accounts, from 1946 and 1947, are especially valuable. In addition, there are Kováč's testimony at the trial of the Slovak fascist criminals after the war, Rabbi Frieder's memoirs, based on his diary, and the reminiscences of Oskar Neumann and others.

From all these sources it emerges that the amount paid and the date of the payment are by no means clear—the figures vary between $40,000 and $50,000, and the dates vary between July and October.[47]

Weissmandel then reports that soon after the deportations had stopped—as a result, he is certain, of the bribes paid—he again asked the Working Group to bribe not just Wisliceny but the SS as a whole in order to achieve a cessation of either the murders altogether or at least the deportations from other European countries to Poland. The Working Group had become aware of the mass murders in August. Fleischmann's letter to Switzerland on August 27 reflects this clearly.[48] The letter, by the way, is roughly coterminous with the report to the United States and Britain by Gerhart Riegner of Geneva (August 8), which is usually—and wrongly—considered to be the first definitive evidence of the "Final Solution" to reach the West.[49] Although at the time it was not known in Bratislava that the murders were committed by gas and that a main death camp was at Auschwitz, there is no doubt that awareness of the mass murders prodded the Working Group to attempt stopping the murders by another approach to Willy.

The step itself was very unusual. The Group had just succeeded, or so it thought, in stopping deportations from tiny Slovakia. Some 24,000 Jews were left in the country, and here they were, trying to call a halt to the "Final Solution," or at least to hamper it decisively. Another unique feature of the situation was that for once, a group of Jewish activists representing all factions in a divided Jewish community—from assimilationists through Neologues and Zionists of all hues to the ultraorthodox leaders—united to rescue Jews outside their community or their country.

According to Weissmandel's account, toward the end of 1942 the Working Group approached Willy, again through Hochberg, and suggested the Europa Plan to stop the deportations to Poland, perhaps to stop the killing in Poland as well. Weissmandel presents the story as though all the members of the Group were behind the project and believed in its practicability. Steiner has quite a different version: "A majority of our Working Group thought it impossible of implementation and too unreal to devote too much energy to its pursuit. Only Rabbi Weissmandel, Gizi Fleischmann and Dr. Neumann insisted on not giving up."[50]

Abraham Fuchs in his work on Weissmandel proves that the first contact regarding the Europa Plan was made in early November 1942.[51] No sum was mentioned at first, according to Weissmandel—either by the Working Group or by Wisliceny—but it was hinted to Wisliceny that the Group was in contact with World Jewry and that a massive bribe would be forthcoming. Wisliceny, on the other hand, in his postwar testimony, says that Hochberg mentioned to him a possible sum of $2–3 million at the very outset. Very soon, however, the Slovak police apprehended Hochberg because he had received or had extorted sums of money and valuables from Jews threatened with deportation, offering to try and release them. Andrej Steiner and others apparently had something to do with playing the necessary evidence into the hands of the police.[52] Wisliceny tried to extricate him from the hands of the police, perhaps—as he said in his postwar testimonies—because he was afraid the secret of the negotiations would come out, perhaps because of some other shady deals that Willy may have been involved in. Hochberg's arrest certainly gave the Slovaks a useful handle on Eichmann's man in Bratislava.

Weissmandel wanted to have Hochberg released. After all, the Working Group had used the traitor to bribe Willy, and if he told the story to his investigators, the Group might well be in trouble. Fleischmann was against such an attempt: to have him removed from Willy's side was very useful. In any case, Hochberg stayed in prison. The Group designated Steiner to take his place with Wisliceny, and Willy realized that he now was in direct touch with the bribers. According to Weissmandel, Wisliceny went to Berlin and brought back the reply from his chief—Steiner assumed this was Himmler—that the SS were interested in negotiations. Weissmandel and Fleischmann do not mention any Jewish offer to the Nazis at this stage but indicate that the Group was waiting to hear the Nazi demands. Steiner has a different story: he explicitly mentions an offer by the Group, in the opening stage of the negotiations, of a payment of $150,000, to be delivered when the first children's transport, which would be part of the agreement, went to Switzerland. If the Jews saw that the Nazis kept to the overall agreement, a second payment of $150,000 would be made, and further payments or goods would be delivered to the Nazis, provided the goods were not related to the German war effort.[53] We should remember that neither Weissmandel nor Fleischmann was in direct touch with Wisliceny; Steiner was, and he wrote down his account in 1946 or 1947, a relatively short time after the events. I suggest that his testimony should be given greater credence in this matter than the others'.

According to Weissmandel, the Group now turned to the Jews abroad. The first to receive an account of the new plan was Nathan Schwalb; on December 4 he cabled to Istanbul that he had received information from Slovakia about "the possibility of stopping the scourge of the deportations . . . they [the Working Group] tell us that he [Wisliceny] will now become the chief official for south-eastern Europe, and that until now he has kept all his promises to the fullest extent."[54] Another letter, over the signatures of Weissmandel and Frieder, dated December 5, was sent to Istanbul, and a letter by

Gizi Fleischmann went to Switzerland.[55] Fleischmann's letter mentioned some small concessions that Wisliceny was apparently offering, such as parcels to be sent to the deportees in Poland, but the central point was the proposal to stop deportations *from* Poland. This was most likely another way of saying that the murders should stop altogether. Whether the proposal was not simply the Jewish one, and not Wisliceny's response, is not clear. Apparently Wisliceny explicitly offered the cessation of deportations from all of Europe except from the Reich territories. The Jews were asked what monies they would offer. Mayer and Schwalb were, it seems, taken by surprise, and the unidentified neutral diplomat who brought Fleischmann's letter to Switzerland returned without an answer. Fleischmann complained bitterly, on December 19, that the will to help was absent. On January 14 she also reported that she had failed to secure help from the Hungarian Jews.[56] Mayer was waiting for a response to his urgent request for instructions from Lisbon. Schwartz and his deputy, Herbert Katzki, hesitated, and did not give an answer in a telephone conversation with Mayer on February 24. On March 1, Katzki told Mayer that nothing could be done—that is, that no money should be sent to Slovakia for the purpose asked for. Richard Lichtheim, the Zionist representative in Geneva, was also of the opinion that the new proposal was "a lie and a deception."[57]

Mayer began to act on his own, however. In late February he told Schwalb to tell the people in Bratislava that their proposal was being carefully considered. He had now promised them a monthly allocation of SFR 20,000, and he promised Fleischmann another SFR 100,000 in après on top of that. It was then, in March, that Wisliceny finally asked for a sum of $2 million, of which 10 percent would have to be a down payment. On March 31, Mayer suggested that he would place $100,000 for Willy in the United States in après money. On April 2 he told Katzki that he would try to "avoid that the negotiations snap and the blame is being put on our shoulders."[58] He also tried to convince a reluctant International Red Cross to send a delegate to Slovakia, because that might protect both the Jews of Slovakia generally and the members of the Working Group specifically. While Mayer was moving toward a greater involvement in the Europa Plan, Schwalb and Alfred Silberschein, another Zionist representative in Switzerland—from the World Jewish Congress—were the only ones there who took the plan seriously enough to demand that money be sent. Except that there was no money in Switzerland, because Mayer had received none, and there were certainly no dollars.

Meanwhile, in Istanbul a Palestine Jewish delegation was being formed (November 1942–January 1943) to establish contact with Nazi-occupied countries. The Working Group wanted money, in dollars, though Weissmandel was fully aware that what the Nazis really wanted was something else; money was just a means, and of course it would have some importance in itself. The Istanbul delegation represented the Zionist bodies in Palestine, and the main form of aid was money; the Group therefore turned to the delegation in their plight.

The reaction in Istanbul has to be understood against the background of the developments in Palestine, whose Jewish leadership controlled the Istanbul delegation. In Palestine, reliable information about the Nazis' mass murder plans had been obtained with the arrival on November 13, 1942, of sixty-nine Palestinian Jewish citizens who had been caught in Europe at the outbreak of war. They were exchanged for a larger number of Germans residing in Palestine and came from different parts of occupied Europe, including several towns in Poland. The travelers brought direct and personal information that left no doubt about what was happening. As everywhere else, the information brought shock, disbelief, and despair.[59] But it also galvanized into action the leadership of the Jewish Agency, the Palestine-based leadership of the Zionist movement. David Ben Gurion, the chairman of the executive; Moshe Shertok (Sharett), the head of the political department; Yitzhak Grünbaum, the head of the Polish committee, who was to head the JA Rescue Committee in 1943; Eliezer Kaplan, the treasurer; and Chaim Weizmann, the president, who resided in London—these were the main figures. Again, the customary present-day accusation is that the JA did too little too late to rescue Jews in Europe, that they placed the creation of a Jewish State above the rescue of Jews, and that Ben Gurion and Grünbaum especially were cold, wrongheaded politicians who ignored the destruction of their people in Europe. Liberal, non-Orthodox, Orthodox, and ultraorthodox Jewish writers and historians have been repeating these accusations for years.[60]

It is fairly clear now that Ben Gurion received detailed information the moment it became available. He appears to have grasped fully the implications of the Nazi murder plans; and, contrary to established views, he became extremely active in promoting approaches to the Allies to persuade them to intervene in favor of European Jews. As one expert, Shlomo Aronson, has pointed out, the Jews were caught in a "multiple trap" from which they were unable to escape.[61] They had to support Allied policies against Hitler, but these policies precluded any attempt to intervene for the Jews specifically. From the Western Allies' point of view, no worse mistake could be made than to come out openly for the Jews, which would lay them open to the accusation at home that they were fighting the war because of the Jews. On the other hand, the Nazi leadership saw the war as an ideological struggle directed ultimately against the Jews; the West rejected this approach, partly because of the unpopularity of the Jews in the West and partly because they were genuinely incapable of understanding the Nazi ideology and its practical influence on Nazi policies.

To demonstrate the seriousness with which the Nazis approached these problems, let me quote from Himmler's speech to top military and SS leaders at Sonthofen on June 21, 1944:

The war we are waging is chiefly and essentially a race war. It is first and foremost a war against the Jew, who incited other nation-states, such as England and America, to enter the war against us, and it is, second, a war against Russia. The war against Jewry and the Asiatics is a war between two races.

(Der Krieg, den wir führen, ist in seinem Hauptinhalt ein Rassenkrieg. Er ist erstens der Krieg gegen den Juden, der andere Nationalstaaten wie England und Amerika in den Krieg gegen uns hineingehetzt hat, und es ist zweitens der Krieg gegen Russland. Der Krieg gegen Judentum und Asiatentum ist der Krieg zweier Rassen.)[62]

Terminology of this kind simply could not be understood in Western chancelleries. Worse still, historians like Arno J. Mayer, in his popular *Why Did the Heavens Not Darken?* argue even today, against all evidence, that Hitler's war was primarily fought against Marxism, rather than against the Jews, who, of course, had invented Marxism.[63] In the eyes of the Western powers the Jews were just one of many suffering groups under the Nazis. They were still very largely understood to be a religion rather than a people, and the persecution of the Jews, despite all the information over the previous nine years, was still largely understood to be a *religious* persecution, because these were terms with which Western civilization at the time could operate. The fact is that even though persecution of Christians by the Nazis may have been a religious persecution, the war against the Jews was a war, as Himmler put it, of "races"—that is, in civilized terminology, a war against the Jewish people, whatever their beliefs or non-beliefs.

Ben Gurion may have derived some satisfaction from the recognition on the part of the Allies that the Jews of Europe were being murdered. A declaration to that effect was made on December 17, 1942, in a statement published in London, Washington, and Moscow. The statement came about largely as the result of the information received from the International Red Cross in Geneva, which, in the person of Carl J. Burckhardt, its vice-chairman, declared to the American diplomat Paul C. Squire, who was interviewing him (November 7, 1942), that the Nazis were indeed killing the Jews, thus confirming the Riegner cable of August. But even more important was the report brought out of Poland by the Polish underground courier Jan Karski (a pseudonym), in late October or early November. Karski met with leaders of the Polish government-in-exile, with Foreign Secretary Anthony Eden of Britain and many others. He reported to them on the destruction of the Warsaw ghetto and on the extermination camps (he believed that he had been inside the death camp of Belżec, though he may actually have entered the slave labor camp not far away).[64] The information he brought was so convincing that the Polish government mounted a serious and intensive campaign to spread the word and demanded action. On December 9, 1942, it presented a strong note to the Allied governments on the subject. The December 17 declaration was the result.

Ben Gurion wanted the Allies to offer the Nazis an exchange: the Germans in the Western Hemisphere in return for letting the Jews go. But this solution was idealistic and impossible, and he quickly turned to another request: that neutrals encourage Jews to enter their countries against a promise by the West to provide supplies to keep the refugees alive and remove them after the war. He also demanded that Germany's satellites be warned to protect their Jews, and he also wanted bombings of German cities to be effectuated openly as reprisals for the murder of Jews, accompanied by a massive leaflet propaganda offensive over German cities. He demanded from the British a relative opening of the gates of Palestine, which had been closed by the British White Paper of May 17, 1939; the White Paper limited Jewish immigration to Palestine to another 75,000, after which it was to cease (unless the Arabs agreed to allow it). There were still 29,000 entry certificates available at the end of 1942, and when Ben Gurion realized that he was failing to persuade the Allies to take the other steps and despaired of success, he concentrated on the idea of bringing in 29,000 Jewish children from the Balkans. Ben Gurion realized the trap the Jews were in and tried to fight for what he thought was feasible within the limits set by the total powerlessness of the Palestinian Yishuv and its isolation from the United States and Britain, from which it was cut off by the war. He certainly saw the tragic prospect of leading the national revival of a people that was being murdered en masse.

The two main figures in the Istanbul delegation were not its nominal head, a trustee of Grünbaum, Chaim Barlas, but the two kibbutz movement representatives, Wenja (Venia) Pomeranz (later Ze'ev Hadari) and Menachem Bader. They were both of two minds about the rabbis' letter, as they called Weissmandel's plea of early December. Although a careful reading of the letter would have shown them otherwise, they and the leadership in Palestine mixed the two stages up and saw in the December letter another plea to save Slovak Jewry. We should also note that at the same time—that is, in November–December 1942—the Palestine leadership was busy with another ransom proposal, from Romania, supposedly offering the rescue of 70,000 deportees in Romanian-occupied Transnistria (a region in southwestern Ukraine and contemporary Moldova) for a sum running into tens of millions of dollars. The two ransom plans seemed to reflect a pattern of offering to save local Jewish populations. By the second half of January, Yitzhak Grünbaum, chairman of the JA Rescue Committee, had sent a cable to Alfred Silberschein of the World Jewish Congress Relief Committee (RELICO) in Geneva, who also was in touch with Slovakia, that the Yishuv felt "positive towards the Rabbis' proposal" and asked him to find out whether the proposal "was practical, and what help was needed."[65]

Not until February 10 do we find documentation showing that Ben Gurion was involved in reactions to the plan. Apparently he misunderstood the information; he spoke as though the discussion was about, not the end to murder, but the rescue of the Slovak Jews. He made it clear that the rescue of 29,000 children, which was then being discussed with the British, and various other "small" rescue plans had precedence, and that for larger schemes the world Jewish community had to be approached for funds, which the Yishuv in Palestine did not possess.[66]

On March 10, 1943, the Istanbul emissaries wrote to Tel Aviv saying that it was difficult to estimate the seriousness of the proposal, though "these means" had prevented the deportation of 20,000 Slovak Jews. Bader apparently did not even mention the proposal in his talk with the Apostolic Nuntius Angelo Roncalli (later Pope John XXIII) on March 9.[67] Ben Gurion came to the double conclusion that the plan was probably an extortion attempt, but that, on the other hand, money had to be sent, because nothing that emanated from the beleaguered Jews in Nazi-occupied Europe could be ignored. He was persuaded to adopt this stand in late February even before he had sent his closest friend and adviser, the JA treasurer Eliezer Kaplan, to Istanbul to find out was what happening. Kaplan returned and reported to the Jewish Agency Executive on March 28, saying that he considered the proposal to be "doubtful"; however, results had been achieved by bribes in Slovakia and Transnistria, and the JA would have to find money, if money was needed. In Kaplan's own meeting with Roncalli, Slovakia was mentioned and a promise was received that Roncalli would intercede with the Vatican to try and save Jews. The Vatican had already acted, and Roncalli's additional plea supported what had already been done. The Yishuv's reaction until May was therefore lukewarm, though not negative: any necessary money would be provided. Not until early in 1943 was the sum of $200,000 mentioned as a down payment for the larger sum that the Nazis demanded. The situation was complicated by disagreement on the merits of the plan not only among the emissaries in Istanbul but among those in Switzerland as well. Schwalb—contrary to the picture of him in Weissmandel's book—was in favor of the proposal from the beginning, whereas Richard Lichtheim, the JA representative, was against it.[68]

The problem, of course, was that the Yishuv did not have anything like the sums Fleischmann, Weissmandel, and their colleagues were thinking about. They thought, in Slovakia, that the free Jewish world would and should be capable of producing millions of dollars with ease—in a way, they had fallen prey, unconsciously, to antisemitic arguments about infinitely rich World Jewry and its power to persuade warring nations to transfer funds wherever they were needed.

In early 1943 the attention of the Group itself was deflected from the Europa Plan to the fate of the remaining Slovak Jews. On February 7, under pressure from the radical wing in the SL'S and the Hlinka Guard, Mach declared at a rally at Ružomberok that "come March, come April, the transports will go again." A letter from the Slovak bishops to the government (February 17) again dealt only with converts, ignoring the danger to the "Jewish Jews" completely. The Group reacted immediately: all contacts with corrupt Slovak officialdom were intensified; Jozef Sivak, the Minister of Education and an opponent of the deportations, and Imrich Karváš, the friendly head of the Slovak National Bank, were recruited to influence the government; and an approach was made to Burzio. It seems that Burzio's intervention played an important role in helping to prevent the deportations. A pastoral letter written by the bishops—not the February letter to the government—was read in the churches on March 21, decrying the deportations in somewhat general, but nevertheless clear, language. The problem, indeed, was the language: the letter was written and read in Latin—hardly the way to move the unsophisticated Slovak believers.

On April 7, Burzio went to see Tuka. In a report to Luigi Maglione, the Vatican Secretary of State, Burzio uses very strong language to describe Tuka: "There is nothing more unpleasant and humiliating than to maintain a conversation with this person, whom some call a sphinx, others a maniac, others a cynical hypocrite . . . a demented man. Nor can one hope that with such a superman arguments touching on conscience can have any force"; he continued in the same vein. Nevertheless, it appears that the interview did have some effect, because in the course of it Tuka declared that if news of atrocities proved to be true, he would not restart the deportations. At a government meeting on April 9, he apparently found himself in a minority, with the majority opposing the resumption of deportations. These did not take place, and a Vatican protest on May 5 designed to prevent any further deportations was answered by the Slovaks on May 28, saying that no deportations of those who had been granted exemptions was envisaged.

Let me add here that Weissmandel accuses the church not only of failing to do anything to save Jews but even of arguing that all Jewish children were sinners and had to pay for the crime of deicide. The documents show that while some of the leading churchmen were certainly no friends of the Jews, others intervened forcefully, and Burzio, whom Weissmandel attacks, too, was in the forefront of the defense of the Jews, not just the converts.[69]

We can therefore say that during the first months of 1943 the pressure from the Working Group on Mayer and Istanbul regarding the Europa Plan weakened. In Fleischmann's extant letters to Switzerland the main issue is, understandably, the threat of the new deportation; and even when Willy visited Bratislava, that threat was foremost on the minds of the Group leaders.

The postwar accounts from Weissmandel down hardly mention this letup, which meant that the people outside—in Switzerland and Istanbul-Palestine—had their attention deflected from the plan.

In the meantime, Wisliceny had been sent, in March, to Salonika to deport the Jews there to their deaths. He did his job without any visible qualms, blaming the situation later on the Jews, saying that they did not utilize the same means as those in Slovakia had (i.e., bribes), and claiming that he had tried unsuccessfully to intervene with Eichmann.[70] The proud Sephardic Jewish community of dockworkers, artisans, and traders—56,000 souls— was sent in cattle trucks to Auschwitz and Treblinka. Being busy in Greece, Wisliceny nevertheless maintained contact with Steiner in Bratislava—having a girlfriend there helped. And in the midst of all this he also had to have an eye operation.

As the Group refocused its attention on the plan, the problem as they saw it was that they did not have the 10 percent of the money that Willy had demanded. But on May 7, when Steiner, Fleischmann, and Wisliceny met, the lack of funds did not seem to be the major worry. Wisliceny reported that Hitler was now adamant about the destruction of the Jews but in a way contradicted his stand by again offering to stop deportations, for $2–3 million. Wisliceny would go to Prague to speak with his superior—presumably Eichmann. Fleischmann and Steiner promised Wisliceny $100,000 if deportations from all over Europe stopped immediately.[71] At a further meeting on May 10, however, presumably after he spoke with Eichmann, Willy insisted on the $200,000 down payment.[72] In the meantime, he said, there would be no deportations from Western countries until June 10, and if the Jews paid $200,000 by then, there would be another stay for two more months.[73] But the money was simply not there. By June, Mayer had sent a total of SFR 180,000 ($42,000), with another $10,000 coming through Hechalutz. One problem was that the organizations to whom Mayer and the others turned— the JDC, the World Jewish Congress—did not encourage them to do anything; the contacts obviously thought that the vaunted plan was just another Nazi extortionary trick. On June 8, Mayer told Schwalb that his answer to the whole proposal had to be negative.[74]

The very next day, June 9, a day before Willy's deadline, Fleischmann phoned Schwalb, and Mayer wavered again, asking Katzki on June 10 whether he had been right in saying no to the Group. On June 18, Fleischmann reported that Wisliceny had postponed the deadline to July 1 and had said that there would be no deportations from anywhere in Europe until July 10.[75] The money, $2 million, could be paid in installments.

A distraught Mayer now called a meeting for June 17 to be attended by some leading figures in Switzerland: Schwalb, Silberschein, and Pierre Bigar of the Swiss Jewish communities. In the end, he agreed to act against the advice of the JDC: he informed Fleischmann that he would try to have $200,000 deposited in the United States for après. But, he added, all deportations from all of Europe must cease, and all murder in Poland must cease as well; emigration through transit countries should be made possible. He also made more money available on an après basis—$23,000 for July–December and another $45,000 in the United States, based on the budget approved for him in New York but which he did not to receive until after September 1943.

Willy had said that he would return to Bratislava on July 1, but he did not arrive, possibly because he was awaiting some communication from his superiors; he said that he would arrive on July 10. In the meantime, Gizi Fleischmann was desperately trying to convince Mayer to send her money for the plan, unaware that he did not have it. Mayer suggested an après arrangement for Wisliceny in America, but Fleischmann rejected it—Wisliceny would consider it an insult.[76]

Wisliceny postponed the meeting with the Group, finally fixing it for August 5. But Mayer had no cash available, and the leaders in Slovakia were desperate. In the meantime, Joseph Schwartz of the JDC had been in Palestine meeting there with JA officials. The understanding was that most of the $200,000 would be shared between the JDC and the JA. On August 1, Shertok sent a cable to Mayer saying that the JA would send $50,000, and that the JDC, Schwartz had agreed, would send $150,000. Then the JA went one better and decided to send $100,000, half the sum, and even more if the JDC did not come through. Mayer cabled on August 11 that he welcomed the proposal and would make the money available for an après arrangement.[77]

In fact, by the end of September most of the $200,000 ($184,000) that the Group had demanded had been sent from Istanbul and Switzerland,[78] even though, contrary to Willy's promises, deportations from Western Europe had not stopped. Their continuation undermined any confidence the Jewish leaders outside might have had in the prospects of the plan.

But the Europa Plan was dying, quite independent of the money problem. On August 27, Wisliceny met with the Group and said that he would have to receive new instructions. He did tell them that his leaders were preparing a transport of 5,000 Jewish children from Poland to Theresienstadt, 2,000 of whom were already on their way. His knowing this information shows that he had actually spoken to Eichmann, because 1,000 Bialystok children *did* arrive in Theresienstadt in August. Eichmann vetoed the idea of emigrating these children to Palestine, for the Mufti of Jerusalem, the leader of the Arab Palestinian national movement, Hajj Amin al-Husseini, who had fled to Germany in 1941, was opposed. The Mufti, he said, was a major player in pushing for extermination of the Jews.[79]

Wisliceny also told his interlocutors some wild stories (for example, that Poland had only recently become the responsibility of his chief, presumably a reference to Eichmann), apparently because he wanted to say something but did not have the authorization to say anything.[80] On September 3, he met with the Group again and announced that the plan had been shelved, though the Germans might return to it at some future time. On September 12, Fleischmann gave him $10,000, but Wisliceny said that he considered the money a deposit on future payments.

The money sent from Istanbul was the result of a radical reevaluation of the scheme in Palestine. It started with a visit by Bader, who went there from Istanbul in mid-May; Bader was now utterly convinced of the supreme importance of the plan, and he persuaded Ben Gurion and the JA Executive to back it. Wenja Pomeranz and Ze'ev Schind (an emissary dealing with "illegal" immigration) wrote a letter to Ben Gurion bolstering Bader's plea. The result was a reiteration of the decision taken in late February to pay ransom if needed and the intensification of a drive in Palestine for rescue money, with Ben Gurion's direct participation. A very high proportion of the money collected went to Slovakia. This aid—again—makes utter nonsense of postwar arguments (including Weissmandel's) that Europe's Jews were abandoned by their kin in Palestine.

Weissmandel's bitter postwar account reveals no knowledge of the money that was sent. His accusations against the Zionists and against the JDC know no bounds. A reader immediately sees is that he is trying to tell the truth and collects documentation to prove his points. He relates in great detail his appeals to the Jewish world, accuses World Jewry of criminal negligence, and simply ignores most of the facts presented above. His view is that the Jews were able to prevent the continuation of the Nazi murder program, but that they failed to do so. He never doubts the sincerity of Wisliceny, although he calls him a murderer and a Nazi. In other words, according to Weissmandel, the Jews were responsible for their own murder. Again, this same argument is repeated by Jewish authors today for reasons that are explicable only in psychological terms.

Weissmandel's view of Wisliceny was shared by Fleischmann and Steiner, who also saw Willy as a gentleman true to his word.[81] The Israeli historian Gila Fatran brings out this aspect of the negotiations and asks how these world-wise Jewish leaders could have believed the wily Nazi official.[82] We should note that whereas Fleischmann was sometimes as bitter as Weissmandel regarding the JDC, refusing to grasp the severe limitations on the sending of funds, she did not share Weissmandel's hatred of the JDC and of the Zionists. When Mayer sent larger sums in the summer of 1943, she wrote to him: "Dear, good uncle, many many thanks for your goodness and helpfulness; may God preserve your health for all of us."[83]

The attitudes of the Jews seem clear enough: Weissmandel and presumably most, though not all, of the Group in Bratislava believed that they had managed to prevent deportations from Slovakia in the summer and autumn of 1942 by bribing Wisliceny and the Slovaks. As a result, they then approached Wisliceny with the Europa Plan. They trusted him implicitly and believed that if only the Jews outside would pay up, deportations would cease. The JDC and the JA were much more skeptical. They saw the plan as an extortion attempt, but they were also faced with other problems. They had no way of transferring sums of money of that magnitude in cash. More fundamentally, there was the major issue of paying ransom for lives. Schwartz and Ben Gurion both knew very well that the Allies would never agree to a ransom policy. They nevertheless sent money for that purpose. It seems fairly clear that Schwartz, Ben Gurion, Shertok, and even Mayer sent it not because they believed that such a rescue was practical but because they did not want to be accused after the war of missing an opportunity to rescue Jews, even if the scheme was very doubtful. Bader and Pomeranz had quite a different view. Bader wrote, in 1943, that just as before the facts about the Holocaust became known, no one believed that the mass murder was possible; now, after the facts were known, no one believed that rescue was feasible. But he argued that it was.

Thus far, we have examined the negotiations from the Jewish perspective, arguing mainly on the basis of Weissmandel's account. What we now have to ask is, Were the deportations really halted by the bribe to Wisliceny? Even more important are other questions: What were the Nazi intentions? What was Wisliceny's real role? Who and what was behind him? Was there a chance at rescue that had been missed?

6

What Really Did Happen in Slovakia?

Dieter Wisliceny was apprehended by the Americans at war's end, taken to Nuremberg, interrogated many times, then handed over to the Slovak authorities. In Bratislava he was again interrogated for a long period of time. Finally, he was put on trial, found guilty of war crimes and murder, and executed in Bratislava in 1948.

To analyze his testimony while taking into account the pitfalls that such testimony presents is obviously very important. He was fighting for his life, and he knew it. He could hardly be expected to make self-incriminating statements; he would presumably glorify his role as much as he could and place blame on others at every opportunity. He was faced with an array of documentation found in Slovakia (not all of it is at our disposal today—some of it has not yet been rediscovered). He was a prisoner, and he did not know what evidence his jailers had. Also, he was faced with survivors, including members of the Working Group who had remained in postwar Slovakia, at least temporarily. Among the survivors, pride of place was taken by Andrej Steiner, who had been the Group's intermediary with Wisliceny. Hochberg, the first intermediary, had been executed in the last stages of the war by Jewish partisans. The reason for Hochberg's arrest in November 1942 and his interrogation by Slovak authorities, as well his subsequent fate, would have been of great interest, but this material was not presented at the trials. What exists in Czech and Slovak archives shows that Hochberg was interrogated on bribery charges. Whether additional questions were asked of him is not known at present.

To come back to Wisliceny: in his testimony he reported on his meeting at the ÚŽ when he and Morávek told the Jews that they were going to be deported (see Chapter 5). He claims that the initiative for the meeting, which is reported in all the survivors' memoirs, came from Morávek, that it "probably" took place at the end of March (actually, in mid-March), and that Morávek made the speech telling the Jews what they were allowed to take with them, and so on.

Wisliceny, in all his testimony, differentiates between two stages of the deportations: the first, in which he says 17,000 young workers were deported, and the second, from April or May 1942, when 35,000 family members were sent away. The figures are more or less correct for the deportations up to July (the total number of Jews deported to Poland in 1942 was 57,837—or 58,534, according to another computation).[1] He then reports that at the end of July, Tuka called him and reminded him of Eichmann's promise that the Jews would be treated humanely; Tuka wanted to hear a repetition of these assurances, demanded separate religious facilities for converts to Christianity, and brought up the idea of a Slovak mission to Poland that would visit the Jewish camps. All of this, Tuka claimed, was the result of Catholic intervention—by the Vatican as well as local bishops. His claim appears to tally with published Vatican documents; the concern for converts was, as we have seen, central, but the Vatican was going beyond that. Tuka also mentioned rumors of the mass murder of Jews, which he, Tuka, did not believe in. At the end of July, indeed, there were already persistent rumors of mass slaughter.

Three days after that interview, Wisliceny says, he went to Berlin to see Eichmann.[2] Eichmann rejected the request for a mission outright, saying that the Slovaks had taken away the Jews' citizenship and now had no right to look after them. Wisliceny argues, as we have already seen, that until that moment he had no knowledge of what was going on in Auschwitz (he claims to have known nothing about the other death camps until after the war), even though he admits having visited Auschwitz in May 1942 in order, he says, to ask Hoess for permission for the Jews to write postcards.[3] He saw a column of Slovak Jewish women there, and Hoess told him these were his best workers. In late June or early July, a Nazi officer told him that he had heard about murder in Auschwitz, and then Wisliceny heard similar stories from Hochberg and from the train crews. That, he says, was the reason that he asked Eichmann what was happening and why he would not allow Slovak visitors.[4] In almost all of his statements Wisliceny repeats the same story: that Eichmann then told him that most of the Slovak Jews were dead and, after Wisliceny demanded the truth and swore an oath of secrecy, showed him an order signed by Himmler in April or May 1942 and directed to Oswald Pohl of the Wirtschaftsverwaltungshauptamt (Chief Economic Administration Office) of the SS, the supervisory authority for the concentration camps, and to Reinhard Heydrich, head of the Central Reich Security Office, which mentioned the Führer's order to murder all Jews. Himmler's letter was in the context of a specific instruction contained in the letter that exempted Jewish workers temporarily from Hitler's extermination order. Wisliceny was well acquainted with Himmler's signature and claims to be certain that Himmler had signed it.

Eichmann, in his memoirs, denies Wisliceny's story and says that there never was a Himmler order to implement the "Final Solution." "Do you believe," he asks his interviewer, "that he sat down in order to write to me: 'My dear Eichmann, the Führer has ordered the physical annihilation of all Jews'? The truth is that Himmler never wrote down a single line in this matter. I know that he always gave oral instructions to Oswald Pohl . . . I never received an order of this kind."[5] But the contradiction between the testimonies is perhaps only an apparent one. Wisliceny never really claimed that he saw Himmler's order to kill all Jews. What he claims he saw was an order temporarily *exempting* certain categories of Jews from a general policy decided on by Hitler. The exemption indicated what the rule was. We should, therefore, be inclined to believe Wisliceny regarding that document. He claims to have been shocked and to have told Eichmann that if these matters were to become known abroad, then God help the German people, if their enemies did something similar to them. Eichmann said this was not his problem; the decision was made by the Führer.

The Slovak mission was not sent. However, a German Slovak journalist, Friedrich (Fritz) Fiala, was sent to Sosnowice to take pictures of the Jews there. In the autumn of 1942 (November 10) he published the pictures and an antisemitic article in the Slovak German newspaper *Grenzbote*. The incident would not be worth mentioning were it not that Fiala became a double agent in Istanbul and a figure in an American spy-ring and returns to our story there.[6]

We now come to the main problem that interests us: Wisliceny's negotiations with the Working Group. Hochberg, he says in his testimony, was a Jew who occasionally did statistical work for him. He does not admit his close relationship with the Jewish traitor, because that would obviously hurt him at the trial before a postwar Slovak court. In one place he says that preliminary discussions with Hochberg took place in the summer of 1942. In another deposition he says that he spoke with Hochberg at a Slovak spa called Rájecké Teplice in September. It is worth quoting verbatim:

The occasion was that transports which had been announced by the Slovak Ministry of the Interior could not go for some reason. On my remarking that this was quite unimportant to me, as I was not interested personally in these transports, Hochberg asked if I meant that. I affirmed that I did, and he said that a certain office [*Stelle*] abroad had asked him to talk with me [to see] if I could not do something to stop the deportations from Slovakia. Who this "office" was he would not say. I stated to him that I would not do anything to force these transports from Slovakia, but that practically speaking I could not prevent the continuation of transports that were arranged by the Interior Ministry, as my activity in the deportations was one of a liaison officer to Eichmann and that I never had any influence over the fate of the persons affected by the deportations.[7]

He then understood from Hochberg that the "Joint" (JDC) was the origin of the appeal to him, and he promised to do nothing to further the deportations himself. Hochberg mentioned the man who had given him the assignment: "Rott" of Zurich. Wisliceny assumed that this Rott was either Schwalb or Mayer, whose names he learned later. Even after the war, according to his testimony, he still believed that Rott had written letters to Slovakia. On two occasions, he says, Hochberg showed him postcards from Rott.

One day, he says, apparently later, Hochberg brought him $20,000, which he deposited with Franz Goltz, the police attaché at the embassy, and he also informed Ludin. Hochberg added, he says, that $3 million were available for this purpose—that is, ransom. Elsewhere he indicates that the money was handed to him in October.[8] He says that he traveled to Berlin, informed a furious Eichmann—who berated him for negotiating with the Jews and for accepting the money—but managed to have Eichmann send a report to Himmler. He argued that "these things" (the murders in Poland) were bound to become known abroad, and played up the opposition of the church. In the end, in November or early December, Eichmann agreed to leave Wisliceny a free hand "until things become settled again [bis sich die Gemüter beruhigt haben]."[9] In November, apparently at the same time, Himmler ordered him to send the money to the Wirtschaftsverwaltungshauptamt (Central Office of Economic Administration) and to hear what the Jews had to say. Wisliceny says that this came down to him in an order that was signed by Himmler's adjutant, Suchaneck.[10] Quite possibly, the two permissions from Eichmann and from Himmler to talk to the Jews amount to the same thing; Eichmann would not have given any permission like that without confirming it with his superiors.

At that time—around November—Wisliceny says, he asked Eichmann to do something about sending Jewish children abroad. Contrary to his expectations, Eichmann agreed and said that he had also received a proposal like that from the International Red Cross via the German Foreign Office. He would concentrate 10,000 children in Theresienstadt and then await Himmler's decision.[11] Immediately thereafter, Hochberg was arrested. Here, as we shall show, the time sequence is not quite accurate. The arrest of Hochberg occurred in November, whereas the negotiations about the children probably occurred twice, once in December and then again in the summer of 1943.

Let us now analyze Wisliceny's stories. It is worth emphasizing that Wisliceny makes it quite clear that Hochberg came to him with the request to prevent further deportations *after* these had stopped for some reason unconnected with Wisliceny, Hochberg, or any negotiations. Then Wisliceny says that Hochberg gave him the money in October or November.

This version is strengthened by Steiner. In his December 1947 testimony (a memorandum to the JDC), Steiner explicitly says that the cessation of the

deportations had nothing to do with the bribing of Wisliceny. In another testimony, probably in 1946, he puts the start of the Hochberg contacts in September, and then, "later," after the deportations stopped, in November, he
says, the Group sent Hochberg with a large sum in dollars ("mit einem
grossen Dollarbetrag") to Wisliceny. We know today, Steiner says, that he
transmitted $20,000 to his superiors.[12]

After Hochberg was arrested, and Wisliceny failed to pry him loose from
the Slovaks, Steiner appeared on the scene. Together, Wisliceny says, they
worked out the proposals for Himmler, the Europa Plan, which concerned
putting a stop to the deportations and letting the International Red Cross
(IRC) look after the Jews in Poland. The proposals were then transmitted to
Himmler, who could not make up his mind about them. My reading is that
the permission given separately by Eichmann and Suchaneck to talk to the
Jews was the result of the submission by Wisliceny of the Europa Plan proposals. The halfhearted permission also reflected Himmler's hesitation, as
Wisliceny reports it. But what exactly were these Jewish proposals?

Steiner's version differs from Weissmandel's, as well as from Wisliceny's.
Steiner says the original proposals included a demand for the non-renewal of
the Slovak deportations; the end of the murders in Polish camps; the end of
deportations from all over Europe; and the establishment of work camps for
Jews in places where the Nazis, it was thought, would insist on anti-Jewish
measures; and the release of 10,000 children from Poland and their transfer
to Switzerland and Palestine.[13] He does not mention the proposal that the
International Red Cross should look after the Jews. Wisliceny, Steiner
reports, returned from Berlin with permission for Polish Jews to write postcards and for the Group to send parcels to Theresienstadt, but with no satisfactory answers to anything else.[14] What Steiner does not say is the obvious:
Wisliceny continued his talks with the Group after he had been to Berlin, and
clearly he must have received permission there to do so.

Unfortunately and very importantly, all the correspondence between the
Slovak Working Group and Mayer and Schwalb in Switzerland was picked
up by the Abwehr (German Military Intelligence) in Vienna; fortunately or
not, it was sent to Bratislava, where Goltz gave it to Wisliceny, because it concerned Jewish matters. From that correspondence Wisliceny knew what the
Jews thought about him, what they called him (Willy), and what problems
they had with money from abroad. Both Steiner and Wisliceny tell the same
story, which means that while the moves of the Jews were known to Wisliceny,
his contacts with the SS leadership remained hidden from the Group.

Finally, Wisliceny says in his testimony of May 6, 1946, that in August
1943 he was ordered, by Himmler through Eichmann, to stop the negotiations and not to have any further contact with his Jewish partners or else he
himself would land in a concentration camp.

Wisliceny's testimonies are problematic, and Weissmandel is not reliable, either. Furthermore, all the information about the early contacts between Hochberg and Wisliceny comes either from Hochberg's reports to the Group or from Wisliceny's postwar testimony. However, its juxtaposition with Gizi Fleischmann's letters written at the time and with Steiner's postwar statements might yield the solution to the riddle. A crucial letter by Fleischmann dated August 27 reports that the *first* payment to Wisliceny was *due* on August 17, and it is probable that indeed the payment was made that day to Hochberg, whether or not it reached Wisliceny.[15] The date of the first talks between Hochberg and Wisliceny would seem to be early August, during a period when there were no transports. These first talks must have taken place. Not only does Weissmandel imply that he had to convince Hochberg, a process that must have taken some time, but there must also have been conversations prior to Hochberg's meeting with Wisliceny on August 17. More talks were held in September or very early October at Rájecké Teplice, after the Yom Kippur transport—six weeks after the first payment to Hochberg in August. The timing would also fit Weissmandel's recollection. On August 17, Hochberg would indeed have met Wisliceny and asked him not to press for deportations, and in October he would have paid him $20,000. The rest of the money was probably pocketed either by Hochberg or by Wisliceny. In fact, some nine to ten months after the event, in the spring of 1943, Fleischmann mentioned that the money had been paid in October, and this dating has to be preferred over Steiner's postwar statement that the payment was made in November.[16]

All this contradicts Weissmandel's story as it was understood until now. The point is that people have different powers of recollection regarding dates. Let me recapitulate: the inspiration to talk with Hochberg came to Weissmandel in early July, and a few weeks passed until, on the one hand, the Group decided to support Weissmandel in his initiative and, on the other hand, Hochberg became convinced that he should approach Wisliceny. Hochberg spoke with Wisliceny in August and received a first payment from the Group. Then six weeks passed, and after another two transports that had nothing to do with the first payment—which may not even have reached Wisliceny—a payment was made to the Nazi. Wisliceny's Rott is Weissmandel's Ferdinand Roth—we must not forget that Weissmandel's book, with the Roth story, appeared in 1960, twelve years after Wisliceny's execution. Wisliceny had no contact with Weissmandel after the war, and his recollection of Rott-Roth is genuine.

Clearly, the cessation of the deportations from the end of July until September 18 had nothing to do with bribing Wisliceny. What, then, was the reason for the pause? Some German documents explain the situation: On June 25, 1942, Ludin and Wisliceny met with Tuka and told him that the Germans would have to stop the deportations because the Slovaks had granted 35,000 exemptions and because the Catholic church continued to intervene. The Slovaks were taken aback, and Ludin reported on this the next day to his Foreign Office.[17] Vatican documents tend to support Wisliceny's and Ludin's argument. Burzio himself and a few like-minded members of the Slovak hierarchy spoke out, privately and in meetings with government officials, against the deportations and especially against the deportation of converts. The figure of 35,000 mentioned in the German document is wrong: A statistical analysis in Gila Fatran's thesis shows that so-called Presidential exemptions (letters by Tiso protecting the addressees from the danger of deportation) accounted for 1,111 persons in 1943. There were 985 mixed marriages, 4,217 converts prior to March 1939, and 9,687 economically "useful" Jews, for a total of nearly 16,000. To what extent these numbers include members of families is not quite clear, however. According to Fatran's calculations, 8,000 escaped to Hungary, leaving 24,000 in Slovakia after October 1942. Some of these were there illegally.

After the June meeting, Tuka, most likely with the support of Mach, tried to get the deportations going again. In an unusual request he asked the Germans to press him to carry on; he obviously needed their pressure to quash opposition from his colleagues. The Germans responded only partly: they said that the cessation of deportations might create a bad impression in Berlin; but in line with Himmler's early warning not to get involved in political problems in Slovakia, they did not go further at that moment.[18]

In July 1942, Morávek was dismissed, and the transports slackened off; in August and for most of September there were none at all. The negotiations with Wisliceny were held during that period.

Another major factor in stopping the deportations was the bribing of the corrupt Slovak fascist chiefs. Wisliceny claims to have emphasized that point with his Jewish interlocutors. Not that it was necessary. After the war the Slovaks denied taking bribes. Koso, for one, claimed that he never received any bribes from the Jews—which was a lie—but he tells in some detail the story of how his wife was bribed by Gizi Fleischmann, denying that he knew about it at the time. This was a lie, too, and it is fairly clear that through his wife this centrally important Slovak official was influenced to desist from anti-Jewish actions.[19] By July the Group had managed to get to the other main Slovak deportation enthusiasts as well: Vašek and Morávek. Vašek and Koso were very amply bribed; Vašek began receiving 100,000 Slovak crowns for every month that no deportations occurred. As a result, his enthusiasm for the deportations declined markedly. In addition, the Group also found supporters in the Slovak government itself, as we have already seen: the Minister of Education, Jozef Sivak, and the head of the Slovak National Bank, Imrich Karváš, who kept them informed without taking any bribes. In addition, Wisliceny may have been shocked, if his postwar testimony is to be believed, when he learned of the "Final Solution" at exactly that time. Objective circumstances, massive bribes to key Slovak fascists, and perhaps the beginning of Wisliceny's hesitation would explain the pause in August. Let me also mention the simple fact that all this was taking place at the height of the murder campaign in Poland. Compared with that, the 24,000 Slovak Jews were small fry; if there were local "problems," the SS could kill them later.

Weissmandel wrongly argued that the first payment was the reason why the deportations stopped in the summer and, further, that the Yom Kippur transport took place because the second payment had not been made in time. The effect of this false rendition of events on Jewish historical consciousness after the Holocaust was enormous, because it implied that the outside Jewish world, nonbelievers in the non-Zionist and Zionist camps alike, had betrayed European—in this case Slovak—Jewry by not sending the money in time.

On the other hand, the ransom payment to Wisliceny may indeed have helped to solidify an already existing tendency. A problem arises here from the blatant discrepancy between the $50,000 in two payments mentioned by Weissmandel and the $20,000 mentioned by Wisliceny. If we try to sort this out, we find that Fleischmann, in her July 27 letter, mentions not $50,000 but SFR 100,000 ($23,000) in *Swiss money*![20] At this time, we remember, the Group was considering what to offer Wisliceny. The ransom payment can hardly have been made after the attempt to bribe Wisliceny, because, as we know, the Nazi official demanded dollars, not Swiss francs. The testimonies of the Group survivors about the sums paid to the Nazi and about the times of payment are contradictory. Steiner compounds the confusion when he says that he himself gave Wisliceny two sums of $10,000 each and one of $15,000—presumably after November, because Steiner had no access to Wisliceny before that. If so, then Wisliceny would have received $55,000 ($20,000 from Hochberg in October and $35,000 from Steiner later on).[21]

Do we therefore have to conclude that Weissmandel's recollection is totally wrong? We must start from the assumption that Weissmandel was reporting what he remembered to be true. He not only had no reason to lie but was probably constitutionally unable to do so. We have already hinted that what happened is probably (1) that Hochberg pocketed the difference between the $50,000 and the $20,000; (2) that about $55,000 was paid, as Weissmandel remembered—$20,000 of which was paid by Hochberg in October and $35,000 by Steiner later on; or (3) that Wisliceny was the person who pocketed the difference. The most likely of these scenarios is the first. In that case, although there was only one payment that Wisliceny received and acknowledged, there were two to Hochberg, and the payment may have helped post factum but was not the reason that the deportations ceased in October. Further payments to Wisliceny were made by Steiner, that is, after November, and were connected with the Europa Plan and not with the Slovak deportations. The fact that two transports went after Yom Kippur had nothing to do with ransom—it was simply a matter of unprotected Jews being available and the bribes to the Slovaks not being currently effective.

Weissmandel not only has his dates mixed up; he also ignores the two last trains completely. Most of the historians who have commented on this affair until now, including myself, have fallen into the trap of believing Weissmandel. One reason may lie in the peculiarities of Weissmandel's book. It was put together after his death by his brother and his pupils, and it is impossible to say what part is Weissmandel and what was added or changed by his fanatical heirs. Also, Weissmandel himself was a bitter man, who had lost his wife and his children at Auschwitz and who vented his fury on those with whom he had ideological differences. He, and his colleagues in Slovakia, had fought the good fight, and World Jewry, because it had abandoned religion and tradition, was the traitor.

Although the Group's conviction that they had ransomed the remnant of Jews in Slovakia by bribing Willy was erroneous,[22] the seed had been planted in both their and Willy's mind. We can see from his testimony how the system worked. The $20,000 should be seen as an opening gambit in the Europa Plan negotiations, rather than connected to the Slovak deportations.

Wisliceny reported to Eichmann; he had no direct line to Himmler, and he never actually talked to him about his contacts in Bratislava. But he was on good terms with Eichmann, he could talk to him, and when he says that Eichmann sent his reports up to Himmler, he is probably speaking the truth, although Eichmann's immediate superior, Gestapo chief Heinrich Müller, must have seen the reports before Himmler did. Müller is never mentioned in the testimonies.

The Europa Plan negotiations (Wisliceny at one point calls it the *Grossplan*) started in November. It is clear that Himmler sanctioned the continuation of the talks.[23] He hedged his agreement by saying that Wisliceny could promise whatever he liked; he, Himmler, would later see what part of the promise should be kept. The reason for agreeing to the continuation of contacts could hardly have been the money. After all, even $2–3 million was a paltry sum in the great war that was going on; $50,000 were simply ridiculous. On the other hand, a large sum could be helpful in explaining to Hitler or others why these negotiations, if they became serious, took place.

The contacts regarding children were renewed in the summer of 1943, when Eichmann and Himmler had to deal with a Swiss attempt to intervene in behalf of children, which we shall look into later. It was then, on August 28, 1943, that about 1,000 children were shipped from Bialystok to Theresienstadt, where they were kept until October 5, obviously for some exchange plan. Steiner, too, in a deposition made on December 2, 1946, to the Slovak

National Court confirms that negotiations about children took place and that Wisliceny at the time said in the name of Eichmann that the Mufti of Jerusalem, Hajj Amin el-Husseini, was trying to prevent that.[24] In addition, Steiner also says that special sums for the rescue of the children were requested from abroad, but the Jewish organizations declined to send these sums for legalistic reasons. As a result, he says, the children were sent to Auschwitz. There is no evidence to support the claim that special sums for the children were requested of the JDC or the Jewish Agency.[25]

The end of the negotiations is presented by Wisliceny in all the testimonies quoted in the same manner: after months during which he could not get an answer out of Himmler—but the permission to negotiate was not rescinded—Himmler finally, in August 1943, forbade any further discussions. Eichmann presented this decision to Wisliceny, along with a threat that if he continued, he would be severely punished—or so Wisliceny says. What emerges from this account is that there were only two Himmler interventions: one, in November, that permitted the negotiations, supposedly taking place with some foreign Jews, and that reserved judgment about how many of the promises would be kept; the other, in August 1943, that forbade the contacts. In between Wisliceny was probably acting—with Eichmann's knowledge (it must be assumed that Eichmann reported to Müller and Himmler)—mainly on his own when he asked for the money, when he promised the end of deportations, and so on. He must have hoped that if he made progress with his contacts, Himmler would pick up the thread and give further instructions, with a pat on the back for his loyal Bratislava representative. The negotiations about the children were conducted with Eichmann, and it was Eichmann, too, not Himmler directly, who expressed a lack of interest in the continuation of the Slovak deportations in the winter of 1942, though it is not very likely that Eichmann could or would have made a statement of "desinteressement" without Himmler's express approval. During the Europa Plan negotiations, then, Wisliceny led the Group negotiators by their noses, pretending that he was entitled to make promises that could be kept.

Who, then, was Wisliceny? Wisliceny was a Nazi murderer—there can hardly be any doubt about that. He was instrumental in deporting the Greek Jews to their deaths and participated actively in the deportation of Hungarian Jewry to Auschwitz in 1944. In the nature of things, he could only be hanged once—in Slovakia, in 1948. Yet his relationship with the Jewish group in Slovakia seems to indicate that he was trying to grab an opportunity to get out of the position the SS had put him in.

What is amazing is that the highly intelligent Slovak Jewish leaders believed him and trusted him more than they did their colleagues outside the Nazi empire, and none more so than Weissmandel. He did not trust Schwalb or Mayer, but he did trust a Nazi.[26] He was convinced that the negotiations failed because the Jews were not able to pay the $200,000. He totally ignored the fact that money was received in Bratislava in the late spring and summer of 1943, and he also believed that Himmler was actively involved in setting all the deadline dates that Wisliceny invented. No doubt, had Wisliceny obtained large amounts of money, the matter would have been raised again. But Himmler was very careful. Negotiating with the Jewish "world government" was a dangerous game.

To be fair, I must add that Gizi Fleischmann was equally convinced, as her letters evince, that had the $200,000 been available between March, or May, and July 1943, the Group could have made an impression on the Nazis and caused a more serious consideration of the Europa Plan.

The conclusions seem to be obvious: in the autumn of 1942 some members of a Jewish leadership group in Slovakia were misled into thinking that they had prevented the deportation of the remnants of their community by bribing the Gestapo representative in their country. They then attempted to use their apparent success to try and stop the deportation of European Jews to Poland generally. Their attempt caused Himmler to intervene and sanction the negotiations in November 1942, for reasons we yet have to determine. Himmler was careful not to intervene again for eight or nine months, though he must have received Wisliceny's reports via Eichmann. Eichmann apparently, and very uncharacteristically, agreed to promises being made to the Jews (which were not kept) mainly at a meeting or meetings at Prague; this, too, fails to make sense unless we assume Himmler's knowledge and acquiescence. At two stages apparently, in December 1942, and again in August 1943, the possibility of somehow letting out some Jewish children was discussed, and indeed, about 1,000 Bialystok children were temporarily held in Theresienstadt between August and October. In late August, Himmler intervened again, this time to stop the negotiations. Why had he approved of them in the first place? Why did he stop them? What did he want?

7

Himmler's Indecision, 1942–1943

To understand Himmler's policy in the matter of contacts with Jews during World War II—specifically during 1942–43—we must try to understand the personality of the man.

Himmler was a pedantic classroom teacher, a gifted organizer and administrator, and a basically weak, superstitious, and unstable man. In his groove as ideologically convinced Nazi devoted to his Führer, he acted with decisiveness and brutality. When confronted with unexpected problems, he prevaricated, hesitated, wavered, or acted erratically, changing his stance and his decisions. The symptom of his indecisiveness was the stomach cramps from which he increasingly suffered. Here he was lucky, in March 1939, to make the acquaintance of a masseur whose miracle-working hands eased the pain and enabled Himmler to work at times when otherwise the cramps would have made that impossible. The masseur was Felix Kersten, a Baltic German (born in 1898) with a Finnish passport, who became a Himmler confidant.

After the war, Kersten published his memoirs.[1] Most historians who dealt with Kersten have pronounced him unreliable, his stories exaggerated and self-serving, the evidence he presents useless, although he received accolades for his work from official governmental sources in Holland, Sweden, and Finland. Yet even his most severe critic, Louis de Jong, states: "Kersten always tended to exaggerate his own role vastly; when Himmler took a certain decision which Kersten welcomed, Kersten had no inkling about the other factors that had influenced Himmler's thinking; apart from that, Kersten also exaggerated the events after the war. However, as a rule, his statement has some relation (sometimes a strong one, sometimes a weak one) with reality."[2] In other words, his comments cannot simply be dismissed—they may contain important information, but they have to be carefully analyzed because their accuracy is often very problematic.

Of all those who were near Himmler and survived the war, Kersten probably came nearest to the man—nearer than Himmler's estranged

wife or his very ordinary daughter. There are at the Institut für Zeitgeschichte in Munich what are purportedly Kersten's notebooks, drafts for
his book, and pages from his diaries. The documents are self-serving—Kersten was undoubtedly an egocentric person out to cash in on real or imagined
acts of saving human lives during the war—and many of them probably do
not date from the war years. Yet there are many comments that can be
checked against documents and facts known from other sources. We can see
that he exaggerated his own role but that the stories are basically true. The
task is to peel off Kersten's colorful additions to get to the core. He is too useful a source to ignore.

According to Kersten, Himmler was too intelligent not to know that things
were not going too well as early as 1942, before Stalingrad. In the winter of
1941–42, the Germans had been thrown back from Moscow and had lost
large numbers of troops, much materiel, and considerable territory. In the
spring the situation appeared to change again in the Germans' favor. Himmler apparently was well informed of the views and opinions of the generals
and those connected with them, however, and not all were optimistic.[3]

In 1943, according to Kersten, Himmler realized that the war might end in
a stalemate or, from Germany's point of view, worse. Kersten says that he
made an effort to persuade Himmler to try to end the war. It seems true that
he talked freely to Himmler—the latter was, after all, dependent on his
masseur for relief from his psychosomatic troubles, which seemed to worsen
each time Himmler had to talk with his beloved Führer: he was terribly afraid
of Hitler. Torn between logic and loyalty, as Kersten presents it, Himmler
began veering toward—well, toward exactly what? To interpret his actions,
let us turn to the developments themselves and see what Himmler actually
did.

A crucially important document exists, a note of Himmler to himself (*Vermerk*) of December 10, 1942, which reads, "I have asked the Führer with
regard to letting Jews go in return for ransom. He gave me full powers to
approve cases like that, if they really bring in foreign currency in appreciable
quantities from abroad."[4] The simplest interpretation is that very rich Jewish
individuals who could offer a ransom in foreign currency—presumably
money that could be brought in or that could be transferred abroad to German representatives—would be released. We know of a number of such
cases, especially after 1942,[5] but there were precedents. On the other hand,
this statement could have been an excellent cover for Himmler later on—he
could claim that he had the power to let Jews go if an important payment was
made, whether it was in money or its equivalent.

In that same month of December, Himmler gave an order to Gestapo chief
Heinrich Müller to segregate Jews who had important connections abroad
from the French Jews and, significantly, Hungarian and Romanian Jews (who

were not yet in the hands of the Nazis). A special camp was to be established for them where they would work but would be kept healthy and alive ("unter Bedingungen, dass sie gesund sind und am Leben bleiben"). The camp of Bergen-Belsen was used for that purpose immediately afterward.[6] Both these documents date from the time when the "Final Solution" was being relentlessly pursued; in fact, the autumn and winter of 1942 were the months of the most massive murder campaign of the whole Holocaust period. It is significant that Hitler gave his approval for the release of Jews in certain circumstances precisely at the time of the greatest massacres. The Bergen-Belsen idea was discussed with the Foreign Office, which sent an official to see whether the camp was suitable for the 20,000–30,000 Jews envisaged for an exchange—it was not quite clear for what: money, German POWs, or something else. It was August 1943 (when Himmler had the Bialystok children brought to Theresienstadt). The Foreign Office informed Eichmann that the camp was totally unsuitable and that improvements had to be made, including some that would ensure that the Jews to be exchanged would not have any knowledge of the conditions prevailing in the camps for Poles and Soviet POWs next door.[7]

One month later, in September 1943, a member of the Office of Strategic Services (the OSS, the U.S. war intelligence agency will be discussed below), under an economic warfare cover, came to Stockholm. On October 3, Kersten, who had just settled in Stockholm and made contact with the Swedish government in his efforts to free Swedish businessmen held by the Germans in Poland, met with Abram Stevens Hewitt socially.[8] At first he thought he might persuade Hewitt to put in a good word for Finland with the U.S. government, so that it might mediate between Finland and the Soviet Union. Kersten says he facilitated a contact between Hewitt and the Finns. Then, on October 24, Kersten suggested to Hewitt that he fly to Himmler and talk with him about peace prospects—Hewitt expressed fears of Soviet expansion, and that seemed to be a common ground on which to start discussions. Hewitt thought that the Germans would have to give up all their conquests, depose Hitler and the Nazi Party, establish a democratically elected government, put the war criminals on trial, and reduce the army so that it could not again become an offensive weapon. Kersten then, according to his book, informed Himmler about Hewitt and asked that Walter Schellenberg, head of Himmler's SD Ausland (Department VI of the Central Reich Security Office—RSHA), the espionage agency of the SS, should be sent to Stockholm to meet with him. Schellenberg came, apparently in early November, and met with Hewitt. Schellenberg's version is that he was not sent by Himmler but happened to be in Sweden at the time. In any case, the two discussed the possibilities, and Hewitt wrote a memo to Roosevelt, which is extant and which corroborates Kersten's description.

After the war Hewitt, in a statement countersigned by the person in whose house some of these encounters took place, again confirmed Kersten's claims.[9] Hewitt reports two long conversation with Schellenberg, arranged by Kersten, in which they discussed the possible terms of a peace arrangement with Germany. The points are essentially the same as those mentioned by Kersten. They also tally with Schellenberg's description, made to British intelligence at a time when he could have had no knowledge of what either Kersten or Hewitt was saying. Hewitt says that he told Schellenberg that he, Hewitt, did not represent the American government but that he would report to it. Hewitt returned to the United States and was told to drop the negotiations.

On December 4, 1943, after Kersten's return to Germany, Himmler said to him that he, Kersten, should not torture him—Kersten quotes Himmler's words. Himmler could not betray Hitler, to whom he owed everything; he could not become a traitor. Schellenberg had reported to Himmler on Hewitt's conditions; they were, Himmler said, almost unacceptable—especially the demand to put people on trial for crimes that, in Himmler's eyes, were not crimes at all, as the actions had all been done on a legal basis. When challenged by Kersten as to the annihilation of Poles and Jews, Himmler said "that, too, happened on a legal basis. Because the Führer decided in Breslau in 1941 that the Jews should be annihilated. And the order of the Führer is the highest law in Germany."[10] Himmler brought up all the typical Nazi objections to Hewitt's proposals but, according to Kersten, was prepared to think about them. More discussions between Kersten and Himmler are reported, and then came the decision of Himmler to send Schellenberg to Stockholm to meet with Hewitt again. This sequence is confirmed by Schellenberg. But when Schellenberg arrived, Hewitt had already left.

Schellenberg himself is one of the figures that have to be discussed when dealing with Himmler's putative attempts to contact the West. Walter Schellenberg was a very young lawyer (born in 1910), a careerist and opportunist, who joined the SS in 1933. He had a sharp and inquisitive mind and quickly rose through the ranks.

As head of the SS espionage service, Schellenberg did work against the Allies, including the kidnaping of British agents in Holland. Later, however, he appears to have become more skeptical regarding German chances of winning the war. He tried to get in touch with Swiss intelligence organs, supposedly to warn them against the possibility of a German attack on neutral Switzerland. Although on the face of it, the attempt of Schellenberg to be and remain in touch with the Swiss Intelligence Service headed by Col. Roger Masson seems to have little direct bearing on our subject, it does help to clarify the context in which Himmler's attempts to sound out possible foreign contacts were made.

Through a subordinate, an SS captain by the name of Hans W. Eggen, a coarse Berlin merchant turned intelligence agent, Schellenberg established contact with Masson and, through him, with the general commanding the Swiss Army, Henri Guisan, with whom he met on March 3, 1943, in the village of Biglen, in Switzerland. Meeting Schellenberg was a major indiscretion on Guisan's part, which, had it become known at the time, might well have cost him his job. Schellenberg thus had Guisan in his power, although Guisan apparently wanted only to make clear to the German that the Swiss would resist any German attack. Schellenberg claims that he warned the Swiss of a German attack that was being planned in March 1943. The Swiss did not need his warnings—they had an intelligence group in Germany (the "Viking" group), who informed the Swiss on March 20, 1943, of the details of the supposed operation. Two days later, information came that the attack would not take place. In fact, there apparently never was a German plan to attack Switzerland in early 1943, and the whole thing was invented by the SS Security Service to facilitate contacts with the Swiss[11]—trying, in a rather crude manner, to gain a foothold in Switzerland, apparently as a springboard for contacts via the Swiss.

Switzerland was obviously a good place to make contacts, and Schellenberg claims that through Eggen and Masson he got in touch with one of Allen Dulles's agents: Dulles was the OSS representative in Bern. Schellenberg also claims to have tried to contact the British consul at Zurich; but nothing came of that.[12]

There are some reports of Schellenberg's attempts to reach the West via the Iberian Peninsula; he claims to have been in touch with the British ambassador, Sir Samuel Hoare, from as early as mid-1942 on, and he does seem to have had some contacts with intelligence personnel at the American legation in Lisbon.[13]

Schellenberg, then, appears as an unscrupulous Nazi intelligence operator—which he undoubtedly was—a bright man, and no ideologue. We can believe him when he says that he recognized from relatively early on that Germany was in trouble, and that he tried to persuade Himmler to change course and contact the West. In his various testimonies Schellenberg argues that he met with Himmler at Zhitomir in Russia in August 1942 and tried to persuade Himmler to prepare for negotiations with the West. He says that Himmler agreed with him but gave him only half-hearted permission to develop contacts.[14] According to one of Schellenberg's testimonies, he and Kersten met at the end of 1943 to persuade Himmler to contact the West in a more planned, decisive manner. Knowing Himmler, Schellenberg says, they decided to approach him through an astrologer named Wilhelm Wulff in Hamburg. They told Wulff what was expected of him, but Schellenberg claimed later that Wulff went one better than that: he supposedly foretold, in March 1944, the attempt on Hitler's life on July 20, his illness of November

1944, and his demise in May 1945. But that did not help to change the SS chief's mind.[15] In sum, what we have so far is one definite move by Himmler—the meetings of Schellenberg with Hewitt, which he approved—and the half measures and cautious soundings through the Europa Plan and the Schellenberg-Masson-Guisan and Iberian contacts.

The crucial question to ask now is whether Himmler had any inkling of the "Generals' plot," which led to the attempt to assassinate Hitler on July 20, 1944. If he did, his tentative soundings may well have been connected to an expectation that the situation in Germany might change radically and that he should prepare options for new political and military moves. There is circumstantial evidence to the effect that he did indeed have such information, and there are fairly explicit postwar testimonies. Each source may be suspect in itself, but put together, they are hard to explain away. Most historians who deal with the problem agree: Himmler had a broad, but not detailed, knowledge of the plot.[16] He must have guessed that there would be an attempt to depose Hitler, but he did not know, nor in all likelihood did he want to know, that an assassination plot was in the offing. It is crucial to find out what and how much he knew, because that may well explain his contacts with and about the Jews.

The most convincing circumstantial evidence of Himmler's knowledge comes from the so-called *Depositenkasse* affair, which exploded in the autumn of 1942. A Czech banker by the name of David was accidentally arrested in Bohemia; a large sum in greenbacks was found in his possession. David told the financial police in Prague that he had been in the employ of two Bavarians, Wilhelm Schmidhuber and Heinz Ickrath, who turned out to be in the employ of Dr. Josef (Sepp) Müller, popularly known as "Ochsensepp," a Catholic conservative opponent of the Nazis (and a postwar Prime Minister of Bavaria), who was then in charge of the Abwehr station in Munich. Müller had been sent by Adm. Wilhelm Canaris, head of the Abwehr, the German Military Intelligence, to the Vatican as early as 1940 to sound out the Vatican regarding possible peace negotiations with Britain. At the Vatican, Müller contacted Ludwig Kaas, former head of the Catholic Center Party in Germany (which had voted in favor of Hitler's Enabling Law of March 1933, only to be dissolved by the Nazis afterward). Nothing came of this initiative, but the Gestapo became suspicious.

Further investigation revealed that Schmidhuber, a merchant and honorary consul of Portugal, and Ickrath, his employee, had established a company in Prague called Monospol, which employed opponents of the regime, including Jews, to travel to Balkan countries and Turkey, buy goods cheaply there, sell them at a profit in Central Europe, and engage in black market currency exchange schemes that furnished money for the Abwehr. One of the countries was Slovakia, and from some of the material, inconclusive as it is, there arises the possibility that Karel Hochberg, the Jewish traitor, may have been one of the sources for some of the black market deals.[17] The whole business was connected to the Munich Abwehr station.

Clearly, financial irregularities were by no means the whole story. The financial police handed the investigation over to the Gestapo. Heinrich Müller sent down, among others, one of his best bloodhounds, Franz Xaver Sonderegger, later aided by Walter Huppenkothen. Sonderegger did not quite believe what he was uncovering:[18] a currency exchange operation designed to create a "black money" reserve for those who operated it. Behind Josef Müller stood Hans von Dohnanyi and his brother-in-law, the Protestant pastor Dietrich Bonhoeffer; behind them stood Col. Hans Oster, the Abwehr's Chief of Staff, and behind all of these stood Canaris himself.[19]

The affair now became more serious. The black money was perceived to be for secret negotiations that the Abwehr group was trying to conduct with Germany's enemies. The Abwehr was a Wehrmacht organ, and a military investigator, a diehard Nazi (and a central figure in the postwar neo-Nazi movement), Manfred Roeder, was appointed to conduct the investigation, supervising Huppenkothen and other Gestapo officers, who remained in the picture. On April 5, 1943, a search was conducted in the central Abwehr offices in Berlin, and Dohnanyi and Bonhoeffer were arrested. While being arrested, Dohnanyi tried to smuggle a note that was lying on the table to Oster, who was present. The note was highly compromising; it hinted broadly at the antiregime character of the group and at some antiregime contacts that were in progress. The Nazis caught Dohnanyi in the act, with the result that Oster was fired as well, though not arrested.

It was clear to Roeder that he had discovered a serious anti-Nazi plot and that Canaris was implicated. The army commander, Wilhelm Keitel, was willing to proceed, but when he asked Himmler's view, Himmler told him to desist. Several of our sources repeat what he is supposed to have said in a note to his men: "Lasst mir doch den Canaris in Ruhe" ("Why don't you leave Canaris in peace").[20] In July, Roeder was transferred to the Luftwaffe, and a more pliant investigator (Kutzner) was appointed. The charge against Müller, Dohnanyi, and Bonhoeffer was reduced from treason to financial transgressions, and in the end only Müller was brought to trial. For lack of conclusive evidence he was acquitted, but all three remained in custody and Keitel demanded a retrial. The wives of Müller and Dohnanyi, both of whom had been arrested as well, were released. It is clear that Himmler had decided not to pursue the affair, and it is equally clear that he had been fully informed about the investigations that had been made.[21]

Bonhoeffer, the only really great hero of the Protestant resistance to the Nazis, was arrested because of his involvement with the group around Oster. What did Oster want? A biography of Oster is illuminating: Oster, who had supported the Nazis in the 1930s like so many of his conservative friends, turned against Hitler's state because of a mixture of moral and political motives. Convinced that the regime was immoral and inhumane and would lead Germany into catastrophe, he tried to throw spokes into the wheels of the Nazi empire. In 1940 he tried to warn the Low Countries of the impending invasion but was disbelieved. He stood behind Ochsensepp Müller's attempts to contact the Vatican, and he tried to get in touch with the West to see whether Germany could not be brought out of the war. At the same time, caught in the vise between his convictions and his duty as an intelligence officer, he helped the Wehrmacht professionally by finding out and reporting the enemy's plans, order of battle, and so forth. From the sources we have, we can tell that Canaris knew about Oster's plots and condoned and supported them, although the two men do not seem to have been cordial.[22]

Canaris also knew and condoned another effort by Dohnanyi and Bonhoeffer, which implicated another member of the conservative opposition, Graf Helmut von Moltke, scion of the military family that had given two Chiefs of Staff to the German Army, in 1870–71 and in 1914. Moltke was a devout Protestant and an opponent of the regime, who built up an oppositional discussion group that used to meet at his estate at Kreisau—hence its name, the Kreisau Circle. At the end of 1941 or early in 1942, Dohnanyi, and through him the others, was approached by a Jewish lawyer converted to Christianity, Friedrich W. Arnold, through Dohnanyi's mother, when deportation to an unknown fate in "the East" threatened Julius Fliess, another lawyer, a Jew, who was also a German war hero and an invalid, and his family. The three then communicated with some other individuals in Berlin who were Jews according to the Nazi racial laws. One was Charlotte Friedenthal, a convert who served as secretary to the central offices of the Confessing Church, the opposition faction of the Protestant Church in Germany; others were added, some of whom had converted and others who had not; also included were their non-Jewish relatives. Some of the individuals were close to Canaris himself.

Meetings with Dohnanyi and Bonhoeffer took place at the Abwehr offices in Berlin. Originally there were seven people to be rescued, hence the project was named V7, or U7 (Unternehmen 7), although the final number was fifteen. Dohnanyi, Bonhoeffer, and Moltke decided to help these people to escape, and Canaris did so by telling Himmler personally (twice!) that they would serve as Abwehr agents in Switzerland—an attempt to smuggle them to Sweden had failed. In actual fact, it was Schmidhuber who went to Switzerland with a plea by Bonhoeffer to Alphons Köchlin, the president of the Swiss Protestant Church organization (Schweizer Kirchenbund), to support the granting of Swiss entry visas, because the Swiss government did not want these Jews either.[23] On September 23, 1942, after the conspirators protected the fifteen from deportation orders that would have meant their deaths, the group came to Switzerland. More than that: the conspirators had managed to have their charges leave with money, much the way transfers were effectuated by Jewish organizations at that time. For transfers the emigrants gave the Abwehr about RM 1 million in money and valuables, and in return received $100,000 (in Swiss francs, presumably) of the Abwehr's money, which enabled them to subsist in Switzerland until the end of the war. The Abwehr, by the way, did not do badly on the deal; the prewar exchange rate had been RM 2.50 for a dollar.[24]

It is extremely hard to believe that Himmler was hoodwinked by this maneuver. If he believed Canaris's story in 1942, the fact that these people were nothing like Abwehr agents must have become clear to him in the following months. Yet it was Himmler himself who gave the instruction to Gestapo chief Müller to facilitate the group's exit. The affair was afterward mentioned in the interrogations of Dohnanyi and Bonhoeffer. According to another Abwehr officer, Erwin Lahousen, the RSHA—probably at Müller's instigation—or Himmler, to cover himself, informed Hitler about the affair. Canaris was called to Hitler, who forbade the future use of Jews in the Abwehr.[25]

Helmut von Moltke went to Istanbul in July and December 1943, just as the Depositenkasse affair exploded, and offered his own peace plan to the Allies. As we shall see, he talked in the name of co-conspirators. Moltke was connected to his own Kreisau Circle, to the Abwehr, to Bonhoeffer and Dohnanyi, and to some of the military and civilian figures who were preparing antiregime actions. In the case of U7, he was saving Jews. Contact with the Allies and involvement with the Jewish issue went hand in hand, it seems, almost by force majeur.[26]

Parallel to these incidents that appear to involve Himmler's knowledge that the conservatives were planning what to a Nazi was betrayal, there is also the difficult and complicated problem of Carl Langbehn, a lawyer and a personal acquaintance of Himmler's. Langbehn's views were in line with those of Schellenberg, and he favored an approach to the Western Allies based on the removal of Hitler. He was also busy intervening with Himmler to free certain prisoners in Nazi camps. Thus, Kersten acknowledges that it was Langbehn who persuaded him to intervene on behalf of seven Swedish citizens accused of spying by the Germans.[27] Langbehn was also a friend of some of the main figures in the conservative resistance movement. According to Walter Schellenberg, he met with Langbehn in the summer of 1942, and Langbehn told him even then that the war was already lost and that the only hope lay in the SS, who should depose Hitler and take over the country. Langbehn wanted an answer by 1943.

The story is in part plausible, but the date is not. It is not very probable that Langbehn asked Schellenberg for an answer regarding his conspiracy and then postponed it for a year! But it is quite possible that Schellenberg was approached. Schellenberg had been aware since 1941 of the contacts woven between the conservative conspirators—in this case, especially Ulrich von Hassel—and Americans to create lines of communication with the West.[28] In any case, it was through Langbehn's efforts, with Schellenberg's approval, that Himmler agreed to have a meeting with Johannes Popitz, a Finance Minister in the Prussian provincial government and a leading figure in the conservative camarilla. The meeting took place on August 26, 1943; Himmler had it bugged, and reputedly even made a record of it on a gramophone disc. He apparently also had Hitler approve of the meeting—in other words, he covered himself again. Yet whatever Himmler might have said or thought, Popitz was fairly open. He did not think that he would convince Himmler to join the conspirators, but he apparently wanted to make certain that Himmler would not intervene against them. If it is true that Hitler approved of the meeting, either he did not bother to find out exactly what had been said, or Himmler did not record some parts of the discussion.[29]

In any case, Himmler must have received a fairly detailed indication that the conservatives were conspiring against the regime. According to Schellenberg, Langbehn was a central figure in the conservative plot, who tried to bring Himmler over to the antiregime side and who simultaneously conducted negotiations in Switzerland with the head of the OSS there, Allen W. Dulles.[30] Himmler cannot have had any illusions about Langbehn. In September 1943, Langbehn was arrested, apparently after his Swiss contacts had been uncovered by the Gestapo, and was executed after July 1944. Schellenberg also claims to have been ordered by Himmler to contact Erna Hanfstängl in Munich, who was loosely connected with the conspirators; Schellenberg says he discussed with her, in general terms, a plot against the regime.

Schellenberg is not exactly the ideal witness, and the Hanfstängl affair is on the verge of the ridiculous. More serious is the story that in 1943 he was in touch with Gottfried von Bismarck, who indeed was closer to the core of the conspiracy. No doubt he reported his impressions. Bismarck wanted to follow a line that would bring Germany to an arrangement with the Western powers—this need not be doubted. Schellenberg also reports talks with some of the military men, such as Maj.-Gen. Fritz Thiele and Gen. Erich Fellgiebel of the intelligence sections in the Army High Command. They, too, were close to the center of the conspiracy, and Schellenberg says that he reported these talks to Himmler.

Schellenberg was also in contact with Prince Max-Egon von Hohenlohe, a German Catholic aristocrat with international family connections who resided in Spain. Through Hohenlohe and his Vatican connections, Schellenberg was in touch with American operatives in Spain, preparing the way, from December 1942 on, for possible peace feelers.[31] Other, similar contacts are reported for the spring of 1943, and Schellenberg claims that Himmler was informed—after all, these contacts were made in his name.

A few weeks before the attempted assassination, efforts were made, according to Schellenberg, to draw Himmler and himself into the conspiracy. Again, Thiele and Col. Georg Hansen are mentioned; Hansen was the new chief of the military intelligence section taken over by Schellenberg after the abolition of the Abwehr in February. In a discussion about the plot with Himmler in early July 1944, Schellenberg says, Himmler responded that he knew all about the plot but that he had to think it over.

It should be stressed, however, that what Himmler was aware of was the political and ideological wing of the camarilla. He did not know, nor did he suspect, the strength of the Wehrmacht group that actually attempted to kill Hitler—perhaps because the Wehrmacht could not be investigated by the Gestapo. When the plot failed, Fellgiebel and Hansen were arrested, and then Thiele. Schellenberg says that he was fearful of his life, but Thiele did not betray him.[32]

Himmler was apparently trying to cover his traces—another indication of his cautious and double-faced character. Indeed, some of the investigations of the July plotters were conducted in the greatest secrecy, maybe indicating that Himmler was afraid lest his passive awareness of the plotters' intentions be discovered. He also tried to use Carl Goerdeler, the political leader of the conspiracy, to contact the Allies via the Swedish banker Jakob Wallenberg. The attempt to use Goerdeler occurred while Goerdeler was in prison, awaiting execution, in October 1944. A contact sentenced to death was not likely to be betrayed to Himmler's detractors or to Hitler.[33]

The OSS also arrived at the conclusion that "the Gestapo" must have been aware of the general outlines of the plot. In a report on the plot dated July 22, Bill Donovan, head of the OSS, mentioned three approaches by the plotters to Dulles, in January, April, and May 1944, in which the Americans were told of the anti-Soviet and pro-Western orientation of the conspirators. The OSS, in line with official U.S. policy, rejected the approaches. Donovan emphasized that "the Gestapo had not stepped in . . . because it planned to wait until the group's plans had been more nearly perfected, or because the Gestapo too wished to have 'an anchor in the West.'"[34]

The indications, then, are that Himmler was aware of a plot. That being so, Kersten's testimony becomes even more important. Kersten maintains that in the summer of 1943, Himmler became more and more hesitant regarding the future prospects of the thousand-year Reich. In the summer he had the 1,000 Bialystok Jewish children transported to Theresienstadt, and this episode took place at the time the so-called Feldscher proposals were being considered. Let us now turn to these proposals.

Early in 1943, Anton Feldscher, an attaché with the Swiss legation in Berlin, transmitted to the German Foreign Office a British proposal that was the result of JA pressure on the British government.[35] The request was to allow 5,000 Jewish children from the General Government (Poland) and the "East" (occupied Soviet territories) to emigrate to Palestine. At the same time, the British, via Sweden, requested the view of the Germans on permitting the emigration of "Judenkinder" (Jew-children) from Western Europe as well. Ribbentrop consulted with Himmler, and the result was an "agreement in principle by the Reich government to negotiate regarding the granting of exit permits, perhaps in exchange for interned [German] persons, but the rejection of the idea of emigration to Palestine. The basic condition is the reception of these children in Britain and the approval of this by the House of Commons."[36]

Eichmann and others were involved in these negotiations that lasted for some ten months and were finally terminated in March 1944. Himmler's line, or perhaps Eichmann's, with Himmler's agreement, was to get four Germans for one Jewish child.[37] Alternatively, the Germans wanted pro-Nazi Irish, Egyptians, Arabs, and Indians to be released to them. The opposition to Jewish emigration to Palestine was explained in a statement from Ribbentrop's office: "The Reich government cannot lend its hand to the ousting of such a noble and valiant people as the Arabs from their Palestine homeland by the Jews."[38] The British declared that they could not accept the children on a permanent basis and rejected the release of much larger numbers of German or pro-Nazi internees in exchange for the children. But the interesting thing is the reply Himmler himself gave to a direct query by Ribbentrop: he stated that, in principle, no emigration of Jewish children could be permitted; it was possible only in exchange for young Germans.[39] The question was not one of irrevocable principle—namely, that Jews or Jewish children would all be killed, not released. Rather, the murder was conditional: if the price was attractive enough, he would talk. Himmler seems to have had the Hitler permission of December 1942 in mind. In this case, the price would not be in monetary terms but in political, military, or propagandistic ones. The British would have to announce the exchange in their Parliament, and Himmler obviously thought that doing so would create an antisemitic wave in "Aryan" Britain.

In this connection, let us turn briefly to the Bialystok children's transport to Theresienstadt in August 1943. Theresienstadt was a combination of ghetto and concentration camp, established in late 1941 to serve as a place to group Jews from the "Protectorate" of Bohemia and Moravia. At first, only Czech Jews were brought there. It was a family ghetto, although men and women were lodged separately, and in 1942 it was turned into a "Altersghetto" (old-age ghetto)—a concentration camp where older people from

German-speaking areas, many of them prominent intellectuals, former military leaders, and people with connections in German society, were incarcerated. Later, Jews from Holland and Denmark were sent there. It could—and was—later shown as a model ghetto to foreign journalists and observers. In reality, people died there en masse of malnutrition and disease. In 1942 the first loads of people were sent from Theresienstadt to Auschwitz to be gassed. The ghetto was just one of the deceptions organized by the Nazis on their way to the total annihilation of the Jews.

In February 1943, however, Himmler gave an order to stop deportations from Theresienstadt. The ban remained effective until the end of August. On September 6 another lot of Jews—4,770 in number—was transported to Auschwitz; they were not gassed but put into a "family camp." Gypsies were also in a family camp, but their placement seems to have been a matter of the SS not knowing what to do with them. In the case of the Jews, the inspectorate for concentration camps ordered that the "quarantine" last six months. The families were separated, but men and women lived in blocks within the same compound; schools were opened for the children; and there was no forced labor—only services within the camp had to be seen to. The food was atrocious, sickness abounded, and only 3,850 people were left after six months, when 3,792 of that number were finally driven to the gas chambers, on March 8, 1944.

In the context of what has been said before, it is easy to jump to conclusions: that the order to stop transports from Theresienstadt temporarily was the result of the Slovak negotiations; that the children's transport from Bialystok and the family camp in Auschwitz were connected, though the Bialystok children were gassed after a few weeks, whereas the family camp still existed; that the family camp was formed to make people available for exchange if needed. If nothing happened after six months, they would be murdered—and they were. In December another transport arrived, and the people were again put into the family camp for six months. The two transports intersected, of course. That did not matter. Hoess had all the lists—he murdered each group when its time came, and there were no mix-ups: *Ordnung muss sein* (there must be order). These conclusions may be correct, but we have no evidence to go on. If correct, such conclusions would fit perfectly into the context of a hesitant, contradictory approach to the problem of putative negotiations with Jews and/or Western Allies.[40]

The spring and summer of 1943 was also when a number of other proposals regarding children reached Himmler. The Swedish government, for instance, transmitted a Dutch proposal to bring 500 Dutch Jewish children to Palestine—at a time when the last Dutch Jews living openly in Amsterdam were being rounded up. The Romanians approached the Germans about Jewish children under eight years of age for the same purpose. These official requests were all refused—and they came before August, when the Bialystok children reached Theresienstadt.[41]

In the autumn, as we know already, Schellenberg represented Himmler to Hewitt in Stockholm. But during the same time Himmler made speeches, among them a famous speech at Poznan in October, when he spoke openly of the murder of the Jews.[42] To understand Himmler, it is worth considering that speech before we go any further.

The Poznan speech was a major statement identifying Himmler with the "Final Solution." In it, he justified the murder of the Jews, and he did so in words that have puzzled historians, philosophers, and theologians. Two passages deserve special comment. In one he spoke of the necessity of killing the Jews who would otherwise have killed the Germans and who still threatened Germany from the outside—it was clear to him that the war was between the Jews and Germany and that the bombing of German cities was the work of the Jews. But although the Jews were being killed, none of their property would be taken, and the SS had remained decent—that was what made them strong. In the second passage he spoke of his conviction that the murder of the Jews was a glorious chapter in German history that would remain secret forever.

This second passage has been interpreted as indicating that Himmler realized something unfathomable had been done, which could never be understood because it was sui generis. Some observers have argued that it is the victims whom we cannot understand because their experiences are so much outside normal human experience. By "understanding" I mean what the German historicists called *Verstehen*, that is, an intuitive feeling of identification. But then we cannot experience even the most trivial pain of another human being. If one's child pricks its finger, we cannot feel its pain, except by analogy with our own experience. So much the more so in the case of a massive trauma like that undergone by the Holocaust survivors. But insofar as experiences can be understood at all, we have an easier task with the victims, because their moral and social universe is identical with ours. It is argued, however, that we can never *understand* the perpetrators, only explain or interpret their actions in a superficial or external way. Their moral universe is totally different from ours, and we cannot cross over. They themselves understood that by deciding to keep the murders secret from all future generations. But this way of looking at the text appears to be unsatisfactory.

In line with Hans Georg Gadamer's hermeneutic approach, we should understand first of all what the Himmler text meant to the person who uttered it and to the persons who heard it.[43] For all of them, it was apparently straightforward. In the future, there would be no Jews, and in the Nazi world of the future no one would understand why the Jews had had to be killed, hence the need to keep the murders secret. Also, at the beginning of the passage Himmler complained about the German people's sentimentality. They agreed, he said, with the party program—namely, with annihilating the Jews (which, by the way, the program did not specify)—but every German "had his own first-rate Jew, an excellent person, even though all the others were swine." Himmler implied that the German people were not reliable as a whole; they were too thick-headed to understand, hence one could not publicize the fact of the murders. They might even oppose them.

Nothing about Himmler's statement is mystical, then. The mass murders, the brutality, the sadism—those were not what was unique about the Nazis. The brutal murder of whole populations, including children, has been with us since the beginning of recorded history and most probably before that. Sadism and brutality scream at us from every page of human history, and they are in no way less horrific than the Nazi variety. If we cannot "understand" Himmler, most of human history is beyond our capacity of understanding. We can put ourselves in the shoes of the perpetrators, as well as the shoes of the victims, because we all have in ourselves the potential for extreme good and extreme evil—at least, what we call good and evil. Himmler's ideas and motives are latent in everyone's subconscious. The real horror of Himmler is not that he was unusual or unique but that he was in many ways quite ordinary, and that he could have lived out his life as a chicken farmer, a good neighbor with perhaps somewhat antiquated ideas about people.

The first passage from the speech brings us even closer to understanding Himmler. When he speaks about the decency of the SS in not taking Jewish property after murdering its owners, is he speaking the same moral language that we are used to? He is indeed. Himmler did not challenge what we call petit-bourgeois morality. He decried theft, though in practice one could steal a little bit; he presumably would have uttered similar platitudes about friendship, loyalty, and family life, though he was in favor of SS men producing offspring outside marriage. Within that framework he changed the biblical "thou shalt not murder" (the traditional English translation of the commandment is wrong: *lo tirtzach* does not mean "thou shalt not kill" but "thou shalt not murder") into a Nazi "thou shalt murder," a positive commandment. In other words, he did not deviate from accepted moral precepts but stood them on their head without changing the traditional framework in which people accepted them.

This peculiar, quite unconscious presentation of ideology makes it possible for us not only to explain but also to understand. Crucial elements of accepted morality *can* be flipped over without the destruction of the moral framework. That would explain why and how the little Himmlers, tens and hundreds of thousands of them, easily made the readjustment to "normal" conditions once the war ended. When conditions changed from Nazi wartime to postwar normality, they flipped back, so to speak, and failed to understand why what they had done in the war had been reprehensible. After all, they had only done their duty, *nicht wahr?*—and doing one's duty belonged to the framework acceptable to all. The Holocaust and the perpetrators of it become eminently explicable.

What is argued here is that Himmler saw no contradiction between, on the one hand, his extreme Nazi views and his desire to murder the Jews altogether, once the decision to do so had been taken, and, on the other hand, his tendency to examine possible tactical concessions, if they brought about important positive results for Germany.

The Poznan speech was by no means the only one in which Himmler expressed his ideology. A look at his speeches in wartime will show that he believed in what he was saying. England had been jewified ("das feige und verbrecherische, verjudete England"), which explained why it had turned against Germany.[44] The Germans were the master race (*Herrenrasse*), and he admonished his audiences to behave like members of it and not be too close to the lower races nor behave in a reprehensible way in front of them (not to be drunk, for instance).[45] Most interesting are his references to Jews. There were still people, he complained, who thought that Jews were, after all, human beings and who behaved toward Jewish women, for instance, as though they were ladies (*Damen*). "The whole German people entered the Eastern campaign with all this mess of superfine, civilized decadence."[46] He was totally committed to the Nazi version of antisemitism, and although apparently he had not originally been in favor of any form of genocide, he was so totally identified with the Führer and the regime that once he received the order to murder, he executed it to the best of his ability. That he hesitatingly sounded out options for a separate peace with the United States or the West generally and in late 1942 and early 1943 hesitatingly supported half measures in the Jewish direction as well did not by any means indicate that he had changed any of his opinions about the Jews.

Let us summarize the way Himmler's thoughts seem to have been developing. In a general way he had knowledge of a plot directed against Hitler. He bided his time. He did not act against the conspirators, though he knew, in a general way, where to find them. He probably thought that if they succeeded, he would gain the upper hand rather quickly and save Nazi Germany from defeat by putting an end, perhaps a temporary end, to the war; by all accounts, he preferred a separate peace with the West in order to concentrate on repelling the Bolshevik threat. Fickle and unstable, he played for years with the idea of contacting the West without ever taking the plunge and confronting Hitler. He allowed himself to be pushed both ways more or less at the same time: he would send Schellenberg off to Stockholm *and* give a fiery, genocidal speech to his officers, *and* he would hold to the annihilation policy against the Jews. The contradiction exists, but both his character and his ideology help to explain it.

We should approach the contacts, or negotiations, that took place with the Jews from this perspective. The first, which we have already tried to analyze, was in Slovakia. It took place a few months after Schellenberg's alleged talk with Himmler at Zhitomir, and it began, from the SS point of view, accidentally, on the initiative of what seemed to be an international Jewish group of possibly great influence. Himmler was not free to act. He had to consider Hitler's radical antisemitism, which might make Himmler look like a disloyal weakling if he was seen negotiating with Jews. Then there was the opposition of the radicals within the SS—Himmler could not afford to appear weak and defeatist to such internal groups. Still, he had Hitler's December 1942 approval of negotiating for foreign currency or, presumably, its equivalent. To see whether there were any real options to contact the Western powers or their Jewish masters through this venue was desirable. Also, contacts with the West, especially with Switzerland, were in the hands of the Abwehr. The SS, he thought, should let the Abwehr develop such contacts, for which the Abwehr, at this stage, would bear the responsibility. Parallel contacts were, in the meantime, established by Schellenberg of the SS.

Himmler's behavior in the Slovak affair, then, can be understood only in the context of his other activities from November 1942 to the summer of 1943. He did not intervene in Wisliceny's efforts during that whole time but simply let him go on on his own. His appointment book shows that he did not meet with either Wisliceny or Eichmann in November or December but that he did meet with Müller. It appears that his interventions were made by oral instructions to Müller, so he could always repudiate his subordinate if Hitler intervened or if radical RSHA people like Heinrich Müller, Ernst Kaltenbrunner, and their ilk took umbrage. The Slovak affair paralleled other very hesitant, very circumspect contacts: Hewitt, and an attempt by the Swiss to have Jewish children released for emigration, to which Himmler gave qualified approval. The crucial event was the transport of the Bialystok children to Theresienstadt at the end of August. This was probably much more a response to the Feldscher project than to the Europa Plan talks. Himmler may have thought that as nothing had come of Wisliceny's efforts for eight months, they should at this stage be terminated, and the Feldscher talks, which were intergovernmental and in which Himmler could have a decisive voice without having to circumvent Ribbentropp's Foreign Office or the Führer's Chancellery, were now preferable. To Himmler these events and choices must have seemed all of a piece—after all, the United States and England were ruled by the Jews, and if Britain was suggesting children's emigration, that would be another way of dealing with the Jewish world government.

Again, the central element here is Himmler's slow realization that the war could not be won and that peace with the West might be preferable to a stalemate. It is highly unlikely that in 1943 he was thinking of the possibility of a German defeat. What we are dealing with, until the beginning at least of the Russian winter offensive of early 1944, are tentacles reaching toward possible options, while at the same time the radical murder of the Jews was being pursued. Could these contacts have been used to save Jews? The fact is, to save Jews in 1943, two sides had to be amenable to acting: the murderers and their Western enemies (the Soviet Union did not evince the slightest interest in the fate of the Jews as Jews). Paradoxically, under certain circumstances Jews might well have been released, or at least temporarily not murdered, given advantages to the Nazis, monetary or political, but the other side, the West, would not even consider such a possibility. For the democracies, as I have already pointed out, the fate of the Jews was not seen as unique; victory in the war was the central and overriding consideration, and the formula of the unconditional surrender precluded all direct negotiations for anything other than that, including the rescue of lives. Himmler might have been willing to sell, given certain conditions. There were no buyers.

8

Dogwood's Chains

The U.S. wartime intelligence agency, the Office of Strategic Services, has received detailed treatment in the historical literature. On the whole, the agency, founded in mid-1942 under the leadership of "Wild Bill" Donovan, has received a good press. It was a fairly large organization, employing some 7,000 people at its peak; yet it had to struggle hard for its existence against the competition of Army and Navy intelligence organs, and it finally lost the struggle, after the death of Roosevelt, its protector. In 1945 the U.S. government still balked at the prospect of a permanent intelligence agency, carried over from its temporary status as a wartime body into peacetime conditions; it was only later that the CIA took over, and saw itself as the heir of the OSS.

The OSS was the creation of Donovan; he signed up his friends and people he thought could help him. Donovan did not care about the ideologies of his employees as long as they did what he expected them to do—fight against Germans and Japanese. The results were mixed. Some appointments were very successful, some were not. The problem in Europe was that the United States had no intelligence infrastructure when the OSS arrived there in the second half of 1942. The U.S. agents were completely dependent on the British, who welcomed them and taught them the basic tricks and at the same time saw them as a superfluous burden and occasionally as potential competitors. While sharing much of their knowledge with their American partners, the British kept the really important secrets to themselves. The Americans had to start from scratch in setting up networks of agents and, generally, engaging in the plodding and mundane work of gathering intelligence.

There were some obvious geographical points of departure for setting up chains of agents and obtaining information about the Axis countries. The Iberian Peninsula was one, and OSS operatives went into Spain and, mainly, Portugal. A headquarters for their operations was set up in Algiers, after the successful invasion of North Africa by the Allies in late 1942. Another place was London, where the OSS could develop its ties with the British, though for a long time in a subordinate role. Yet another place was Switzerland, where Donovan placed the man who was probably his most successful operative: Allen W. Dulles, who spun a whole web of contacts in Germany and, to a lesser degree, in some of the occupied countries. There was, however, one more place that had to be used: Istanbul.

Turkey remained neutral in the war until August 1944. The Turkish Army was too weak to be relied on to withstand the Germans or the Russians, and the government was therefore eager to keep out of the war and maintain a determined neutrality. The Turkish counterintelligence agency, the redoubtable Emniyet, was among the best, and it maintained full control of what was happening in its country, which soon became a playground for the opposing intelligence groups of the belligerents. The OSS entered the game in Istanbul in earnest with the appointment of Lanning Macfarland, a Chicago banker, as chief of mission in Istanbul and his arrival there in April 1943. He was under the command of the main Mideast base of the OSS in Cairo under Lt. Col. John E. Toulmin, but his position was a very important one in itself.

OSS-Istanbul had to deal with the Balkans and extend feelers northward as far as possible, perhaps into Germany itself. Its Special Intelligence (SI) and Special Operations (SO) agents had to penetrate Greece, Bulgaria, Yugoslavia, Albania, and, it was hoped, Hungary and Romania, for aid to partisans and for political and sabotage missions. Among the other tasks were information gathering on a large scale and contacts with opponents of Nazism in all of southeastern Europe. For these, the OSS had no people ready to serve. In Istanbul they were lucky. They found Alfred ("Freddy") Schwarz, alias Dogwood.[1]

Dogwood's name frequently appeared in postwar accounts of the OSS. He had been a Czech Jew, it was said, possibly a double agent, whose network of operatives, code-named for flowers, had failed to produce useful results; the work had ended in the betrayal of some anti-Nazis in Austria and elsewhere, and the group was dissolved in August 1944. Dogwood was dead, it was said. Well, the truth was quite different on almost all counts.

Alfred Schwarz was indeed a Czech Jew. Born in northern Bohemia in 1904, he studied philosophy, psychology, and civil engineering in Prague but left his studies to devote himself to problems of advertising and commerce. In 1928 he decided to go to Istanbul, where he quickly succeeded in building up an import firm for machinery: mechanical, shipping, and agricultural. Most of his imports came from Germany, Austria, and Czechoslovakia, and he built up strong ties with important industrialists and merchants in those countries. He also learned Turkish and became a confidant of Turkish government figures. He claimed to have been involved in the development of a Latin script for the Turkish language and to have been in contact with the founder of modern Turkey, Kemal Pasha "Atatürk."

When war came, Schwarz decided to devote time to fighting the Nazis.

Turkey had absorbed a number of German anti-Nazi intellectuals, who became teachers, lecturers, and professors at Turkish universities, bringing with them a much higher standard of academic excellence than had been known in Turkey before. Not all of them, of course, were reliable anti-Nazis, but many were. Schwarz knew them and could pick their brains regarding the developments in Germany and Austria; the non-Jews, who still had contacts in their home countries, were very useful sources of information.

At first, Schwarz was recruited by the Czechs and the British, but apparently not as an ordinary agent. He was wealthy and seems not to have received pay for his services, except apparently once more for expenses. What exactly he did for the British is not clear; British intelligence archives are hermetically closed, and British intelligence personnel still alive at the time of writing are under the Official Secrets Act oath and will not talk. Occasionally, though, his ties to Col. Harold Gibson, the head of the British Secret Intelligence Service (SIS, MI6) in Istanbul, become evident. When the Americans came, the British offered them Schwarz, with his agreement, perhaps at his request, but he appears to have remained in touch with the British afterward as well.

On July 20, 1943, Schwarz became Dogwood. He initially based his network on the German intellectuals in Turkey; only later did he extend his ties into the Balkans. He reported to the OSS man appointed to be his contact— Archibald Coleman, code-named Cereus. Coleman was a journalist who had been employed on intelligence missions in Mexico and Portugal with no great success, and Dogwood did not value him very highly. Macfarland was not Dogwood's type, either. Dogwood thought that the Americans were uneducated, lacking the sophistication that a Central European would have appreciated. Dogwood's secretary was Walter Arndt, a Polish citizen, partly Jewish, who had been born in Istanbul and whose father was a professor, first in Turkey and then in Britain. Young Arndt had volunteered to fight in the Polish campaign of 1939, and had managed afterward to escape from Poland on the strength of his Turkish connection. In Istanbul, he joined Dogwood—he was very useful, he knew Polish as well as German and English, and he was also in close touch with Coleman and the OSS group. Lansing Williams, whom Dogwood despised for his drinking bouts, was the OSS administrative and financial agent supervising Dogwood's chains of contacts.

It seems that Dogwood was not circumspect enough with his main informants, the Istanbul German émigrés, some of whom may have been double agents. The useful contacts were individuals such as Franz Josef Ridiger ("Stock"), an Austrian businessman; Alexander Rustow ("Magnolia"), a professor at Istanbul University and a German anti-Nazi; Hans Wilbrandt ("Hyacinth"), another German intellectual, and some others. The reports emanating from the Dogwood network provided a high proportion of the

OSS-Istanbul reports: 31 of 117 in December 1943, then 83 in January 1944, and so on.[2]

From his postwar testimony it appears that Dogwood was primarily interested in mediating between the Americans and trustworthy German anti-Nazis, so that the terrible war might come to a speedy end, toppling the Nazi regime and returning democracy to Germany while preserving Central Europe from a communist takeover, which Dogwood, like many others, foresaw.[3]

One can understand Dogwood's enthusiasm when, in July 1943, Helmuth von Moltke, a central figure in the anti-Nazi resistance in Germany, came to Istanbul. Moltke contacted Dogwood through Paul Leverkühn, head of the Abwehr station in Istanbul, as well as through Rustow and Wilbrandt. On December 30, 1943, in a report on the whole affair that reached the U.S. State Department, Dogwood characterized his contact as representative of "an influential group of German anti-Nazi staff officers and high officials (associated loosely with other liberal elements, and exponents of labor), who in order to save Germany from complete annihilation are determined to work together, and collaborate with the Allies, for the defeat and destruction of the Nazi regime."[4] What they wanted was an Anglo-American occupation of a defeated Germany. Moltke knew the American ambassador in Cairo, Alexander C. Kirk, from before the war; he knew Field Marshal Jan Smuts of South Africa, and he knew Dorothy Thompson, the American journalist. Dogwood's own view is clearly stated in the report: "The magnitude of the promise held out by the proposed collaboration can hardly be overstated. No limited intelligence effort and no scheme of partial assistance by German staff members . . . can offer even a remotely comparable chance of ending the War in the West at one stroke, and save perhaps many hundreds of thousand lives of Allied soldiers and civilians in occupied countries."

Moltke wanted the Western Allies to use overwhelming force in the West; then he and his fellow conspirators would rebel against the Nazi regime, facilitating the occupation of Germany by the Anglo-Americans and preventing a Soviet advance. If the Allies invaded Europe with an overwhelming force, no one could argue that Germany's defeat was caused by treason. The conspirators would topple Hitler and surrender unconditionally to the West. In an "exposé" attached to his report, Dogwood analyzed the group and the offer. He repeated Moltke's request that the Red Army should stop on a line from Tilsit to Lwów (Lvov), that is, from the northeastern corner of east Prussia to what today is the western Ukraine (eastern Galicia). In prewar Poland, Lwów had been the capital of this province.

During his second visit to Istanbul (December 11–16), Moltke hoped to meet with Kirk, but Kirk, apparently on his own initiative, refused. He informed Moltke by letter that nothing short of the unconditional surrender of the German forces would terminate the war; dickering with German opposition factions would not be useful.[5]

Moltke's readiness to fly to Cairo was ignored. Instead, he met with Brig. Gen. Richard G. Tindall, the U.S. military attaché in Ankara, who reported on his meeting to the State Department. The conservative conspirators' chief worry was the threat of a communist takeover engineered by a Soviet occupation force. But more emerges. The existing literature has portrayed Moltke as almost a pacifist, only very loosely connected with the military anti-Hitler conspiracy and concerned more with the moral and political problems that the resistance movement had to deal with. Quite a different Moltke appears in these documents: a close ally of the military resistance, a moderate Prussian conservative aristocrat, and a devout Christian. What also emerges is that his contact with Canaris and the Dohnanyi-Bonhoeffer group established the link between the conspirators and Canaris's Abwehr. In fact, Dogwood told the American ambassador to Turkey, Laurence A. Steinhardt, what we already know—that the contact with Moltke had been facilitated by the head of the Istanbul Abwehr, an old friend of Donovan's, Paul Leverkühn. When Moltke's mission failed, Leverkühn wrote a letter directly to Donovan, proposing much the same thing as Moltke had done. Donovan wanted to submit the Moltke proposal to the Joint Chiefs of Staff in Washington, and penned a memorandum to that effect (April 2, 1944). The next day the top body of the OSS met to consider the memo, then advised Donovan not to submit it, even though they knew that Moltke had been arrested in January as anti-Nazi. Not until July 29, 1944, after the failure of the plot to assassinate Hitler, was the Donovan report on the Moltke mission put on Roosevelt's desk.[6]

The American officials' naïveté and lack of information could not be portrayed better than in the letter accompanying Dogwood's communication to Steinhardt by one of the embassy officials, a Charles P. McVicker, Jr. The letter is dated October 24, 1944—that is, after the assassination attempt against Hitler on July 20. Dogwood knew exactly who he had been dealing with. In his earlier submissions he had accurately characterized the resistance group, and now he told McVicker that he had a letter from Moltke listing the names of friends, which he could show the ambassador; he then stated that many on the list had already been executed. Hence, he said, Moltke had been genuine.

The fact that Dogwood had such a list—it has not turned up so far—is very interesting. It meant that Moltke relied on his OSS contact sufficiently to expose the most secret and most life-endangering document of all, a roster of acquaintances who were planning the overthrow of the Nazi regime. To McVicker all this was news. The date of his memorandum to the ambassador, however, explains the situation: Dogwood had ceased to be connected to the OSS after July 31, 1944—fired, according to OSS records, but he said that he had resigned. He was very bitter toward the OSS and toward the United States generally. He argued, and continued to argue until his death in Switzerland in August 1988, that a tremendous chance had been missed to end the war then and there. Had the Americans only supported the German conservatives, multitudes of people would have been saved, including huge numbers of Jews, and the agony of a Soviet occupation of half of Europe would have been avoided.[7]

Donovan apparently was of the same opinion as Dogwood. He made a fairly crazy attempt at personal diplomacy designed to present Roosevelt with a proposal that the President would be willing to accept. He sent a journalist to Istanbul, Theodore Morde of *Reader's Digest*, without White House knowledge or support, to talk to the German ambassador, Franz von Papen. Through the mediation of Rustow-Magnolia, Morde met Papen on October 5, 1943, between the two Moltke visits. The idea was to persuade Papen to attempt a coup against Hitler, billing him as the future ruler of Germany. At a second meeting on October 6, Papen responded: Germany should remain the most important economic power in Europe, and Austria should remain German. When Morde returned to Washington and the White House found out what he had been up to, he was disowned and forbidden to travel. Donovan presented his report to the President, but it was rejected out of hand.[8]

Dogwood went beyond his attempt to facilitate Moltke's talks in Istanbul. On September 8, 1943, he submitted a memorandum to the Americans suggesting the establishment of a new political organization of democratic Germans in exile called the Deutscher Freiheitsbund (German Freedom Movement). This DFB would support subversive groups in Germany and organize military intelligence, but its main task would be to prepare for the establishment of a peace-loving, democratic Germany after the war. In fact, Dogwood had already set up the DFB, but it failed to make any impression on the Allies. His memo on the subject was never answered or acted on.[9]

A number of questions in connection with the Moltke affair have to be addressed here: Did the Abwehr and did the conservative conspirators contact the West, inter alia, through Jews, or was their activity in any way connected with the murder of the Jews? Did Himmler's organization have knowledge of these contacts? Why did Moltke and, one might add, Dogwood, fail?

The Abwehr was using Jewish and half-Jewish agents—of that there can be no doubt. Besides Alfred Zierer, whom we have met, there was "Richard Klatt," a Viennese "half-Jew," who was really a former sports journalist by the name of Fritz Kauders who was working out of Sofia and whose reports were considered to be very important by the German General Staff. In Sweden there was Edgar Josef Klaus, a Latvian Jew, who tried to mediate between the Germans and the Soviets.[10] These contacts were apparently seri-

ous ones, but we know that some very low-grade contacts existed as well; to
these we shall return later.

Essentially, Jews occupied only a minor position in the Abwehr's scheme:
they were victims, more than allies. The Nazi conviction that the Jews ruled
the Allied world and that therefore Jews could play an important role in any
negotiations or contacts was absent. The murders, too, played a very minor
role in what appear to have been the considerations of the Abwehr people.
The conspirators were, basically, German patriots who regarded the Jews as
objects whose fate depended on others. Study of the conservative opposition
to Hitler makes it clear that a very strong antisemitic feeling pervaded these
opposition circles—they would have agreed with Himmler's stance in the
closing days of the war that, whatever happened, Jews had no place in a
future Germany. There were exceptions, of course, such as Dohnanyi or
Bonhoeffer, but most of these people were what one would today consider
radical antisemites.

Did Himmler have an inkling of these contacts? The answer to this question remains hazy. The Depositenkasse affair shows that Himmler received
information that must have led him to assume that such contacts existed. It
was, after all, the business of the Abwehr to establish some contact with
enemy agents, and Himmler knew of the general trend of thinking among the
conservatives. The answer therefore should probably be a qualified yes.

Finally, why did Dogwood fail? There the answer is simple and cruel. The
proposal that Moltke brought and which Dogwood so ardently wanted to see
accepted by the Americans never had a chance. The Casablanca decisions of
the Western Allies in February 1943 made unconditional surrender the only
way Germany could get out of the war—surrender to all the Allies, not just
to the West. The secret services sometimes went beyond their brief in these
matters, but the top leadership was determined: the Allied front included the
Soviet Union, and any surrender would have to be made to all three major
powers. The basic idea of the German opposition, to keep the Soviets out of
Europe, was impossible to achieve in these circumstances. Had the Western
Allies accepted the Moltke proposals, what might have happened was a
palace revolution in Germany at a time when the German Army was still
fighting outside the German heartland. In other words, there might have
been a repetition of the situation in the autumn of 1918, an excellent breeding
ground for another stab-in-the-back legend, which would almost inevitably
have arisen: that the victorious German Army under Nazi leadership had
been defeated not by the enemy but by a dastardly aristocratic conspiracy
back home. The rejection of Moltke's and similar plans by Roosevelt was
therefore well-nigh inevitable.

This does not mean that Dogwood-Schwarz was wrong. He was right in
one sense: he, like Moltke, foresaw the danger of a Soviet takeover of East

and Central Europe and the consequence of rejecting the proposals—the death sentence for uncounted multitudes of soldiers and civilians, including the Jews, who were particularly threatened and with whom Dogwood identified passionately.

The Moltke connection was not, however, the only chain of communication that Dogwood forged. Another contact was called Cassia. Cassia was Franz Josef Messner, general director of the Semperit rubber and chemical works in Austria and a staunch Catholic. In 1939, Messner had spent time in Brazil and had acquired Brazilian citizenship, but he decided to return to Vienna after the outbreak of war because, his widow claims, he could not leave his employees behind and just save himself. On his way back he was arrested by the French, interned in Morocco, and liberated only after the collapse of France. The incident helped him to establish his credentials with the Nazis in Austria.

At the end of 1941 various groups organized resistance in Austria; most of the activists were communists or belonged to other left-wing groups, but some were Catholic. Left-wing contacts were maintained through Helene Sokal, a Jewish scientist, and Thomas Legradi, who had some protection because he was the employee of a Swiss firm. Another major figure was the deacon of Saint Stephen's Church in Vienna, Heinrich Maier. The communists and socialists committed sabotage, helped anti-Nazis avoid conscription, aided deserters from the German forces, helped foreign slave workers, prepared anti-Nazi leaflets, and so on. A coordinating group reflecting the different ideologies was established, and in late 1942 a memorandum was smuggled out to an Austrian Jesuit priest living in Lucerne, Otto Keller, who was in touch with an Austrian Jewish exiled lawyer by the name of Franz Hollischer, who was organizing an Austrian refugee group there. The memo reached the British, and they acknowledged it by radio from London, several times, with the code name "May 1, 1942."

Reading about the group gives a mixed impression of professional underground work by the leftists and bad blundering by naive, amateurish Catholics. Messner joined the group after Maier had persuaded him to do so. They decided to provide the Allies with information about arms-producing factories, especially ball-bearing plants. The drawings, however, were unprofessional, as was the information on production. One of Messner's aims was to prevent the bombing of the Semperit works, so he did not provide information about war plants situated next to Semperit factories.[11] Through the mediation of Ridiger, Messner visited Istanbul in January 1944 and, despite surveillance, reached Dogwood. Christened Cassia, he signed a document (on February 4) in which the aim of a free Austria was set forth, and an obligation was expressed to help the OSS in its work. He also agreed to be given a radio transmitter, so that he could be in direct touch with the

OSS. After his trip to Istanbul, Messner went to Switzerland, where he met with Allen Dulles, who commended the Istanbul OSS on picking such a fine gentleman as Messner.[12]

The radio for Messner was given to Fritz (František) Laufer, the same Abwehr and later SS Security Service (SD) man whom we have already met. Dogwood knew him to be a double agent, but he thought that he was nevertheless reliably anti-Nazi. Laufer became a flower in Dogwood's chain, called Iris. He betrayed Messner, had him arrested, and thereby caused the disintegration of the whole chain. Messner was arrested on March 25, 1944, in Budapest, apparently as he was about to receive the radio.[13] Maier, Sokal (who married Legradi after the war), Legradi, and some of the others had already been caught by the Gestapo—as a result, it seems, of yet another betrayal from within. After a trial in October, most of the members of the ring who were caught—the communists and leftists mainly avoided capture—received death sentences. Maier was executed in November; Messner on April 23, 1945, in Dachau. Legradi received only a jail sentence because of his Swiss contacts, and Sokal escaped from prison and continued her underground work until liberation.[14]

Dogwood, in his efforts to develop reliable agents, stressed contacts with "serious" people. Forty years later he maintained that he never actually engaged in espionage, setting up spy rings, and the like; no, he had always concentrated on psychological warfare and the political side of affairs. This statement is simply not so. Dogwood tried to develop spy rings that would bring about important changes, whether in the political or the military field. The contact with Moltke can serve as a good example. Another example is his attempt to penetrate Papen's office, mainly through the German–Slovak journalist Fritz Fiala, whom we met in Slovakia as an ardent Nazi. Fiala was sent to Istanbul as a journalist in January 1943, and he developed his opposition to the Nazi regime as a result, apparently, of the Allied successes at Stalingrad and in North Africa. As Dahlia he graced Dogwood's flower garden, but his reports were rather thin. Careful examination shows that his information was inaccurate, old, or misleading. It is not unlikely that he was indeed a double agent, trying to have the best of two worlds. He seems to have misled Dogwood completely. A final examination of the record by the OSS counterespionage unit (called X–2) in August 1944 took a very dim view of Dogwood's reliance on Fiala. However, when Fiala applied for asylum with the Americans in that same month of August, because Turkey had declared war on Germany, he was granted protection and was evacuated to Egypt. After the war he was tried as a war criminal before a Slovak court.

Dogwood had other questionable agents, and he tended to protect them from OSS investigations once he became convinced that they were useful. Increasingly, because of this approach, he got into trouble with his OSS superiors. Dogwood was a man of very decided opinions, and he seem to have felt something very close to contempt for OSS personnel.

Dogwood's organization worked under the cover of the Western Electric Company, with Walter Arndt as Schwarz's manager and with a secretary. Lansing Williams was supposed to look after money, but he was less than useless. Dogwood maintained contacts with other groups, such as the British SIS in Istanbul. He was especially close to the Jewish representatives from Palestine, first Teddy Kollek (later mayor of Jerusalem) and then Ehud Avriel. He may even have received some of his information from Avriel and Kollek and passed it on as his own. He proposed to his OSS superiors that a much closer relationship should be established with Kollek, but his advice went unheeded. OSS relations with the intelligence people of the Jewish Agency were friendly at first, but they soured in 1944, not only in Istanbul. By the summer of 1944, Toulmin had decided that he wanted nothing to do with these Palestinian Jews, because they had ulterior motives—that is, they were willing to fight the Germans, but they also wanted to satisfy their own political agenda, which could not be permitted.[15] It probably never occurred to Toulmin that the Americans, the Greeks, the Poles, and all the other Allies also had an agenda for which they were fighting.

Among Dogwood's flowers, the Hungarian ones became, in 1944, centrally important. In a way they caused the destruction of his whole centerpiece. Let me present them and their activities in Istanbul; later I will tie them to what was happening in Hungary.

In 1943 the name Iris appeared on Dogwood's lists. Iris, as we know, was Fritz (František, Franz) Laufer, alias Direktor Schröder (alias Ludwig Mayer, alias Karl Heinz), a Prague Jew, reportedly a waiter who had become an informer for the Germans in their war against the Czech underground. Laufer then went to Budapest and for a while became a Czech agent. When it became clear in November 1941 that he was betraying the Czechs to the Abwehr, the Czechs so informed the Americans. He then became an Abwehr informer.[16] The Budapest Abwehrstelle (Ast) was itself a branch of the Vienna Ast, headed by Count Rudolf von Maregna-Radwitz, one of Canaris's men. Vienna was responsible for espionage in the Balkans and Turkey, and the relevant branch, IIIF, was headed by Baron von Manteuffel. Vienna was involved with Munich in the Depositenkasse affair, and the Prague money-laundering operation Monospol was also operated from Vienna via Munich. The Budapest office was headed by Lt. Col. Rudi Scholz, and the chief of the Levant operations, that is, the Turkish end, was under Dr. Schmidt or Schmied (pseudonym). The Budapest office, however, boasted a number of agents, all of them from the underworld or not far removed from it, with the exception of Capt. Erich Klausnitzer, a German whom we have already met and who was also listed in the Vienna main office. Of the Budapest agents, two were Jews—Laufer and "Bandi" Grosz—and Winninger was a "half-Jew." Erich Wehner (Werner, Wenda), alias Eric Popescu, may also have been a "half-Jew." Laufer visited Istanbul, according to Dogwood's recollections, two or three times in 1943 and once in 1944. Grosz ("Trillium") came eight times altogether. "Josi" Winninger came a number of times, but it is unclear whether he was a Dogwood flower as well. Grosz and Winninger, probably Wehner, and possibly even Laufer were also used as couriers for the Palestinian emissaries in Istanbul.

Laufer had been in Istanbul as early as 1941, and he was handed his first letter from Dogwood in March 1943—actually, the letter was given to Teddy Kollek, who gave it to Grosz, for Laufer. According to Schwarz, Laufer also came to him sometime in 1943 and asked him to get him out of Nazi Europe.[17] Laufer was threatened as a Jew, and he wanted the Americans to save him and his young wife. Schwarz says that he sent him to other OSS personnel, but they would have nothing to do with him. Schwarz describes Laufer as a heavyset young man with reddish hair and blue eyes; he thought that, as a Jew, Laufer would be an ideal OSS plant in the Abwehr. Laufer apparently gave some information to Dogwood, which made Dogwood view him as a reliable agent. What is clear is that Laufer was taken over by the SD when the Germans occupied Hungary in March 1944. If Grosz is to be believed—and we do not know for sure if Grosz knew that Laufer was a Jew—Laufer was going around dressed in Security Service uniform, and it was he who gave Grosz instructions, together with the Security Service commander in Budapest, Gerhard Clages, about Grosz's task of paving the way for contacts between the SS and the OSS. Schwarz added another piece of interesting information on Laufer's last visit to Istanbul, which Schwarz at first placed in 1943 or early in 1944; he later said that it must have been between the German occupation of Hungary on March 19 and the arrival of Grosz and Brand on May 19. Schwarz said very definitely that at the meeting Laufer proposed a trade of Jewish lives for trucks—again, this was *before* the Brand mission.[18]

Laufer had betrayed Messner in Budapest toward the end of March, but apparently the Istanbul OSS was not aware of that in April–May. It seems that Dogwood received Laufer in April, and Laufer tried to persuade Ridiger, who had served as contact man to Messner, to come to Budapest. Ridiger refused.[19]

Dogwood knew Grosz, who had become his agent Trillium. In his reminiscences, he at first denied having met Grosz in Istanbul in May 1944, when Grosz came there with Joel Brand; then he remembered that he did meet him, but claimed that he had met with him only in the presence of Ehud Avriel, Kollek's replacement as the JA's intelligence operative in Istanbul. The reticence about Grosz is understandable: he was a petty criminal and an

unsavory character by all standards. Born in 1905 in Berehovo, in Subcarpathian Russia, the easternmost province of prewar Czechoslovakia (generally known by its Czech acronym, PKR, for Podkarpatská Rus), the ugly,
small, red-haired man with his protruding teeth made his career as a rug
dealer and then a smuggler. He married a non-Jewish woman in 1937, and he
converted—not that he cared, apparently, for any religion at all. He was convicted of a customs offense in 1930 and then caught as a carpet smuggler in
1934 and later sentenced by the Hungarians to serve time in prison. In 1938,
after the Anschluss, he sold passports to Austrian Jews. In 1941 he was again
sentenced in Hungary, this time to a year and a half in prison, and offered his
services to the Abwehr to avoid jail. He was employed by the Stuttgart Ast,
with another agent called Franz Kleer, and was sent to Switzerland (May
1942) to gather mainly economic information. Apparently he was no great
success, and he was then sent to Sofia (June 1942) to work for German Air
Force Intelligence, with "Richard Klatt," the "half-Jew" from Vienna. Returning to Budapest, with the jail sentence constantly hanging over him, he began
working for the Hungarian Military Intelligence (from August 1942) but did
not rupture his contacts with the Abwehr. He was a clever smuggler, and the
Abwehr used him for information trips to the Balkans and, ultimately, to
Istanbul.[20]

Together with Winninger and Popescu, but to a greater degree, Grosz
transported money and letters from Istanbul as a courier for the Palestinian
emissaries throughout 1943. He transmitted the cries for help from Budapest
and from Bratislava via Budapest. He was also active for the Hungarians:
Anton von Merkly, of the Hungarian intelligence, asked Grosz to contact the
British in Istanbul and tell them pointblank that Hungary was willing to go
over to the Allies provided the Russians were kept out. There is no date to
this story, and in the absence of British documentation I can say only that it
sounds plausible enough.

Early in August 1943, Grosz contacted Dogwood—he had first met him in
July—with the same message: that Hungary sought a separate peace. Altogether, Grosz traveled to Turkey eight times, beginning in March 1943; the
count includes his May 1944 mission with Brand.[21] He had also been in touch
with Polish and Japanese intelligence, and he even knew George Earle, the
American "naval attaché" and eccentric wealthy exhibitionist, who claimed a
direct connection to Roosevelt and whom the OSS avoided like the plague.[22]

It is clear from the Dogwood material in the OSS Archives that Schwarz
relied on Grosz to provide him with information. Indeed, Grosz had information which he collected and distributed—that, after all, was how he made
a living. Grosz, as we have seen, was in touch with Klatt in Sofia, who provided the Germans with the so-called Max-Reports, which were highly val-
ued by the German military but were in fact concoctions, usually based on

the guesses of two individuals in Sofia, one of whom may have been connected to the Soviet embassy there. The uniqueness of Grosz, and the central place that he occupies in the story of Nazi-Jewish negotiations, lay in the way he became the only real contact with the West in Istanbul from the point of view of the SD and ultimately Himmler. To understand that, let us go back to the problems the Abwehr had at the end of 1943.

The situation of Canaris had become more and more dangerous. His chief aide, Oster, had been neutralized. Bonhoeffer, Müller, and Dohnanyi were in prison. And the achievements of German intelligence were less and less impressive. The Germans had failed to place agents in Britain; their attempts to penetrate the United States had misfired. Their intelligence information on the Soviet Union was pitiful. They had not been able to forecast the Allied landings in North Africa in November 1942, and their political reporting on what was going on in the Allied countries was reduced to gossip and guesswork. Nor had their attempts to contact the West brought any real result. It is true that in Switzerland, Hans-Bernd Gisevius, a member of the conservative Canaris clique and a German diplomat there, had become a trusted friend of the Bern representative of the OSS, Allen Dulles.[23] But nothing emerged from that contact: the United States was interested in defeating the Germans and spurned any efforts at changing the Nazi rule in Germany that would not bring about total unconditional surrender to all the Allies at the same time. Even then, the effort presumably would have to be a purely German one, and no promises could be made regarding any American help or sympathy.

Faced with this situation, Canaris sank deeper and deeper into despair. He no longer took an active interest in the day-to-day operations of his office; he just tried to keep himself afloat. Hitler grew more and more disillusioned with his intelligence chief, whom he had admired. But he still declined to listen to hints, especially from the SS, to fire Canaris and dissolve the Abwehr. Within the SS this was the preferred solution: to hand over the political espionage, perhaps also the military espionage, to an ideologically reliable Party apparatus.

The Istanbul Ast was headed by Paul Leverkühn, another of Canaris's friends. The continued existence of the Abwehr was dependent on a more or less even continuation of its work. But disruption was unexpected and fatal. Erich Vermehren was a junior clerk at the Istanbul Ast. He was married to the daughter of one of the best-known German authors, Countess Elizabeth Plattenberg-Twardowski. The young Mrs. Vermehren-Plattenberg was a devout Catholic, and a determined opponent of Nazism. She converted her husband to her faith, and the couple soon found that they could not continue to work for Nazi Germany, not even in the framework of the Abwehr; they did not have an inkling of the Abwehr conspiracies, of course. Early in 1944 the Vermehrens decided to abandon the German ship. They contacted the

British SIS and the American OSS and asked to be taken out of Turkey. The Western agencies were taken by surprise—they had never expected anything like that and had never been in touch with Vermehren before that. In addition, the Emniyet was not likely to view this violation of Turkish neutrality with favor. However, the arrangements were quickly made, and on February 2, 1944, Vermehren and his wife were whisked out of Turkey. Immediately thereafter, two more Abwehr contacts fled to the Allies. Their defection was a major blow to Abwehr operations.[24]

The repercussions were immediate. When Hitler received word of what had transpired, he exploded—as might have been expected. On February 10, Canaris was fired, and the Abwehr was abolished as an independent organization. As a transitional solution, Georg Hansen was appointed temporary head of the military end of the Abwehr, but most of it was absorbed by Schellenberg's SD, the SS Security Service within the RSHA, now commanded by Ernst Kaltenbrunner under Himmler's general supervision. The final takeover was in July.[25] Information about this radical change was slow to percolate down the ranks of the Abwehr itself, because the takeover was done carefully, in order not to damage contacts and lines of communication. From the point of view of Himmler's Western contacts, however, the change was of decisive importance. The Abwehr's lines into the Western camp were now in the hands of the inexperienced SD. In many places, such as Budapest, the Abwehr crews were divided between those who were taken over and those who were not—in the case of Budapest this resulted in the physical annihilation of the latter.[26] Leverkühn was recalled from Istanbul and an important RSHA officer, Hans Freund (alias Milo), was sent to straighten things out.[27] Freund could rely on the apparatus of the SD, run by Ludwig Moyzisch, that had existed in Istanbul beside the Abwehr apparatus.[28] Security was tightened. Just then the other catastrophes, already mentioned, hit the Istanbul Abwehr. Karl von Kleczkowski, an Austrian journalist, and his half-Jewish wife, threatened with a recall to Germany, followed in Vermehren's footsteps and defected to the Allies. Next came the defection of Wilhelm Hamburger, a young Austrian, the son of another director of the Semperit works. The father had been an early Nazi, but the son apparently did not share his views—or else the father changed his. In any case, Hamburger wavered, then hesitated, but faced with an order to return to Germany, he, like Kleczkowski, took the jump and, like the others, was taken out of Turkey. Worse was yet to come. Moyzisch's secretary, Nelly Kapp, who was involved in a romantic affair, decided to follow suit, bringing with her important intelligence material. In line with Nazi practice, relatives of the escaped Germans were apprehended—Vermehren's mother, Petra, in Lisbon, as early as February 11.[29]

Another set of contacts that involved Istanbul were those of Franz von

Papen, the man who had brought Hitler into power. A reactionary Catholic politician, he was the German ambassador to Turkey. By 1943, Papen realized that Germany was likely to lose the war, and he, like so many others, was looking for a way out. Papen was not part of the conservative resistance group in Germany; he was a loner, an outsider, a man with tremendous personal ambition and great vanity, and he tried to impress American contacts with his importance, hoping to play a central role in the overthrow of Hitler and in a future right-wing, anticommunist German state with U.S. backing.

One source claims that prior to the abolition of the Abwehr, Leverkühn was Papen's main source of information.[30] Papen apparently thought that if the Republicans won the November 1944 presidential elections in the United States, there was a good chance that the United States would then concentrate all its war efforts in the Pacific, giving Germany a chance to survive and even defeat Britain. That is what Papen reputedly told Hitler. There is no independent confirmation of this anywhere. However, Papen did believe in a future understanding between Germany and the United States on an anticommunist basis. Leverkühn probably maintained friendly contact with Papen, whereas Moyzisch supervised Papen as closely as possible. Again, given the control that Himmler and Schellenberg exercised over Moyzisch, they were probably well informed about Papen's stance. And again, they did nothing to stop Papen.

Dogwood was involved in none of this, but it formed the background to his activity during the first seven months of 1944. His major effort during this time, apart from the Cassia arrangements, was the attempt to mediate in a Hungarian bid to leave the war by negotiating through military channels with OSS representatives. It will become immediately clear what connection this has with our main theme.

The Hungarian government under Prime Minister Miklos Kallay (1942–44) had begun to feel its way toward a separate peace with the Western Allies after Stalingrad. Several attempts were made through emissaries, diplomats, and military people to prepare a Hungarian exit from its alliance with Nazi Germany. Thus, in August 1943, an official of the Hungarian Foreign Ministry, Laszlo Veress, was sent to Istanbul to talk to Allied diplomats. On September 9 he met with the British ambassador, Sir Hugh Knatchbull-Hugessen. The ambassador presented him with a demand for unconditional surrender, to be kept secret until it could be implemented. The Hungarian Army was to be slowly disengaged from the Russian front. Veress returned to Budapest with a radio transmitter. In February 1944 the Kallay government sent four Hungarian intellectuals—among them the Nobel Prize–winner Albert Szent-Györgyi and the lawyer Ferenc Vali—to Istanbul to pave the way for peace talks.[31] In September 1944, Gen. Istvan Naday was sent to Allied headquarters in Italy.[32] However, obstacles appeared—the same ones

that the German conservatives faced in their attempts to achieve an understanding with the Anglo-Americans. The West was unwilling to accept the
basic proposition that Hungarian diplomats reiterated time and time again:
that the Red Army should be kept out of Hungary. Caught between the Nazi
devil and the communist deep blue sea, the Hungarian ship was refused aid
by the West. Roosevelt and Churchill were not going to risk their delicate
relationship with Stalin to pander to anti-Nazi German generals, much less
so to the Hungarians. What the Western diplomats whom the Hungarians
reached were willing to tell their interlocutors was that the Hungarians
should turn against the Germans and surrender unconditionally to the
Allies—to all the Allies.

In 1943, as the situation worsened from their point of view—as Hungarian forces in Russia were beaten and were caught up in the German
retreat—Hungarian attempts to make a separate peace became more frantic.
The Germans had their sources of information on their allies and followed
the Hungarian antics with ever-growing displeasure. Toward Germany, the
Hungarians, with Regent Admiral Miklos Horthy at the helm, professed
undying loyalty to the common anti-Bolshevik cause. It was in that context
that Minister of Defense Lajos Csatay and the Foreign Minister, as well as
the Chief of Staff, Gen. Ferenc Szombathelyi, authorized another attempt,
this time one that would lead to the intelligence services in Istanbul; it would
be based on a military approach, which, they probably hoped, might be more
persuasive. Hungarian intelligence (Section 2 of the General Staff, under
Gen. Istvan Ujszaszy, Col. Gyula Kadar, and Lt. Col. Anton von Merkly)
delegated as their representative Lt. Col. Otto Hatz de Hatzsegy (Jasmine as
a Dogwood flower); he was a member of the Hungarian gentry who had done
a tour of duty in Ankara and was now, in late 1943, Hungarian military
attaché in Sofia. Hatz was born in Banjovo (Bosnia) in 1902 of a poor family;
he knew German, Russian, Bulgarian, and some English and French. He had
been involved in recruiting Muslim Bosnians for the Hungarian Army. A
Hungarian patriot and an accomplished fencer, Hatz was typical of his class
and his generation.[33]

His main helper was Ferenc ("Ferry" or "Feri") Bagyoni (Dogwood's
Pink) of the Hungarian intelligence, the man who in early 1943 had recruited
Grosz for the Hungarians. Bagyoni was convinced that Grosz and Kleer were
fooling the Germans and were ready to establish contacts with the Allies to
help extract Hungary from the war. Bagyoni was sent to be an aide to Hatz
when the latter was sent to Istanbul, and himself contacted the Palestinian
emissaries. He then became, together with the Abwehr people, an important
courier for the Palestinians.[34] Like the Germans, the Hungarians thought
they should play the Jewish card in their attempts to reach the West.

Dogwood had heard of Churchill's plan to invade the Balkans, which had

been abandoned but which indeed was then being used by the West in a dis-
information campaign, supposedly as an alternative to the invasion of France
by the Allied powers. Churchill had originally wanted to defeat the Germans
in the soft underbelly of their Balkan dependencies, but he had also been aim-
ing at reducing the threatening influence of the Soviet Union in a post-Nazi
Europe. Dogwood completely identified with this idea. As a minor, if centrally situated, figure in a clandestine operation, his views neither mattered
nor were shared by his immediate superiors in the OSS—the organization
carefully avoided dealing in high politics. Dogwood, not an American and not
really employed by OSS, had his own ideas, and he tried to advance them as
far as possible. When he was approached by the Hungarians to serve as an
intermediary with the OSS, he thought that his great moment had come and
that he might prevent the destruction of Jews and the conquest of the Balkans
by the Soviets and help end the war much more quickly than a continuing
bloodbath would.

For Hatz, the problems were many. He had to camouflage his approach
from the Germans, but he also had to contact the OSS through someone who
knew that organization and who would also have contact with the British.
The only person he could think of was Bandi Grosz, who, as we know,
worked for Hungarian intelligence, presumably supplying them with information about the Abwehr as well: it was surprising how pliant an informer
could be if he had a jail sentence hanging over his head. Grosz, in addition,
was the carrier of a Hungarian passport and in a sense was dependent on the
goodwill of the Hungarian G-2. It was Grosz who introduced Hatz to the
Anglo-Americans.

The introduction of Hatz to Dogwood and Coleman was made by Grosz in
September 1943, when Hatz was in Turkey ostensibly visiting the Izmir
trade fair. Another person who was involved in the initial contacts was Lothar
Kövess (Dogwood's Jacaranda), a shipping merchant and scion of an important family of Hungarian politicians and a known British intelligence agent.
On the other hand, he also had a number of close Nazi contacts, and although
another OSS figure, Archibald Walker, had employed him at the Socony Vacuum company and vouched for him, a question remained open: whether he
was playing both ends against the middle by ingratiating himself both with
the Abwehr and with the Nazis, the Hungarians, and the British.[35]

In the meantime, Hatz had already met with Teddy Kollek and with a
British agent. Grosz then introduced him to Dogwood. The Americans
wanted to know what kind of cooperation the Hungarians would be prepared
to offer. On September 29, Hatz was given a list of American demands which
specified that no political negotiations or concessions could be discussed but
that complete military and intelligence collaboration would prove Hungarian
sincerity. Another meeting took place in early October, at which time a trans-

mitter was handed to either Kövess or Bagyoni, and on October 5, Hatz flew from Sofia back to Budapest.[36] At a meeting in which Hungarian Chief of Staff Szombathelyi and Kadar of the Hungarian Intelligence Agency participated, he was ordered to continue his contacts. He also brought with him the radio transmitter to be used in contacts with the OSS. The Hungarians were afraid to use the transmitter, so Kadar hid it in the piano of his mistress, the actress Katalina Varga-Karady. When the Germans occupied Budapest, they found it and arrested everyone connected with it.[37] How they knew that the transmitter existed is not clear—but Hatz himself could have told them, or Laufer.

At the next meeting in Istanbul in November, with Dogwood, Kövess, and Macfarland (Hatz says that he specifically asked to have Grosz excluded because he did not trust him), Hatz made the suggestion, obviously as an opening gambit, that the Hungarian General Staff provide a "designated American representative [with] detailed military intelligence concerning the German Army and German operations." In exchange, Hungary asked that the United Nations bear in mind during the peace negotiations that Hungary had made an overt act of assistance to the Allied cause. Hatz also indicated that if the Allies—meaning the Western Allies—invaded Hungary, Hungarian troops would occupy airfields to enable Allied parachutists to land.[38] Hatz also asked for a "portable radio" so he could communicate with Istanbul. He also said that the Hungarians would send an Allied-approved Hungarian officer to Istanbul to act as collaborator with the Allied services. Such an officer was immediately appointed—apparently in the person of Ferenc Bagyoni—because the Hungarian military attaché in Istanbul, Bartalis, was unreliable.[39]

Interestingly enough, it appears that Hatz made no more approaches to the British, and Donovan left to his Chiefs of Staff the decision on how the British should be brought in.[40] Now, the problem for Hatz was how to arrange his relations with the Germans. He went back to Sofia and, on December 1, met with Otto Wagner (code-named Delius), the local Abwehr chief. He told Wagner about Kollek and the two American agents. He presented the discussions to the Abwehr man as though he, a staunch anticommunist, had tried to convince the Americans that their policy was mistaken. The Americans, Hatz pretended, had responded by saying that if Bolshevism was to take the place of Nazism, they, the Americans, would consider the war lost.[41]

On December 14, Hatz again met with his superiors in Budapest—Kallay, the Prime Minister was possibly among them—and received what in effect was a carte blanche to carry on his talks in Istanbul. It appears that he omitted to tell them about his tête-à-tête with Wagner.

Hatz returned to Sofia on his way to Istanbul on December 16 and reported to Josef Beckerle, the German ambassador, on his past meetings, as well as on his forthcoming one with the Americans, saying that he would reject any idea of spying on behalf of the West. On the eighteenth he met with Coleman and Dogwood, who told him that the Hungarians did not have much time to make up their minds. Hatz proceeded from Istanbul to Sofia, and there again contacted Wagner and Beckerle, to whom he related most, but not all, of what had transpired in Turkey. He said, falsely, that he had rejected the American offer. He also embellished the story of his conference in Istanbul with all kinds of fairy tales about an argument over Bolshevism with his conversation partners.[42] Beckerle reported the conversation to the German Foreign Office on December 22, 1943. The cable was caught by Ultra, the British code-breaking agency, and Macfarland was warned by both his superiors and by the British, who did not tell him how the OSS had got wind of Hatz's treason.[43]

Hatz then returned to Budapest and reported to his superiors, telling them about his Istanbul talks but not apparently about his Sofia meetings. Kadar and he met with Kallay, who was unhappy about the military angle and the concrete American demands. There was no way the Hungarian Army could disengage itself from the Russian front without the Germans taking severe countermeasures. Nor was there a way to conduct partisan operations on the open Hungarian plain. Hatz was told to keep the discussions in Istanbul going and to make the Americans understand the limits of Hungarian actions. Miklos Horthy, Jr., was also informed so that he could tell the story to his father the admiral.

Kadar then decided to take the bull by the horns, and he and Hatz went to see Canaris in Munich; the meeting took place on January 9, 1944. They told their story again, and a very wary Canaris warned them against the Allies— and against the Germans as well. The Hungarians should not see the Allies in Istanbul anymore; he knew that Hatz was playing a double game, and he did not want to expose himself. It should be remembered that this was one month before Hitler abolished the Abwehr.

The next meetings took place on January 19 and 22, with Dogwood and some of the others (Coleman, Kövess, Arndt, Macfarland, and Col. Vala Lada-Mocarski of the Cairo OSS, who was slated to be dropped into Hungary); the OSS people emphasized to Hatz that they were interested only in military matters, not political ones. The Americans, amazingly, naively, and irresponsibly, confronted Hatz with their knowledge of his double dealings (had Hatz and the Germans drawn the proper conclusions from this episode, they might well have discovered the secret of Ultra—namely, that their codes had been broken). Hatz responded that the Allies had committed indiscretions and that the Germans had heard of his meetings; therefore he had bluffed by telling the Germans inaccurate versions of his Istanbul talks. At the meeting on January 22, Hatz indicated that providing military information might not be ethical, and the Americans told him that ethics were not involved: if the Hungarians wanted to have their efforts recognized after the war, they had to cooperate now and rebel against Germany.[44]

Returning to Bulgaria, Hatz again met with Wagner, and Beckerle reported the meeting in a February 1 cable. Hatz told Wagner that Kadar had given him the order to meet the Americans one more time and tell them that the Hungarians were breaking off the contacts. He then told Wagner just about everything that had transpired between himself and the Americans, but peculiarly enough he seems to have mentioned only Coleman and Schwarz (he knew Dogwood's real identity). He included in his report the statement that the Americans knew of his reports to Wagner and Beckerle. This information should have told the Germans that their code had been broken, with potentially incalculable results for Allied warfare, but it apparently went unnoticed. Wagner also reported that "Hatz believes that the focal point for opening contacts between Hungary and the Allies is the central role of Jewish conspirators."[45]

Macfarland had been warned by Donovan several times about Hatz's betrayals and also about Grosz's links with Hungarian intelligence, but he continued the talks with Hatz regardless. On February 5 he wrote to Donovan justifying his action. He said that "we" had concluded a simple agreement with Hatz in the form of a memo. He was talking only about military cooperation and subversive activities with Hatz; it was the British, he said, who were introducing political subjects. Hatz was only a courier, who had not learned anything about the OSS or its plans.[46]

The last meeting of the OSS with Hatz prior to the occupation of Hungary by the Germans on March 19 was held in Istanbul on February 27, 1944, with Hatz, Macfarland, Kövess, and Dogwood present. At that meeting, Hatz promised that the Hungarians would provide the Americans with full economic intelligence data to prove that Hungary was in effect paying the Germans in order to prevent a German occupation. The OSS would welcome for military reasons the list of Hungarian enterprises and their production figures, and it would also be given the Hungarian Army's order of battle and state of mobilization. By that time both parties knew that the Germans might occupy Hungary, and Macfarland explained to Hatz that Hungary was expected to resist such a development; Hatz was skeptical. He thought that there could be little resistance if the Germans marched in. He promised to provide the OSS with full details of the Hungarian war against the Russians and also said that if the Allies invaded Yugoslavia—this was what Dogwood was praying for—the Hungarians would probably lay down their arms and even become co-belligerents with the Allies.[47] Apparently, Bagyoni or Kövess met with some OSS people again on March 9, when they were given two radio sets, one for Bagyoni's use in Budapest and the other for Laufer. Hatz informed Wagner-Delius about one of the sets, which Bagyoni then carried to Sofia. From there Bagyoni took it to Budapest via Vienna. Hatz says he wanted to trip up Laufer, whom he had identified as a Nazi agent, but apparently that did not work. It seems that the set landed in Laufer's hands and that Laufer used it to lure Cassia-Messner into the trap that caught him (he was arrested). The other set was given to Grosz, who says he dropped it into a river. The OSS was not very successful in its attempts to establish contact with Hungarian oppositionists.[48]

In April 1944, Hatz, Kövess, and Bagyoni were recalled to Budapest, where they were arrested on May 3.[49] Bagyoni later argued that they had been betrayed by Laufer. Hatz was released on May 26 after a confrontation with Wagner-Delius in the presence of Clages—itself a very peculiar development, for the Gestapo were not known for special leniency in cases where contacts with the enemy were suspected. Still, Kövess, Hatz, and Bagyoni—the latter somewhat later—were released unconditionally. On June 8, Hatz again appeared in Istanbul, and despite warnings from Donovan he was again met by both OSS and American diplomats. He had good explanations for everything, but it no longer mattered.[50] He became the personal adjutant to the Hungarian Minister of Defense on July 1. Bagyoni escaped to Sweden in September. Hatz, who in October became the operations officer (Ia) of the Seventh Hungarian Corps, went over to the Russians on November 7. After liberation, he was the military commander of Budapest until April 1945 and was then arrested by the Russians. He spent the next decade in Soviet prisons, returning to Hungary in 1955. He became a trainer to the East German and Hungarian fencing teams, and died in Budapest in 1977.[51]

The Hatz episode was connected with another one, which is also relevant to our main theme. Through the Hungarian diplomatic mission in Bern, Ujszaszy and his colleagues, unaware that Hatz had betrayed them, asked the OSS for (or agreed to) an American mission to reach Hungary to work out practical steps toward collaboration with the Hungarian Army and prepare for surrender. The OSS sent the "Sparrow mission." The Sparrows were headed by a flamboyant colonel named Florimond Duke. He had never parachuted before, but the three Americans set out on March 15 from Italy and landed safely in Hungary. By prior arrangement they were "arrested" by the Hungarian counterintelligence and brought to Budapest, where, on the eighteenth, they met with Ujszaszy, who promised cooperation but said that Horthy was out of town. Indeed he was—at Klessheim, with Hitler, listening to the Führer's diatribes on Hungarian treachery. The next morning the Germans marched in; within a few days the Americans had been handed over to the Germans as prisoners of war, and Ujszaszy was arrested—the Sparrow had been shot down.[52]

Hatz was not likely aware of the inter-German struggle between the

Abwehr and the SS, at least not to its full degree. By making his report not only to the Abwehr but to Beckerle, he in effect prevented the Abwehr from utilizing his contacts. Beckerle was an *Obergruppenführer* in the SA, a rival of the SS, and Ribbentrop's man. Ribbentrop was eager to trip up both Himmler and the Abwehr, and Canaris could not do anything with the Hatz mission, which he must have known would incite a German countermeasure. The affair was not mentioned explicitly in the Klessheim talks between Hitler and Horthy, but the general theme of Hungarian treachery was broached. One way or the other, Grosz and Laufer were involved, however, which meant that the SD did in the end pick up the pieces, for Grosz and Laufer became SD agents. They obviously told the SD everything they knew about the Hatz affair, and judging by the fact that Hatz was arrested and then freed by the SD, Hatz himself must have confirmed it. Not surprisingly, the next step, the attempt by the SD itself to reach the West via Dogwood, took the Hatz case into account.

The importance, then, of the Hungarian interlude to our main theme lies in two main points: one, these maneuvers were carefully watched by Himmler's men to discover how the contacts were established and what they might lead to; and two, from the SD perspective it probably appeared that the most fruitful approach was via the Jews, who seemed to be in charge of all the intelligence channels—Laufer, Grosz, Dogwood, and the Zionist emissaries were proof of that.

With the end of the Cassia connection, the exposure of the unreliability of Grosz and the treason of Laufer, the fiasco with Fiala, and the end of the Hatz negotiations, Dogwood was left with very little.[53] His involvement with the Brand-Grosz ("trucks for blood") mission, which will be dealt with below, was minimal. He appeared as a failed intelligence operator, if not worse.[54] His personal behavior, his self-assurance and feeling of superiority in relation to Coleman and Macfarland, his cultural pretensions, his secretiveness about his contacts—all these things hastened the termination of his activity with OSS.

Macfarland became discredited, largely through the failure of the Dogwood chain. On June 10 he was still trying to defend it. He admitted the failures but argued that the Dogwood office was used as a "cut-out for many unrelated agents." Although security had not been good—in other words, the Dogwood chain could be penetrated—it had not been disastrous. Within a month, however, the chain had collapsed.[55]

Unrelated to the Dogwood disaster was the failure of a second chain. It had been started in April 1942, a year before Macfarland had arrived, by Archibald Walker, the Socony Vacuum representative in Turkey. Called the Rose chain, it became discredited as well. The information gathered by its agents came from travelers to and from the Balkan countries, and Walker reported through the Reports Division of the U.S. consulate general in Istanbul, as well as through the OSS; for a long time, nothing serious had emerged from Rose chain reports. At the end of July, after much hesitation, Macfarland was forced to end the connection with Dogwood, who again became a simple Istanbul businessman, Alfred Schwarz. Many years later, Schwarz maintained that he had left the OSS in disgust, whereas OSS records have it that he was fired. The truth is probably in between. In August 1944 an investigation headed by the redoubtable Frank G. Wisner, head of SI in Istanbul and then head of X-2 counterespionage, discredited the Dogwood chain. Wisner's critique was sharp and decisive. The Dogwood episode was closed.

Coleman's association with the Dogwood chain had been terminated by the OSS as early as February 1944. By that time, relations between the SI section of the mission and Macfarland (Dogwood's Juniper) had become strained, and the SI people doubted whether the Dogwood chain was really useful. Coleman himself was seen as a failure, too, and in September he was on his way back to the United States under suspicion of having misused his position in Istanbul.[56] Macfarland was relieved of his post as of August 7, and Frank G. Wisner was appointed in his stead. Typifying the attitude that the Mideast OSS staff had toward Macfarland is a letter of February 16, 1945, by the OSS chief in Cairo, Harry S. Aldrich. Macfarland "is liked by practically everyone, including myself, but I have seldom found anyone who did not think him completely insecure." His work in Turkey caused "considerable damage to OSS's work and reputation there." A satiric song was composed about Macfarland that was sung everywhere. "To be completely frank . . . I summarize my opinion of him by saying that I have long considered him, as far as the interests of OSS go, a menace."[57] So much for Macfarland.

Alfred Schwarz–Dogwood was an important link in the chain of efforts to penetrate German-held Europe, on the one hand, and to end the war through a negotiated peace, on the other hand. He became a focal point in German attempts to contact the Western powers; both the conservatives of the Canaris-Moltke brand and the SD, through Laufer and Grosz, used him as a conduit. He understood, or half understood, the complexities of the internal German situation. His own notions were very clear: he thought that a shortening of the terrible war might save uncounted lives, very many of them Jewish. In his mind, the Holocaust—which he knew was happening—the continuation of the war, and the threat of a communist takeover in Eastern Europe were all combined in that they could all be ended or avoided with a single stroke. After his disappointment with the American reaction to Moltke, he thought that the Hatz negotiations might lead to a similar result if the Allies decided to invade the Balkans, rather than staging a frontal attack on the Germans in France. When he failed to achieve anything at all, he withdrew into boundless bitterness and hatred of the Americans, whom he accused, to the end of his days, of being responsible for not seeing that they could have prevented senseless slaughter, including that of their own soldiers. The point is that, given the situation in Europe, to have followed his advice might have created the basis for a regeneration of Nazism in Germany and ultimately not have prevented Soviet supremacy in Eastern Europe. Given the policy of alliance with the Soviets, who were then on the verge of liberating Eastern Europe, including the pitiful Jewish remnants, from a still very powerful German Army, his ideas were bound to be rejected.

After the capitulation of Romania on August 23, 1944, Wisner went to Bucharest to open shop there for the OSS. After the war, he became the prime mover in getting Byelorussians, possibly also Ukrainians, who had served with the SS into the United States as an anti-Soviet move. He apparently was also involved in helping former German Nazis into the Western Hemisphere.

In 1946 the U.S. Army Counterintelligence Corps (CIC) in Austria investigated the former Gestapo group in Vienna to find out who had betrayed the Cassia ring and how. One of the interrogated Gestapo men tried to implicate Schwarz as a double agent, but even the CIC realized that that was too weak a reed to rely on. The CIC was searching for Schwarz in Austria—he stayed on, quite publicly and openly, in Istanbul, then indeed moved to Austria, became a bank director, and finally settled in Lucerne, in Switzerland. He did not recant his views. To the end, he was convinced that the Americans should have supported the German conservative underground in order to shorten the war. He also believed that an Allied landing in the Balkans would have avoided the kind of disaster that overtook Eastern Europe with its conquest by the Soviets. He did not live to see the collapse of East European communism in 1989. He probably would have said, "I told you so."

The Brand-Grosz mission was engineered by the SS mainly to establish contact with the Americans, and Grosz was supposed to be in touch with Dogwood, building on the contacts that had been established by the Abwehr (again, chiefly by Grosz) and by the Hungarians through Hatz—all of which was known to Himmler's men. What we have established, then, is that Istanbul was the obvious place for Himmler's half-baked efforts to open options with the Western powers to be made; indeed, they were made there, especially after the takeover of the Abwehr in early 1944; the central figure on the American side was a Czech Jew, Dogwood; and the main figures sent by the SS-SD were two Jewish criminals, Grosz and Laufer. When we consider that Himmler, contrary to Hitler's directives, continued to use Klaus in Sweden, who was also taken over from the Abwehr, a pattern seems to emerge: repeated attempts to approach the West at least partly through low-grade Jewish agents.[58] The possibility of offering some Jews in exchange for the establishment of contacts with the West appears in the Brand mission and by implication in the Grosz mission as well. The pattern fits with Himmler's conviction that the Jews were behind all Germany's enemies and that offering Jewish lives might be one of the ways for Germany to achieve a temporary halt in its war against the United States and Britain.

9

Satan and the Soul—Hungary, 1944

In 1953, Dr. Israel (Reszoe, Rudolf) Kasztner, the man who is identified with the attempt to save Hungarian Jewry by negotiating with the Nazis, was persuaded by his center-left political friends in the new State of Israel to bring a libel suit against one Malkiel Grünwald, an old man who had said in an obscure Israeli publication that Kasztner was a criminal: he had negotiated with the most terrible enemies of the Jewish people and had saved a trainload of Hungarian Jews in return for abandoning to their fate the rest of the Jews of Hungary. In the process, he had misappropriated funds the Jews paid to him in return for promises to be saved. The trial began in early 1954, and Grünwald was defended by a brilliant right-wing lawyer, Shmuel Tamir, who quickly turned the trial into an arraignment of Kasztner, who had to defend himself against these and other charges that were brought before the Tel Aviv Court, presided over by Judge Benyamin Halevy. At the end of a prolonged trial, which exacerbated emotions and aroused enmities more dramatic than any that had been evinced in Israel since its independence and which had a lasting effect on Israeli society, Grünwald was acquitted on all charges except that of having libeled Kasztner for money mismanagement, where the issue was left undecided because of lack of evidence against Kasztner. Halevy, in his sentencing, pronounced a verdict that reverberated in Israel until the late 1980s: "Kasztner sold his soul to Satan."

The problem that we are facing here deals with a major aspect of the Holocaust—the problem of the rescue or otherwise of Jews and how people thought it might be achieved. But the problem also affected Jewish society in Israel and abroad in the generations that followed the war and is likely to affect future generations, too. The basic issue from a Jewish point of view was and is, Was it justifiable to conduct negotiations with the Nazis to save Jews? And if it was, what were the limits to such contacts? What was, and what should have been, the reaction of leadership groups in threatened Jewish communities? And, most important, was there a chance of rescuing Jews by negotiations?

To intertwine moralizing or sermonizing—as distinct from facing moral issues—with problems of historical interpretation is dangerous. We should first of all define the historical issues and the moral ones behind them. Let me present the factual development and attempt an interpretation, then, with great reserve and circumspection, say something about the wider issues of ethical behavior as they appear to develop from the analysis, and finally connect all that to our central theme.

Hungarian Jews were a very special group of people.

According to their own, superpatriotic legends, they had been in Hungary before the Mongol Hungarians ever came there; they had supposedly come with the Romans. Some archaeological finds show that Jews had indeed been in the Roman province of Pannonia, or modern Hungary. Later, much later, Jews came from Byzantium (Constantinople), and after the conquest of Hungary by the Turks in the sixteenth century, Turkish Jews followed. All this was almost totally irrelevant in modern Hungary: Hungarian Jews were in fact comparatively recent immigrants. They had arrived from Bohemia and, mainly, Moravia starting in the eighteenth century, and from Polish Galicia starting in the early nineteenth century. In 1772 and 1795, parts of southern Poland were acquired by the Austrian Empire, which also ruled Hungary. In effect, Hungarian Jews were of Polish or Bohemian-Moravian origin. In Hungary, unlike in other European countries, the Jews did indeed fulfill a central role in the development of the economy, and the antisemitic "charge" of Jewish economic leadership had a true ring to it.[1] Jews even entered into agriculture, partly as lessees of land, partly as medium or large landowners, partly as petty farmers. They were a minority there, but their presence was felt. Trade and small crafts were largely in the hands of Jews. In industry, Jewish entrepreneurs developed what few natural resources there were, and large-scale industry and banking were influenced by people of Jewish extraction.

Assimilation went, in some ways, further than elsewhere in Europe. In Hungary, as in Germany and elsewhere in Western Europe, the Jewish religion was liberalized, and soon the majority of Hungarian Jews were so-called Neologues, in many ways equivalent to contemporary Conservative Jews in the United States. As in some cases in the United States, the rabbis may have been Neologue, but the congregants were religiously indifferent for the most part, although they did want to keep something of the tradition. These Jews considered themselves Hungarians of the Jewish persuasion; they tended to be devoted to Hungary and its culture, which they helped develop as writers, artists, and intellectuals in other creative spheres. Not only the Neologues were superpatriots. So were the Orthodox, about one-third of Hungarian Jewry. Jews came to frown on Yiddish, the language spoken by the Jewish immigrants, and ultraorthodox seminaries began using Hungarian. Hungarian Jewry split into two main groups in 1868; the two communities barely even spoke to each other.

The younger generation of Jews before and during World War I was radicalized; some were prominent in the founding of left-wing movements. In 1918–19 a short-lived communist government ruled Hungary, headed by Bela Kun, a Jew; a majority of the Ministers had Jewish parentage but totally repudiated their Judaism. The right-wing reaction to this regime brought to power the government of Adm. Miklos Horthy, who assumed the title of Regent in the absence of an agreed-on royal figure to occupy the throne of Saint Stephen in Budapest. A "White" terror gripped Hungary, and the Jews were probably the main sufferers proportional to their number.

At the end of World War I, by the terms of the Treaty of Trianon, Hungary found itself deprived of outlying provinces where ethnic non-Hungarians were in the majority, such as Slovakia, Subcarpathian Russia, Transylvania, and the southern regions that became part of Yugoslavia. A restored greater Hungary became the dream of right-wing chauvinist groups. In their frustration, they turned against the Jews as the most vulnerable "foreign" element in the country; there was also a large German minority, but many Hungarian Germans were Horthy supporters, and the Army was full of Hungarian German officers.

Between the world wars, antisemitism was part of the government creed, even though Horthy and his clique had Jewish connections, and the titled landowners and gentry had in no small part intermarried with Jews. Rich Jewish families and the upper level of the Jewish intelligentsia were accepted into Hungarian society, and a *numerus clausus* act of 1920 (limiting Jews in the professions to their percentage in the general population) was later disregarded. As Hungary began moving into the German orbit in the 1930s, antisemitic propaganda increased. To accommodate to German thinking and also to take the wind out of the sails of the rising fascist right wing, the government passed discriminatory legislation in 1938 and again in 1939, which reimposed the *numerus clausus*. Legislation was passed in 1940 to remove Jews from the officer corps of the Army, and a labor service under humiliating conditions was instituted for Jews instead of regular Army service. For the Hungarian Jews who had fought bravely for the Austro-Hungarian monarchy in World War I, this was a serious blow.

In 1938–40 Hungary, under Germany's aegis, reacquired southern Slovakia, Subcarpathian Russia (PKR), northern Transylvania, and, in 1941, the Banat region of Yugoslavia. In the newly acquired territories, especially in the north and the east, Orthodox Jews were preponderant among the Jewish population and were not necessarily Hungarian speakers. With these conquests, the Jews numbered 725,007 souls in 1941; of these, 400,980 lived within the pre-1938 borders (so-called Trianon Hungary). In addition, there were many converts to Christianity—61,548, according to the 1941 count.

In Trianon Hungary the Jewish birthrate was declining, and the situation there was comparable to that of pre-Hitler Germany. Most of the Jews— 65.5 percent—belonged to Neologue communities, 29.2 percent to Orthodox communities, and 5.3 percent to in-between communities, the so-called Status Quo group. This was in 1930, before the Orthodox received reinforcement from the new territories. Both main communities were led by Jewish aristocrats: Court Councilor Samu Stern led the Neologues, Fülop von Freudiger the Orthodox. Fascist-type antisemitic parties gained ascendancy. The Arrow Cross (Nyilas) Party of Ferenc Szalasi gained 49 of 226 parliamentary seats in 1935 and increased their strength again in 1939, to about a third of the lower house.

The situation of the Jews went from bad to worse, but compared with the fate of Polish or German Jewry, they were incomparably better off. The Jewish labor battalions that the Army set up numbered 52,000 men in 1940. Hungary joined Nazi Germany on June 27, 1941, to attack the Soviet Union, partly, no doubt, because its neighbor, fascist-dominated Romania, had joined the Nazis, too, and Hungarian nonparticipation would have endangered Hungary's hold over newly acquired northern Transylvania, which the Romanians wanted back. The Jewish labor battalions, mostly commanded by rabidly antisemitic officers, were sent into the Ukraine. Of the roughly 40,000 sent, some 5,000 returned in 1943, and a few thousand were taken prisoner or escaped to the Russians. The rest were killed, mostly by Hungarian and German troops, or starved and beaten to death. The result was that young Jewish men were simply not there when the German onslaught on Hungarian Jewry came in 1944.

After Hungary entered the war, the government of Laszlo Bardossy decided to deport those Jews who could not prove Hungarian citizenship, especially from the new areas in the north and east. A decree of July 12, 1941, provided legal cover, but many of the 18,000 Jews who were deported to German-occupied Ukraine did in fact have Hungarian citizenship or had lived in their towns and villages for generations without bothering to acquire official government documents to prove it. The deported people were sent to the area of Kamenets Podolskiy. The Germans at first did not want to accept them—not unlike Eichmann in early 1942 in response to the Slovak offer to deport Slovak Jews. On August 25, the SS general Franz Jeckeln agreed to accept the Jews and deal with them by September 1. On August 27–28, some 14,000–16,000 Hungarian Jews and several thousand local Jews were machine-gunned by the SS, Ukrainian collaborators, and Hungarian sappers. When Hungarian Interior Minister Ferenc Keresztes-Fischer, one of the few liberals still in power, learned of the massacre, he ordered a stop to the deportations. Yet another massacre, on a much smaller scale, occurred in the Novi Sad area of Hungarian-occupied northern Yugoslavia, where 3,309 civilians, mostly Serbs but including 700 or so Jews, were murdered in January 1942.[2]

Early in 1942, a rabidly antisemitic Hungarian major-general, Joszef Heszlenyi, offered to continue with partial deportations, knowing full well what the fate of the deported Jews would be. The Germans were asked to accept 100,000 Jewish deportees in the Ukraine. The Nazis declined, citing transport difficulties. When the Hungarians returned in July to ask the Germans to reconsider, the German Foreign Office turned to the RSHA and asked whether it could now accept these Jews—to murder them, be it remembered. Eichmann finally answered in Himmler's name on September 25 (Himmler later explicitly acknowledged that he had been the authority in whose name Eichmann had written): The Hungarian proposal was a partial solution only, and it was not worth activating the whole evacuation machinery when the Jewish question in Hungary would remain unsolved. Eichmann was prepared to wait until the Hungarians were ready to hand over *all* their Jews.

Another approach, and a very peculiar one, was made by Gedeon von Fay-Halasz, private secretary of Prime Minister Miklos Kallay in his second role as Foreign Minister, to Dieter Wisliceny, who was visiting Budapest in early October 1942. On the thirteenth, Fay, an ally of Heszlenyi's, repeated the request to deport 100,000 Jews, perhaps together with the projected deportation of Jews from Romania. He held out the prospect of deporting all Jews from Hungary but said that the deportation would have to be done in stages, with Budapest Jews being the last to go. Wisliceny, who said that he was visiting Budapest privately, replied that he would report on the meeting. This time, Himmler himself intervened. In a letter to Ribbentrop on November 11, 1942, he suggested following up the Hungarian overtures by "solving" the Hungarian Jewish "question." But then the German ambassador to Budapest, Dietrich von Jagow, voiced doubts: Did these overtures occur with the knowledge of the Hungarian government? In any case, nothing further happened, and the Hungarian proposal appears to have been withdrawn.

None of the research on Hungarian Jewry has shed light on this episode, which after all lasted for a whole year. The Hungarian General Staff or some people within it seem to have acted on their own bat and without Kallay's knowledge.[3] Kallay was taking a more reserved stand toward Germany just then in order to prepare for an approach to the Western Allies to extricate Hungary from the war, and it has been argued that he tried to improve the condition of the Jews. To suppose that he would have endangered his own policy by a massive deportation of Jews is not very reasonable. Yet how could proposals like these be floated over a period of a year without the knowledge of the Hungarian government? The events just related remain a mystery.[4]

In the spring of 1942 about 7,000–8,000 Slovak Jews fled to Hungary. They and a trickle of Polish Jews, who were escaping the mass murder campaign in Poland by crossing the mountains into the PKR and thence to Budapest, had great difficulties finding places of refuge in Hungary. Not only was the Alien Police after them, but the support they received from the Neologue community and even to an extent from the Orthodox was grudging and minimal. Fortunately, many Slovak Jews had relatives who helped, and the Polish Jews were sometimes helped, though again grudgingly in many cases, by the official Polish Diaspora in Hungary—Hungary had given refuge to Polish escapees from German-occupied Poland, in line with the traditional friendship that existed between Hungary and Poland.

One of the most contested questions, which has a direct implication for our theme, has been, Did Hungarian Jews "know" about the murder of Jews in other countries—in other words, were they aware of what we call the Holocaust? Three elements of awareness have just been touched on. First, Jews deported in labor battalions to the Ukraine saw what was happening to all Jews there; 5,000 of them came back in the summer of 1943 and presumably told their stories to their families and communities. Hungarian non-Jews, officers and men on leave, also told the folks at home what was happening in the Soviet Union. Second, 2,000 to 2,500 Polish Jews escaped to Hungary between 1942 and 1944. They had seen the Holocaust with their own eyes, and they settled mainly among Jews in the cities and towns. They told their stories to whoever wanted to listen, but many did not want to hear. Third, Slovak Jews escaped in 1942 but maintained contact with Slovakia afterward. In Slovakia the certainty of death following deportation became clear in the summer of 1942. Again, thousands of Slovak Jews in Hungary told their Hungarian Jewish friends and relatives what they knew from their families in Slovakia.

In June and July 1942 and again in December, the Hungarian service of the BBC, which was widely listened to in Jewish and Gentile intellectual and middle-class circles in Hungary, broadcast information about the mass murder of the Jews.[5] In addition, individuals, such as the nun Margit Szlachta, who went to Rome in late 1942 to tell the Vatican that the Jews were being murdered, spread the story among their friends. We should not forget, of course, the impact of the Kamenets-Podolskiy massacres on Hungarian Jews. The fact that these Jews had been killed was common knowledge, and the idea that deportation meant death really started from there.

Information regarding the fate of the Jews in Nazi-occupied Europe was not lacking before March 1944, then. One very interesting piece of evidence is supplied by a Hungarian writer who, in the winter of 1942–43, met with Kasztner (and Joel Brand, an important member of Kasztner's committee) in the presence of two refugees from Slovakia, who recounted the fate of Slovak Jews who "had been deported and murdered by the Germans. We were not surprised, since we had already heard much about the massacres from Hungarian soldiers and Jewish conscripts back from the Eastern front." The writer had heard the same from refugees leaving Central Europe and Poland and from the BBC and the broadcasts by the world-famous anti-Nazi German author Thomas Mann. "No Hungarian Jews, not even in the most remote village, could be unaware of the menace."[6]

The question, however, is whether this information was internalized and turned into knowledge. It is quite likely that in villages and among uneducated people in towns the information would have been either unavailable or hazy; but it is difficult to believe that it did not reach most Hungarian Jews. Because it was life-threatening, it was largely rejected. In the Kasztner trial in Israel, Kasztner was accused of not providing Hungarian Jews with the information about Poland that he possessed. A chief answer to that charge surely is that Kasztner was not the only one who had that information—most Hungarian Jews had it, too, but they did not believe it, or refused to act on it, or did not see any way to act on it. Kasztner himself was an unknown person from the recently acquired territories; not only did he have no way of transmitting whatever information he had to the Jews of Hungary, but even had he been able to pass it on, his warnings would hardly have been heeded: he had no authority in Hungary.

In addition, we have to remember that the Nazis and their Hungarian allies practiced deception with real virtuosity. They told people before deportation that they would be shipped to work camps in Germany and even provided them with the names of these supposed camps; because there was nowhere to run and their good Hungarian neighbors had absolutely no interest in their fate, they were conditioned to believe these stories. The lies and the conditioning to accept the lies were another major factor that prevented the information they had from turning into active knowledge.[7] There was (and is), however, an understandable tendency on the part of survivors and their kin to blame external factors for their reactions in the face of the deportations and to deny that they had the knowledge of mass murder.

Rudolf Kasztner (born in 1906) was a journalist from Cluj (Kolosvar in Hungarian) in northern Transylvania, a member of the center-left Zionist group Ihud, the Diaspora extension of the Palestine Jewish Labor Party known as Mapai. Before the annexation of Transylvania by Hungary in 1940, Kasztner had been a parliamentary correspondent in Bucharest, and after he became a Hungarian citizen, he moved to Budapest. There he found a very weak Hungarian Zionist movement—in contrast to the strong Zionist presence in Romania—and within it an even weaker Ihud component. Hungarian Zionists probably did not account for more than 5 percent of Hungarian Jews, the reason being that, as we have seen, most Hungarian Jews were patriotic Hungarians, whereas the Zionists preached that the Jews were a nation and should go to Palestine. Theodor Herzl, the founder of modern Zionism, had been a Hungarian Jew, but that did not rub off on his community. When he came to Budapest, Kasztner nevertheless found some other spirits like him, among them an adventurer by the name of Joel Brand.

Brand was born in 1906, also in Transylvania (in Naszod). He was educated in Erfurt, Germany, where his family had moved in 1910 or 1911. Later he became a communist agent, working for the Comintern as a sailor and an odd-job man in the Americas and the tropics. He became a middle-rank communist functionary in Thuringia and was arrested when the Nazis came to power. Released in 1934, probably because of his foreign citizenship, he returned to Transylvania, then settled in Budapest. There he became a Zionist, joining a Mapai (Ihud)–controlled youth movement. He tried to train for emigration to Palestine, but he was not of the stuff that pioneers are made: he had a restless nature, loved the city, with its cafés and bars, and was known to drink.

To obtain a certificate of immigration into Palestine, he contracted a fictional marriage in 1935, but the marriage became a real one. Hansi Hartmann, his wife, opened a small glove factory, for which Brand was the commercial representative. Spending his time in cafés and clubs, he made the acquaintance of Joszef Krem, a Hungarian espionage agent who was eager to make some money. When the Kamenets-Podolskiy deportations involved Hansi Brand's sister, Brand turned to Krem, who for a fairly large sum of money got Brand's relatives back. Brand then contacted other families, and their relatives were also brought back by Krem, again for money. From then on, Brand became actively involved in smuggling and aid to refugees. He joined Kasztner and Samuel Springmann, another center-left Zionist and the owner of a jewelry shop, who began to function as the treasurer of the group. In December 1941, Kasztner tried to organize a refugee aid group with the help of Hungarian Social Democrats, but the non-Jews were not interested. He tried and failed again in the autumn of 1943, when he met with some Social Democratic representatives, such as Illes Monus, editor of the party newspaper *Nepszava*. But the Socialists were not willing to endanger themselves for the sake of the Jews.[8]

From a Hungarian Jewish point of view, people like Kasztner and Brand were marginal—they were totally unknown in the community, and they were foreigners. Springmann, for instance, was a Polish Jew. In addition, they were Zionists. It was a different story when Otto Komoly, a respected Budapest engineer, reserve officer, and war veteran, became the chairman and the rallying point of the group. By early 1943, the Aid and Rescue Committee had been organized; known by its Hebrew name of Va'adat Ezrah Vehatzalah, it included representatives of other Zionist groups—Komoly himself, a General Zionist (member of the Liberal Zionist Party), Moshe Krausz and Eugen Frankel, who were religious Zionists, and Ernst (Ernö) Szilagyi, representing the left-wing Hashomer Hatzair.

In October 1942, Springmann got in touch with Bandi (Andor, Antal) Grosz. When the Istanbul JA representatives asked the Budapest Zionists to establish an aid committee, Grosz became the main courier, visiting Istanbul as an official of the Hungarian Danube Navigation Company. It was Grosz, apparently, who was the bridge between the Vaada, as we shall call the Hungarian Aid and Rescue Committee, and the Abwehr group in Budapest. The other chief courier was "Josi" or "Josko" (Josef) Wieninger or Winninger (alias Duftel), who for money even took letters and funds to Polish ghettoes. The chief contact with the Abwehr people was Brand, who became responsible for rescue work from Poland and Slovakia.

According to Brand, the Abwehr asked him to transmit to the Palestinian Zionist emissaries in Istanbul a list of anti-Nazi Germans, presumably so it would reach the Western Allies.[9] While this may or may not be a Brand fantasy, there is no doubt that the connection was fruitful for both sides: Winninger, and probably Grosz and Erich Wehner (Eric Popescu) as well, photocopied the letters that went both ways and transmitted them to the Vienna Ast. As long as the Abwehr was an independent organization run by opponents of the regime, there was relative security, but things turned sour when the Abwehr was taken over by the SD. The Abwehr group in Budapest was, in the main, a bunch of greedy agents, who lined their pockets but whose only contact with the West through Istanbul was Grosz—the other two apparently knew only the JA emissaries. Grosz, as we have seen, became a U.S. agent and was also in touch with the British and the Polish intelligence in Istanbul.

On March 14, Winninger told Brand that the Germans were about to occupy Hungary. The information was brought to the JA in Istanbul on the seventeenth. But it was too late. On March 19, a Sunday, relatively weak German forces occupied Hungary. There was no resistance.

Operation Margarethe, the German occupation of Hungary, was connected with the Hungarian treatment of the Jews, although that was not the prime cause of the occupation. On March 17–18, Hitler had summoned Horthy to a series of discussions at Klessheim castle in Austria. The main point discussed was the participation of Hungary in the anti-Soviet campaign and the knowledge that the Germans had of Hungarian attempts to negotiate a separate peace with the West. But the Jewish question occupied an important part of Hitler's attention. It was clear to him that the influence of the Jews was anti-German and that it was growing. Hungary would have to deal radically with its Jews. The broad hint was made by Ribbentrop that in Poland the Jews were being killed. Horthy was forced to agree to an occupation of Hungary, and his new Prime Minister, Döme Sztojay, was certain to introduce antisemitic measures. Horthy probably did not foresee what actually happened, though it is highly doubtful whether he would have resisted it even had he known all the consequences. Together with the SS troops came Eichmann's Sondereinsatzkommando (Special Action Commando), whose task it was to deport Hungarian Jewry to its death. Two new undersecretaries in the Ministry of the Interior headed by Andor Jaross, Laszlo Endre, and Laszlo Baky, sympathizers with Szalasi's Arrow Cross, facilitated Eichmann's task.

Let me mention here that the occupation of Hungary came six weeks after Hitler had ordered the firing of Canaris (February 1944) and the absorption of the Abwehr into the SD, a development that appreciably strengthened Himmler's position in the Reich. This change was in process just as the occupation of Hungary was effected—by SS troops. The hierarchy set up by the German bureaucracy in Hungary reflected these facts. The German ambassador and plenipotentiary was Edmund Veesenmayer, an ardent Nazi who held a high rank in the SS and who had quarreled with Ribbentrop—in fact, he had resigned and had been called back by Ribbentrop—but was on good terms with Himmler. The commander of the SS security organs in Hungary was Otto Winkelmann, and the RSHA officers spread out, thinly but effectively, all over Hungary; they were coordinated on Jewish matters by Theodor Horst Grell, who was attached to Veesenmayer's official diplomatic representation. Amt IV of RSHA, the Gestapo, was represented by a number of officers, but Eichmann was independent of most of them, reporting directly to Müller and probably to Himmler as well when necessary. Another very important representative of the RSHA was the head of the SD (Amt VI) in Budapest, Gerhard Clages, who held the same rank as Eichmann (*Obersturmbannführer*—lieutenant colonel).

When the Germans came, Winninger quickly abducted Brand and hid him in the apartment of Rudolf (Rudi) Scholz, or Schulz, of the Abwehr, so the SS could not get at him.[10] Grosz was not that lucky; he was picked up and brought to the SD in Budapest. However, he later joined Brand at Scholz's. Winninger used the opportunity to "liberate" some money ($8,000 or $20,000, depending on the source) and valuables from Brand.

Eichmann's unit included Wisliceny, who had come from Slovakia equipped with letters from Weissmandel (in the name of the Working Group) to three individuals in Budapest who were thought to have enough guts and devotion to negotiate with the SS as the Slovak group had done. The three individuals were Freudiger, whom Weissmandel must have thought to be the best representative of the Orthodox camp; Baroness Edith Weiss, an influential member of the richest and economically most important Jewish family in Hungary, who might be of help on the Liberal side; and Rudolf-Reszoe

Kasztner, to represent the small Zionist group, apparently at the suggestion
of the Slovak Zionists. But Edith Weiss was in hiding; and Freudiger turned
out to be a frightened man who wanted to save his own skin and his immediate family and Orthodox friends. Freudiger approached Wisliceny two days
after the occupation of Budapest in order to intervene in favor of his brother
who had been arrested. He did not try to do anything else except intervene in
favor of a group of Orthodox Jews whom he boarded on the "Kasztner train"
(see below), and in August he managed to flee to Romania with his friends
and family after bribing Wisliceny and a Romanian representative in
Budapest. There remained Kasztner.

On March 21 the Germans forced the Jews to establish a Judenrat for
Budapest, which in German eyes represented all the Jews in the country—
just as the Amsterdam Judenrat represented all Jews in Holland. At its head
was Samu Stern, and in it were representatives of Neologue and Orthodox
trends, assimilationists, and later also converted Jews. Kasztner was not then
or ever afterward a member of the Judenrat; his nonmembership was a matter of principle but was also because he represented a tiny minority. There
was a nominal representative of the Zionists on the Judenrat, however;
Komoly joined a completely different Judenrat in late October 1944.

Much of the initiative in the persecution came from the Hungarians, so
Eichmann did not have to do much pushing at all. On March 29, Jaross suggested the introduction of a yellow badge for Jews, and this became law on
April 7. On April 4, ghettoization plans were prepared, and on the seventh
the instructions were sent out to the provinces.

German industry was starved of workers. Germans were being recruited
into the Army because of the very heavy losses on the Russian front. Labor
tsar Fritz Sauckel was recruiting workers from all over Nazi Europe, by persuasion at first, but then mostly by force. Millions of workers were forced
into Germany, and they were treated in accordance with their origins: the
Ostarbeiter (Eastern workers) from the Soviet territories were treated worst,
then came the Poles, then the others. But all this recruitment was insufficient. In the spring of 1944, Hitler himself was involved in consultations
regarding a radical increase in aircraft production. Germany was developing
jet fighters and missiles, as well as trying to replace the losses incurred in
defending Germany from ever heavier attacks by Anglo–American bombers.
The so-called *Jäger* plan for aircraft production and related war matériel was
developed, which required more unskilled and semiskilled workers. The idea
of demanding 50,000, then 100,000 Jewish workers from Hungary arose. The
SS policy of murder and the demand for Jewish labor coalesced, but they
appear to have been adopted separately as far as Hungary was concerned.
The SS plan was the application of the "Final Solution" to Hungary, whereas
the Jäger demand for workers was a temporary need. The two accidentally

came together. From the Nazi point of view, the coalescence helped, because it made a good excuse to demand of the Hungarian government, especially Horthy, an agreement to the deportation of Jews: 100,000 Jews and their families, or, in other words, all of Hungarian Jewry, would be deported for labor in Germany. The physically fit would become slave labor; the rest would be murdered.

On April 28 the first train with Hungarian Jews left for Auschwitz; large-scale deportations started on May 14. The first regions from which the Jews were deported were the newly acquired territories of the PKR and Transylvania. The Russian advance was threatening Hungary in these areas, and military exigencies could be summoned as excuses for the horrors that were now taking place. We should remember how sudden it all was. On March 18, Jews were Hungarian citizens, though of a lesser sort, living in relatively free surroundings and going about their everyday business; four weeks later—everywhere but in Budapest—they were being squeezed into temporary ghettoes, usually abandoned quarries or brick factories, without sufficient food, in overcrowded and unsanitary conditions, sometimes with no roof over their heads. Four weeks after that they were searched, abused, humiliated, beaten, and forced into locked cattle cars on the way to Auschwitz. This was done not by German troops but by Hungarian gendarmes under very light but effective supervision by Eichmann's people, including Wisliceny.

Between May 14 and July 7, according to German figures, 437,000 Jews were deported to Auschwitz. What was left were the 250,000 Budapest Jews, the men in the labor battalions, and converts trying to escape deportation by hiding as Christians. Of those deported to Auschwitz, about a fourth were either introduced into the Auschwitz concentration camp or, more usually, sent to Germany to work there in armament factories. The exact number cannot be stated, but after the war a total of 72,000 Jews returned from German camps, including those who had been in the labor battalions. If at least 50 percent had died in the camps and on the death marches at the end of the war, and if a proportion of these people had been in labor battalions, then the probable number of those selected for work was about 100,000–110,000, or 25 percent of those deported. This figure would also accord with the postwar testimonies of Rudolf Hoess, the commander of Auschwitz. The other three-fourths were murdered: children, older people, mothers with children, and many men were gassed and cremated, and their ashes were strewn over the grounds at Auschwitz.

The official Judenrat leaders were of the upper-middle-class Jewish elite; they were loyal and law-abiding Hungarian citizens whose life-styles and views made them utterly unprepared for the calamity. They did have information—not only in the many ways already described but also through the so-called Auschwitz protocols. Vrba and Wetzler, two Auschwitz inmates, fled from Auschwitz on April 7, and their report was written up a couple of weeks later. It must have arrived in Budapest, perhaps through Kasztner, at the end of April, and been handed over to leading members of the Judenrat. But people like Stern were completely helpless. They tried to turn to "their" government, especially to Horthy himself. Horthy did not want to intervene or help, and the real power, in any case, was not in his hands. He undoubtedly could have made a stand, but he was politically, temperamentally, and intellectually incapable of such a thing at the crucial time. Abandoned by the government, handed over to the mercies of the SS, unaccustomed to and incapable of illegal work, the Judenrat obeyed the Nazis, though small attempts at circumventing Nazi orders are recorded.

There can be no doubt that members of the Hungarian government knew, by and large, what the fate awaiting the Jews in Poland was. They had obtained their information from the same sources as the Jews, and many of the Hungarian perpetrators were, moreover, in close touch with the Germans throughout the whole period. At first they probably did not know the precise details of what was happening in Auschwitz, but in May and June a number of people received copies of the Vrba-Wetzler protocols, apparently mainly via Joszef Elias, head of the Jo Pasztor Misszio, the Good Shepherd Mission, a Protestant missionary organization. He says that he received the protocols from one Geza Soos, a Hungarian Foreign Ministry official who ran a small liberal resistance group. Soos must have received the document from Kasztner or Komoly, because Elias claims that he got it in late April or early May, and according to one version Kasztner was in Bratislava in late April when it was given to him. Elias's secretary, Maria Szekely, translated the document into Hungarian, and six copies were prepared. Horthy's daughter-in-law received one, and the others were given to Cardinal Justinian Seredi, Bishop Laszlo Ravasz of the Calvinist Church, Bishop Sandor Raffay of the Lutherans, Komoly, and Soos himself. They certainly did not keep the information to themselves. In addition, Ernö Petö, a prominent Judenrat member, claimed that he gave the protocols in Hungarian to Horthy's son, to the papal nuntius, Angelo Rotta, and to Finance Minister Lajos Remenyi-Schneller. They all received the copies before the deportations started.[11]

The Auschwitz protocols certainly had an immediate impact. Late in June, Horthy and his gang may possibly have acknowledged to themselves that Hungarians had been the active element in sending hundreds of thousands of Hungarian citizens to gas chambers. They began to feel the effect of pressure organized by Roosevelt's War Refugee Board (WRB).[12] Jewish organizations also became very active in trying to help their Hungarian brothers and sisters.

All this activity caused the eruption of neutral and Allied intervention, direct and indirect, which ultimately caused the cessation of the deportations. On June 26 a Council of Ministers meeting took place which was the start of

the turnabout. At that meeting the Hungarians decided to approve the emigration of 7,800 Jews. Some 7,000 of them had Palestine papers arranged
through Swiss mediation, and some had Swedish and other protection
papers. The Germans made a show of agreeing to the idea of limited Jewish
emigration, because they saw in it a way of compelling the Hungarians to
agree to the deportation of the rest of Hungarian Jewry in return for a
promise—which would be kept or not—to let some Jews out.

Moshe Krausz, head of the Palestine Office dispensing Palestine immigration certificates, saw the German agreement as a great victory, as support for
his opposition to the Kasztner line of negotiations with the Germans. Krausz,
who had found refuge with the Swiss legation, which represented British
interests in Hungary, very cleverly turned the 7,800 supposed individual exit
permits, which had not yet been given by the Germans, into permits for
7,800 families, or about 40,000 potential emigrants. He persuaded the Swiss,
under Vice-Consul Charles Lutz, to issue appropriate protection documents,
of the kind that later were copied by Raoul Wallenberg for the Swedes and by
other neutrals for smaller numbers of Jews. In the end, as we shall see, there
was no emigration, but others got hold of the idea of issuing protection
papers and turned it into a means of saving large numbers of Budapest Jews.

What were the options that Hungarian Jews had, and what specifically
were the options of the Vaada?

The Vaada was under no illusions about Nazi intentions. Within the
group, a difference came to be felt between the "adults"—youngish profes-
sionals like Komoly and Kasztner—and those in the Zionist youth movements. In Hungary the main youth movements were Hashomer Hatzair;
Maccabi Hatzair, which had developed from a sports organization; Bnei
Akiva, the religious youth movement; Noar Tzioni, a more liberal centrist
group; and Dror, another left-wing group. These groups swiftly developed
liaisons, and they generally took a common stand on issues. The total membership was very small: children up to sixteen years of age no longer counted,
and most of the young men over eighteen were recruited into the labor battalions. The youth movements would probably have collapsed had there not
been an influx from Slovakia, and, to a small extent, from Poland, that provided leadership. Even so, the total number of members cannot have been
larger than 400–500. The point, however, is that these young people were
determined and clear-sighted, and they quickly came to the conclusion that
their own adult leadership was not going anywhere with its policies. A difference, though not a split, developed between the two groups, with the youth
movements advocating illegal rescue work and the Vaada trying the negotiation method.

At first, while the deportations threatened to take place and then did, the
two groups combined to warn the provincial communities that were being

ghettoized of the mortal danger they were in. They persuaded the Judenrat to
open a special department for the provinces and sent out youth movement
members, usually to the communities from which they originated. Essentially, what had happened in Slovakia repeated itself here: in all cases without
exception, the message was rejected by the local leadership. Calls to resist or
flee went unheeded; even family members of the emissaries often refused to
be saved by fleeing to Budapest. In Ungvar (Uzhorod, today Uzgorod), the
capital of the PKR, a letter arrived from Weissmandel, directed to his Orthodox friends but also to the whole community, urging them to resist deportation or to flee, and that, too, went unheeded.[13] In most communities, calls for
resistance or flight were, it must be admitted, impossible to obey. There
really was nowhere to hide in the open Hungarian plains, and the Gentile
neighbors were mostly hostile or cowed, or both. The churches were violently and murderously antisemitic;[14] the greed of the neighbors who hoped
to loot Jewish property once the owners were gone was overwhelming. To
the question that was asked in 1954 of Kasztner—Why did you not warn the
Jews? the first answer was that most of them already had the information, and
the second answer should have been—yes, a serious attempt was made, and
it failed. People did not want to listen. But Kasztner, unaccountably, did not
say this in 1954.

The option of flight from Hungary seemingly existed. The youth movements, with the agreement of the Vaada, tried the borders to Yugoslavia and
Romania. Joel Brand and two youth movement members (Yitzhak Kanal and
Perets Revesz) wrote to Istanbul in early January 1944 discussing these
options, including hiding in the Carpathian mountains, that is, in the PKR,
which could have been a solution for a few hardened youth.[15] Yugoslavia was
German occupied, but the Tito partisans were gaining ground, and attempts
were made to find a way to reach them. Almost all these failed, and the people who tried were mostly caught or died in the attempt. No more than fifty
to seventy youths made it through. The Germans were guarding the
approaches to partisan territory very closely indeed. Hungarian Jews also
faced language barriers and the understandable distrust that the partisans had
of all Hungarians.

Romania was easier to cross into, both because the German military presence was less prevalent and because a large Jewish community on the other
side extended a helping hand. The distance between Cluj and the Romanian
border was only ten miles, and in Romania lay Turdea, where an unusual
couple of young men were doing all they could to prepare a friendly reception. Aryeh Hirsch, of the Zionist Noar Tzioni movement, and Finkelstein,
the local Orthodox activist, joined to make the reception possible, mainly by
bribing local officials and preparing train rides to Bucharest. Cluj was indeed
an obvious place from which to flee, because of its proximity to the Romanian

border. The account of one Rabbi Moshe Weinberger (Carmilly) that he tried
to rescue numbers of Cluj Jews by fleeing across the border is apocryphal. In
the end, only a small number of Cluj Jews tried to save themselves by crossing the border, despite the fact that the situation in Hungary was obviously
one of great danger.[16]

After the war, one of the main accusations against Kasztner was this: his
own community in Cluj would have fled en masse to Romania if only he had
given a warning. Quite apart from the ease with which the Hungarians and
the Germans could have stopped a mass flight is the fact that there is evidence of Polish Jews who found refuge in Cluj and who were telling their stories to anyone who would listen. The problem was that people are disinclined
to listen to life-threatening stories. The Cluj situation also shows, however,
how impossible it was to talk of a mass flight of Jews from places that were
farther from the border. The youth movements and the ultraorthodox in
Budapest did indeed try group escapes, and we have a fairly accurate description of the effort from the vantage point of the youth movements. In the end,
4,000–4,500 Jews managed to cross illegally, mostly helped by *passeurs*.
Many others were caught and deported to Poland. The Romanian government pretended to guard its frontier and execute all those who crossed; but
its attitude became more and more lenient, probably because the WRB intervened through the International Red Cross. The Romanians responded on
June 2, 1944, to the WRB that they had to make public declarations threatening Jews who crossed the border with death but that "their safety would be
looked after by the Rumanians."[17] In August 1944, Romania switched sides
and joined the Allies.

Let us return to the options of the Vaada: they tried to warn Jews, and they
tried to organize flight through the youth movements affiliated with them.
There was a third option—namely, to emulate the Warsaw Jews and stage an
uprising. Indeed, this was what the Istanbul emissaries told their Hungarian
friends to do. In December 1943, Kasztner met with the youth movements
and counseled them to obtain weapons, build bunkers, and prepare false
papers. The members of Bnei Akiva, the religious movement, were the only
ones who did not take his recommendations seriously, but the others tried.
The Noar Tzioni group (center-liberal), under the influence of their Polish
comrades, prepared a series of bunkers. A renowned resistance fighter who
had escaped to Hungary from the Bedzin ghetto in Poland, Hayka Klinger of
Hashomer Hatzair, met with the leadership of the youth movements after her
arrival on January 19, 1944. A commander was nominated, Moshe Schweiger
of the Vaada, and some arms were accumulated and hidden.[18] Places of refuge
and bunkers were prepared.

When the Vaada surveyed what it could do, on the eve of the German
occupation, the results were pitiful. Its youth movement component num-

bered a few hundred at most. Hungarian Jewry was totally unprepared for an armed struggle. Most of the young men were in labor battalions; in addition, as we have seen, they were mostly loyal citizens, and the fight would have been in large measure against Hungarian gendarmes. There was no Hungarian Jewish underground organization, nor was there a Hungarian antifascist underground to speak of, certainly not one that would have joined in an uprising. One practical proposition, submitted to the Judenrat by Imre Varga, a physician and an ex-officer, a convert to Judaism, was to blow up a center of German administration in Budapest. When his proposal was rejected, he committed suicide.[19]

Another important point perhaps was that—unlike in Warsaw, where the Jews had been closed within a ghetto, concentrated in a collective imposed from above—Budapest Jews were living in different parts of the city.

Finally, there was no time. Everything happened at breakneck speed, and an underground organization preparing a rebellion needed time. The resistance option was rejected with regret, not only by the Vaada but by the youth movements as well. Rescue, not resistance, was the watchword that both components accepted. On April 3, Schweiger was arrested; later he was shipped to Mauthausen. Whether he was picked up accidentally or whether he was a marked man because the Abwehr had read the correspondence between Istanbul and Budapest cannot be established. The resistance option was no option at all.

If the Vaada wanted to save all or at least many of the Hungarian Jews, the alternatives of hiding, flight, and resistance had to be ruled out. I have already mentioned the absence of a Hungarian antifascist underground. There were opposition groups, to be sure, such as the political leadership of the Small-holders Party, the Social Democrats, and two rival communist groups. None of these went beyond the talking stage, or at most the stage of very minor attempts at sabotage. The heroic Hungarian antifascist underground is a fig-ment of the postwar Hungarian imagination. In fact, toward the end of the fighting in Budapest even the communists depended on the Zionist youth movements for forged documents. There was no organized Hungarian resis-tance to turn to.

These, then, were the options that had to be discounted. What remained? Two choices, basically: either despair and attempts to save individuals, as many of them as possible, or negotiations with the murderers. At a later stage, after the ascent to power of Szalasi's fascist regime on October 15, 1944, the youth movements added another realistic option: saving large num-bers of Budapest Jews by illegal means and by collaboration with the neutral diplomats.

What the Vaada did was negotiate, on the strength of the letter that Wis-liceny had brought with him from Bratislava. Not that negotiation was accepted unanimously—far from it. Moshe Krausz and, to an extent, Ernst Szilagyi opposed the very idea of dealing with the Nazis.[20] Krausz suggested turning to the Hungarians and to the neutrals and considered Kasztner a traitor. He himself fled to the safety of the Swiss legation, where he established an excellent relationship with Charles Lutz, the Swiss vice-consul. Lutz had served as a Swiss diplomatic representative in Tel Aviv before the war and was very friendly toward the Zionist enterprise. The results of this contact made themselves felt later on, but at the moment, in the spring of 1944, Krausz's line was the tangible expression of a deep-seated enmity between himself, on the one hand, and Kasztner and Komoly, on the other hand. Krausz, who was the head of the Palestine Office charged with allocating the few legal certificates for Palestine that the JA managed to send to Budapest prior to the German occupation, was accused of not having distributed them justly or properly; and although with the Germans in Hungary the emigration possibilities had disappeared, the old rancor was still there.

Any attempt to approach Hungarian politicians had to be made by Komoly, the Hungarian Jew. Kasztner began to concentrate on the "German line," as it was known internally. Probably on March 24 he and Brand met with Wisliceny, Capt. Erich Klausnitzer of the Abwehr, and the other Abwehr people who had mediated the contact between them and who had demanded payment for that service.[21] Klausnitzer appears immediately afterward as part of the SD outfit, and this may be of considerable significance. Kasztner and Brand offered $2 million—the sum that they understood had been talked about in the Europa Plan negotiations—for a guarantee that the Hungarian Jews would not be ghettoized or deported, and they offered $200,000 as a down payment, again on the Slovak precedent. Wisliceny promised that there would be no deportations but doubted whether $2 million would suffice. The inducement was that the money, Kasztner said, would come from abroad, after the major Jewish organizations had been apprised of the talks. Throughout the whole period Kasztner presented himself as the JDC representative without any basis for doing so. Wisliceny also offered to discuss large-scale emigration, though he rejected a request for the immigration of a relatively small number of people to Palestine.[22] Right afterward, Kasztner and Brand proposed an emigration plan for 150,000–160,000 people; the number was based on their knowledge that the JA still had about 30,000 immigration certificates coming to it in accordance with the White Paper of 1939. In their minds they turned these individual certificates into certificates for heads of families, multiplied the result by five, and derived a fairly large figure. This proposal is rather important because Kasztner was accused, after the war, of trying to save just a few hundred Zionists.[23]

The same day, Brand says, Kasztner, Komoly, Szilagyi, and Rosenfeld, another minor Zionist leader, met to discuss what to do next. They saw that they should concentrate the affairs of the official Zionist organization in their hands and had an appropriate resolution passed. Then they decided that Komoly would try to contact the Hungarians, and Kasztner would negotiate with the Germans. But, Brand says, the Hungarians did not agree to any talks.[24]

The first $200,000 was supposed to have been paid on April 9, but "only" $92,000 was available, in Hungarian pengö supplied by the Judenrat, whom Kasztner had informed of the situation.[25] Wisliceny was no longer present, and instead, Otto Hunsche and Hermann Krumey of Eichmann's staff were there to receive the money. On April 21, another $77,000 was paid, and Hunsche was indignant at the lack of seriousness on the part of the Jews. They had not fulfilled their promise; the Nazis, on the other hand, were gentlemen. Dr. Josef Schmidt (or Schmied),[26] another member of the Abwehr team, added that deportations were now unavoidable but that 600 people might be able to emigrate. A totally ineffective move appears to have been made by the WRB through Switzerland to support this contact; the interesting thing is, however, that the WRB made a point of mentioning the effort, although in making it, the board was in effect sanctioning ransom negotiations.[27]

This first stage in the negotiations seems to have been just another extortion attempt. From later developments it becomes apparent that Eichmann reported to Winkelmann but that there was little inclination to follow up on this form of contact.

On April 16 or 25, according to Brand, Eichmann summoned him to his headquarters on the Schwabenberg in Budapest and there offered him the famous "trucks for blood" proposal.[28] Or did he? What he apparently said was that he would be prepared to release one million Jews in return for an appropriate payment in kind or otherwise. The trucks, as well as other items, such as tea, coffee, and soap, came up only as examples of the kind of things the Nazis might request. Krumey, Eichmann's underling, spoke to Brand about machine tools, leather, and other commodities. But the demands soon solidified into 10,000 trucks and quantities of consumer staples. Brand was asked where he wanted to go to offer the proposal to the Jews and the Allies, and he chose Istanbul.

Why did Eichmann choose Brand over Kasztner? Did he know that there were differences between them? We know today that there certainly were, and Kasztner said in his final postwar report that "the question of whether sending another person might not have influenced the outcome of the Istanbul negotiations will remain unanswered."[29] The choice of the adventurous rescuer over the experienced politician-journalist may have been influenced by the fact that the Nazis knew something about Brand from his previous incarnation—or it may have been purely fortuitous.

For what followed we only have one testimony, namely, that of Kurt

Becher. According to Becher, who was the person responsible for the economic exploitation of the Jews, either Eichmann or his nominal superior, Winkelmann, asked him to check these Jewish offers. Becher says the request came two weeks before Brand left for Istanbul. He says that he went to see Himmler at Salzburg on another Jewish matter—the Manfred Weiss affair (see below)—and told him what he had heard from Winkelmann and Eichmann—that the Jews had offered goods, mainly 10,000 trucks—and Becher asked him for permission to have Brand go to Istanbul. Himmler agreed and charged Becher with going back to Budapest and finding out more about these possibilities.[30]

The sequence is not very clear, because it is highly unlikely that Eichmann offered to send Brand to Turkey or talked about the trucks himself without acquiring authorization from someone higher up, presumably Himmler. Nevertheless, the likelihood that Becher, who handled economic matters, talked to Himmler about sending someone to Istanbul to see whether a deal was possible is reasonably high.

In any case, Eichmann met Brand again a few days after the first meeting. From Brand's account it seems that Veesenmayer and Winkelmann were present, certainly the former. That would give the meeting extraordinary importance, because it would link other elements of the SS with the Eichmann offer.[31] A few days later, most likely on May 8, Eichmann again summoned Brand, and gave him, to his consternation, $32,750 and a bundle of letters from Switzerland.[32] These things had been sent by Saly Mayer in Switzerland to the Swedish embassy for the Vaada, but the SS had forced Grosz to go there and obtain it under false pretenses, or possibly Grosz had had the idea of fetching the money and ingratiating himself with the SS by delivering it to them. The Nazi coup was repeated on May 14, when, according to Brand's testimony, Clages handed Brand $50,000 and SFR 270,000, together with letters calling on the Jews to get in touch with underground Hungarian organizations. These amounts raise some questions, because the total sum transferred by Mayer to Hungary in April and May did not exceed $86,000. But we know by now that Brand's testimonies are often contradictory.[33]

At this meeting, too, Gerhard Clages of the SD, Eichmann's rival, was present—another indication of the broader basis of the contacts with the SS. Eichmann offered to blow up Auschwitz and free the first "ten, twenty, fifty thousand Jews" after receiving information from Istanbul that agreement had been reached in principle, or so Brand put it in his June 22 interview with the U.S. emissary Ira Hirschmann (see below). In Brand's postwar book and in the Kasztner trial in 1954, this offer became a promise to free 100,000 Jews. Eichmann also added that the trucks should be properly winterized and that they would not be used against the West.[34] Eichmann himself—in the interview that he granted to the Dutch journalist Stassen prior to his capture by the Israelis—said that the "basic objective of Reichsführer Himmler [was] to arrange if possible for a million Jews to go free in exchange for 10,000 winterized trucks, with trailers, for use against the Russians on the Eastern Front. . . . I said at the time, '[W]hen the winterized trucks with trailers are here, the liquidation machine in Auschwitz will be stopped.'"[35] It is dangerous to place any credence in Eichmann, but something of the sort must have been said. Whether that was Himmler's basic objective may be doubted.

A problem arises as to whether Eichmann told Brand to return by a specific date. Apparently he said that Brand should return soon, and he possibly mentioned two or three weeks. But Brand's testimony is contradictory on this very important point, and on one occasion (the June 22 interview with Ira Hirschmann), he declared that Eichmann "said I could take my time if I saw that I had possibilities of success."[36] In his interrogation, he said that the discussion with Eichmann took place at their last meeting, on May 16, at which Winkelmann and Veesenmayer were—again?—present. There Brand said he would need about a week or two, unless he had to go to Palestine. Eichmann replied, "Good. But be as quick as possible."[37]

Again, Brand's testimony is questionable in detail. It does not make much sense to claim that Winkelmann and Veesenmayer were present at two meetings. Brand mentions that Becher was present at one of the meetings, the first, and then corrects himself and says that possibly he was present at the second meeting as well. Becher himself implies that he was present at all the decisive meetings with Brand.[38] It can probably be assumed that Veesenmayer, plausibly also Winkelmann, was present at one meeting at least, and Becher at perhaps two or three.[39]

Obersturmbannführer Kurt A. Becher arrived in Hungary in March 1944, ostensibly to buy horses. What kind of horses he bought will be discussed later, but for the moment it is important to note that Himmler involved three of his men, all of the same rank, in the Brand negotiations: Eichmann, whose job it was to send the Jews to their deaths; Clages, the intelligence officer whose task it was to reach the West; and Becher, who had to see to it that the SS did not lose any money or goods, God forbid. Kasztner put it succinctly: "There was an exemplary collaboration between the various SS organs: the *Judenkommando* ([Eichmann's] Jewish unit) murdered, the economic staff [Becher] cashed in."[40]

Probably around May 7, the SD in Budapest finally decided to liquidate the Abwehr there. The service accused the Abwehr of corruption, and we find internal SS reports that tell a story of interrogations and a clear hint at executions. After Winninger and the others were arrested, Erich Wehner was finally caught late in June. The SD accused all of them of having distributed JDC money from Istanbul to Poland, Vienna, Bratislava, and Budapest. Who gave the SD the necessary inside information about the group?[41] The reader may have guessed who: none other than Bandi Grosz, according to his own admission later in Cairo to his British interrogators. But he was not alone. Grosz apparently told the SD about Brand's contacts with the Abwehr, and Brand was called in to testify as well. He did, meeting Fritz (František) Laufer for the first time on May 1 (or, to put it differently, he was arrested on that date and brought to the SD), and told the SD officers everything they wanted to know. There was a second interrogation of Brand on May 4, and a third around the tenth.[42] Two Abwehr men were taken over by the SD at that point, and both Grosz and Brand testify to their presence at the meetings: they were Erich Klausnitzer, of the Vienna Ast, and Fritz Laufer.[43] One day before Brand left for Istanbul, he again met with Laufer, who asked him how long he would be away, and then said that he would set no time limit but that he (Brand) would have to be as quick as possible.[44] The central position of Laufer in the SD apparatus and in the mission preparations is evident.

Grosz, in the meantime, was being groomed for the other mission to Istanbul, and an unwilling Eichmann, apparently forced by Clages, announced to Brand that Grosz would be going with him. Grosz was told by Clages, Klausnitzer, and Laufer on May 13 and 14—or so he testified in Cairo—to "arrange a meeting in any neutral country between two or three senior German security officers and two or three American officers of equal rank, or as a last resort British officers, in order to negotiate for a separate peace between the Sicherheitsdienst [SD] and the Western Allies." If that failed, he was to arrange a meeting with the British through the mediation of the Zionists in Istanbul. According to Grosz, he was told that his mission was the central one, Brand's the subsidiary one. "Brand's mission was really only a sop to the [German] Foreign Office, and camouflage for the mission with which the SD was contemplating sending Grosz."[45] This makes a great deal of sense: Brand, the ideological Zionist, could hardly be trusted with a complicated intelligence mission. Grosz, precisely because he was a clever, low-grade operative with criminal tendencies, would do what he was told in order to save his skin. He could also be very easily dumped when the need arose. Moreover, Brand apparently accepted this interpretation—implicitly at the time and explicitly after the war. As he put it in his testimony at the Eichmann trial in Jerusalem in 1961: "My impression was . . . that Himmler used the Jews as a bribe, as it were, in order to have a visiting card with which to enter into bigger things. . . . [Eichmann] made it clear to me that the deal originated with Himmler."[46]

In Cairo, Grosz testified that he himself asked Clages "why he, a petty smuggler, should be chosen to do this instead for instance, Herr (Franz) von Papen [the German ambassador to Turkey]." Clages replied that he wanted to negotiate not with diplomats but with military people. The problem was with Ribbentrop's Foreign Office: if Brand was successful and brought trucks, or goods, or money, the Foreign Office could not turn against the SD and complain about the change of policy toward the Jews. Brand's mission, according to Clages, was a cover for the SS, who were moving against Ribbentrop. The main mission was Grosz's. He would have to arrange the required meeting through the Zionists and, failing that, through an American agent in Istanbul by the name of Schwarz.[47]

How do we know that Himmler was the prime mover in the Brand-Grosz story? Simple logic suggests that no one else could have given the orders that resulted in the mission. But we also have direct evidence: a cable from Veesenmayer to the German Foreign Office on July 22, 1944, says explicitly that Brand and Grosz were sent to Turkey on the order of Himmler.[48] Two of the main Nazi figures also testified to Himmler's involvement, though we must be very careful when handling Nazi testimonies. Eichmann said in his interrogation that the order came from Himmler but did not elaborate. Becher was more forthcoming: "So I came into contact with Mr. Joel Brand. . . . Trucks were a big problem. So trucks were discussed, 10,000 trucks that is. There were many discussions. Himmler said to me: 'Take whatever you can from the Jews. Promise them whatever you want. What we will keep is another matter.'"[49] The testimony of Grosz is in many ways proof of the seriousness of his mission and of the personality behind it. One significant expression reported by Grosz in his interrogation was the reference to Himmler as "Heinrich mit [dem] Augenglass [Heinrich with the eyeglass]," a nickname of Himmler's that was current only among SS officers and which shows that Grosz indeed had discussions with men like Clages.

What are we to make of this? Some interpreters of the evidence have argued that the whole thing was a maneuver to outwit the Jews or a trick to sow discord between the West and the Soviets. The first argument is unacceptable because the SS did not need to outwit the powerless and helpless Jews, who in any case knew by that time precisely what was awaiting them— murder. The second point certainly is true, but it has to be seen in a much larger context, which we have already discussed. Another argument is that if the Allies had rejected the proposal, they would have been accused of not saving Jews when it was possible to do so.

The clumsiness of the approach has been a wonderment to all observers. An analysis of the available material leads us to a number of conclusions. For one thing, it seems very obvious that Eichmann was Himmler's reluctant messenger; his own inclination clearly was to carry on with the murders and not be diverted to negotiations with the Jews. On the very day that Brand left for Vienna and Istanbul, Eichmann traveled to Auschwitz to make sure that the Auschwitz commander, Rudolf Hoess, would be ready to receive the first transports, which began leaving Hungary on May 14. Hoess apparently told him that he could not "process" such large numbers all at once, and indeed some of the transports from the PKR had to be guarded for days before they were herded into the gas chambers. As a result, Eichmann ordered that there should be no selections and that all of the arrivals should be gassed.[50]

The presence of Clages and most probably Veesenmayer at some of the Brand-Eichmann meetings makes it apparent that it was Himmler who changed the extortion policy of the first stage into an attempt to get to the West in the second stage. Himmler operated on two parallel lines. One was the open one, through Brand, most probably based on Hitler's assent in December 1942 to liberate Jews for ransom. So, ransom was demanded for the Jews, but what was even more important was the hidden agenda: some kind of negotiations would have to take place if the talks were even to begin. Brand understood this very well. He realized, of course, that the Allies would not send trucks to their enemies, but he also thought that the German desire for a contact with the West should be utilized to call a halt to the murders.

What Himmler wanted to achieve can only be guessed. He would not have committed any of his thoughts to paper. But it should be remembered that the Brand-Grosz mission arrived in Istanbul two months before the assassination attempt on Hitler, and we know already that Himmler was aware of a plot, though he did not know when it would come to fruition and what form it would take. Let us assume that he wanted to prepare for a possible approach to the West if the opposition gained ground or if Hitler became convinced that such an approach should be made. The Abwehr no longer existed, so the SD was given the task of preparing such contacts. Himmler and his goons, even the more intelligent among them, such as Schellenberg, were pretty inexperienced in such matters. They would try to utilize former Abwehr contacts and see where these would lead them.

It may be significant that at precisely the same moment that the Brand-Grosz mission was being discussed, indirect contacts took place in Stockholm between Peter Bruno Kleist, employed by both the Abwehr and the SS (June 28) and the WRB's Iver Olsen, who was also a full-time OSS operative. Nothing came of this offer to save 2,000 Latvian Jews in return for money, but no such clumsy contacts could have been made without Himmler's approval.[51]

Let us reiterate. The Jews, in Himmler's ideology, were the real enemies of Nazism. They ruled the Western Allies and they controlled Bolshevik Russia. They had to be exterminated, but if Germany was in an unfavorable military situation, could this war of annihilation against them not be temporarily suspended in order to gain a breathing space? A basic desire to murder all the Jews does not contravene a readiness to use them, or some of them, as hostages to be exchanged for things that Germany needed in its crisis; the negotiations could be held with either the foreign Jews themselves or with their non-Jewish puppets. There would be plenty of time to return to the murder policy once Germany was on its feet again.

Who could the SD turn to? The destruction of the Abwehr left very few confidential paths open. It had to take into account the bitter enmity between the SS as a whole and Ribbentrop's Foreign Office. Diplomatic channels were practically out of the question. Contacts with the British and U.S. intelligence services—the counterparts of the SD—in Lisbon and Madrid, insofar as they had existed, were now largely lost. There remained Istanbul, where the Zionist emissaries were present as well. A messenger had to be sent who could easily be disavowed, and he had to know how to get in touch with the right people. Brand was useless for this task, but he could be a good cover for the real mission. If that main mission failed, then the Brand proposals could serve as an opening gambit; the SD could see what the reaction to them was. The heavy-handedness of the offer and its obvious attempt to split the Allies were not out of character for Himmler and his friends. We can find plenty of parallels in other areas. Himmler was far from capable of diplomatic niceties, and Schellenberg was not much more than a very intelligent but inexperienced lawyer-policeman, who was tackling a task much too big for him.

If the mission failed, Himmler was covered: the Brand proposals were in line with what Hitler had permitted him to do in December 1942; and the Grosz mission could easily be denied by pointing to the messenger: the lowest character possible, a low-grade Jewish spy. Who would the Nazi elite believe—a convicted Jewish criminal or the loyal Reichsführer? What, however, if it succeeded? Well, in that case intelligence officers of both sides would meet and prepare talks by politicians. If Hitler was still in charge, he would be offered what he may have wanted: a chance of making a separate peace with the West in order to concentrate on the Bolshevik menace. If he was no longer around, Himmler himself would take charge and negotiate for a settlement with the West that would look reasonable by his standards.

Is there, finally, a possibility that Grosz invented all or most of the items included in the offer? Is it possible that he invented the discussions with Clages and Laufer? To be sure, Grosz was a totally unreliable person. However, during his interrogation in Cairo, which is our main source, he was in constant danger of either being returned to Turkey and thence into the hands of the Nazis or facing a firing squad in Cairo as a spy. He did not know what his interrogators knew or did not know, but he had to assume that they had ways of checking what he told them. He may have invented some details or kept others secret to put himself in the best possible light. It is, however, highly unlikely that he invented the main thrust of his mission. The names that he mentioned of SD people whom he met were accurate, and the phrase "Heinrich mit dem Augenglass" shows that his testimony is generally reliable.

To analyze the details of Brand's and Grosz's proposals is much more difficult. From later developments it appears that Himmler really thought he might get trucks or goods of some kind or, as a last resort, money. During the negotiations with the Swiss in 1943 he and Eichmann had insisted on an exchange of four Germans for one Jew; that offer was meant seriously and was no less preposterous than the trucks idea a year later. Himmler's total misunderstanding of Western politics and of the psychological frame of mind of Western military and political leaders was evidenced by the proposal not to use the trucks against the West. He must have thought that an open offer would cut through the diplomatic turbidity and that the West might rise to the bait.

The crucial question is, Would he have let the million Jews go free? In the Cairo interrogations and in the discussions that took place later within the British government an issue came up that may have played a part in Himmler's calculations. If large numbers of Jews had been released—let us say only the first 10,000 or more promised by Eichmann in return for the agreement in principle by the Western Allies—the result would have been, in effect, the stopping of some, if not all, military activity, especially in the air, as these people were being gathered and then transported through Central Europe. Such a ceasefire may well have been one aspect of Himmler's plan. On the other hand, we should remember what Becher and Wisliceny said about Himmler: that he had told them to squeeze as much out of the Jews as possible and that he would later see whether the promises would be kept.

The Grosz mission was much simpler: it consisted only of an invitation to American or British intelligence people to meet with SS officers in a neutral country. The aim behind it, as Grosz stated, was to prepare for negotiations for a separate peace, though the immediate proposition was much more modest: a meeting between intelligence officers of both sides. That would give the Reichsführer—*Reichsheini* as he was called behind his back—a number of options.

This, then, was the content of the Brand-Grosz mission from the German side. What were the motives and arguments on the Hungarian Jewish side?

They were much more obvious and less complicated. It was clear to the Vaada that deportations would begin soon, although the Vaada members, including Brand, were taken aback when they began before Brand had even left Budapest. With all the other options closed, the possibility of receiving outside help as a result of negotiations with the Nazis looked like the last real hope. Brand, as we have noted, did not believe that the Allies would give the Nazis trucks, but the very fact of negotiating might save many lives. The problem with the attitude of Kasztner and his friends, which was not unlike the attitude of the Slovak Jewish leaders, was that they almost believed in the antisemitic notion of a tremendous Jewish power and did believe that Jewish leaders could move freely during the war and would be able to persuade leaders of the Allied nations to do what they wanted to see done. They believed

that American Jewry in particular was tremendously rich and almost all-powerful and that money and goods would not be a problem. They also had an
unlimited trust in the leaders of the Western powers, who would surely do
everything they could to prevent the annihilation of the Jewish people. Isolated in Nazi-occupied Europe, they saw in Roosevelt and Churchill
demigods whose avenging campaign against the Nazi evil would naturally see
in the hunted Jews not only souls to be saved but allies to be supported. Perhaps, in their hopeless situation, they had to believe these things in order to
survive, but when their beliefs had to be tested against the cold realities of a
world war, they proved to be so many illusions.

The Western powers responded in the context of the Normandy invasion,
which occurred in the middle of the events that we are dealing with, on June
6, 1944, and the end phase of the Soviet offensive, which brought the Soviet
armies to the Vistula River in Poland and the Carpathian mountains in the
south, on the edge of Hungary itself. At that crucial moment, to antagonize
the Soviets because of some hare-brained Gestapo plan to ransom Jews was
totally out of the question. On the other hand, Roosevelt had established the
WRB just a few months prior to the Brand mission. If there was a chance of
saving lives through contacts that neither harmed the war effort nor caused
a split in the Allied front, perhaps it could be considered. The hesitancies
and waverings between May 22–25 and July 13 were caused by the unavailability of Grosz's testimony as presented in his interrogation in Cairo. When
his own mission became known in London on July 13, the situation changed
radically.

10

The Mission to Istanbul

On May 17, 1944, Joel Brand and Bandi Grosz left Budapest in an SS car for Vienna. There they spent the night in a hotel reserved for SS personnel. Brand had with him recommendations from the Judenrat and from the Vaada legitimating him as the representative of Hungarian Jewry. Grosz had notes, which he carefully memorized and then destroyed. The next day Brand received his passport, in the name of Eugen Band, but without a Turkish visa, which he never even requested, because he was sure the emissaries in Istanbul would see to a minor problem like that.[1] Grosz had his Turkish visa, whereas Brand cabled to Istanbul that he was coming. He did not say anything about his new name; he said he wanted to meet the central figures of the Zionist movement. When the answer from Istanbul came that "Chaim" would be waiting, he assumed naively that Chaim Weizmann, the president of the World Zionist Organization and the Jewish Agency was meant, not Chaim Barlas, head of the Istanbul group of Zionist emissaries.

A German courier airplane took the two to Sofia, where their credentials were checked by the local Gestapo, and on May 19 they flew to Istanbul. Grosz was whisked away from the airport by a Turkish "business associate" from the Hungarian firm that served as a cover for his intelligence operations, whereas Brand was threatened with arrest and deportation.[2] In the end, the emissaries managed, with great difficulty, for him to pass the controls and be given a temporary permit to stay. Brand, then or later, never really understood the powerlessness of the Palestinian Jewish group. The fact that the name in his passport was different from the name the emissaries had given the Turkish authorities—Eugen Band as against Joel Brand—did not seem to him to be of any relevance; surely they should have been able to deal with this.

Who arranged the departure of Brand and Grosz to Istanbul? Kurt Becher says that he did, and apparently experts in the RSHA forged the papers.[3]

A dramatic, very emotional meeting occurred at the Pera Palas

Hotel, when Brand told the whole group of Zionist emissaries about the situation of Hungarian Jewry and about Eichmann's proposal. They were stunned and overwhelmed: What should they do now? It was clear, especially to the two main figures, Wenja Pomeranz and Menachem Bader, the two kibbutz emissaries, that everything had to be done to prevent the mission from being a failure. They cabled to Jerusalem that Pomeranz would be flying to Palestine to report on a crucial new development. On May 24, Pomeranz, who in the end went by train, arrived in Palestine, where he was immediately received by Moshe Shertok, head of JA's political department.

Shertok, too, realized the tremendous importance of the development, and the two went to Ben Gurion's house. Pomeranz brought with him a message from the emissaries, written on a piece of paper in a toothpaste tube. The message was a cry of despair: "We are waiting, in desperation, for your decision, upon which depend perhaps tens of thousands of lives. We are not free to make it here." And Barlas asked: "What should we tell the persecutors about 'goods' and ransom? Will someone from the JA Executive come here, and who? Would it be wise to send Brand to Jerusalem and would there be a guarantee that he can return—which is the condition for his mission? Should he negotiate in Ankara as well, apart from a talk with Mr. Avni [code-name for U.S. Ambassador Laurence A. Steinhardt]?"[4] After a long talk with Ben Gurion, a meeting of the Jewish Agency Executive (JAE) was hastily summoned to hear Pomeranz.

The idea of negotiating with the Germans for the release of Hungarian Jews had occurred to JA Executive members even before Brand's mission. On April 2, two weeks after the German occupation of Hungary, Yitzhak Grünbaum of the JA Executive suggested to his colleagues that they turn to the German representatives in Istanbul to stop the murders not only in Hungary but all over Europe. In effect, Grünbaum was trying to carry on where the Europa Plan had left off. The JA Executive, including Ben Gurion, rejected the idea, but largely for pragmatic reasons. Negotiations with Germany without the knowledge of the Allies were an impossibility, and the wrath of the British and the Americans, the only ones the Jews could turn to, would descend on the Jewish negotiators. A resolution was adopted to contact Ira Hirschmann, the WRB delegate who was supposed to return to Istanbul shortly (he came there first in February), and have him propose that the Balkan Jews not be deported to Poland but concentrated and looked after by the Red Cross. The contact in this form was never made, perhaps because Hirschmann returned in June, and by then Brand had arrived.[5]

Ben Gurion and Shertok argued that the British had to be informed officially, through the Mandatory Government in Palestine; they would in any case receive information about the mission from their own intelligence sources, and if any negotiations were to be entered into, the British and

American governments would have to be the ones to do so, and the sooner they were brought into the picture the better. In fact, the emissaries in Istanbul had immediately approached Arthur Whittall, the Istanbul MI6 agent, and his superior in the British secret service, Col. Harold Gibson, with the information, and had asked them to facilitate Pomeranz's trip. In a parallel move, Barlas informed U.S. Ambassador Steinhardt. Yitzhak Grünbaum, nominally responsible for rescue activities, objected, however; he did not trust the British—they would torpedo the whole project. After a vigorous debate, Grünbaum was outvoted.

On May 26, Ben Gurion and Shertok went to see the British High Commissioner for Palestine, Sir Harold MacMichael, no great friend of the Jews, Zionism, or the JA. MacMichael nonetheless reported the contents of the proposals and his discussion with the Jewish leaders to London accurately. In his report he quoted the Jewish representatives as saying that Eichmann was prepared to release 5,000–10,000 Jews before receipt of the goods and to exchange Jews for German POWs. It will be remembered that Brand in his written statements sometimes spoke of 100,000 Jews being released upon the receipt of a confirmation that the plan had been accepted, and he did not mention any exchange of Jews for German POWs. This discrepancy again shows the unreliability of Brand's testimony regarding details of the proposal.[6] According to MacMichael, quoting Shertok and Ben Gurion, Brand said that the deportations had not started yet—again contradicting other statements by Brand, in which he made it clear that he knew that the deportations had started on May 14.

Already in that preliminary discussion, MacMichael asked the pertinent questions. Was this not an attempt to split the Allied front? Could one really trust the Gestapo to come up with a plan to save Jews? Was it not unthinkable to even consider giving the Nazis trucks in the middle of the war? Ben Gurion's answers foreshadowed the JA stance: No goods could be shipped to the Nazis, but negotiations had to be undertaken, because lives might be saved. All three agreed that Shertok should fly to Istanbul and meet with Brand, who would have to return to Hungary soon; Eichmann had supposedly given him a time limit of two weeks. The High Commissioner turned to Brig. R. G. Maunsell, the chief of British intelligence in the Middle East, to find out more about Grosz and about the background to the Brand mission.[7]

In the meantime the Turkish authorities were very unhappy about the stay in their country of Jews who, in their eyes, were obviously Gestapo agents. The Turks were bent on deporting Brand, who had stayed at the hotel under a mild house arrest from May 23 to May 26; he had tried to go to Ankara to see Steinhardt, but he could not get a ticket without a valid visa. Avriel and Bader sought desperately for a way to prevent the calamity of a deportation; they talked and bribed and talked again, but on May 26, with Shertok not yet in Istanbul, the Turks took Brand into custody prior to his removal from Turkey. Avriel managed, with great difficulty, to obtain an agreement from the Turks that Brand could stay the night at the hotel, but he would be deported on May 29. The Turkish decision, which may also have been influenced by von Papen's pressure, was made at the cabinet level and was in accord with perceived Turkish interests.[8]

This Turkish attitude may also explain why the British embassy in Ankara failed to obtain a visa for Shertok to visit Istanbul, despite apparently honest attempts by MacMichael to send him there. As a result, Shertok asked, in a cable to Istanbul, that Brand return to Hungary and tell the Nazis that his proposal was being seriously studied by the Jews and the Allies. In a second cable, having learned of Brand's reluctance to return to Hungary, Shertok demanded that Brand not come to Palestine but remain in Turkey.[9] This, as we know, was an impossible demand, given the Turkish reluctance to keep him in their country.

Brand thought that if he returned ignominiously to Nazi-held territory, without Grosz, he and his family would be the immediate victims, but more important, Hungarian Jewry would be doomed. He resisted the idea of a return to Hungary at this stage with every fiber of his being. On May 27, with the deportation scheduled for the following night, Bader wrote that he hoped Brand would not be executed as soon as he was delivered into Nazi hands. Brand gave him his last will.[10]

The next day an attempt was made to persuade the British SIS in Istanbul to give Brand permission to go to Palestine, but the British refused, and for three days, on instructions from London, they persisted in this refusal. By that time they had heard the general contents of Brand's message from Ehud Avriel, and they wanted no part of that very difficult situation. They were prepared to request the Turks to deport Brand and Grosz to British-held territory, but they refused to state that the two were Jews seeking asylum. They were, then, asking the Turks to give them two enemy agents, and of course the Turks refused. The British handled the situation this way intentionally to prevent Brand and Grosz from landing in their lap.

What Grosz was doing during that time is not clear, but we may assume that he contacted some of the British agents. His wife had been brought out from Hungary earlier, and he was staying with her. He must have been in contact with the OSS immediately after his arrival, because Macfarland sent a message to Washington on May 21 saying that Grosz had told the Americans about the arrest of Hatz and Kövess in Budapest. Grosz also spoke with Dogwood, on May 30, and thus informed the Americans of the gist of what he had brought with him.[11] What Dogwood did with the information is not known, and so far no documentation has turned up to enlighten us on this point.

On May 29, Bader persuaded Brand to accept a fictitious agreement between "Moledet" (Fatherland)—a code name that Bader adopted to represent the JA for the benefit of the Nazis—and Brand. In that document, with which Brand would return to Budapest, appeared the statement that the Jews accepted the Eichmann offer in general terms, provided the deportations were discontinued. The Germans were promised a ransom of SFR 1 million if they stopped deportations: $400,000 for each 1,000 Jewish emigrants to Palestine and SFR 1 million for each 1,000 Jewish emigrants to Spain. In return for permitting the Allies or World Jewry to supply the Jews in the camps, the Germans would receive equivalent supplies for themselves. German plenipotentiaries were to discuss all the terms with people now on their way to Istanbul—that is, Hirschmann and Shertok. The document was a very weak reed to lean on, but Bader could not think of anything better.[12] Still, maybe it would help Brand survive.

After accepting the document from Bader, Brand went to Grosz's room in the hotel and asked him to accompany him to Budapest. Grosz threw Brand out of the room: "Joel can delude himself that he has something in hand to return with. But I have not yet succeeded to do what they asked of me, and without me succeeding, the agreement which you offered to Joel has no value."[13] That night, before dawn on May 30, a dramatic meeting took place in the hotel between Brand and Bader. Bader, a fatherly figure, tried to console Brand regarding the inevitability of his return to Budapest. In the end, the exhausted and desperate man gave in to the inevitable: "At last, after hours of struggling, he accepted very quietly the decision that they had to return [to Budapest]."[14]

These details are important because of a story that spread in Israel at the time of the Kasztner trial. It was said that the emissaries, who were representatives of the Jewish Agency—which was the real defendant in the Tel Aviv dock in 1954—had forced Brand, who wanted to return to Hungary, to go to Palestine instead, where he was arrested by the British. The JA, like the European Judenräte, was eager, it was said, to collaborate with the enemies of the Jewish people—the British, in this case. That caused the failure of the Brand mission. Brand himself was the originator of the story, apparently because he cut a much more heroic figure if he had been bent on going back to Budapest. In his book, which was published after the trial, he repeated the story. The theme was picked up not only by Tamir, the lawyer facing Kasztner, but also by a very popular author, Amos Elon, whose best-selling novel on the subject repeated the false version. In a scurrilous passage Elon in fact accused Bader of causing the failure of the mission by collaborating with the British, who did not want to see Brand return to Hungary.

The exact opposite is true: Brand desperately wanted to avoid a return to Budapest, for excellent reasons: he would have been murdered, and the mission would have failed. Bader unsuccessfully tried to help him. In October 1944, Brand told Hirschmann as much: had he returned from Istanbul, "it would have been interpreted as a definite refusal by the Allies of his proposals, and he saw only dangers of additional reprisals from this eventuality." As it was, he said, "at least he accomplished something with the cessation of the deportations and the 1700 refugees [the Kasztner train—see below] who did come through."[15]

Grosz, as we have seen, refused point-blank to return to Hungary. When he was threatened with deportation, he begged the British "on bended knee" to arrest him in their territory.[16] The British knew exactly who he was and thought he might be useful in helping them understand the workings of the German intelligence services. On May 31, in a reversal of the earlier British stand, Secret Intelligence Middle East (SIME), the Mideast branch of the SIS, decided to accept the two into British-held territory. The Turks, who had resisted the British request on May 29, relented, and gave visas permitting entry into Syria to both Grosz and Brand. SIME's decision to accept the two was later questioned by an unhappy London MI6 center, but on June 1, Grosz left for Syria, where he was arrested and taken to Cairo. Brand was given the chance to meet with Shertok in Istanbul and waited for a few days more.

In the meantime, Shertok tried to procure a Turkish visa. Not surprisingly, the Turks were not eager to have another figure complicate the situation. The visa was refused. MacMichael reported to London on May 26 that Shertok would be going to Istanbul, and when there was no response from the British ambassador in Ankara, he cabled him that if the visa was not received by May 30, he would send Shertok without one. The Ankara embassy cabled back that under no circumstances was Shertok to come without a visa. As we know already, Shertok then sent a cable to Istanbul telling Brand not to leave until he came. The reason he gave was that as an enemy citizen, Brand might not be able to return to Hungary once he had been in Allied territory. But the British consulate in Istanbul—in effect, the SIS—told Brand that he had to leave, implying that if he did not, he might have to return to Hungary without seeing Shertok.[17] On June 12 or 13 the British ambassador told Steinhardt that a Turkish visa had been telegraphed to Jerusalem around June 5; this probably was after Brand had already left Istanbul. At any rate, Shertok did not get the visa in time.[18] MacMichael then promised Shertok that he would be able to meet with Brand in Aleppo and that Brand would then be allowed to return to Hungary.[19]

Meanwhile, in Istanbul, two American reports on the Brand-Grosz mission were penned on June 4 by Reuben B. Resnik, JDC's local representative, and by U.S. Consul Leslie A. Squire; apparently they had interviewed Brand together and agreed on their conclusions: that the Brand proposal was another Gestapo plot and that the two emissaries were not very impressive. Brand, Squire argued, had had contacts with the Hungarian intelligence agency, which was notoriously pro-German (Squire was wrong on that point), and he was linked to the Gestapo because the Gestapo knew of his illegal life-saving activities. Squire accurately reported Brand as saying that 12,000 Jews were being shipped to Poland each day to be murdered. As to the content of the Brand proposals, Squire knew only about Hungarian Jews that were to be liberated, not about one million Jews to be selected from all over Europe, as Brand put it in later interrogations. Squire understood Brand's main point of negotiating in order to gain time, but he was completely fazed by the Germans. Surely the Gestapo could not believe that these proposals would be accepted by the Allies. Therefore, they must have been designed for propaganda purposes, mainly to create a split between the West and the Soviets. He rejected the notion that a serious attempt was being made to start peace talks, or that the Germans were trying to blame the Allies for the nonsurvival of the Jews, pointing to the Allies' rejection of the German proposals. Squire also, like so many others, thought the proposals were designed, among other things, to relieve the Germans of the "burden" of "providing" for the Jews. The State Department reacted to the Squire memo with great praise.[20]

The British attitude was given expression at a meeting of the War Cabinet Committee on the Reception and Accommodation of Refugees, which met in London on May 30. The consensus was that the German proposals were a piece of political warfare and an attempt at blackmail. After all, if the Germans had anything serious to offer, they could do so via the Swiss, who were the "Protecting Power" representing British interests to the Germans. To transfer huge numbers of Jews to Spain in effect meant to cease war operations—and the discussion about this took place, we should not forget, a week before the Normandy invasion. Perhaps the Germans wanted to exchange Jews for German POWs in Allied hands—which was unacceptable. At the same time, the government had to take into account the pro-Jewish sentiments expressed by the churches and the public in Britain: a "mere negative should not be opposed to any scheme which promises rescue of Jews." The thought was offered that the Americans might be misled into sympathizing with the proposal, because the President's War Refugee Board "backed by Mr. Morgenthau had, partly for electoral reasons, committed itself to the 'rescue' of Jews." This commitment might lead to the danger of "an offer to unload an even greater number of Jews on to our hands."[21]

The British submitted an aide-memoire to the United States on June 5. In the very first paragraph of that document they reiterate what they saw as a real danger: if one million people left Nazi-held territory, military operations would have to be suspended, enabling the Germans to concentrate all their forces against the East—thereby implementing what probably was Himmler's intention. Another comment was that if Jews were let out, there would be an outcry in the Allied countries; people would ask about Allied military and civilian internees, who faced "terrible conditions" (they did not, of course).

The positive side of the British attitude was the statement that "if the German Government were willing to release Jews in position of extreme distress or danger" (as though there were Jews in Nazi Europe who were not in "extreme distress or danger"), Britain and the United States would be willing to examine the possibility of accommodating these people in the Iberian Peninsula. This offer was written a day before D day, after which any German movement of people to the Spanish border became illusory. In addition, the British said that no representative of the JA or any other Jewish body could possibly meet Germans, but the JA could convey to Hungary the attitudes of the Allies. According to the aide-memoire, Weizmann, when he was informed, reacted by saying that the proposal seemed to be an attempt to embarrass the Western governments. He had, however, reserved judgment.[22]

Interestingly, two points were missing from this early exchange, because the British were simply not aware of them: one was Eichmann's statement that the trucks would not be used against the Western Allies, and the other was the Grosz mission. Both were transmitted to Whitehall slightly later.

On June 9, Pehle informed Stettinius that Roosevelt had "agreed with our thought that we should keep the negotiations open if possible" to gain time "in the hope that meanwhile the lives of many intended victims will be spared."[23]

The reaction of the Jewish bodies in the free world was somewhat confused at first; but largely because of Shertok's conscientious reporting of the proposals and of the opinions of the JA Executive, the chief figures in the Jewish world responded intelligently. Nahum Goldman, a European Jew, immediately understood Shertok's policy of negotiating for the sake of negotiating, and upon hearing of the proposal from the new under secretary of state, Edward R. Stettinius, Jr., on June 7, advised him along those lines.[24] Trucks were out of the question, but money should be offered, or the International Red Cross could take over the supply of food to the Jews. Goldman's idea to leave the Jews where they were and place them under the supervision of the Red Cross, a policy that would answer the British objection that it was impossible to move that many people, was later adopted by others.[25]

At the same time as Shertok's interventions, Ben Gurion turned to Goldman and asked him to transmit to Roosevelt a plea "that suitable arrangements be made to discuss the proposal with representatives of the enemy group from which [the proposal] emanated, and that the door should not be closed." He then made it clear that the JA thought the WRB was empowered to negotiate with the enemy and that he thought this authority should be utilized to contact the Nazi organizations that had made the offer. Ben Gurion was aware that the Brand proposals had nothing to do with the German Foreign Office. In all the Jewish interventions, the same demand was included: to permit Brand to return to Budapest.[26]

The Allies had yet another partner in their responses: the Soviets. Goldman, for one, understood that it was better for the Soviets to hear about the Brand mission from the West than for them to find out about it through their intelligence people in Istanbul. The Americans insisted on informing the Soviets, over British objections: it was perfectly clear to the British that the Soviets would veto any approach to the Germans and that involving them would mean the end of the mission. But on June 9 the State Department sent a cable to Moscow asking the U.S. ambassador to fill in the Soviet leadership. The inevitable answer came back on the nineteenth: Andrei Vyshinski, the Deputy Foreign Minister, had said that the Soviet government did not "consider it permissible or expedient to carry on any conversations whatsoever with the German Government" regarding the Brand proposals.[27] Did the State Department, then, turn to the Soviets because they knew what the response would be, or did they do it despite that knowledge? The answer is by no means clear. After receiving a negative Soviet reply, continuing the Brand contacts seemed impossible. Had the Americans presented the offer as a way to try to save lives, instead of asking officially, Soviet objections could have been either partly answered or partly ignored, or both. The Soviets seem to have killed the original Brand mission.

On June 5, Brand left Istanbul, and on June 6 he crossed the Syrian border, accompanied by Avriel. To the consternation of both, Brand was arrested by the British, who at first absolutely refused to have Shertok meet with him. For four days Shertok fought a battle of telephones and cables, until at last, on June 11, the British relented and let him speak to Brand for a whole day in Aleppo. Shertok's record of the conversation and that of the British officer who insisted on being present were preserved. Brand was also able to talk privately, not only with Shertok but also with members of the JA intelligence group—Shaul Avigur, head of Mossad, and three others.[28]

Brand told Shertok of the Eichmann offer, as well as giving him a detailed picture of the internal and external situation of Hungarian Jewry. He also reported Eichmann's statement that the trucks would not be used against the West—he later regretted having made that disclosure. When asked what would happen if he returned with a positive answer, what would happen if he returned with a negative answer, and what would happen if he did not return at all, Brand said that he did not believe that he would save the Jews if he returned with a positive answer. This reply stands in stark contradiction to Brand's statements in his book and in his postwar testimony, where he argues that if only he had been permitted to return, he could have saved multitudes. To Shertok he said that if he returned with a negative answer, the Germans would initiate total destruction—a peculiar statement in view of Brand's knowledge that the Germans were in fact deporting Jews to their deaths, having started on May 14. If Brand failed to return altogether, he said, they would murder his friends and most of his family. They might keep some of his family alive to show them off as the relatives of the villain Brand, who had left them in the lurch and saved his own skin. Abandonment and self-preservation are exactly what some of his friends and family—wrongly—accused him of doing.[29]

At the close of the long meeting, Shertok appears to have settled on a strategy: he would ask the British to have neutrals enter into negotiations over the Nazi proposals and to keep the negotiations going as long as possible in the hope that in the meanwhile the murders would stop and, who knows? maybe the war would end. Brand had to be permitted to return to Budapest. But Brand was carted away to Cairo rather than to Budapest, there to undergo, along with Grosz, a series of interrogations by British intelligence officers— interrogations that went on for weeks.

The British government had received word of the Brand mission both from its representatives in Turkey and from MacMichael. The United States received a cable from Ambassador Steinhardt on May 25, and in Washington the WRB agreed with the JA that negotiations might help to save endangered Jews. In both capitals, the Nazi offer was discussed quite seriously. The context in which the Brand proposals were discussed in the United States was established by the more energetic role that the Americans were playing in attempting rescue through the WRB.

On March 7, before the German occupation, the U.S. legations at Bern and Lisbon had transmitted a note to the Hungarian government threatening the Hungarians with retribution if they persecuted the Jews.[30] On March 24, just five days after the occupation of Hungary, Roosevelt issued a public declaration warning the Hungarians not to lend a hand in the persecution of Jews or other civilian populations and threatening retribution for those who did. The warning was repeated in a diplomatic communication to the Hungarians on April 12.[31] How basically ineffective this approach was can be gauged from the fact that after the declaration was issued, 437,000 Jews were deported to Auschwitz, essentially by Hungarian forces.

The British government refused to join in the appeal. The United States exerted some pressure on the Vatican—the Allied forces were advancing toward Rome, which they liberated on June 4—and Papal Nuntius Angelo Rotta did indeed protest to Michael Arnothy-Jungerth, the Hungarian Foreign Minister, on April 27. The Holy Father, he said, was very sad because he saw that Hungary, a Christian nation, was going against the teachings of the

Gospels. On May 15 he again protested against the deportations, which had just begun. But he could not persuade the Cardinal Primate, Justinian Seredi, who instead wrote a pastoral letter that agreed with antisemitic measures and aimed to protect Jewish converts to Christianity from deportation. The letter was suppressed by the government, though it was read out in some churches, belatedly, on July 1.[32]

The Vatican became more determined after the liberation of Rome, and on June 25 the Pope implored Horthy to prevent further pain and suffering on the part of the Jews. On June 30, Gustaf V of Sweden cabled Horthy to save the remnant of Hungarian Jewry "in the name of humanity" and the good name of Hungary. However, the bombing of Budapest by the U.S. Air Force on July 2 was apparently at least as influential as these interventions. Horthy, who had been given intercepted U.S. messages threatening the bombing of the capital—the cables had probably been played into the hands of the Hungarian intelligence—saw Veesenmayer on July 4 and prepared the ground for a retreat from the deportation policy. He was convinced that the bombing of the city had been the American response to the deportations.

One of the intercepted cables was that of the WRB representative in Switzerland, Roswell D. McClelland, dated June 24, which proposed the bombing of railways leading to Auschwitz in Hungary and Slovakia. The idea had been suggested in a message that Weissmandel sent through Schwalb on May 18. How paradoxical to think that the suggestion of an ultraorthodox rabbi to bomb railways found its way not only to the WRB but also to Horthy, on whom it may have had an influence in stopping the deportations. In addition, the cable served as the basis of another message, this one from the British ambassador John C. Norton to the Foreign Office; it landed on Churchill's desk on June 26. Churchill's comment was, "There is no doubt that this [the murder of the Hungarian Jews, or the Holocaust generally] is probably the greatest and most horrible crime ever committed in the whole history of the world, and it has been done by scientific machinery by nominally civilized men in the name of a great State and one of the leading races of Europe."[33]

Horthy, however, was also influenced by the knowledge that the extreme right wing, with Baky and Endre as the most prominent politicians among them, was preparing a coup with the help of the gendarmerie. He ordered loyal army units into the capital and, after strengthening his position, ordered a temporary stop to the deportations on July 7, assuring Veesenmayer that he would continue with the last stage, the deportation of the Jews of Budapest, as soon as possible. Eichmann managed to deport another trainload after July 7, against Horthy's wishes.

Other neutral states and organizations also pleaded with Horthy, not knowing that he had already made up his mind to stop the deportations. On

July 6 the president of the International Red Cross, Max Huber, addressed a letter of protest to Horthy.

Meanwhile, Brand was brought to Cairo on June 14. MacMichael very cynically disregarded the promise that he had made to Shertok to return Brand to Budapest and forbade Shertok even to mention it. At this point, Brand did want to return, because he felt that the time he had been given by Eichmann had run out. Also, he had given his message to Shertok, whom he recognized as a top-level representative of the Jewish people and whom he could rely on to present the deal to the Allies.

In Istanbul, Brand had insisted that Grosz return to Budapest with him, but Grosz was now in British custody, which would be a sufficiently good explanation if Brand returned alone. But the British, who had originally been so reluctant to have Brand, now wanted to squeeze out of him information on Hungary, on the German intelligence system, and on "Zionist armed activities" (in Hungary, no less!), which might, so they thought, threaten their rule in Palestine. They wanted to compare his testimony with Grosz's, hence their refusal to abide by their undertaking and allow Brand to go back.

Kasztner and the Vaada in Budapest were going frantic about Brand's failure to return and advised the emissaries in Istanbul that all was lost if Brand stayed in the Middle East. Shertok and other JA officials now turned the issue of Brand's return to Hungary into one of their central demands—it was an obvious way to keep the negotiations going. They were supported by Joseph J. Schwartz of the JDC, who was in Turkey at the time and who argued for Brand's return with the U.S. government.[34]

Another aspect to Brand's not returning needs to be mentioned. That Brand had had no choice, that it was not due to any cowardice on his part that he did not return, that he did not just abandon his family, that he was being held in Cairo against his will—all these were not only unknown and unacceptable in Budapest but remained so with Holocaust survivors until today. His colleagues and for a time even his wife did not forgive him for his supposed treachery, and the result was a deep rift between him and the surviving Vaada associates.

After returning from Aleppo, Shertok participated in yet another special meeting of the JA Executive at Ben Gurion's house, on June 14, where the future policy of the Jewish leadership was discussed and decided on. The center of activity could not be Cairo, or Istanbul, or Jerusalem—Shertok had to go to London to discuss the Brand mission with the British government. Moyne thought so, too, and Ben Gurion pushed for the same thing in Palestine. "Take your tuxedo and your top hat, Moshe," he is reported to have said, "and fly to London." Shertok would try to sell to the British the idea that some officially neutral but actually pro-Allies body should negotiate with the Germans on neutral ground. Shertok was thinking in terms of the Inter-

governmental Committee on Refugees, whose vice-chairman, Gustav Kullmann, was a Swiss citizen; or the International Red Cross, or perhaps the WRB,
which Shertok (wrongly) thought had permission to negotiate with the enemy.
Ben Gurion rejected Grünbaum's condition for negotiating with the Germans—namely, that the deportations and the murders should stop. The main
goal, Ben Gurion thought, should be to enter into negotiations. All the rest
would come later.[35]

The next day, June 15, Ben Gurion and Shertok again met with MacMichael.
The purpose was to inform the British government in London, to whom
MacMichael would report, of the JA's position. Coarse and unfriendly though
he was, the British official nevertheless immediately transmitted to London the
main points: negotiations through the medium of neutral citizens or the WRB
and the return of Brand to Budapest.

The big argument within the JA Executive was over relations with the
British. Grünbaum especially did not trust the British and was certain that
they would sabotage any effort to save Jews. Ben Gurion opposed him; he
saw that the mission would have no chance of success if the Western Allies
were not persuaded to support it. An independent Jewish effort was doomed
to instant failure. Both were right, of course. But what emerges here is a picture diametrically opposed to the one painted by popular historical literature,
which shows Grünbaum as a person who did little and cared less and which
depicts Ben Gurion as almost a collaborator with the Nazis, a callous and
uninterested man who cared only about the future of Jewish Palestine and
not about the Jews in the Diaspora. The true picture is, as we have already
seen, quite different. Both men were deeply involved. The JA Executive met
seven times in the month after Pomeranz came from Istanbul, three times in
special sessions in Ben Gurion's home. Ben Gurion saw the Brand affair as
currently the central event for the JA, devoted his time and energy to it, and
declared to MacMichael, as well as to the JA Executive, that Jews should be
taken anywhere, not just Palestine.[36]

Here we should introduce Ira A. Hirschmann, the WRB delegate then on
his way to Istanbul. Hirschmann was a key executive in the New York
Bloomingdale department store company and a supporter of the so-called
Bergson group, a radical right-wing Zionist group that had managed to
obtain a great deal of exposure on the plight of the Jews of Europe through
aggressive advertising and the creation of committees of Gentile friends of
considerable influence in American public life.

Why Roosevelt appointed Hirschmann to be the WRB's troubleshooter in
Turkey is not clear; Roosevelt had no liking at all for the Bergson group and
its policies—but he made the appointment, and Hirschmann went to Turkey
in February and again on June 11, in the wake of Brand's arrival there. His
own account of the events reads very much like an "I was there" story; *he*

saved, *he* negotiated, and *he* achieved. In fact, his rescue attempts, though made with the best intentions and with great energy, failed completely. He neither achieved a breakthrough regarding the flight of Jews from the Balkans nor succeeded with the Brand affair; he makes much of his interventions with the Romanian and Bulgarian ambassadors in Turkey and claims that through his contacts he saved the Jews in those countries from last-minute Nazi attempts at murder. There may have been a marginal influence on the Romanians (none in Bulgaria), but it was the Red Army bursting into the country that made the Romanians rebel against Antonescu and join the Allies, and it was the weakness of the German forces there that enabled this changeover to be effected without serious harm to the Jews.

Hirschmann's importance in the Brand affair lies in the fact that he interviewed Brand in Cairo (June 22) and that his report strengthened American resolve not to close that chapter completely. Hirschmann was very impressed with Brand, and like others, he thought that the scheme should be kept alive, even though the detailed German proposals were unacceptable. Lord Moyne, the British Minister Resident in the Middle East, agreed. Moyne even suggested that Brand might be sent back with a noncommittal reply that would enable the Jews there to continue talks. Hirschmann gained the impression— probably a very true one—that Eichmann had come to the trucks proposal more or less accidentally and that whether the exchange was for trucks or something else was not the central issue for the Germans. He also saw in Brand's description an indication that the Germans who had sent him were hoping to start separate peace negotiations. In the Hirschmann interview, Brand spoke of Eichmann's offer to let out "ten, twenty, fifty thousand Jews" if the Allies accepted his proposition in principle. One item in the Hirschmann-Brand talk is of great interest: Brand said that "Schröder" gave him a list of goods that the Nazis were interested in. The British confirmed who Schröder was: Fritz Laufer, Dogwood's Iris.[37]

The limit of Hirschmann's influence is evident in the rejection of most of his suggestions, including one that would have sent an American representative—he obviously hoped that he himself would be chosen—to London to confer with the British, together with Shertok, with whom he had met in Cairo on June 22 and who arrived in London on June 27.[38]

The British government seemed to be relenting on the question of Brand's return to Hungary. The JA intelligence chief, Reuven Zaslani, reported from Cairo that the head of British intelligence, Maunsell, had no objection to Brand's return from a security point of view; and Moyne, in his talk with Hirschmann, expressed the same view.

Toward the end of June (the twenty-sixth), British Foreign Secretary Anthony Eden composed an internal memorandum in which he weighed the possibilities. The proposal had clearly emanated from a high Nazi authority, possibly Himmler or even Hitler. It was either blackmail, or it intended to put the onus of mass murders resulting from an Allied rejection squarely on Western shoulders. A counterproposal by the Allies was indicated. "Up to the present His Majesty's Government have, while refusing to discuss the particular plan brought by Brand, tried to keep the question in play in order to stave off the threat (contained in the Gestapo proposals) of wholesale murder against the remaining Jews, particularly those in Hungary, and avoid the charge of indifference to the whole Jewish catastrophe and any measure calculated to mitigate it."[39]On July 1, about six weeks after Brand's arrival in Istanbul, Eden informed the Americans that the British were willing to let Brand return with the message that the Allies would consider practical steps to help Jews. The British suggestions reduced the Eichmann scheme to a ridiculous minimum: 1,500 Jewish children should be received in Switzerland; the 5,000 children from Bulgaria or Romania who had been promised Palestine entry certificates should now be released for emigration (this suggestion ignored the Nazis' condition that released Jews should not go to Palestine, because of Germany's obligations to the Palestine Arab leader, Hajj Amin el-Husseini, an ardent Nazi supporter); and German safe conduct passes be given to ships, presumably in the Balkans, carrying Jewish refugees. Nothing was said about what the Allies would give in return.[40]

In Washington, John W. Pehle, the WRB director, informed Secretary of the Treasury Henry Morgenthau, Jr., who was the active member of the War Refugee Board, about the Brand mission only on June 19.[41] On the same day the State Department finally replied to the British note of the fifth. According to a WRB draft, the U.S. note stated, quite correctly, that the detailed proposals Brand had brought were less important than the chance to save lives by talking. The note indicated that the Americans were aware of the dangers inherent in the idea of moving large numbers of people through Europe at that time, but they insisted nevertheless that the Allies should offer temporary havens for "Jews and similar persons in imminent danger of death." As to the Brand proposals generally, all the American documents reflect the insistence on keeping the door open and having Brand return to Hungary.[42]

What now developed was a significant difference of opinion between the British and the Americans. A British response of June 26 disagreed with the statement that "all" Jews who managed to escape should be looked after and instead proposed a list of certain groups that would be helped if they managed to leave Nazi Europe (some rabbis, 5,000 children and women from the Balkans to Palestine, and so on). They reiterated, however, that a negative answer should not be given, and offered to release Brand and return him to Hungary with some kind of story.[43] Interestingly, the British response was given after the negative Soviet reply; in other words, the British were willing to risk a minor unpleasant incident with the Soviets. They proposed to handle all negotiations through the Swiss and reject all suggestions of ransom.

Helpful in a very limited way though the British attitude was, behind it stood a sense of official annoyance at being bothered with Jews. When asked to see Weizmann and Shertok on June 28, Eden minuted: "Must I? Which of my colleagues looks after this? Minister of State [Richard Law, the "hero" of the failed Bermuda conference in April, 1943] or Mr. [George] Hall? At least one of them responsible should be there if I have to see these two Jews. Weizmann doesn't usually take much time."[44] Hall saw these two Jews first, on June 30. Weizmann and Shertok asked for Brand's return, for negotiations through the Swiss or the WRB, for radio warnings to Hungarian railway men, and for the bombing of Auschwitz. Shertok also demanded, in contradiction to what had been decided in Palestine by the JA Executive, that the Germans should be told that the talks would be dependent on their stopping the murders.[45]

The British received information about the Auschwitz report of Vrba and Wetzler through their mission in Bern on June 26, albeit in a very brief version, and the Americans received the information on July 6 in a more extensive form.[46] For the British, the information was repeated; on July 2 it came from Sweden and from the Czechoslovak government-in-exile in London.[47] Churchill commented on the June 26 cable: "Foreign Secretary. What can be done? What can be said?" And Eden turned to his advisers: "Department for urgent advice please."[48]

The Foreign Office officials no longer doubted the reports' accuracy but thought nothing could be done to help. From the first days of June, Jewish representatives from the JA and from the American Va'ad Hahatzalah (VH, or Rescue Committee of [Orthodox] Rabbis) had demanded the bombing of Auschwitz and/or the railways leading to it. The reports from Sweden were brought up at a cabinet meeting on July 3, and Eden commented that "distressing as the situation was he doubted if there was any effective action we could take." Repeated warnings to which the Allies could give no effect were self-defeating, he thought.[49] To his Prime Minister he replied that he would find out the reaction of the Air Ministry regarding the bombing of Auschwitz.

At a meeting that was finally arranged between Eden, Weizmann, and Shertok, another aide-memoire was presented by the JA to the British (July 6). It reiterated, but with much greater force, what the JA had told Hall. Ransom payment was explicitly demanded, and a declaration assuring the neutrals that Jews accepted into their countries would be looked after by the Allies was asked for. The railways leading to Auschwitz and Auschwitz itself should be bombed. The officials at the Foreign Office demurred. "We can't have this. . . . These Jewish proposals for a meeting [with Germans over ransom] are impossible." Only in consideration of American sensitivities did the Foreign Office hesitate to "dismiss the Gestapo proposals with contempt" as they ought to have been dismissed in the first place. Ian L. Henderson, one of the top Foreign Office staff, commenting on the Hirschmann report, said on July 9 that "the Nazis know that His Majesty's Government and the US Government are affected by the political weakness of being under Jewish pressure, whereas the Russians are not," and that they therefore use black-mail methods on the West.[50] And Home Secretary Herbert Morrison (Labour) commented on July 1 that it was "essential that we should do noth-ing at all which involves the risk that the further reception of refugees here might be the ultimate outcome."[51]

At the actual meeting, Eden managed to mislead even the experienced Shertok: he professed the greatest sympathy for the plight of the poor Hun-garian Jews. Yes, His Majesty's Government would certainly do everything in its power; the matter would be discussed in the War Cabinet, the question of negotiations included.[52] Eden sought to finish off the Brand mission while at the same time expressing sympathy for the victims, but behind his words lay a fear that the minutes of British officials on internal documents evince. Despite the statement of the Germans that they would not allow masses of Jews to reach Palestine because of German commitments to the Jerusalem Mufti, the British suspected that proposal was a major German–Zionist plot to introduce a million Jews into Palestine. That, of course, they would pre-vent with all the means at their disposal.[53]

Interestingly enough, as has already been pointed out, it is that very Ger-man demand to exclude Palestine as the destination for Jews and the JA's ready agreement to it that show how erroneous the historical analyses are that predi-cate Zionist policy at that stage on an exclusive Palestinocentrism, as though the JA had been against finding havens for Jews in places other than Palestine.

On July 1, even before receiving the JA's aide-memoire and reacting to Shertok's proposals, Eden informed the Americans that he had told Shertok (he had not met him yet!) that there could be no contacts between the Allies and the Germans such as Shertok had suggested and that no quid pro quo could be offered to the Germans; after the Soviet veto, no such discussions could take place. But Shertok had suggested that a neutral person represent-ing the Intergovernmental Committee for Refugees or the International Red Cross be the intermediary. He called it a "carrot" to be dangled before Ger-man eyes because it would mean that the Americans and the British were willing to discuss the release of Jews with them. Eden did not react to that at all. The German proposals, Eden indicated, were intended "to elicit a rejec-tion, which then would be represented as justification for extreme measures against Jews." (What more extreme measures could be taken than wholesale murder?)

On the positive side, the British repeated their proposal to negotiate through the Swiss about specific small groups of people to be emigrated from Nazi Europe. Pehle replied (on July 5), over Secretary of State Cordell Hull's signature, that what should be aimed at was a general guarantee to neutrals, specifically to Switzerland, that the Allies would look after and remove from their territory "all" Jews who managed to flee there. In a separate communication to Moscow (on July 7), Pehle indicated that he was looking for an intermediary, a Swiss it would be hoped, so that further information could be obtained from the Germans.[54] The British again demurred; the statement was too all-inclusive and could land the Allies in an open-ended situation from which there would be no escape.

The Americans also told the Soviets, on July 7, what they and the British had just learned: that Eichmann had offered not to use the trucks against the West. It was the British who opposed telling the Soviets the truth in order to keep the door open for further developments that might perhaps lead to the saving of some lives. But the Americans, intent on keeping on good terms with the Soviets, insisted on giving the Russians the information. They added that the Western powers were reluctant "to shut the door completely to any offer. Other offers of this nature are expected and eventually one may be received which can be given serious consideration," and suggested that contacts be established through the Swiss. But giving the information about the trucks to the Russians just about finished the practical possibilities connected with the Brand mission.[55]

In the meantime, the impact of the negative Soviet response had sunk in at the WRB. On June 21, Pehle cabled Steinhardt in Ankara and Averell Harriman in Moscow not to do anything about the matter and to await further instructions. Hirschmann, who was informed of his boss's attitude, receded into the background—from now on he was neutralized.[56]

The American views were, as we would suspect, by no means unanimous. The WRB or some officials at the State Department might be unwilling to close the door to further negotiations even after the negative Soviet response; others had a different view.[57] Within the OSS in the Middle East evaluations of the Brand mission might be positive or negative. But distinctly anti-Zionist or even antisemitic views were also expressed. Thus, in an army CIC report, probably dating from mid-June, Dogwood was suspected of being a Nazi agent because of his contact with the Istanbul Zionists and with Grosz, Laufer, and Brand. Zionists were accused of having their own implacable political intentions toward Palestine, and they were supposedly willing to negotiate with the Nazis to bring Jews to the Middle East to the detriment of the Allies.[58]

With the Soviet veto all chances of proceeding with the Brand mission seemed to vanish. However, Shertok's negotiations in London began *after* the Vyshinski note; and both the British and the Americans were reluctant to close the door completely to a chance of saving some lives at least, with the British adopting a much more restrictive stance than the Americans. It looked as though some kind of Swiss intervention could take place, with the British obviously thinking of official approaches, such as had been made in the Feldscher affair, while the Americans were looking for private or semi-private unofficial conduits. At this point in early July the Nazis made some surprising moves.

This particular stage apparently started with Ferenc (Feri) Bagyoni, the Hungarian courier attached to the military attaché in Ankara, who, as we have seen, had been used by the Zionist emissaries for transmitting their messages to Budapest. In the name of Krumey, Eichmann's henchman, Bagyoni suggested on June 10, only five days after Brand had left for Aleppo, that one of the emissaries go to Budapest to continue the negotiations. The emissary's safety and return would be guaranteed. Kasztner cabled from Budapest on June 20 that the Germans would like to meet Joseph J. Schwartz of the JDC in Portugal. Their representative would be Schröder. Schröder was identified as Laufer, although another Schröder, an SD operative, was also in the Iberian Peninsula. The JDC asked the U.S. State Department for permission, and Pehle, over Hull's signature, energetically refused (July 27).[59]

On June 23, Kasztner repeated Bagyoni's offer to have Menachem Bader meet with the Germans, and after a few more messages, he asked Bader, on July 7, to meet with a German agent calling himself Colonel Stiller; the purpose of the meeting was to have Bader travel to Budapest to continue the Brand negotiations. As proof of the seriousness of the Nazis, Kasztner informed Bader of the train that had carried close to 1,700 Jews to Switzerland (actually, to Bergen-Belsen; see below). Bader met with "Stiller," who claimed to be associated with the Istanbul German consulate and who offered Bader a plane ride to Berlin (or to Vienna, according to Bader's postwar testimony) to discuss the Brand proposals there.[60] Bader turned to his superiors, Shertok and Ben Gurion. Ben Gurion replied that British approval had to be obtained, because Bader was a Palestinian citizen. Ben Gurion had to yield to the British mainly, it seems, because the German offer to Bader had originally been brought to his attention by Anthony Simmonds, commander of the A-Force, a British Air Force intelligence unit with which the JA cooperated. Naturally, the British refused to let Bader go, and he was so informed by Shertok.[61] But Ben Gurion did not give up. Contrary to his official stand, he agreed that Eliezer Kaplan—treasurer of the JA and his close personal confidant, who was in Istanbul at the time—should see whether Bader could be sent to Hungary or Germany despite the British ban. After some wavering, Kaplan apparently decided that it could not be done.[62]

On July 15, Kasztner sent Bader a cable indicating that the Nazis had suggested Schwartz and Bader to him as possible negotiators and that in fact

Kasztner was trying to save the Brand mission. On the same day the Germans made a parallel attempt to save the mission, this one aimed at Eliyahu Dobkin of the JA, who was in Portugal at the time, but it, too, fell through quickly.

Several questions present themselves. First, who was Colonel Stiller? Second, who exactly sent him to Bader? And third, what was the meaning of the invitation?

As might be expected, no person by the name of Colonel Stiller is listed among the German personnel in Istanbul. It would have been very important to confirm that the agent who went under that cover represented the SD, as was likely, but no documentation has been found to prove it. He could hardly have represented the Foreign Office, which opposed the mission, and the Abwehr did not exist anymore. Kasztner's involvement might indicate that Schröder was Laufer and that Stiller was probably a Security Service man. What is most interesting is that Bader was not invited to go to Budapest but was invited to go to Berlin or Vienna by German courier plane—Brand and Grosz had come by such a plane. The offer could only have meant a centrally organized attempt to bring a Jewish representative to an SD headquarters. There is no doubting Bader's testimony, but no trace has been found of such an attempt in any German archive or testimony. We just do not know.

During those hectic July days, Shertok and Ben Gurion tried to move the Western Allies. Shertok suggested again, unsuccessfully, that the British should ask Gustav Kullmann, the Swiss deputy director of the Intergovernmental Committee for Refugees, to serve as liaison with the Germans. And Ben Gurion addressed a personal appeal to Roosevelt through Goldman on July 11 in two consecutive cables. He pleaded "not to allow this unique and possibly last chance of saving the remains of European Jewry to be lost." He asked for negotiations, and he now said, like Shertok in London, that, as a condition for holding the talks, the Germans should cease deporting Jews. It is highly improbable that Roosevelt saw this desperate plea.[63] In any case, he did not reply.

The end of this first phase came when the report on the Grosz interrogation, completed on July 4, reached Whitehall on July 13. The Grosz-Brand mission was immediately seen for what it was: an undisguised attempt by the Gestapo—the British failed to sort out the different SS branches—to enter into negotiations for a separate peace with the West. A perusal of the questions and replies showed that the forces behind this trial balloon were important and serious, and the report was brought before the British Cabinet Refugee Committee that very morning. The reaction was predictable: Eden said that until then the object had been to spin out the contacts in the hope that some proposals would emerge that the Allies could accept. But now "a report had just been received" that showed that the mission by Brand and

Grosz had been "intended as cover for a separate peace intrigue." The purpose was to embroil the Western Allies with the Russians. Churchill himself intervened and let the committee know that negotiations via the Swiss were no longer feasible, given the nature of the mission. It was proposed at the committee meeting that Brand might be sent back with no message at all.[64]

The Brand mission was now seen to be sullied: Brand had come with the duplicitous Grosz. All notions of letting Brand return with anything in hand had to be dropped, and the Germans would have to be shown that the propaganda effect could be turned around. On July 19 the *New York Herald Tribune* carried an item that had been leaked by the British government (under a July 18 dateline), exposing the Brand story as a Gestapo plot designed to secure a negotiated peace or a split in the United Nations, and the fact was mentioned that the Germans had asked for trucks that would not be used on the Western front. The *London Times* called the story one of the "most loathsome" of the war. Only the defeat of Germany would provide security for Jews and other oppressed peoples in Europe. Wickham Steed, in a BBC broadcast on July 21, went further: he reported the arrival of "a rich industrialist, a Hungarian Jew, accompanied by two German officials, to Turkey to negotiate with the British. . . . It is needless to say that this humanitarian blackmail was not accepted."[65] The leak and the media response was thought to have definitely killed the initiative.

To the Americans the British were explicit—though they never, as far as we can tell at this point, gave them the Grosz interrogation record. The British concluded (July 18) that the Brand mission "was intended as cover for an approach to us or to the Americans on the question of a separate peace." Brand therefore could only return with a negative answer—if indeed he wanted to go back. Weizmann was to be informed that "we had decided to have nothing further to do with Brand's suggestions."[66]

The reactions to the publication of the Brand proposals—in a distorted form, by the way—varied, of course. In Palestine the JA Executive expressed bitterness, even hatred, of the British, who had betrayed the trust placed in them and condemned Hungarian Jews to death by making the offer public. In Germany, Ribbentrop, who had again been bested by his rival Himmler, sent a furious cable to Veesenmayer; the general content can be summarized in the popular American expression "What the heck is going on?" Ribbentrop had no idea, and Veesenmayer had not told him. The problem was the date on which Ribbentrop's cable was sent: July 20, the day when the assassination attempt on Hitler was made. Most Germans had other worries that day. Veesenmayer's response on July 22 does arouse some important questions, however.

There is no hint that Veesenmayer himself was involved in any way in the negotiations with Brand. The implication is that Winkelmann was, and that the purpose of the Brand mission—Grosz is not mentioned—was to exchange "some Jews [*einige Juden*]" for goods in short supply in Germany. Grell informed Veesenmayer, the latter says, that the negotiations in Turkey were going well and that the publication of the news in the press was probably an attempt to disguise the affair vis-à-vis the Russians, but in reality the Western powers were ready to enter into such a deal.[67] It might be surmised that the other sources that Veesenmayer mentions, those who supplied Grell with his information, were Clages and Eichmann for the most part. Toward Ribbentrop at least, the negotiations were presented in a positive light from the Germans' point of view, even after their disclosure by the Allies. Because Himmler was mentioned as the person behind the initiative, it would appear that he was interested in keeping the plan rolling, which would explain why the effort to reach the Allies—by sending Schwarz, Dobkin, Bader, Laufer, anyone—would be continued. In the absence of SS sources, this version of events is about the closest we can get. The proximity of the dates to July 20 probably means that Himmler slipped the mission plan through without too many questions being asked.[68]

The Brand mission seemed to be finished from the Allied viewpoint, though not from the German, but events did not bear this conclusion out. Kasztner continued to attempt to have someone from the free world meet with the SS representatives; he did not know about the failure of the mission, and he must have been encouraged by what Becher and others told him from the German side, though its disclosure in the press became known in Budapest.

The British felt uncomfortable with their negative position. To accommodate at least some of the Jewish demands, they turned to the Soviets on July 13 and suggested that as the Russian Army was closing in on Hungary, the Soviets should threaten reprisals for the mistreatment of Jews in Hungary. There was no response.[69] Still, Kasztner did not give up, and the negotiations that Brand had suggested did, in a way, take place. On August 21, 1944, Becher and three others, including Kasztner, met with Saly Mayer, the JDC's man in Switzerland, on the Swiss-German border bridge at Saint Margarethen. But that meeting belongs to a later chapter.

How did Himmler deal with publicity about the Brand story in the Western press? It should again be emphasized that the story broke a day before the attempted coup on Hitler's life. But even Ribbentrop, who raised more than an eyebrow, was simply told that the Reichsführer SS had tried to obtain badly needed war materials from the West in exchange for some Jews—Himmler was covered by the Hitler directive of December 1942 and by his careful orchestration of the Brand mission. No one mentioned Grosz—the Allied press just hinted at the separate peace offer, but that was not taken seriously by Himmler's enemies within the Party. And, of course,

Himmler was charged by Hitler to find, interrogate, and execute the conservative opposition. That task took precedence over everything else.

The Brand mission had a sequel in the Middle East. Brand had been held incommunicado in Cairo since June 14 (or 12; the date is not certain). The British took their time over the question of what to do with him. He went on two hunger strikes and planned both a breakout and suicide. On October 5 he was released. The British offered the JA one of two choices: Brand could return to Hungary with a negative answer, or he would be released to Palestine and stay there. The JA people saw that Brand could no longer accomplish anything in Hungary, certainly not with a negative answer. He would presumably have been immediately killed. They chose to save his life and had him released to Palestine, a bitter man who then joined the extremist Stern Group, an anti-British organization that also fought the JA, calling the leaders Quislings.

Years later, the questions around Brand did not lose their poignancy. From what we know about him, he was an extremely courageous man, who passionately wanted to help Jews escape from death and who in his efforts to smuggle people into Hungary proved himself to be an ingenious operator. He was gifted with a great natural intelligence; he was also a man who liked easy living, who loved adventure, and who felt at home in cafés and bars, in underground conspiracies and card-playing circles. His truthfulness was not always impeccable. He died in 1964, probably of a liver disease connected with alcohol consumption. He was attacked by his erstwhile friends of the Vaada; these attacks, and his vehement responses, were part of a serious misunderstanding by all the Jewish actors in the situation in which they found themselves. We shall have to return to this painful episode later.

What happened to Grosz is only partly known. He also went to Palestine, having been released by the British after the war was over. He claimed that he had been an honest courier for the Istanbul emissaries, and after the establishment of the State of Israel, when some former emissaries became central figures in the new government, he asked for money. Kollek, Bader, and Avriel—whether because they felt compassion or because he was an unpleasant fellow whom they wanted to get rid of—supported the idea of giving him some money, provided he left Israel. It is not clear whether he received any. Suspicion of his motives and role mounted. At the Kasztner trial, he was asked to testify, and there he simply said that he had been sent by the SS to arrange for preliminaries to separate peace negotiations. The attorneys and the court in effect laughed at him, as though thinking, "You, you ugly little criminal?" But for once he was telling the truth. In January 1955, Teddy Kollek suggested giving him $15,000 if he agreed to leave Israel. He died in Munich in the early 1970s, having left Israel in or after 1955.[70]

The mission was perhaps given its best epitaph by David Ben Gurion. On

July 10, 1944, the fortieth anniversary of the death of Theodor Herzl, the founder of modern Zionism, Ben Gurion said:

What have you done to us, you freedom-loving peoples, guardians of justice, defenders of the high principles of democracy and of the brotherhood of man? What have you allowed to be perpetrated against a defenceless people while you stood aside and let it bleed to death, without offering help or succour, without calling on the fiends to stop, in the language of retribution which alone they would understand. Why do you profane our pain and wrath with empty expressions of sympathy which ring like a mockery in the ears of millions of the damned in the torture house of Nazi Europe? Why have you not even supplied arms to our ghetto rebels, as you have done for the partisans and underground fighters of other nations? Why did you not help us establish contacts with them, as you have done in the case of the partisans in Greece and Yugoslavia and the underground movements elsewhere? If, instead of Jews, thousands of English, American or Russian women, children and aged had been tortured every day, burnt to death, asphyxiated in gas chambers—would you have acted in the same way?[71]

11

The Bridge at Saint Margarethen

When Brand did not return and the deportations from the provinces assumed the proportions of the most terrible disaster, Kasztner thought at first that he had failed totally, that everything was lost. In a desperate letter to Nathan Schwalb in Geneva on July 12, 1944, he wrote:

You will understand the mental condition in which I am writing this letter. The dream of the big plan [the ransom plan and the Brand mission] is finished [der Traum des grossen Planes ist ausgeträumt]; the hundreds of thousands went to Auschwitz in such a way that they were not conscious until the last moment what it was all about and what was happening. We who did know tried to act against it, but after three and a half months of bitter fighting I must state that it was more like watching the unfolding of a tragedy and its unstoppable progress, without our being able to do anything of importance to prevent it. . . . The speed of the collapse was so wild that help and actions of succor and rescue could not keep up with it; even thoughts were too slow. I cannot give you a picture of the annihilation or of its impact; I could only feel it. The thing that happened here between May 15 and July 9 is like the burial of the last scion of an aristocratic family as they lower him into the grave and turn the face of his ancestors' shield to the wall.

Kasztner tried to explain to Schwalb what he had tried to achieve and what he saw as the main points of Brand's mission: to offer goods so Jews unfit for work would be sent to Spain and thereby saved. Eichmann had explicitly told him that that, too, was the Nazi proposal: "To extract necessary labor from Hungarian Jewry and sell the balance of valueless human material against valuable goods."[1]

Kasztner more or less explicitly expressed his bitterness about Brand's failure to return. Had he returned, Kasztner says, possibly more people could have been saved. Regardless, Kasztner had to defend Brand's actions in his talks with those Germans who had been willing to consider a change in their policy toward the Jews.

After Brand had gone, Kasztner and Hansi Brand were caught between the SS and the Hungarian secret police; the Hungarians wanted to know details about the Brand mission—what he was sent to propose and to whom and especially how much money the Jews had paid to the SS. On May 10, Kasztner was arrested by the SS so that he would not be able to tell the Hungarians about the mission. He was released after Brand had gone, but on May 27 he, Hansi Brand, Sandor Offenbach, the treasurer of the Vaada (Springmann had managed to leave Hungary before the German occupation), and Offenbach's wife were arrested, and Hansi Brand was tortured to extract information from her. She withstood the torture and apparently told the Hungarians nothing. Kasztner was brought to the PKR area, but before the Hungarians tortured him, the whole group was freed by the SS; the Germans had no wish to let the Hungarians in on their secrets.

Kasztner clarifies how the problem of the negotiations with the Germans was handled. The reins remained securely in the hands of the Vaada, but there were discussions and consultations with the Orthodox under Fülop von Freudiger and Gyula Link. While negotiating with the Germans, "we did not forget the flight to Romania, to Slovakia, and attempts at hiding people." Only 200 to 300 people could be hidden, and Kasztner estimates the number of those who fled abroad at 1,000—much too low, as we know now.[2]

An important section of the letter deals with the famous Kasztner train, to which we must turn our attention. The idea of sending a train out of Hungary was brought forward when, at the first meeting between Kasztner, Brand, and Wisliceny, there was a discussion of the possibility of permitting 600 people with Palestine certificates to go to Palestine via Constantza in Romania. Wisliceny said that the Germans were interested in large-scale Jewish emigration, not in the departure of small groups, but that the idea could be explored. When Kasztner took over the negotiations, he broached the subject again. Eichmann originally (May 22) agreed to the emigration of 600–750 persons and later (June 3) to an enlargement of the number. In July, Kasztner reported that the $200,000 in pengö paid to the Nazis in April had been for this emigration program; in the end, the Germans demanded much larger sums of money.

In line with established German policy, Eichmann opposed the idea of the Jews going to Palestine, because of the obligations that Nazi Germany had toward its Palestinian Arab ally, the Mufti of Jerusalem. The impact of the Mufti was a radicalizing factor in Nazi anti-Jewish murder policy. The number slowly grew; Kasztner wanted to include people from the provinces, including a special contingent from his birthplace of Cluj. He was permitted to go to Cluj and was told how many could come from there. On June 10 he took 388 people, members of his own family, some friends, and other individuals to Budapest. In addition, some more people came from other provincial towns. They and all the other people who were candidates for Kasztner's train were put into a camp on Columbus Street in Budapest, where they were guarded by SS men.

What was the purpose of the train in Kasztner's own mind? We have to take the date into account: Brand had left and had not returned, and Kasztner was seeking a way to reopen contact with the SS so that as many people could be saved as possible. An idea germinated: a train that would leave for Spain—that was Eichmann's dictum—would be a first breach in the policy of total murder. It could signal a change in German policy; other attempts at rescue had failed, in any case. Mainly, Kasztner hoped that the first train would be followed by a second and a third; once a pattern was established, perhaps an attempt could be made to stop the murder machine altogether.

On the other hand, the Nazi agreement to have the train leave Budapest could be another trick; the passengers could debark at Auschwitz, just as all the others had. The gamble was a tremendous one, and to convince others that it was worth the try, Kasztner put his own family in the train. As Hansi Brand said in her testimony at the Eichmann trial in Jerusalem: "If he [Kasztner] put his own children [on the train], perhaps these people really will be brought to a neutral country. That made me calm, because I hoped that these people, whom we persuaded with such difficulty to get on the train, would be brought to freedom despite everything."[3] In contrast, Kasztner's opponent, Moshe Krausz, bitterly accused Kasztner of sending people to their death and of falling victim to an obvious deception by the wily Nazis.[4]

In the end, 1,684 persons took the train, and it was indeed, as was said at the time, a Noah's ark. Who selected the passengers? A small committee headed by Komoly, and including Kasztner; Hansi Brand; a former president of the Orthodox group in Cluj, Zsigmond Leb, and others.[5] Kasztner was undoubtedly a central figure, but he was by no means the only one. As Kasztner states in his postwar report, Eichmann originally demanded $200 per head, then $500. That famous humanitarian, Kurt A. Becher, demanded $2,000 and ultimately settled for $1,000.[6] To send 1,684 people required something like SFR 7 million. The amount was to be paid in foreign currency, in pengö, and in gold and jewels. One hundred fifty people bought their places, because there was a ransom price, but the vast majority of the people on the train did not have the necessary money. Rich people would have to pay for the others. A special committee handled all these money matters; it was composed of Komoly, Szilagyi, an engineer by the name of Reichart, Hansi Brand, and Offenbach. Kasztner was not included. On June 20, Hansi Brand and Andreas Biss handed over three suitcases with the money, jewels, gold, shares of stock, and watches to Gerhard Clages to give to Becher. According to Kasztner himself, the heads of the families of some fifty individuals had paid large sums directly to Becher, then insisted that their family members be included on the list for the train. The arrangement sounds fine—except that Becher included these fifty people among the total of 1,684 for whom $1,000 per head would have to be paid, so he collected a double price per head for these people.[7]

Representatives of all communities, trends, opinions, ages, and origins were included in the train. There were the extreme anti-Zionist Hasidic Rabbi of Szatmar, Joel Teitelbaum, and his whole court—rescued by the Zionist Kasztner—leaders of the Orthodox and Neologue communities, Zionists of all hues, members of Zionist youth movements, Polish and Slovak refugees, and ordinary Hungarian Jews who had managed to corner Kasztner or some other member of the committee and make their case. A group of Orthodox leaders had been included by Freudiger, who bribed Wisliceny for that purpose. Some people who did not belong to any of these categories jumped on the train or sneaked onto it and became part of the ark.[8]

The train left Budapest on June 30. When it was stopped near the Hungarian-Austrian border, where it could head either to Auschwitz or westward, panic struck. Teitelbaum and his clique sent off desperate pleas for someone to rescue them—and them alone—but the decision was in Eichmann's hands. What made him send the train to Bergen-Belsen is not clear, but the decision must have come at least in part from further up the ladder—from Müller or Himmler himself. At the time, the Allied beachhead in Normandy was expanding, and travel toward the Spanish border became more and more problematic. The train reached Linz in Austria, and there people had to go into showers—many were convinced that these were gas chambers. Their concern, by the way, is as good a proof as any that the Auschwitz protocols had received widespread, though unofficial, publicity within Hungarian Jewry, or what was left of it. On July 8 the train reached Bergen-Belsen, which had been established as a transit and exchange camp for Jews by an order of Himmler dated December 1942. Ultimately, as we shall see, the passengers were to be released to Switzerland.

After the war and in connection with the train, Kasztner was accused of two main crimes: first, of having pushed the idea of the train instead of warning people of deportations—thereby enabling Eichmann to buy him off and ensuring undisturbed deportations and the consequent deaths of hundreds of thousands—and second, of saving his own family and friends at the expense of multitudes of others. These charges seem farfetched. We have seen already that Hungarian Jews had the information, certainly in a place like Cluj where, as said above, Polish escapees had found refuge and told their stories. The second charge is surprising, in a way: Would it not have been quite contrary to ordinary human nature, had Kasztner not tried to rescue his family? He was still relatively safe in Budapest. Should he have sacrificed his own family?

The train was organized in June, when the deportations were in full swing. All contact had been broken off between Budapest and the provincial ghettoes, except by the courageous emissaries of the youth movements, who tried to warn the ghettoes but were, as we have seen, rejected everywhere they went. Also, Kasztner was an unknown personality outside Cluj. A warning by an unknown adult Zionist would hardly have been heeded more than the warning by the youth movement members. The idea, moreover, of Kasztner going around the ghettoes in June—illegally, we must presume—is too absurd even to consider, but door-to-door visits would have been the only way to do what he was told ten years after the event that he should have done. Lastly, and in connection with these considerations, Eichmann hardly needed the silence of an unknown leader of a minority group within the Jewish community, who could not get to the provinces, in any case, to conduct the deportations by the Hungarian gendarmerie, who exercised their brutal rule everywhere in Hungary.

From the Nazi point of view, what could have been the purpose of letting close to 1,700 people escape? The money collected was after all a very minor amount compared with the money involved in other actions that the SS were undertaking then (see below, the Becher blackmail). To be sure, Himmler was covered by Hitler's oral instruction of December 1942, but there must have been other considerations as well. Further instructions must have come from Himmler, because Eichmann would never have let 1,700 Jews go without express orders from his superiors. The release of a trainload of Jews makes sense if we combine it with the hesitant steps taken by Himmler two months later in Switzerland to start negotiations with the people whom he thought were the representatives of World Jewry.

For the Jews the train also represented another element in the unfolding story: the "Final Solution" might not necessarily be the last word. Given a Nazi empire in deep trouble militarily, the principle of total murder could possibly be bent if the passengers of that Noah's ark landed in Switzerland and were not shipped from Bergen-Belsen to Auschwitz.

The train, then, was one attempt that Kasztner made. But it was by no means the only one. Kasztner later thought that he had, by his negotiations, saved another 18,000–20,000 Jews. Behind these rescues was a desire on the part of Ernst Kaltenbrunner, now head of the RSHA, to provide his Viennese colleagues with industrial labor, which was in scarce supply. Combing out Germans for recruitment into the German Army, together with the lack of more slaves from the East, more and more of whom were being liberated by the Russians, made for new and desperate needs.

Eichmann offered Kasztner a chance to send 30,000 people to Austria instead of Auschwitz. In fact, only 18,000–20,000 Jews, mostly from Debrecen, Szeged, Baja, and Szolnok, were sent to the areas around Vienna to work. The Nazis could have sent the women, the elderly, and the children to Auschwitz. In this case they did not do so, perhaps because of the Kasztner negotiations. By keeping these people alive temporarily—Kaltenbrunner pointed out in his correspondence with Blaschke, his Viennese underling, that the labor was indeed temporary—essential labor needs could be satisfied and the prospect of further negotiations could be kept open. In the end, some of the 18,000–20,000 were shipped to Bergen-Belsen, some to Theresienstadt, and the rest stayed on near Vienna. About 12,000 survived.[9]

Kasztner's main effort had to do with that same Nazi officer, Kurt A. Becher, whom we have already met in connection with the Brand mission. Becher had been sent to Hungary, ostensibly to requisition horses for the SS. What happened when he came to Budapest is a most peculiar story indeed. By "pure accident," or so Becher claimed afterward, he was "assigned" the mansions and offices of the richest Jewish family in Hungary for his quarters; they were on 114–16 Andrassy Street in Budapest. The family was part of the group that controlled the Manfred Weiss industrial concern. Becher probably came to Budapest more or less with the occupying troops, because on March 21 the first important director of the firm, Ferenc Kelemen, was arrested, and by April 5 Becher was in full control. Purely by accident, then, and out of his deep love for humanity, he became involved in rescuing members of that family from prison and from Mauthausen concentration camp.

The Weiss concern was the most important industrial enterprise in Hungary. Founded and developed by Jews, it produced armaments, machines, and a large variety of other products. It was controlled by a system of interlocking directorates. In the course of its development, the Jewish industrialists became part of the Hungarian aristocracy, some of them converted to Christianity, and many non-Jews joined them, either as family members or as business associates.

Early on March 19, Hans von Mauthner, a nephew of the Weiss barons, was called up by one of his uncles and informed of the occupation of Hungary. Mauthner phoned all his relatives, most of whom managed to hide. The head of the family, Ferenc (Franz) Chorin, and his brother-in-law, Baron Moricz Kornfeld, had heard the news independently and fled the capital to the monastery at Zirc, where they were hidden by a friendly abbot. But Chorin committed the mistake of calling his home by telephone a few days later, not knowing that it had been taken over by the Nazis, and he was caught. In the meantime, Ferenc Kelemen had been squeezed dry by Becher, who learned about all the holdings and directorates of the Weiss group. Chorin's capture came while Kelemen was being interrogated, beaten, and tortured at the Gestapo headquarters in the Astoria Hotel. Chorin was brought to the Gestapo jail on Foe utca, where, according to the testimony of a fellow prisoner, he was with difficulty prevented from swallowing cyanide. On March 26 he and other prominent and wealthy Jews—among them, Moricz Kornfeld and Leo Goldberger—were transferred to a Gestapo "facility" at Oberlanzensdorf, near Vienna. At that point Becher appeared on the scene and, with Himmler's approval, offered to take Chorin out in order to discuss with him how to manage the business. Chorin was delighted to be "rescued," and went with Becher to a Vienna hotel on May 1, whence he was shipped back to Budapest. The others were sent to Mauthausen on May 4. Becher had presumably acted out of a heartfelt concern for the older man's health.[10]

What followed was a series of complicated discussions, described by Becher as "friendly," between Chorin, representing the Weiss family, and Obersturmbannführer Becher. Not about horses, to be sure, but about "equipment [*Ausrüstungsgegenstände*]" and about handing control of the industrial concern to the SS in return for their lives. The idea of handing over the property did not come from Becher—oh no, it came from Chorin. In fact, Chorin was kept under strict house arrest at his own villa, which was occupied by Becher and his girlfriend, Countess Hermine von Platen. After a few days, when Chorin saw that his family would sooner or later be caught and arrested, with Mauthausen or Auschwitz as their final destination, he either offered Becher what Becher had wanted him to offer or responded to a suggestion by his gentleman blackmailer.[11]

Becher, in his postwar testimonies, pretended that he had been afraid to submit the proposal to Himmler because it would involve the escape of some forty-eight or fifty Jews from Nazi Germany. In fact, Himmler himself had given Becher permission to liberate Chorin after his first arrest. The deal that Becher was working out was exactly what Himmler had wanted—after all, we do remember the permission to make such deals that Himmler obtained from Hitler in December 1942. With Himmler's approval, Becher began arranging the complicated agreements that were necessary to transfer the control of the Weiss works into the hands of the SS.

In postwar statements Becher presented his part in this affair as pure humanitarianism on the one hand—he was trying his best to rescue these poor persecuted people—and, on the other hand, as fulfillment of the orders of Himmler, who was apprised of what was going on and not just agreed but prodded Becher to conclude the bargain. Some of the extended family who held the controlling shares in the company were not Jews. The Jews in the Weiss family had forfeited their property to the Hungarian government through the confiscatory legislation passed in the wake of the German occupation. But the "Aryan" part of the family could not be forced to hand its assets over to the Hungarians. That portion of the property could be acquired by the SS. Himmler needed a firm like that to establish the SS's own economic power base, which could begin to compete with Goering's economic empire, the Hermann Goering-Werke. What was being forced on the hapless Chorin was an agreement to give up the shares belonging to the non-Jewish branches of the family. Chorin himself was a Jew, and Baron Kornfeld, Baroness Edith Weiss, and others were converts or children of converts, and hence "Jews." The family lawyer—a converted Jew by the name of Wilhelm Billitz, who was married to an "Aryan" Hungarian and therefore was exempt from anti-Jewish persecution—saw no other way than to agree to the black-mail offer of the humanitarian SS officer.

The main point in the four "agreements" that Becher forced Chorin to accept was that, because the Jewish members of the family could not expect to be trusted by the German Reich to increase production for the German war effort and because their property rights as Jews were restricted in any case, the non-Jewish members were "willing" to hand over their own shares to the Germans, who would serve as trustees for twenty-five years. Origi-nally, the talk was of thirty-three years, but the time was reduced. All the vast properties held by the family were then listed—that was what Kelemen had been held for—and the SS was guaranteed a payment of 5 percent of the business turnover of the whole concern. That percentage was a vast sum, which probably would have thrown the business into bankruptcy within twenty-five years. The fourth agreement detailed what the SS was willing to do: fly most of the family to neutral countries, leaving five people behind as hostages. Control over the company was to be vested in a largely fictitious directorate, but the practical management was to be supervised by two SS officers. Becher was one of them.

On May 17 all the family members with signatory rights were summoned to a villa heavily guarded by SS troops. They were kept waiting until about midnight, when a dapper Becher appeared with Chorin and Billitz in tow. Chorin and all the rest signed on the dotted line, with only Chorin's wife, Daisy, objecting. Chorin explained to her that "we cannot do anything else, we are completely in their hands."[12]

Chorin and the other Weiss family members were transported to Vienna on May 18; there they remained for several weeks, living in sleeping cars at a small train station near the city. Becher had some problems getting them out—after all, the German Foreign Office was not supposed to know of the deal made by the rival SS. While in Vienna, five more persons, one "Aryan" and four Jews, had to give up shares that had somehow been overlooked before—36,630 shares of very important Hungarian enterprises. Becher had promised the group a sum of $600,000 but then told them that he could offer only $170,000. In return, the generous SS officer permitted another five fam-ily members from Budapest to join the emigrants. Nine people chose to go to Switzerland. They flew from Stuttgart on June 25, without the promised passports or visas, and were accepted by the Swiss only after considerable difficulties. The second group, of thirty-two persons, with Chorin and most of the Kornfelds, left Stuttgart for Lisbon with passports and forged visas in the company of Becher's underling, Karl Stapenhorst (Billitz was one of the thirty-two, but he had to return from Lisbon as one of the hostages). They arrived on June 26.[13]

Becher had pulled off a great coup for the SS. He had acquired a tremendously wealthy and profitable industrial concern by pure blackmail and had liberated a number of Weiss family members, keeping a few as hostages so the others would be prevented from saying what they knew. What is more important, however, is that Hitler supported Himmler in the acquisition of the Manfred Weiss works and instructed Ribbentrop to tell Veesenmayer in Budapest to tell the Hungarians that the affair was finished as far as the German ambassador was concerned. "We stand in a battle of life or death, and it is our main aim to consecrate all the means at our disposal for a victorious finish of this struggle."[14] The direct involvement of Hitler in the affair, for which we have evidence, indicates, first of all, how closely he followed everything connected with Jews and, second, how much leeway he was giving Himmler regarding the permission he had granted in December 1942. In the Weiss case, Himmler did not go beyond a narrow interpretation of that permission.

The Hungarians, when they learned about the Weiss affair, were furious. The pro-German Prime Minister, Döme Sztojay, protested; he demanded the participation of Hungarians in the directorate, so that the largest Hungarian industrial enterprise should not be totally under German control. Himmler agreed to have one Hungarian director among a number of Germans, which was largely a cosmetic change. In the end, three directors were Hungarians and five were SS officers. The decisive argument was that SS divisions were in Hungary at the time. So the acquisition of the Weiss works by the SS remained in effect.[15] Everything, including staged meetings of shareholders, was done according to "correct" business procedures. Becher personally represented Himmler in the bitter and difficult discussions with Sztojay. Himmler would not yield on any material point, despite a pathetic appeal to him by Sztojay on July 9 and despite Veesenmayer's opposition to the transaction (because he was left out?).[16] Becher was an accomplished diplomat and businessman, as Sztojay rightly said in his letter; Himmler could justly be proud of him. He was.

It is a moot point whether Becher pushed for the deportations in their first stage, as Eichmann claimed at his trial in Jerusalem, or whether he was just a beneficiary of the deportations. Clearly, the Weiss family could not have been blackmailed without the threat of deportations hanging over their heads. A panicky atmosphere of imminent death threats was most conducive to pliancy on the part of Becher's victims.

Becher did not engage only in large-scale blackmail and robbery on behalf of the SS. He also knew how to deal with smaller fry. In a letter of April 22, 1962, Gyula Link, whom we have met as one of the main financial supporters of Orthodox rescue attempts, detailed to Joel Brand his experiences with Becher. Link paid the *Wirtschaftsstab* (Becher's economic staff) 2,000 woolen blankets and SFR 100,000, and was supposed to pay SFR 15,000 monthly to not wear the yellow star, thus protecting himself, his family, and two Slovak Jewish women hiding with him against ghettoization and arrest. Every month the conditions grew worse. The refugees and then his brother were excluded from the agreement; he had to wear the star; he was moved to a ghetto house. Ultimately, he fled to Romania but hoodwinked Becher by paying the last SFR 17,000 on the day of his flight in order to mislead him.[17]

Becher also forced Jewish artisans to produce goods for the SS—without payment, of course. His office made merchants and artisans set up workshops at their own expense and use their own materials and tools in order to produce for the SS, and the Budapest Judenrat was forced to pay the artisans and merchants. The artisans were promised that they would not be deported. In the end, when Becher was forced to flee from a Hungary being liberated by the Soviets, he took with him a group of wealthy individuals and families who had paid for their rescue by giving up their properties and materials to Becher's SS. Many poor craftsmen and craftswomen survived along with them. Becher did indeed save their lives—at the price of blackmail and robbery.[18]

It is important to note that Becher became part of the German preparations for the Brand mission at more or less the same time as he laid his hands on the Manfred Weiss firm. Billitz asked him to intervene to save Jewish lives, says Becher. When Becher testified to that effect in 1961, Billitz had been dead for many years, so no confrontation with a witness was possible. A Swiss journalist, Kurt Emenegger, argues that Billitz was probably poisoned by Becher's men because he knew too much of the inner workings of the Becher gang. Becher, by his own admission, became part of the German background to the Brand affair because of the economic proposals that were connected with it, which sounds much more plausible than the story of saving human lives. With Veesenmayer, Eichmann, and Clages involved, for Himmler to ask his successful economic expert to participate was logical—or perhaps Becher suggested the idea to his boss. According to Andreas Biss, it was Clages who suggested to Biss and Kasztner that they get in touch with Becher, because Becher might help them. That is what happened: Kasztner began to talk not only with Eichmann but with Becher as well. The serious relationship with Becher apparently started when Kasztner bribed him with $20,000 to intercede with Himmler against further deportations after Horthy stopped them in early July.[19]

We have seen that in the wake of the failure of the Brand mission, Kasztner tried to arrange meetings between representatives of the SD and JDC's Joseph Schwartz, or Eliyahu Dobkin of the JA, or Menachem Bader, the delegate from Istanbul. According to a well-researched paper on the subject by Paul L. Rose, when Kasztner finally received on July 10 the so-called interim agreement between Brand and Bader of May 29, he rushed with it to Eichmann and Becher, who were impressed by its contents. Perhaps, had the Istanbul emissaries sent the agreement earlier—or if they did send it, had it arrived earlier—they might have strengthened Kasztner's hand in his dealings with the Nazis. In any case, it appears that the memorandum made the SS negotiators—Becher and Clages primarily, we can assume—more eager to find a way to reach the West via the Jews.[20] Yet on July 17, Kasztner was told by Eichmann that if Brand did not return forthwith, he, Eichmann, would send the whole Bergen-Belsen transport to Auschwitz and have them all gassed there without a selection.[21] Kasztner was frantic, and Biss reports that for the first time he saw his friend burst into tears, completely desperate.

The efforts to have someone else from the free world meet the Nazis have to be explained in this context. Such a meeting was envisaged as an alternative to the meeting represented by the combined Brand-Grosz ideas, which was a meeting with U.S. government spokesmen. Whether Becher supported these initiatives is difficult to say, but he must have been involved. The German negotiator was to have been Laufer, the Jewish SD man, so perhaps the alliance of these two Himmler agents, representing SD and SS economic interests, was directed against the third Himmler agent—Eichmann.

Komoly was to have gone to Lisbon, or perhaps to Istanbul, because Kasztner was again arrested, on July 18, by the Hungarians, who wanted more information about his German contacts. For about ten days, while Kasztner was held by the Hungarian gendarmes, Freudiger contacted Becher, offering him 250 trucks, which he tried to have delivered from Switzerland, or at least Swiss money. For that purpose he was in touch with Isaac Sternbuch and his siblings and circle in Montreux, Switzerland; they were the representatives there of the Va'ad Hahatzalah and were less concerned about legal procedures than the JDC was. However, neither the WRB man in Bern, Roswell D. McClelland, nor Saly Mayer had any desire to agree to the transaction. The VH was incapable of delivering the trucks, and Becher again turned to Kasztner upon the latter's release.[22]

The time has come to say a bit more about Kurt A. Becher, who is a key person in our tale. Becher was a young Hamburg merchant (born in 1909), who loved horseback riding. In 1934 he became a member of the mounted unit of the Allgemeine SS (General SS), in 1937 he joined the Party, and on September 27, 1938, he started his SS career. He received his training in the *Totenkopf* (Death's Head) cavalry regiment at Dachau. In his 1946 testimony to the Americans he admits that he underwent (further?) training with the Totenkopf unit at Oranienburg. We know that the unit was the "Brandenburg" brigade, which had little to do with military training or riding. It was a concentration camp guard unit, to which General SS men were assigned for a few weeks of hardening. It seems that Becher served a few weeks (until November 5) as a camp guard at Dachau and Oranienburg concentration camps, which was not something to boast of after the war.[23]

Becher was *gottgläubig,* which means that he did not belong to either of the two Christian denominations, Protestant or Catholic, but was an ideologically sound National Socialist. When the war broke out, he joined his SS Totenkopf "Standarte" in Poland (Totenkopf units alternated between field duty and concentration camp guard duty). By his own admission, he did not see any action in Poland, but his unit, like all other special SS units, must have been engaged in terrorizing Poles and Jews. Becher remembers nothing of this, naturally. He received more training as an SS NCO at Dachau in late 1939. From February 1940 on, he served as cavalryman in the Totenkopf cavalry unit in Poland. He became a lieutenant in January 1941.

His duties in Poland were very pleasant; his unit robbed and stole wherever it could, along with other SS units. In Warsaw he was part of a group that was investigated by the SS juridical authorities for corruption and *Rassenschande* (sexual cohabitation with non-Germans). Although he himself did not appear in the indictment, his immediate superior officer, Hermann Fegelein, and Fegelein's brother did. In his postwar testimonies he could not, for the life of him, remember anything about the Warsaw ghetto. His friend, Franz Konrad, however, who was hanged by the Polish authorities as a war criminal in 1951, testified (on October 2 and 4, 1948) that Becher came to him when Konrad was in charge of plundering the ghetto and demanded a certain percentage of the goods taken from the Jews for his superior, Fegelein. In 1940–42 Warsaw was a good place for an SS man to enjoy life. It is funny how memory grows fuzzy after a lost war.[24]

His personal life reflected his whole personality. In 1936 he married Margot Peters, daughter of a merchant, and in due course she bore him four children. His extramarital sex life was quite impressive, and before 1944 he was living with Countess Hermine von Platen. Margot was an intellectual, non-Nazi type; Hermine was an excellent horsewoman, not terribly well educated, and with an aristocratic title—just the type for Kurt Andreas, even though, to tell the truth, Hermine started adult life as a barmaid and acquired the "von" later. There were two other mistresses in Budapest, so Becher did not need to feel lonely among the Hungarians and the Jews. He divorced his wife in 1947 and married Hermine, but Hermine died soon afterward, and Becher married Maria Smend. After her death in 1959 he married for a fourth time, a young horsewoman, Ilsebill Funk, who produced a daughter for him.

Becher strikes the observer as an opportunist, a man who believed in Nazism not because of any deep intellectual or emotional conviction but because of a strongly developed herd instinct. He most certainly expressed belief in German victory until the end of 1944. Why did he save large numbers of Jews in Hungary while remaining the Nazi blackmailer, thief, and antisemite that he always was? Did something in his background make him eager to provide an alibi for himself?

The mainspring of his actions was undoubtedly his loyalty to Himmler. As late as 1945 he praised Himmler's character to Schweiger, after Schweiger's liberation from Mauthausen. Becher wanted to succeed as a loyal SS officer. But his insistence on meeting Americans and his attempts to save the Reich through such contacts are indicative of his understanding of Himmler's vacillating policy—loyalty to the Führer, on the one hand, and a desire to change directions and ally Germany with the West in order to save the Nazi regime, on the other hand. The alibis worked very well. Kasztner, Schweiger, Biss (who became one of the Va'adah's main contacts with the Germans), the hostages that he took along to the Swiss border at the end—all these people testified in his favor and lauded him after the war.

Why did Becher act the way he did? Did he attempt to provide himself with an alibi for something that he was seeking to hide? Let us investigate.

In 1941, when the Germans invaded the Soviet Union, three newly established SS units went in behind the advancing German armies with "special security tasks." They were two SS motorized brigades and one SS cavalry brigade. They were not part of the German Army, nor were they part of Heydrich's security forces (including the Einsatzgruppen, or action units—the murder squads who killed Jews on a large scale). The special new formation was called the Kommandostab Reichsführer SS, and it was under Himmler's personal command. Very well equipped and trained, these 18,000 or so men were given the task of "cleansing" the rear areas of partisans, communists, and Jews. The cavalry brigade, under the command of Hermann Fegelein, Hitler's future brother-in-law (he later married Eva Braun's sister), cleared the Pripjet marshes between Byelorussia in the north and the Ukraine in the south, which motorized units could not penetrate. Between July and September, they killed a measly few hundred "partisans" and communists but did manage to murder 15,000 Jewish men, women, and children for the greater glory of the Third Reich.

Untersturmführer (Lieutenant) Kurt Becher was sent in as commander of Platoon 3 of the cavalry company of the First Regiment before he was called upon to be the Ordonnanzoffizier (administrative officer) of the brigade on August 5. Before August 5 the regiment was busy killing as many Jews as possible. After the war, Becher not only claimed that he had never killed any Jews because he was only an administrative officer—this was a patent lie, as we

have just seen—but he also claimed that he had no knowledge of the extermi-
nationist policy toward the Jews until three years later, in August 1944!

An administrative officer has to know in detail the orders and commands
of both superior authorities and the commanders of the unit. Becher's unit
was officially told to kill all "partisans." Jews were to be killed because they
were the instigators of partisan warfare. But the Pripjet marshes held no partisans to speak of, nor, for that matter, were there many partisans anywhere
else in the just-conquered areas of Byelorussia and the Ukraine. In fact,
antipartisan warfare was simply a cover for the murder of Jews. As Franz
Konrad, an officer in the same First Regiment, said: "Everyone who looked
like a Jew was killed as a partisan."[25]

Becher participated in "many scouting missions and fulfilled other difficult tasks." He must have done his job very well, because he earned medals
for it and was then recalled to do important economic work in the SS offices
in Berlin.[26] There is no signature of his on any reports of murders, and
Becher claimed after the war that he had just been doing administrative and,
presumably, planning work. Whether he "only" administered and planned
murder or whether he also participated in it, which is at least likely, there is
no doubt that he had plenty to hide later on when the fortunes of war turned.
After his exertions under Fegelein's command, however, he had to regain his
health. He had contracted venereal disease (as part of his administrative job,
presumably), but thank God (not the Protestant or the Catholic one, but the
one that an upright gottgläubig Nazi patient with venereal disease believed
in), he was cured and went to do important work in Berlin.[27]

Kurt Emenegger, the Swiss investigative journalist who researched the
Becher affair in the early 1960s, claims more than that. He claims that by a
special order 17 Himmler nominated Becher personally to coordinate the
activities of the infamous Einsatzkommandos (the subunits of the Einsatzgruppen, the Nazi murder squads for the destruction of the Jews) with the
activities of the cavalry brigade in cooperation with Fegelein. Emenegger
claims that in a January 1943 letter from Himmler to Becher, Becher was
praised for his undaunted devotion in the struggle against subhumanity
("unerschrockenen Einsatz gegen das Untermenschentum"). Emenegger
detailed a story that is typical of many prosecutions in postwar West Germany. His research team obtained the texts of the two documents (Himmler's special order of 1941 and his letter of appreciation to Becher of 1943)
and asked the appropriate government attorneys in Essen and Düsseldorf
where the actual documents were. Let Emenegger speak:

"Our informant, Dr. Max Merten, a Berlin lawyer, told us that the 'owner,' or
rather the trustee with whom these incriminating documents were located,
was Investigative Judge Dr. Hans Behm, district judge in Essen. Thereupon

the Frankfurt prosecutor Dr. Steinbacher, as well as the Frankfurt investigative judge, District Judge Schneider, demanded the documents from Dr. Behm. Dr. Behm claimed that he did not know about the documents and did not possess them. The Frankfurt people had to be satisfied with that. Dr. Grimm, Dr. Behm's successor in presiding over the case of Wagner and von Thadden [another anti-Nazi case], also declared that he had no knowledge of the documents we sought and could not find them among the papers taken over from Dr. Behm."

Then one of Emenegger's collaborators, Ernest Zaugg, "tries a last time."

"He goes to Essen, with a witness, and suddenly asks the Essen general prosecutor, Dr. Ludwig Kuhnert, if he knows anything about special Himmler order 17 and its contents? And whether it is correct that this document had already been sent to the Hessian general prosecutor, Dr. Fritz Bauer in Frankfurt?

"Zaugg had not promised himself much from his questions. If Dr. Behm and Dr. Grimm do not know anything about the documents, then the prosecutor will not know anything either. Dr. Kuhnert's open answer was the more perplexing: Yes, he is acquainted with the document, since 1953 in fact! Not under the name of order 17, but the contents are identical with those that Zaugg presented. The document, he says, had been found in connection with the Wagner / von Thadden case. He could not remember whether the document in the files was an original or a photocopy.

"'Where, then, is this damned document?' asks Zaugg. Again, Dr. Kuhnert does not hesitate. It was taken away by a Mr. Richter of the Frankfurt prosecutor's office.

"Needless to say, the next morning Zaugg and I were already sitting in the office of the Hessian general prosecutor. Dr. Bauer's surprise is real, after we had reported everything to him. Really, now. . . .

"The first thing, naturally, is for Dr. Bauer to call Dr. Kuhnert in Essen. He turned on the microphone, so we could listen in. We clearly hear Dr. Kuhnert's distinct, though hesitant, affirmation: Yes, he had talked with Zaugg about the document. Yes, he knows its contents, which are essentially identical with the one we mentioned.

"Dr. Bauer asks whether the Essen general prosecutor has knowledge of the letter of 1943, in which Himmler lauds Becher for his devotion in the struggle against subhumanity. Yes, he, Dr. Kuhnert, knows of such a letter from Himmler to Becher. This, too, like special order 17, had been found in the Wagner / von Thadden file.

"However, Dr. Kuhnert does not now remember where the documents had got to. As far as Richter is concerned, Zaugg must have misunderstood him. Perhaps he had told Richter to look for the documents in Bonn. . . .

"In the papers that Mr. Richter brought from Essen—he himself is serving in the Bundeswehr [West German army] in the meantime—there is no trace of the documents."

The Frankfurt people were looking for the missing documents in vain. In the meantime, Dr. Merten from Berlin had been asked whether he knew about the contents of these papers, and he affirmed that he did, and repeated their contents to the investigators.[28] Emenegger asks, rightly, who made these documents disappear and how? And this at a time when Becher was a multi-millionaire in Bremen with excellent connections to the highest as well as, we might suspect, the lowest places?

Let me add that Emenegger, in a private discussion with myself, said that he had called Merten in Berlin and that Merten had promised him access to the documents if he reached Berlin within a day. But Emenegger could not persuade his superiors at the journal to agree to spend more funds, and by the time he arrived Merten told him that the documents had gone. How, by whom, where, he would not say.

The circumstantial evidence appears fairly convincing: Mr. Kurt A. Becher has something to hide. What is more important, however, is the light that Emenegger's story throws on the ambiguities of the Third Reich. Becher followed his admired master, Himmler, in making clumsy attempts to reach the West. He was a convinced if superficial and opportunist Nazi, the stuff so many mass murderers were made of. Becher was a killer probably, a murderer probably, a robber and blackmailer most certainly—and a savior of maybe hundreds of thousands of lives. He saved those lives to benefit himself in the long run and, at first, anyway, to improve the prospects that the Nazi Reich would survive. Like so many others, he may even have returned to a relatively normal morality when the Nazi Reich was in its death throes.

In the main, his job was to provide horses, not only for the few cavalry units of the SS but also for other uses, because the campaign in the East required a great deal of horsepower. His relationship to Fegelein brought him to Himmler's attention, who saw in him a talented young man to be used for economic tasks. In between the murder bouts in Russia and the extortions in Hungary Becher led the quiet life of a provider of horses for the SS. After the major extortion of the Weiss works, Becher saved Jewish lives.

What we have here is essentially the problem of the ambiguity of evil: a man who originally—as a young wheat merchant in Hamburg—is neither good nor evil but just an ambitious young man trying to become rich, becomes an accomplice of mass murderers and is himself involved, perhaps on the margins, perhaps more deeply, in the corruption, the extortion, and the mass murders that are going on. Becher was probably just conventionally antisemitic. There is no evidence of any special hatred of Jews, and in his dealings with Kasztner and others he expressed no more than the usual Nazi haughtiness, and later not even that. But most murderers in eastern Poland, for instance, were not ideological antisemites, either.

Becher, like so many others, seems to have identified with the Third Reich, accepted the absolute leadership of the Führer, idealized his particular "führer," Himmler, and rejected moral autonomy or personal responsibility. He was not responsible: Himmler or Hitler was. If Himmler said that Jews had to be killed, then the killing had to be done—as profitably as possible for one's own career and pocket. Neither hatred of Jews nor love of killing was at issue. If Himmler or Hitler or the Nazi doctrine had argued for the mass murder of all left-handed individuals, that job would have had to be done, too. For historical reasons it was the Jews who were the main enemy. When Becher slowly became aware of the consequences of the mass murders, he may even have felt that they had been a mistake.

No less interesting than Becher's wartime exploits is his postwar career. A clever opportunist, he became one of the richest men in Germany. He was denied the socially desirable status of a member of Bremen's prestigious merchant guild in 1961—that was the start of Emenegger's investigations—because of rumors about his past.[29] But he attained just about everything else. Did his conscience bother him? Of course not. Had he not saved many, many Jews? Why were these people so ungrateful? He, like many others, distanced himself from Nazi ideology and practice in the postwar world; the total inversion of the moral universe, not any deviation from it, made it possible for the Bechers, the executioners, extortioners, and robbers to return to a decent bourgeois life. To this day they do not acknowledge what they did.

Let us now return to Kasztner and his desperate attempts to save as many Jews as possible. His new hope was Becher, and Becher was interested, very interested, in milking money or goods or political negotiations through his contact with Kasztner. The Hungarians were reluctant to continue with the deportations, which would have meant the murder of the Jews of Budapest, who were the only ones left in the country. Horthy had stopped the deportations given the confluence of several factors: pressure from the Americans, from the neutrals, from the Vatican; the bombing of Budapest; the approach of the Russians to the frontiers of the country; and the threat of a putsch by the Hungarian gendarmerie and the outright fascist elements. The government of Döme Sztojay did not last for long, and the new government under Geza Lakatos was trying to extricate Hungary from the war.

Opposed as they were to each other, Ribbentrop and Himmler now pursued similar policies toward Hungary. Himmler—and Eichmann perhaps more than Himmler—wanted to deport the rest of the Jews as quickly as possible. Ribbentrop, the convinced Nazi, wanted no less. But the Hungarians, eager to repair their image in the eyes of the West, announced on July 17 that they would be willing to let certain categories of Jews leave the country. Among them were the Palestine certificate holders, or, rather, those to whom Krausz had promised certificates, which he did not possess. He increased the number from 7,800 to some 40,000 by the well-tried method of declaring that the smaller number represented family heads and would have to be multiplied by four or five to include the families. In addition, the Swedish had promised an exit to 400 or 450 people with Swedish connections, and other, smaller categories had a chance to leave. The British government, afraid of an influx of 40,000 Jews into Palestine, tried to limit the offer to the 7,000 or 8,700 originally suggested, but it was too late: the Hungarians were willing to let 40,000 Jews go.[30] For all of these Jews, the Hungarians asked the Germans to grant exit visas.[31]

The Nazis saw their opportunity. They at first opposed any exit of Jews, and Ribbentrop gave an appropriate instruction to Veesenmayer as early as July 7.[32] Similar instructions followed. Undaunted by Horthy's stopping of the deportations, and indeed on the very days that he did so, the Germans and their fascist Hungarian allies (especially Interior Minister Jaross) were actively preparing the deportation of Budapest Jews.[33] On July 24, Eichmann requested the RSHA to intervene; he wanted the German government to declare openly that no emigration to Palestine would be permitted, for reasons that we already know. The Germans officially agreed to the Hungarian request to grant transit visas to the emigrating Jews, but made their agreement conditional upon the agreement of the Hungarians to deport all the other Jews of Budapest.[34] The emigration of a minority would be paid for by the deportation to death of the rest.

In the following days, this policy was reiterated again and again.[35] However, Eichmann had no intention of letting those relatively few Jews go. He told his superiors that he had convinced the German embassy to procrastinate in granting transit permits. Once the deportations started, all Jews would be included. On another occasion, he announced that the deportations would take place in a very sudden ("schlagartig") way, and before anyone realized it, the Jews would disappear. If the Jews managed to go westward, and he must have meant Spain, he would see to it that they would be stopped in France by "appropriate measures [geeignete Massnahmen]."[36] The deviousness of the inter-Nazi relations is perhaps exemplified by Himmler's decision on August 4 to oppose the Jews' exit to Palestine and by implication not to other places.[37] Here again, Eichmann appears as the extreme hardliner and Himmler as the more cautious, vacillating chief.

After the Hungarian decision to stop the deportations and the German agreement—on the face of it—to let a number of Jews emigrate, Hitler intervened. On July 17, he wrote a note that Veesenmayer was ordered to present to Horthy. In the sharpest language possible, Hitler threatened renewed intervention in Hungary as a result of Horthy's betrayal, manifested in the latter's stated desire to dismiss Sztojay and his attempts to abandon his German ally and to stop the deportations of Jews. "The Führer expects that now measures will be taken against the Budapest Jews, with those exceptions that the Reich government had conceded to the Hungarian government on the suggestion of Ambassador Veesenmayer. No delay in the general Jewish measures will be allowed to take place; otherwise, the exceptions agreed to by the Führer will be revoked."[38]

The Hungarian government, then, was under pressure from two opposing sides: from the neutrals, who reiterated Allied warnings about the continuation of deportations, and the Germans, who wanted to deport the remaining Jews as quickly as possible. On August 14, Veesenmayer reported a breakthrough for the German side: the Hungarian government had decided to deport the Jews starting on August 25. On the nineteenth the Hungarians again confirmed their agreement. Eichmann demanded that the deportations begin the next day. But Horthy had not yet given his approval. The Germans needed to decide whether to keep their side of the bargain and allow small numbers of Jews to emigrate. They did not, of course, agree to the Krausz figures. They were talking about 7,000 individuals who might be permitted to go to Palestine via Romania, although Himmler was against the Palestine destination. Eighty-seven people would be allowed to go to Sweden—the Swedish ambassador and Raoul Wallenberg, who had arrived in Budapest on July 9, had not been able to push the number any higher. Nine Jews would be allowed to go to Portugal, three to Spain, and five to Switzerland. Eichmann did not exclude the possibility of some armed Jewish resistance, and a large number of Jews—he put it at 100,000—would hide, or had already done so, once the deportations were under way.[39]

On August 19, Veesenmayer's representative, Grell, reported that the Hungarian Minister of the Interior had told Eichmann that the deportations would definitely start on the twenty-fifth, although Horthy had agreed to only a limited "evacuation." The government, however, had decided that all Jews would be deported except for Jews converted before January 1, 1941, and a special group of 3,000 people under Horthy's protection. On the twenty-fifth, the Jews would be concentrated in three large camps. The first six trains with 20,000 persons aboard would leave for Auschwitz on the twenty-seventh, to be followed by daily trains carrying 3,000 people each. The concentration of the victims would be done solely by the Hungarian gendarmes.[40] On the twenty-fourth, Eichmann was told by the Hungarian Ministry of the Interior that the amassing of Jews would begin on the twenty-eighth and that the Jews would remain in five camps established for that purpose. They would not be sent to "Germany." Eichmann declared in an angry response that he would ask the RSHA to recall him since he was no longer needed.[41]

During the night of August 24, Winkelmann received a cable from Himmler personally, according to which all preparations for the deportation of Jews should be immediately stopped. The news was transmitted to Veesenmayer, who informed Ribbentrop.[42] What had happened?

Kasztner was only partly aware of the negotiations and the tensions between the Hungarians and the Germans. He knew, as we have seen, that the tragedy of the deportations, which had annihilated the Jews of the provinces, could strike Budapest any day. He was therefore desperately eager to achieve a breakthrough in the negotiations that would enable him to get the Germans to stop the murders, temporarily at least, in order to gain time. He was sure by now that he could achieve such a breakthrough only through Becher, and he decided to gamble on that card. All his plans for Jewish partners to negotiate with the Nazis—Bader, Schwartz, and Dobkin—had failed. At the end of July he thought of Saly Mayer, the JDC man in Switzerland.

In the meantime, another incident was making life very difficult for Kasztner. Ten years later it surfaced at his trial and helped destroy him. The JA had managed to persuade the British intelligence services to drop Palestinian Jewish parachutists behind enemy lines. They would have two tasks: helping Allied, mainly British, airmen who had been shot down over enemy territory, to escape, and providing military information. They would also have a mission to aid Jews: organizing resistance among the Jews of Europe, or at least bringing them moral and possibly material support.

The whole idea was part of the Allied intelligence methods of warfare; not dissimilar activities had had some measure of success from Yugoslavia to France to Burma. In all, by the end of the war thirty-three Jewish parachutists and agents were infiltrated, of whom seven died. Most of these courageous men and women did not succeed in their missions. Not that they did not try—they tried very hard and showed tremendous courage in doing so. But the circumstances were against them. They came late in the war; in many cases, they were dropped in the wrong places; sometimes they could find no Jews anywhere near where they landed—the Jews were no longer there—and they simply had bad luck. Three parachutists were destined for Hungary: Joel Nussbacher (Palgi), the only survivor; Franz (Peretz) Goldstein; and Hanna Szenes. Hanna Szenes, a young poet whose mother still lived in Budapest, was first dropped into Tito's territory in Yugoslavia, whence she was supposed to make her way into Hungary. She was apparently betrayed even before she crossed the border; in any case, she was caught and brought to a Budapest jail. The other two, who crossed the Hungarian border from Croatia on June 13, trod a similar path. At first, they went to Budapest, but the Hungarians and the Germans were already shadowing them. When they went back to receive a transmitter, they were arrested.[43]

In Budapest, Palgi and Goldstein managed somehow to escape the Germans, and they went to—Kasztner. After all, both of them had been born in Hungary, and they were Zionists; Kasztner was now their leader. Kasztner did not know what to do with them. The Germans would suspect that they had contacted him. It was one thing to pay ransom in some form; it was quite another thing to become involved with two Jewish-Palestinian-British agents cum parachutists in the middle of a war. Kasztner told them to make up their minds whether or not to give themselves up. Hanna Szenes was already in jail, and they could do nothing for Budapest Jewry. Certainly there was no chance of organizing armed resistance at that late stage. The two young men hesitated, then gave themselves up. Palgi managed to jump from the train that deported him, probably to Mauthausen; he survived—he did not go to Kasztner anymore. Goldstein perished, probably at Mauthausen.

Should Kasztner have hidden them? Did he tell the Germans that they had contacted him before they gave themselves up? If he had hidden them, would he not have endangered all Budapest Jews? On the other hand, how could he knowingly send two young men from Palestine to their deaths? In the history of the Holocaust there are a number of such cases, and they were solved in different fashions by different people. The death of Goldstein, combined with the accusation that Kasztner did not do enough to save Hanna Szenes, or perhaps simply abandoned her to her fate in order to save his policy of negotiations, was weighty and serious. The indictments may have been justified: Kasztner may have caused the two men to fall into Nazi hands, and he had done nothing decisive to rescue Szenes, who became a hero in post-Holocaust Palestine-Israel.

Kasztner, then, developed his relationship with Becher—not that he was under any illusions about Becher's character. We have several documents that reflect the relationship with fair accuracy: Kasztner's notes on meetings with Becher and Wisliceny, which he dictated to his secretary (Lilly Ungar), who kept copies of them.[44] On July 15, Becher opened the discussion by saying that they were meeting on neutral ground—probably meeting in his office and not on the Schwabenberg (a Swabian hill in Budapest), where Eichmann's headquarters were located. Kasztner responded that for him there was no neutral ground; only hostile territory existed for him "here." To this Becher, that humanitarian lover of Jews, replied, "You are an uppity dog [Sie sind ein frecher Hund]." Kasztner confronted Becher with instances of German deception from Wisliceny on and said that at least 300,000 Hungarian Jews had already fallen victim to murder in Auschwitz. He said that the Germans could not have expected that the trucks would be arriving two weeks after Brand left for Istanbul. No, said Becher, but six weeks had now passed, and no trucks had showed up. Kasztner said that a journey to Lisbon (they were thinking in terms of negotiations with Schwartz or Dobkin at the time) made sense only if the Germans fulfilled a number of conditions: stopping the deportations and the gassings at Auschwitz and finding out how many were left alive of those who had been deported and what the price was for returning them to Hungary. Becher said that Kasztner should find out all about these conditions from Eichmann. Kasztner then insisted on the release of his train as a precondition for talks and threatened Becher with armed resistance by the Zionist youth, who were out to save Jewish honor, if the negotiations produced no results. But Kasztner also indicated that no one had told the deportees what fate awaited them (this was not true, as we have seen— attempts had been made to tell them) because the Jewish side had hoped the negotiations would bear fruit.[45]

At his meeting with Wisliceny on August 12, Kasztner expressed his hope that the deportation of the Jews from Budapest could be prevented through Becher. Wisliceny replied that if Becher elicited an instruction from Himmler not to deport the Budapest Jews, Eichmann would have to obey. Kasztner still insisted that further trains should leave the Reich; and because France, and hence the way to neutral Spain, was now closed because of the Allied invasion, only the road to Constanza, Romania—on the route to Palestine— was now open.

Kasztner then met with "Schröder," or Laufer. Laufer was interested in "his" people being among the first to go to Switzerland, a position that might indicate either that the SD had spies among the people on the train or that some of Laufer's family were on the train. In a phone conversation—all these contacts were made on August 12—Kasztner arranged for the journey to the Swiss border to negotiate with Saly Mayer (see below). The final sentences of the phone conversation are decisive for our understanding of both Kasztner and Becher. Kasztner asked whether the Budapest Jews were safe from the threat of deportation. Becher answered that "until we finish our talks, there will be peace in the city. If the talks have a negative outcome, the situation in the city could turn critical."[46]

The contemporary notes on these conversations are very valuable; they probably reflect the relationships as closely as we might wish. What emerges is the totally businesslike way in which Becher and Eichmann dealt with the problem of human lives. Becher, no less than Eichmann, insisted on *Leistungen* (results; achievements; payments), and he seems to have seen Kasztner as just another Jew from whom to pry something his "highly to be respected [*hochzuverehrender*]" Reichsführer would be happy with; he could, of course, have argued after the fact that he had to reap some results in order to succeed with Himmler. His tone and attitude to Kasztner belie such an explanation, however. Himmler himself decided on details: how many people from the

Bergen-Belsen transport would be released, how to evaluate the Jews' Leistungen. He was obviously responsible for countermanding the orders to deport the Jews of Budapest, too, but Becher would make his orders dependent on what the Jews could offer. Kasztner emerges as a strong character, unafraid to talk back in the Nazis' own language to gain what he wanted: the Bergen-Belsen transport and the promise not to deport the Jews of Budapest. We have the feeling that he was not quite aware of the danger facing Budapest Jews—he probably did not have a detailed picture of the preparations that the Germans were making. But his instincts told him that the danger was mortal and that action was required.

As events were unfolding, a new figure emerged on the Jewish side, Andreas Biss, a cousin of Brand's but no great friend of his. Biss was a wealthy manufacturer who had converted to Christianity in his childhood but now identified with his fellow Jews. He became a close adviser of Kasztner's and financed a big share of the Vaada's activities. His apartment became a gathering place for Vaada members, and his advice was sought and given. When Kasztner was arrested, Biss took his place. He, too, met with Becher and became an admirer of his. On July 22, Biss wrote a memorandum for Himmler which he gave to Clages for transmittal. In this memo Biss proposed stopping the murders of Hungarian Jews, not necessarily of all the others, in the Germans' own interest. Despite the claims of Biss to the contrary, nothing resulted from his memo.[47]

Biss was a very important agent in the process that led Becher to the next stage of the negotiations. In the absence of Kasztner and Hansi Brand, he met with Becher and kept his interest in the talks alive, and he also intervened with the Germans to free Kasztner from the Hungarian jail.

In the swirl of events Kasztner was frantically looking for someone to carry on the talks that Brand was supposed to have had with representatives of the Jews or the Allies. He had no knowledge of the U.S. refusal to let Joseph J. Schwartz of the JDC negotiate with the Nazis. Therefore, on August 1 he suggested that the talks with Schwartz take place in Switzerland, and that Saly Mayer be one of the participants. Schwartz picked up the idea and asked the WRB what they thought of it—Mayer was a Swiss citizen, and the American restrictions did not apply to him. The WRB asked for an opinion from its man in Bern, Roswell D. McClelland, who thought it was a good idea, provided the Swiss government agreed to it. He adopted the aim that had also been put forward by Shertok: "to draw out the negotiations and gain as much time as possible without, if feasible, making any commitments." He did not think that Mayer could offer ransom, "especially in exchange for goods which might enable the enemy to prolong the war."[48]

Mayer's freedom of action was thus circumscribed from the very start. Nevertheless, he accepted the difficult task of deceiving the Nazis when

Schwartz first suggested it to him, probably in late July, and he prepared himself for it.

Saly Mayer was a most unlikely person to undertake the mission. Born in 1882 of a southern German family, Mayer had been a lace manufacturer but had retired early, partly because he nursed political ambitions within the Jewish community and partly because he had a very unhappy family life. He was a very conservative man, very strict with himself and with others, and his education was limited. He considered himself an Orthodox Jew—he kept to the dietary laws, did not work on a Sabbath—although his knowledge of Judaism was unimpressive. From 1936 to 1942 he served as the head of the Union of Swiss Jewish Communities (SIG). He resigned his presidency in the face of serious criticism for accepting without too much protest the restrictive policy of the Swiss government toward Jewish refugees; he had argued that a small community of 17,000 souls in a beleaguered neutral country should make the best of its good relations with the government, including the Alien Police. Ever since 1940 he had served as JDC representative in Switzerland, but until 1942 he had received very little money to use to aid Jews under the Nazi regime. We have seen his role in the Slovak negotiations, and he was quite knowledgeable about the needs of Jews in Hungary because of his contacts with different groups there. Also, his friendship with Nathan Schwalb, the emissary of the Zionist youth movements in Switzerland, helped.

The funds that Mayer had at his disposal in 1944 were much more substantial than those he had had in 1942–43. American Jews had reacted more generously to JDC appeals because of the information that reached the United States regarding the fate of European Jewry. He received $6,467,000, of which $3,763,000 was preempted for the upkeep of Jewish refugees in Switzerland and for fulfillment of obligations to help Jews in France and Romania. That left $2,700,000 for the rest of Europe and Shanghai, where Jewish refugees were supported from Switzerland via the Red Cross. The sum was very small, but, as in 1942, he could not say that to the many who were looking to him for relief, and even the Jewish Agency, thus earning the undying enmity of their representatives. His rationalization of this behavior was that the talks were so delicate that any publicity might endanger lives; also, he was obligated to both the Swiss and the U.S. governments to keep his negotiations strictly secret. He did not, by the way, like the idea of control by the WRB; he called the board his nurses and governesses. Schwartz agreed, but there was no way out: "They are not even nice-looking nurses, but it cannot be helped."[49]

Mayer was a loyal Swiss citizen, and he wanted to obtain the agreement of his government to the forthcoming negotiations. He turned to Heinrich Rothmund, chief of the Alien Police (August 8), who in 1938 had been instrumental in persuading the Germans to introduce passports for Jews bearing the red letter "J" in them to distinguish German Jews from other German subjects. Mayer asked for permission to have Jewish refugees enter Switzerland, first those from the Kasztner train and then the Strasshof people (the group of Hungarian Jews, mentioned earlier, who had been deported to Vienna rather than to Auschwitz). Rothmund replied that only children and adults with relatives in Switzerland would be permitted in and that Mayer was forbidden to offer ransom in his talks. The Swiss government was afraid that its neutrality might be compromised. The Red Cross told Mayer that it could on no account associate with people who were using illegal means to rescue Jews.[50]

On August 21 the WRB, over the signature of U.S. Secretary of State Cordell Hull, instructed Mayer that he could not offer ransom, could not offer goods, and could not negotiate in the name of JDC, because that was an American organization. He should come as a Swiss citizen and as a leader of the Swiss Jewish community and negotiate with the aim of gaining time.[51] Mayer received the cable after his first meeting with the Nazis, which took place the same day.

On the same August 21, 1944, Saly Mayer met four men who had come from the Nazi side of the border: Obersturmbannführer Kurt A. Becher, Hauptsturmbannführers Max Grüson and Hermann Krumey, and Kasztner. He supposedly represented the Swiss refugee organization that distributed JDC funds to Jewish refugees in Switzerland (it existed on paper only and consisted largely of Saly Mayer). They met in the middle of the border bridge at Saint Margarethen because Mayer refused to enter Germany, and he did not particularly want his "partners" to enter Switzerland.

Becher repeated the demand transmitted by Brand for 10,000 trucks and supplemented it with a request for agricultural machinery. In return, the Nazis would let Jews leave for the United States (not Palestine, because of the Arab veto) on the same ships that would bring the machines and trucks. To show their seriousness, the Nazis had brought 318 people who had been on the Kasztner train from Bergen-Belsen to the Swiss border on the day of the meeting. Mayer gave a vague lecture about morality, and they agreed to meet again: Mayer had to ask his backers what they thought of the suggestions.

Mayer reported to McClelland along these lines. Becher, in his August 25 report to Himmler, said that Mayer had been convinced of the Nazis' seriousness by having 300 "pieces" (*Stück*—that is, the Bergen-Belsen group) delivered into Switzerland; he had, Becher said, demurred about the trucks and had suggested minerals and industrial goods—he would seek American agreement to this. He would tell the Nazis the next time how much money he had at his disposal and submit a list of materials that would be immediately available. For Mayer to have said something like that was quite in character; any mention of trucks, after the failure of the Brand mission, would have immediately terminated the negotiations. Everything else that Mayer suggested, if that was what he said, was an obvious attempt at procrastination. But Mayer had offered money, and he had offered goods, contrary to his instructions from the Swiss and the Americans, which is probably why he did not mention those offers in his own report.

On the night of August 24, Himmler told his people in Budapest not to deport the Jews—we remember that the action was planned for August 25, then for the twenty-eighth. Veesenmayer, in obvious disbelief, reported the order to Ribbentrop and received the answer that Himmler had indeed so ordered. It is extremely hard not to connect the two events, although Becher's cable to Himmler bears the date of August 25. In his testimony Becher claims to have seen Himmler shortly after the meeting on the Swiss border and to have convinced him not to deport the Jews of Budapest. He does not explain why he then sent him a cable to report on the negotiations. Because nothing that Becher says can be taken at face value, the contradictions remain unresolved.[52] In fact, it would appear that these talks, initiated and promoted by Kasztner, were the direct cause of the rescue of the Jews of Budapest. Becher also claims that around that time he persuaded his chief to issue an order to Ernst Kaltenbrunner, head of the RSHA, and Oswald Pohl, head of the economic office of the SS responsible for the concentration camps, forbidding the further killing of Jews. There is no evidence to support this claim.

Postwar criticism of Mayer's behavior has centered on his refusal to offer serious ransom payments or the delivery of goods; he has also been accused of hiding behind the official U.S. policy. The options have to be weighed scrupulously, as indeed they were by Mayer himself. He could offer serious ransom proposals and goods, but he had no way of delivering on offers because he lacked money. All his funds were kept in Swiss banks, and wartime regulations were so strict that any large-scale use of even these limited funds in contravention of the policies of both Switzerland and the United States was simply impossible. On the other hand, to gain time, he had to offer *something*. He must have decided very early on—in fact, before the first meeting—to walk a tightrope. He would offer ransom payments and goods and but postpone delivery by all kinds of devious means, and keep McClelland, who served as a watchdog over him, in the dark about what he was really saying to the Germans. In other words, the respectable, sixty-two-year-old Swiss citizen and erstwhile small politician (he had represented a liberal party on the Saint Gallen city council) cheated his government and the U.S. government in order to lead the Nazis by their noses, as Becher put it later. The purpose was to save Jewish lives—at a certain point he even widened his interest to include all slave laborers in the Nazi domain. Let us see how he did it; let us also try to discover what the purposes of the Nazis may have been.

12

The Swiss Talks
and the Budapest Tragedy

The idea of letting the remaining Jews leave was not taboo in Nazi Germany in early 1944. On April 3, Veesenmayer in Hungary asked Ribbentrop what had become of the idea that the Foreign Minister had suggested to the Führer: presenting all the Jews to Roosevelt and Churchill as a gift.[1] He was not answered, but he doubtless knew what he was talking about.

We can only surmise the reason for this surprising move by the arch-Nazi Ribbentrop. The simplest explanation seems to be that after the failure of the Feldscher negotiations, Ribbentrop thought that the Allies would refuse a German proposal to hand all the Jews to the Allies and that a refusal could be used as good propaganda material, counteracting all Allied arguments about the Nazi treatment of Jews: You make such a to-do about these people, yet you refused to accept them when we offered them. But if this is the explanation, we have yet another example of a reversion to prewar arguments and policies—even if the intent was purely propagandistic. Another example is the cable from the German Foreign Office to Veesenmayer in Hungary on July 6, which directed him "to prevent, if possible, an emigration of Hungarian Jews and, insofar as it may be permitted, make it dependent on a significant contribution." On September 5 the Foreign Office specified what the Germans would demand in return: "a certain number of Reich German internees" (in Allied hands).[2] In other words, the policy of the "Final Solution" would continue, but it could be temporarily modified if the price was right. And this was Ribbentrop's office, which usually followed a strict Hitlerian line.

Other negotiations or contacts began developing at the same time that Kasztner was trying to make the talks with Mayer a reality, and they, too, lead back to Himmler. In Switzerland there existed the HIJEF, or Montreux committee, led by two brothers, Elias and Isaac Sternbuch, and Isaac's wife, Rachel, who were representatives of the

VH in America and bitter enemies of Mayer and the JDC.[3] Isaac Sternbuch established contact with Swiss pro-Nazis in order to offer ransom proposals to the Germans. These contacts led the group to a Swiss representative of the German Messerschmidt works, Carl Truempy. Truempy was also in touch with a committee of Jewish refugees from Hungary led by Mihaly Banyai, and on July 13 he tried his hand at negotiating in Vienna with some SS officers regarding a possible flight of 20,000 Hungarian Jews to Romania. Nothing came of that, nor of another attempt to talk with a high SS officer, Wilhelm Haster, through a contact in Bregenz, on the Swiss-German border (August 12). Haster reportedly told Truempy that the Bergen-Belsen group from the Kasztner train would be released if payments were made. Truempy also approached Mayer, who tried to use him to clarify a problem that acutely bothered him: Was Becher speaking in the name of Himmler? Would any money paid to Becher actually rescue Jews? Through Truempy, Mayer transmitted a memorandum to Himmler in which he asked point-blank what the Nazi policy toward the Jews was. We do not know whether Himmler saw the memo; in any case there was (of course) no answer.[4]

Truempy was used by Sternbuch in an attempt to liberate the anti-Zionist Hasidic Rabbi of Szatmar, Joel Teitelbaum, from Bergen-Belsen. The VH representative, Leo Rubinfeld, told Truempy: "The aid organization to which I belong is not interested in the [other] people who came with the Hungarian transport to Bergen-Belsen."[5]

Having seen Mayer's initial stand in the negotiations with Becher, we may not be surprised that, contrary to his American and Swiss instructions and despite the loathing (not too strong a word) that he and Sternbuch felt for each other, he supported Sternbuch's efforts. Sternbuch wanted to send tractors to the Nazis—in accordance with a proposal sent to him from Hungary by Freudiger—if he could rescue Jews that way. Mayer put SFR 260,000 at the disposal of the Montreux committee and then, in September, paid SFR 69,200 of that money for forty tractors. The tractors were shipped, without any noticeable effect on Nazi policy.[6]

After the first meeting on the bridge at Saint Margarethen, Mayer met with the Nazis (without Becher, who was represented by Grüson and Krumey), Kasztner, and Wilhelm Billitz on September 3, 4, and 5. He had received word (September 1) that a credit of $2 million had at last been made available to him in the United States, but it could not be used without WRB agreement—so it was of little use for ransom payments. To the Nazis he promised a $5 million credit in Switzerland, with which they would be able to buy goods, provided *all* the Jews under Nazi rule, not only those in Hungary, were kept alive. Hoping that the Nazis would take a long time to determine what goods they wanted, Mayer also expected to consult with Schwartz, who planned to visit Switzerland soon.[7] On September 5, Grüson demanded that someone with full political powers join the negotiations—Mayer did not have the *pleine pouvoir* (full power to negotiate) that the Nazis had hoped for.

We can see here what the two sides were after. Mayer went far beyond his brief and did not report to McClelland nearly all that he told the Nazis. Grüson, on the other hand, expressed Himmler's real intention: to reach someone with full political powers with whom options for a separate peace could be discussed. The talk about money and goods was all right, as far as he was concerned, but it was mostly camouflage. Himmler said as much four months later in the only notation that we have in his own hand.

For three weeks after the meeting nothing much happened. There was no money or goods, and there was silence from Mayer. Becher saw himself betrayed and must also have feared for his own skin when facing his much-to-be-revered Reichsführer. Kasztner sent frantic messages to Mayer, and finally, on September 26, Mayer sent a cable to Budapest reiterating his agreement in principle (after he had already agreed to it in practice on September 5!) to put money into an account in Switzerland, which the Nazis could then use. Biss and Kasztner brought the cable to Clages and Becher. Both were delighted and promised to inform Himmler.[8]

On September 29 another meeting took place, again without Becher, and with a new SS officer, Herbert Kettlitz. Kasztner and Marcus Wyler-Schmidt, Mayer's lawyer, left us accounts of this meeting that differ completely.[9] Kasztner says that Mayer promised $15 million in credits in three monthly installments, whereas Wyler-Schmidt says that Mayer offered $2 million if the Germans stopped their anti-Jewish policy, improved the conditions for all foreign slave workers, and stopped the current deportations of Jews from Slovakia. Difficult though it may be to choose, Wyler's account seems the more probable, especially since Mayer himself noted in his quaint way that he had told Kasztner the whole truth (*Emess,* in Yiddish): I "have only five million [dollars in Swiss francs, which was his total budget at the time,] of which 100,000 already spent, another [$]2m in USA. [Cordell] Hull: no goods, no ransom money, but keep negotiations going."[10] Mayer succeeded in doing exactly this, even though he had failed to produce anything tangible in the way of ransom money, goods, or political contacts in the United States.

In the meantime, the Allies had occupied France and a large part of Belgium, and the big Soviet summer offensive had carried the Red Army to the gates of Warsaw. Romania had changed sides on August 23, 1944. Tito's army was slowly conquering parts of Yugoslavia, and the Anglo-American forces were crawling up the Italian boot. Nazi Germany was in very deep trouble. Himmler had liquidated the conservative opposition to Hitler after the unsuccessful assassination attempt of July 20. Himmler must have realized that he had to be more energetic in his attempts to sound out the Western powers.

Mayer procrastinated, trying to move the negotiations from ransom and the supply of goods to Red Cross attendance on the Jews in Nazi territory. In the meantime, other initiatives began to take shape, especially two, one in Switzerland and one in Sweden, each initiated by one of the sides.

In Switzerland, Jean-Marie Musy—a former Swiss President, conservative Catholic right-winger, and former Nazi sympathizer who wanted to improve his public image—became a go-between with the Nazis. In April 1944 he had managed to pry a Jewish family loose from the SS-controlled French prison at Clermont-Ferrand and bring them to Switzerland.[11] Sternbuch asked him to negotiate with Himmler, whom he had met before (in 1940), and gave him a document saying that the Americans were ready to let Jews into the United States. The contact with Himmler was established through Schellenberg, probably through the latter's Swiss middlemen. On November 3, Musy met with Himmler. Himmler, Musy reported, said he had about 600,000 Jews and could release them without asking Hitler for permission if he received trucks and other goods in exchange. Musy said he offered over SFR 1 million.[12]

Musy's report sounds genuine enough—and so do Himmler's conditions. They had not changed since May, when Brand was sent to Istanbul, and they were based on the same assumptions: if an impressive number of goods were sent in, Jews would be released (some of them? it is hard to imagine that the Nazis would have let *all* Jews go). The transaction would change the military situation and open up political avenues to the West. What emerged, however, was internecine fighting among high SS officers—Schellenberg against Becher—which mirrored the dissensions between Sternbuch and Mayer. On the German side, Himmler was the one whose favors were sought, whereas on the Jewish side the ultimate authority was the WRB in the person of McClelland. Himmler was not sure which way to go. McClelland favored Mayer.

On November 18, Musy wrote to Himmler, promising—in the name of the VH—SFR 20 million to pay for the release of Jews in Germany or the occupied territories; the VH would also see to it, Musy wrote, that goods would be available to be bought for Germany with the ransom paid. Sternbuch did the same as Mayer: he had Musy write that a list of the goods would have to be prepared, obviously in order to drag out the negotiations.[13]

While the Swiss negotiations were going on, Kleist returned to Stockholm (in October) with a new idea: to evacuate 100,000 Estonians to Sweden and thus rescue them from the advancing Soviets. In addition, he said, freeing Jews in Germany in return for money was impossible, but he would advocate good treatment for the Jews, so the Nazis would have a good press in the West. What he wanted in return was an overture by the WRB–OSS people in Sweden, but that never came.[14]

Mayer knew about Kleist's contacts and decided to again try to negotiate with Becher. He convinced McClelland that the time had come to dangle a more important carrot in front of the Nazi's eyes than just empty promises and obtained Swiss visas for Becher and Kettlitz. Becher was to meet with McClelland, and Kettlitz was to make a list of goods, which Mayer would supposedly enable him to buy. The meetings at the border resumed—on October 29, November 2, and November 4. According to Wyler (Mayer's lawyer), Becher already realized he would not procure trucks but hoped that other goods might be acceptable; they would save German blood, and therefore Jewish "blood" would be given in return. There was talk of hundreds of thousands of Jews who would be able to leave (but not to Palestine). The price would be SFR 20 million if the money was made available within two or three weeks. Kasztner said that Mayer had been totally ineffectual, talking a lot about moral obligations. Kasztner's account was written up after the war, when a deep hatred developed between him and Mayer, whereas Wyler was trying at the time of the events to justify Mayer's actions in every detail; it is therefore not easy to reconcile the accounts. In this case again, Wyler is probably nearer the truth.[15]

Mayer can hardly have been as ineffectual as Kasztner says, because on November 5, Becher went with him to a meeting with McClelland at the Hotel Baur in Zurich. Mayer read a long, stern lecture to Becher and spoke of the inevitability of the Nazi defeat. He demanded the end of the killing of civilians, Jews and non-Jews alike, the departure of orphaned children to Switzerland, and permission for the Red Cross to look after the inmates of concentration camps. The bait was a WRB cable over Hull's signature opening a credit of SFR 20 million ($5 million) in Mayer's favor. He did not tell Becher that the money could be used only with the permission of the U.S. government (that is, it would not be used for ransom payments or goods for Germany). Becher agreed that henceforth children and elderly people would be spared and that the Red Cross could examine the different categories of Jews—whatever that meant.[16]

What transpired at the Hotel Baur on that November day is quite amazing: an official representative of the U.S. government met with a high SS officer on neutral ground, ostensibly to discuss humanitarian issues. The meeting was in contravention of official U.S. policy, according to which the only purpose of any negotiations with the Germans would be to settle the latter's unconditional surrender. Indeed, I know of no comparable action on the part of the Americans during World War II.

Himmler had seemingly achieved his aim—his representative had finally met an American diplomat. But the results were very disappointing from a Nazi point of view: the American, through Mayer, had let him know that the war was lost and in effect had asked the Germans to accept any terms the

Allies might set. The discussion turned on Jews and other inmates of camps under Nazi control but had further implications. In the end it was a fruitless meeting. The Americans would not pay ransom, and the Nazis would not deliver or protect Jews. The Nazis, as we have already seen on previous occasions, wanted to negotiate and held out the prospect of maintaining Jewish lives in return for political advantages. But the Americans were unwilling to endanger the certain prospect of total victory because of some humanitarian projects.

By that time, the purpose of these negotiations from the Jewish point of view, which was supported by McClelland, was to prevent the murder of the remaining Jews at the last moment. By November 1944, evacuating them from Germany was not the solution. The most practical thing to do would have been to have the International Red Cross look after them until they were finally liberated, and that was indeed the direction in which the McClelland–Mayer team was thinking. To arrange Red Cross supervision, the bait of the $5 million was essential, and Mayer thought that it could ultimately be used to pay the Red Cross for a feeding and clothing program in the camps. Realizing that it would be unthinkable to feed and clothe just the Jews, Mayer had broadened the agenda to include all the inmates and all the slave laborers. He must have realized that $5 million were insufficient for such a task, but the money could serve for starters. Mayer was shattered when the WRB backtracked on November 21, withdrawing the promise of the $5 million.[17] To top it off, he was informed that Schwartz would be permitted to visit Switzerland, but not to participate in the discussions with the Nazis. Clearly, what lay behind these moves was the fear of Soviet and, perhaps, British reactions.

All these moves and countermoves took place against the somber background of a renewed anti-Jewish action in Budapest. Eichmann—with the agreement of the Hungarian fascist government of Ferenc Szalasi, which had assumed power after an unsuccessful bid by Horthy to sign an armistice with the Soviets (October 15)—began deporting Budapest Jews to the Austrian border on November 8 to work there on a line of fortifications against the Soviets (see below). Kasztner was frantic and kept asking Mayer for the money, which would serve as a bait to prevent further deportations. Mayer could neither help nor tell Kasztner the truth. On November 18, Kettlitz cabled that Mayer had no money and would not have any, and advised his superiors to turn to Sternbuch. Sternbuch responded by asking the VH in the United States for a credit of SFR 10–20 million ($2.5–5 million). The WRB asked McClelland for advice, and McClelland advised against a positive response (December 9).[18]

Becher now, at the end of November, thought that he had to report to his chief and went to Berlin. While he was there, he received a cable from Kasztner saying—untruthfully—that the SFR 20 million were available and that Mayer was working hard to overcome technical difficulties. That cable, Kasztner says, saved the situation.[19] The story is patently untrue. Kasztner himself told Marcus Wyler at a meeting on the Swiss border on November 30 that Becher had told him in a phone conversation, after receiving the cable, that Kettlitz's information had been revealing and that Kasztner should not tell him fairy stories.[20]

No cable from Kasztner but the cold calculation of a Nazi was behind Becher's moves. He had to convince Himmler to carry on with the negotiations, because without them he had neither an alibi nor a remote chance of perhaps supplying the SS with what his chief wanted: some goods, and negotiations leading perhaps to a separate peace. Himmler desperately wanted contact with the Americans and would not lose anything by permitting his most obedient Becher (*gehorsamster Becher*—as Becher used to sign letters to Himmler) to carry on with his Jewish contacts in the hope that they would lead somewhere. In addition, we may surmise, a bond had developed between the Nazi extortioner and the Jewish negotiator. Kasztner had become a kind of walking life insurance for the Nazi, who must have seen the end approaching, and Becher had become Kasztner's only remaining contact (Clages had been killed in Budapest on October 15) for reaching Himmler and alleviating the lot of the remaining Jews. After the war Kasztner helped his good friend Kurt A. Becher.

What most likely impressed the Nazi leadership no less than the convoluted negotiations with Mayer was the demand of the Romanian government, in November, that the Nazis return the Jews deported from Transylvania; the territory had been reconquered by the Romanian Army, now fighting on the side of the Allies. If the Jews were returned, the Romanians would then permit the Germans residing in the area to leave for Germany. The murder of the Transylvanian Jews at Auschwitz made the proposal impractical, but the Germans realized that they could barter Jews for things they wanted. The background of the Romanian offer, or demand, has not yet been cleared up, except that obviously some Jewish request was behind it, as was the desire of the Romanians to get rid of their Germans.

Himmler's reaction to the Romanian offer is of some importance. Reading Kettlitz's negative report from Switzerland, which reached him through Becher, and despairing of success in that direction, he tried to contact the Swiss directly, through SS Obergruppenführer (general) Gottlob Berger, one of his closest and most trusted aides. He offered to exchange Hungarian Jews (he still had Budapest Jews, though no Transylvanian ones) for Germans in Allied hands, especially Romanian Germans, because information had reached him that the Russians were about to exile these people to Siberia. The Swiss said that they had no diplomatic relations with the Soviet Union, hence could not be involved.[21]

It is typical of Himmler, given his political intentions, that he did not approach the Russians (who could have made the deal work), but the Swiss, who represented the Western Allies in Germany. His choice of approach may indicate that he was making another attempt to reach the Western powers, but with a generous offer—which would presumably have won Hitler's support because it was a matter of exchanging "blood for blood," to use Nazi terminology. The lives of the remnant of Hungarian Jewry were on the line. Of course, the Allies would never agree to such an exchange, especially not the Soviets, who were now in control of Romania. Interestingly, no evidence has been found that this offer reached the Jewish organizations.

Parallel to that development came Himmler's order (the date is unclear, probably early November or late October) to dismantle the gas chambers at Auschwitz. Becher takes credit for that move, but it is more likely that the approaching Soviet troops and the prospect of their occupying Auschwitz and discovering what had happened there was the real cause.

The talks on the border were becoming useless. Kettlitz was evicted from Switzerland and told Becher, as we have seen, that he could not procure any money from Mayer (November 27); in the wake of this information, Becher issued an ultimatum, which would expire on December 2 (originally, on November 24): if no ransom money was available, the Jews would suffer, and the Budapest Jews would be the first to do so. Truempy, who was informed of this move by his Nazi contacts, informed the President of Switzerland, Eduard von Steiger. The Nazi group met with Rubinfeld, Sternbuch's man, who had to tell them that his group had only SFR 1 million, but he promised that he could obtain more. On December 1, in his first talk with Kasztner without witnesses, Mayer again told him the truth: he could possibly collect SFR 4 million (presumably from Swiss Jews, for the most part) but would be acting against Swiss and American instructions. In any case, the Nazis demanded much more, and he simply did not have it. He wanted to resign his task in despair.

At that point Kasztner's strong personality came into play: he convinced Mayer to carry on, and argued Kettlitz and another Nazi officer, Erich Krell, into sending a cable to Becher reporting that SFR 5 million was available and that the continued imprisonment of the Bergen-Belsen transport was the cause of many of the problems that had been encountered. Becher responded on December 4 that no evil would befall the Jews of Budapest, but he also demanded the rest of the money that he had been promised—SFR 15 million. On the night of December 6 the remaining 1,368 Jews of the Kasztner train from Bergen-Belsen crossed the Swiss frontier.[22]

Mayer now turned to Schwartz, who was visiting Switzerland, and asked the JDC directly for the $5 million he needed as show money and as a possible payment to the International Red Cross if his plan worked out. After much negotiating—the total income of JDC for 1944 was $15 million, and all of that had been committed—Schwartz agreed. McClelland, too, at Mayer's insistence, reapplied for the $5 million from the WRB (December 13). After a great deal of hesitation, on January 7, 1945—almost a month later—the WRB finally permitted the transfer of the $5 million of JDC money to Mayer, to be used only as show money or with the agreement of the WRB. Finally, Mayer latched on to negotiations that had been initiated by his rivals at the World Jewish Congress with the Red Cross, and obtained an agreement from the Red Cross to supply Jews in concentration camps with food and clothes.[23]

The idea of using the Red Cross was also discussed at the second meeting that Jean-Marie Musy had with Himmler, on January 1. Again, the VH would give Musy SFR 5 million, but in this case the Red Cross would support the German population ravaged by the war. It is fairly obvious that Himmler's purpose here, and in the parallel negotiations with the Swedes (more below), was to contact the Western Allies. Sternbuch reported to his organization on January 17 that he could set 30,000 Jews free if $5 million (dollars, not francs) were sent to him. He claimed that Musy had arranged for 1,400 Jews to be set free each month in return for $25,000 for each such transport. He would use the $250,000 that he had in Swiss banks for the first transport. The WRB was suspicious: Was ransom involved here? McClelland replied (January 28) that Musy had received what seemed to be a personal payment of $11,000 from Sternbuch, and had extorted another $2,000 from a private individual. Two brothers of Recha Sternbuch had been released on Himmler's orders. On January 15, Musy had another meeting with Himmler, who says he told Musy that the Jews had been employed in heavy labor involving loss of life, but now they were being employed to do ordinary labor because of the current negotiations.

What the Americans and the British wanted to do with the Jews was, Himmler wrote to himself, of no interest. It was clear, he said, that Germany did not want them in its territory or any territory under its influence. If Jews were sent to Switzerland, Germany would demand a guarantee that they not go to Palestine, because Germany would never do such an indecent ("unanständig") thing to the Arabs ("those poor people, tortured by the Jews").[24] On January 21, Musy again traveled to Germany, and on February 7, the Theresienstadt Jews—1,210 of them—arrived in Switzerland as a result of his negotiations. A day before that, Musy and Sternbuch met with McClelland and asked for permission to use $1 million for the liberation of all the remaining Jews in Germany. Clearly, McClelland wrote, this was an indication that Himmler desperately wanted to contact the West.[25]

Musy, in Himmler's name, demanded that the Swiss and American press react positively to the Nazis' "humanitarian" gesture of February 7. At the same time, the WRB authorized the JDC to send close to $1 million to Sternbuch, but, as in the case of the $5 million sent to Mayer, the money in effect could not be used because ransom payments were forbidden. By now Himmler had been promised $6 million, and he was in a quandary. On January 18 he wrote a note to himself: "Who is really the one with whom the American government actually maintains contact? Is it a rabbinical Jew or is it the Jioint [*sic*—the JDC]?"[26]

The struggle between the factions within the SS grew more chaotic as the end of the thousand-year Reich approached. Schellenberg and Becher later accused each other (and Schellenberg and Musy accused Mayer) of collaborating with the radical faction around Kaltenbrunner and Heinrich Müller and causing Hitler to intervene against further releases of Jews. The Führer had done so after the February Theresienstadt transport, which was widely reported in the Swiss press. In the face of these difficulties, Himmler decided nevertheless that each of his underlings should continue to explore his line in the hope that one of them would bring him the desired results.[27] Becher intensified his attempts to extract money from Mayer—real money, not promises—in meetings held on February 1, 7, and 11 in order to prove to Himmler that it was he and his contacts whom Himmler should rely on. Mayer was still trying to secure Nazi consent for the Red Cross to provide food and clothing to camp inmates, rather than to the German population. On February 11 he promised Becher to have him meet McClelland for a second time. But events overtook them, and there were no more meetings.[28]

The intervention of the neutral countries—Switzerland, Sweden, and to a lesser extent Spain, Portugal, and Turkey—as well as the Vatican and the Red Cross, made an appreciable contribution to the cessation of the deportations from Hungary in early July. The line advocated by Moshe Krausz, the man in charge of the Palestine office and Kasztner's bitter enemy, had two elements: to turn to the Hungarians *and* to turn to the neutral states and organizations. The first part of this proposal proved useless, as we have seen; but the second gained in importance as time went on. It started with the friendship that Krausz developed with Charles Lutz, the Swiss vice-consul, who had been the Swiss representative in Tel Aviv before the war. Now Lutz was the representative of Switzerland as the Protecting Power of Great Britain. His work included the granting of Palestine entry permits (certificates).

Throughout July and August, Lutz, with the support of the Swiss ambassador, Maximilian Jäger, tried to effectuate the emigration of a large number of Jews. His efforts were based on the Hungarian offer that was intended to offset the anti-Hungarian sentiment in the West, which was connected with the reports about the Hungarian deportations. Krausz informed Istanbul on July 13 about the new Hungarian proposal to emigrate *some* Jews, and the Hungarian chargé d'affaires in Bern told the Swiss and the Allies on July

17.[29] The Hungarians, according to Krausz, were talking about 8,234 Palestine certificate holders and 1,000 children. The Germans talked about 7,000 individuals, the Swiss about 7,800 families, and there were a number of figures in between. The Germans, as we have seen, were prepared, on the face of it, to permit these people to leave, provided they could deport the rest to Auschwitz.

Krausz did not content himself with the Swiss. He found a sympathetic ear with Minister Carl I. Danielsson of Sweden and in mid-May cabled the Swedish Red Cross to send somebody like Count Folke Bernadotte, a nephew of the King of Sweden, to Budapest to protect Jews, especially children. The result was that Waldemar Langlet of the Swedish Red Cross came on June 11 to strengthen the legation. After some negotiations between the WRB and Sweden, in which the JDC was also involved, Raoul Wallenberg was approached, and he agreed to go to Budapest on a life-saving mission. He arrived on July 9, on the day that the Hungarians stopped the deportations, so he had time to acquaint himself with the country, the problems, and the personalities. Schools were set up for Jewish children—in accordance with government orders, 10 percent of those in attendance were Christian children—and they were supervised by Langlet.

Authorizations for foreign protection multiplied in the summer. In August the Swiss had officially sanctioned 8,700 such papers, but more were issued: 4,500 Swedish, 2,500 Vatican, 1,500 Spanish, and 700 Portuguese papers were issued to Budapest Jews. Basically, these papers promised entry into the relevant countries (in the case of the Vatican, it just stated that the bearer was under the protection of the Budapest Nunciature). The papers were not really legal papers, and the Hungarian government did not formally recognize them.

Krausz set up shop in the so-called Glass House, which was an extension of the Swiss legation, donated to it by its Jewish owner, who was a glass manufacturer. In August the International Red Cross established a section dealing with aid for children, and Otto Komoly was put in charge. This restructuring enabled the Vaada to legalize many of its operations. Efra Teichmann (Agmon) of Hashomer Hatzair was in charge of the economic division, dealing with provisions and clothing in the main. The collaboration between the youth movements and the Vaada improved considerably. The central figure in the youth movements, Raffi Friedel (Benshalom), represented them in the Glass House; his being on Swiss extraterritorial grounds provided yet another protection to the Zionist youth.

In the early autumn the neutral diplomats in Budapest saw clearly that the Germans had no intention of permitting Jews to leave Hungary. After the deportations had been avoided on August 25–26, Jews remained in special houses (2,168 dwellings) in crowded ghetto conditions, but their situation had eased considerably. Since August 24 there had been a new government in Hungary, led by Gen. Geza Lakatos, that was trying to move from allegiance to Germany toward surrender to the Allies. The Hungarians were still talking to the Germans in terms of deporting Jews, but this was just make-believe.

In the fall of 1944, Horthy was growing more and more panicky. Romania had switched sides on August 23, and the Germans had had to retreat to the Hungarian border. Soviet troops were entering Hungary, and the Germans had no way of stopping them. A clandestine mission was sent to Moscow to negotiate a surrender, and Horthy decided to emulate the Romanians. On October 15 he announced over the radio that Hungary was leaving the side of the Germans. However, the Germans were prepared for such a development. In a series of swift moves, they took Horthy's son hostage and forced Horthy to resign and hand over the government to the fascist Arrow Cross leader, Ferenc Szalasi. In the shoot-outs that accompanied the revolutionary changes, Gerhard Clages was killed. The immediate result of this counter-revolution was a reign of unbridled terror. Armed gangs directed their attacks mainly against the surviving Jews in the city, numbering probably close to 200,000. In the first few days some 600 Jews were murdered, partly by shooting them on the banks of the Danube, so they fell in dead or wounded.

Eichmann reappeared in Budapest immediately after the takeover by the Szalasi gang. He had been given the task of recruiting slave workers from among the Jews in Budapest—50,000, if possible. Only a few men of working age were available, because most of the men were in labor battalions. Eichmann, with the agreement of the Szalasi government, took women, the very young, and the elderly instead. On November 8 the sorry trek to the Austrian border began—the overwhelming majority were marched on foot. At the border Wisliceny was to take them in charge and hand them over to the sappers who were building fortifications against the advancing Russians. The scenes on the road between Budapest and Hegyesalom, the Hungarian-Austrian border town, were heartrending. People died like flies. They were being driven relentlessly in cold, rainy weather by Hungarian gendarmes and Arrow Cross louts; they were refused food and drink and very often had to sleep in open fields. Many contracted severe illnesses on the road—typhoid, pneumonia, and so on—and died. Others died of exposure, often after they had arrived at the border.

The survivors were supposed to work at the border, but many were in no condition to do so, and in the end quite a number were simply sent back by rail by the disgusted German officers responsible for the fortifications. Others were put to hard labor, and again many perished. SS officers on the Austrian border opposed the forced marches. Among them were Rudolf Hoess, the former commandant of Auschwitz, and Hans Jüttner, another mass murderer whom Kasztner tried to save after the war because he had opposed the continuation of the marches. These officers wanted to build the fortifications, and the exhausted and dying women and old people from Budapest were hardly the ones to help.[30] The marches were finally stopped on November 27 (they had slackened considerably after November 18), after Becher, among others, intervened in Budapest, using the authority of Himmler.[31]

Pressure from the neutrals did have some limited effect on the deportations and marches. People with *Schutzpässe* (papers of protection) were often, but not always, released before or even during the marches—in a few cases even after they had arrived at the border. Most of those who remember Raoul Wallenberg tell about his heroic efforts to save people who had Swedish papers on them, and in some cases he bluffed his way to saving others as well. The difference between Wallenberg and the other neutrals, mainly Lutz, did not lie in the numbers saved. Lutz's signature was on many more papers than Wallenberg's, and the Swiss saved many more people than Wallenberg did— in the Glass House and some other Swiss-protected facilities alone there were 21,000 people. But Lutz rarely went out himself to face the Nazis and their Arrow Cross allies. Wallenberg did. He gained access to some highly placed Hungarian politicians, and with his brash courage he faced Nazi officers who did not quite know how to handle him. He became an admired Scarlet Pimpernel figure, and fact and fiction mixed in the descriptions that Jewish survivors gave of him. His fame was certainly justified by his extraordinary exploits.

Sheer numbers and efficiency make the Swiss rescue effort more important. Both of the chief rescue operations, the Swiss and the Swedish—and the allied efforts of the other neutral countries, the Vatican, and the International Red Cross, were dependent on another factor, which ultimately was decisive: the Zionist youth movements. The movements grasped the opportunities presented by Krausz and the neutrals.

The youth were guided by a group of people from the different movements—there was not even a formal committee, but the leading figures were well known to the members. As the horror of the Arrow Cross actions and the marches unfolded, the youth organized children's homes, saved people from prison in daring coups, and provided vast numbers of false papers. According to a reasonable estimate, at least 100,000 such papers were provided—not just forged Schutzpässe, but food coupons, military papers for those who were camouflaged as "Aryans," papers of domicile, work documents, and so on. Among the individuals in charge were people like Shraga Weil of the Hashomer Hatzair movement, who became one of Israel's best-known painters. In Budapest he used his talents for painstakingly forging documents. These factories for forged papers were also used to supply documentation to the small Hungarian underground.

The Arrow Cross government knew that most of the papers for Jewish adults, as well as for children, were forged. Late in November the government declared that they would no longer recognize them. On one occasion they even forced Lutz and his wife to go to a concentration point, where Jews were being gathered for a march, and separate the false papers from the genuine ones.

The actions of the youth movements were by no means haphazard. A conscious decision had been made in January 1944 not to organize an uprising, as in Warsaw; the leaders realized that such an attempt would fail, nor would it help anyone to survive. Unlike in Poland, survival was possible in Hungary after October 15, and the movements did everything in their power to help people survive, though in situations of extreme danger, members did not hesitate to use weapons. Youth who were endangered or who were sought by Arrow Cross gangs hid in bunkers and had arms with which to protect themselves. One of these groups, consisting of eighteen youngsters, fought a battle at a place called Hungaria Korut against Arrow Cross besiegers until the remnants were forced out by tear gas. One Hashomer Hatzair member especially, Joszef (Joshko) Meir, took part in sabotage and the derailing of trains, but armed attacks, including some street fighting, were marginal compared to the rescue actions they undertook.

The Szalasi government declared on November 13 that all Jews must move into a ghetto area in the center of the city. The move had been largely accomplished by December 2, when the Russian ring around the city was tightening. The ghetto could easily be destroyed, and the task of the neutrals and the youth movements was to prevent that.

The youth, especially those protecting the children's houses, and the Arrow Cross murderers fought a major battle of wits. The youth set up thirty children's homes (they maintained contact with sixty-two additional homes run by various organizations and neutral representatives), many in houses that had previously belonged to the Jewish community. In one case, the Social Democrats donated a house, and one of their leaders, Miklos Kertesz, helped to run it; in it resided 1,500 children. Most of the houses were protected by the International Red Cross, others by the different neutral representatives. The children were brought there in part by the parents, but because being seen on the streets was risky, youth movement members dressed in Arrow Cross uniforms rounded up children—with the consent of the parents if the parents were still alive—and brought them to the safety of the new establishments. Attempts were made to keep the children's lives as normal as possible, but the fear, the lack of food and heat, and the increasing dangers made that task difficult.

Showing or flying the insignia or flags of the neutrals might be a partial defense, but it did not always help. Many children were murdered when the wits of the movement representatives or the teachers, nurses, and mothers in the houses could not prevail against the Arrow Cross hunters. Apart from avoiding murder, there was the perennial problem of food, medicine, clothing, and coal or wood in the severe winter weather. Efra Teichmann was responsible for the food, and he performed miracles of ingenuity—cajoling and bribing Hungarian peasants, truck drivers, horse-and-cart owners, officials, and policemen to let his food supplies into the starving city before the Soviet ring closed. The International Red Cross, represented by Friedrich Born, the Swiss delegate, and Komóly, supplied medicine, but that, too, had to be supplemented by the youth.[32]

In fact, the International Red Cross did have an important place in Budapest, and Friedrich Born used his position effectively to save Jews. He persuaded Veesenmayer to grant exit permits for 8,000 Jews—connecting with the Horthy offer of July—and although no one left, the public declaration of the Arrow Cross government on October 23 that it would abide by the agreement helped to bridle somewhat the enthusiasm for murder in the ranks of the fascists.

The neutrals protested against the treatment of the Jews, but because they did not want to recognize the fascist government, they could not make their formal protests effective. The exception was Spain, but the Spanish ambassador had fled the city, and in his stead an Italian, Jorge (Georgio) Perlasca, took over the embassy and hoodwinked the Arrow Cross government into believing that he represented Spain. Under his management, Jews were accepted into the embassy building, and a children's home was protected under the Spanish flag until the Russians came.

Andreas Biss tells how Becher was instrumental in averting a major tragedy in early December, when Budapest was about to be completely encircled. The Szalasi government had decided, so the Jews understood, to kill off all the Budapest Jews before the government forces were themselves defeated. Biss went to Becher and asked him to intervene, but Becher answered that he had to show something to his superiors to justify such an intervention; he asked for thirty trucks. These trucks were actually German vehicles that had been supplied to Slovakia, and Becher asked that they be bought back and delivered to the SS, not to the Wehrmacht. A shady merchant by the name of Alois Steiger, or Steger, asked for SFR 700,000 to deliver the trucks. Biss managed to pay SFR 188,000 or so and promised in the JDC's name (the JDC was blissfully unaware of this) that Steiger would procure the rest from Switzerland. Steiger then went to Becher, so Biss says, and reported that the trucks were available. Becher intervened with the German and Hungarian authorities (December 9, 1944), and the Jews were saved.[33] Biss no doubt believed his own story, but there is no proof that Becher intervened, though he may have; nor do we know whether Steiger paid for the trucks or whether he and Becher were in collusion to squeeze some more Swiss francs from the Jews. Steiger, at any rate, demanded the money "back" from the JDC after the war—and did not receive it.

Becher left Budapest; Eichmann had left earlier. The struggle between the two had become obvious, and Becher claimed after the war that he had complained to Himmler, who then invited both of them to meet him in the Schwarzwald area sometime in December. Himmler, Becher says, yelled at Eichmann and demanded obedience of him: if he had ordered Eichmann to kill Jews before, Eichmann had done so; if he now ordered him to serve as a nursemaid to Jews, he had to do that, too.[34]

Pest was liberated on January 18, and Buda a month after that (February 13). By that time, 40,000 Jews had been deported from the city in the marches, and between 10,000 and 20,000 had been killed.

The picture of events that emerges from this story is not quite the same as the one that has been presented so far. For one thing, the role of the Zionist youth movements was crucial. It is true that they could not have achieved what they did without the support of the neutrals, but neither would the help of the neutrals have been effective without the Zionists. They saved tens of thousands. The glory and the fame were given, understandably, to those heroic Gentile individuals, such as Wallenberg, who made great sacrifices— in his case, he gave his life as well—to save Jews from death. The point is, however, that there were not only "Righteous Gentiles" in Budapest—Wallenberg, Lutz, Born, Rotta (the papal nuntius), Perlasca—but also "Righteous Jews." They did not seek fame any more than their Gentile counterparts did—and they created lasting friendships with the Gentiles—but after the war, when the story was told, they were simply forgotten. After all, they did what was expected of them—they saved Jews—and so Raffi Benshalom, Zvi Goldfarb, Dov Weiss, Efra Teichmann, Pil (Moshe Alpan), and the others faded away, becoming citizens of Israel: kibbutz members, industrialists, workers, engineers, and, in the case of Benshalom, noncareer diplomats.

The record needs a second correction that is extremely difficult to make because Wallenberg, the self-effacing Swedish banker, was a truly heroic figure. Still, had he remained alive, he probably would have been the first to discount some of the stories, and especially the grand totals, that were bandied about. He would have said that if he saved 4,500 people with his papers and thus enabled the youth to forge quite a few thousand more, why should he be credited with saving 100,000 Jews, as some of the accounts have it? Were there that many people during the Holocaust who saved 4,500 persons? He played second fiddle to Charles Lutz—but that does not mean that his fiddle was unimportant or that its tune was not very beautiful.

In the end, Lutz and the Swiss protected the 21,000 already mentioned and, in addition, 26,000 in the ghetto who had official or forged papers and

10,000 in the labor battalions, who received the papers by various means, and recommended 5,000 others to various other neutral legations, for a total of 62,000 people saved.[35]

By the end of 1944 Himmler's policy of trying to contact the West and using Jews, among others, to achieve that goal, had become explicit. He was now in an inferior position; the Reich was collapsing, and his attempts failed. The Jewish negotiators—Kasztner, Mayer, Sternbuch—managed to bluff their way—despite tremendous obstacles erected by the Allies and the Swiss—into saving most of the Jews of Budapest, except those lost in the terrible marches of November, and the excesses of the Hungarian fascists, and the desperate hunger and sickness of the Russian siege. Their attempts to reach out to the Jews held in Nazi camps were unsuccessful. In the few weeks before the end of the war, in these last days of Nazi rule, was there a chance to save more lives by negotiating with the murderers?

13

The Final Months

On October 23, 1944, in expectation of a massive Soviet offensive, Kurt A. Becher was nominated chief of the evacuation staff of the Nazi occupation authorities in Hungary.[1] "Evacuation" meant that he was in charge of cleaning out Hungarian property. According to our source—Gyula von Szilvay, then director of the Hungarian Foreign Trade Ministry—the property shipped away was put on 25,000 wagons and trucks and had a total value of SFR 6,000,000,000. According to the same source, most of it was Jewish property.

The Hungarian official in charge of abandoned Jewish property, Albert Tutvölgyi, resigned in March 1945 when he saw that these properties were being confiscated by the Nazis. Szilvay mentions details—whole factories and the contents of warehouses being evacuated to Germany by a company that Becher set up for the SS, called Omnipol. An interesting example was uncovered by OSS agents in Switzerland: a Hungarian industrialist, Thomas de Pechy, arrived in Switzerland in early March 1945 with a load of merchandise to sell to Swiss customers. His merchandise turned out to be products of his establishments, which had been evacuated by Becher. Becher very generously agreed that de Pechy could sell the goods in Switzerland, provided he received a rake-off of 25 percent. Becher's move was not only rapacious but also rather stupid. De Pechy got an assurance from the Swiss that they would not pay any money to the Germans. In this case, Becher lost.[2]

Becher had specific Jewish treasures in his possession—apart from the evacuated goods—deriving from the Va'adah's payments and from confiscations that he and his staff had made in Hungary before they fled to Austria at the end of 1944. He gave one piece of luggage to Moshe Schweiger, whom he released from Mauthausen in order to have a convenient alibi; there had been three pieces originally, filled with money from the payment handed over to him for the Kasztner train. The bag was handed over to the American CIC on May 30, 1945—after the war. But on May 24, Subsection B of the 215th CIC Detachment found an even larger treasure hidden away under the beds in the house that Becher had occupied before the Americans arrested him: 18.7 pounds of gold, 4.4 pounds of platinum, and jewelry. And on June 25, Becher's other alibis—Jews whom he carried with him to Austria to serve as proof of his humanitarianism—gave the CIC another treasure, consisting of gold and paper shares, which they said had been in Becher's possession.[3] He apparently planned to make investments in Austria with the other goods that he managed to take from Hungary. Even if Szilvay's figures are exaggerated, it is clear that if Becher did good in Hungary, as he claimed after the war, he certainly did very well.[4]

As the Soviet Army was closing in on Budapest, the desperate Hungarian Nazi regime was tending toward a last, crazy "revenge" against the Jews. The neutrals were trying their best to forestall more murders, acting under the leadership of the papal nuntius, who, together with the Swedes, sent a strong communication to the Szalasi government on November 17, on behalf of all the neutral missions, demanding that the (largely forged) protection papers be honored. The fascists then tried to divide the Jews in the ghetto into two groups—those protected by the neutrals (33,000 people, according to one count) and those not so protected (86,000 people). The ghetto was closed on December 10. A huge number of Jews, possibly as many as 100,000, were killed by the Arrow Cross government between October 15 and liberation, including those who died in marches and some of the 119,000 just mentioned. Even before the Soviets finally encircled the city on December 27, starvation was spreading. Hundreds of thousands of Hungarians also suffered from it, but they had lived on relatively adequate rations before and had easier access to food than the beleaguered Jews, who had been on a starvation diet for months. Children died by the thousands, and adults followed. Horses, rats, everything remotely edible, was eaten. The Arrow Cross squads murdered Jews wherever they could. Otto Komoly was killed by them, too, apparently on January 1.[5]

What interests us here is whether the German forces' nonintervention vis-à-vis the Jews is in any way connected with the Becher-Kasztner negotiations, or indeed whether Kasztner's claim that the German Army intervened in a positive sense stands up to examination. The results are not conclusive. During Becher's interrogation by Allied officers in Nuremberg on July 7, 1947, Kasztner suddenly appeared, and a surrealistic discussion took place between the two of them in the presence of a stenographer. Becher could not remember a thing about the last days in Budapest. Kasztner more or less forced him to "remember" that he had intervened with Himmler in favor of the Jews and that, as a result, the Germans in Budapest had rescued the rest of the Jews there.[6] By January, when this intervention is supposed to have taken place, there was every reason for Becher to do something to save these Jews. Whether or not he did, we do not know.

The last months of the war and the fate of the surviving Jews in Nazi camps are intimately connected with a phenomenon that has scarcely been discussed in the historical literature until now: the death marches. The Nazi principle, reportedly enunciated by Hitler, was that enemies of the Reich should not fall alive into the hands of the Allies; all concentration camp inmates were enemies of the Reich.[7]

While prisoners had been marched under terrible conditions before, the mass evacuation of inmates from camps really began with the 68,000 or so prisoners who were marched out of Auschwitz on January 18, 1945. In almost all the other camps the same procedure was followed. In long columns, on foot, people were marched criss-cross through the contracting Reich territory or loaded into open railway cars without food and water and then carried slowly through the countryside. The ostensible purpose was to move them into camps that were not (yet) "threatened" by Allied troops. In fact, considering the way the marchers were treated, the aim must have been to have very few left when the destination was reached. In the testimonies of almost all survivors these marches occupy a very central place: usually between 20–30 percent of the story. The marches were worse than the camps, if that was possible, certainly in the recollections of the survivors.

The marches took place between January and May 1945, when the Allies had absolute control of the skies, and not a cockroach could move without being spied by Allied aircraft. Interestingly, these marches are very rarely mentioned in the records of the Allied intelligence organs and governments, and absolutely nothing was done to stop them—by putting railway engines out of action, for instance, or by calling on some of the many teams who parachuted behind enemy lines to be in touch with Allied POWs. Sometimes POWs were marched in the same echelons with the camp inmates, except that the POWs received a certain minimum of food and were not murdered on the road, whereas the camp inmates were. The conclusion is that the Allied commanders received information about these marches and did not do a thing about them. The Jewish organizations had but the vaguest notion of this major tragedy; communications were chaotic in those last months of the war, and the Jews were not privy to the information gathered by the Allied intelligence agencies.[8] No one, including the negotiators with Himmler, helped the hundreds of thousands of marchers; at least 60 percent of them died.[9]

The final phase of Himmler's quest for negotiations with the West was connected with the Swedish government's actions to rescue some 600 Norwegian students, who had been deported to Germany in 1943–43—making a total of 6,000 or so Norwegians who now were languishing in concentration camps—and 1,600 Danish policemen, who shared the same fate. The motivation for this Swedish action was undoubtedly Scandinavian solidarity, with the promise of further friendly relations between Sweden and its neighbors.

A first intervention occurred on December 1, 1943, when the Swedish embassy in Berlin asked the German Foreign Office to have German actions against Norwegians in Norway stop. The German reaction was sharp and uncompromising: the Swedes—Ribbentrop's office said, after checking with a furious Hitler—had no business intervening on behalf of Norwegians under German rule.[10] The Swedes refrained from bringing up the question again for ten months, during which time they were active in facilitating the sending of food packages and other individual help to imprisoned Scandinavians.

On September 7, 1944, they turned again to the Foreign Office. The situation was completely different now because of the German defeats in the East and the liberation of France and Belgium in the West. The Swedes were in a position to threaten the Germans that a rejection of their humanitarian requests endangered Swedish-German relations. The Swedes intervened especially in favor of sick Norwegian and Danish detainees, who, they argued, should be sent to Sweden as well; the others should be either returned home or sent to Sweden. The Germans stated that they would refrain from further deportations from Norway to Germany, provided the fact was not published. In November they agreed to return sick Norwegian students to Norway. On November 30 the Norwegians proposed, through their embassy in Stockholm, that a Swedish Red Cross rescue team should receive Scandinavian detainees in Germany upon the expected German collapse; such a team, they said, should be headed by Count Folke Bernadotte, deputy head of the Swedish Red Cross and a relative of the King, Gustaf V. But the Swedes preferred to continue their talks via the German Foreign Office, because there had been some success and because the German collapse, though inevitable, was not yet imminent—the Swedish military attaché thought in mid-December that for the moment the Germans were holding their own. A couple of weeks later, with the last German offensive in the West (the Battle of the Bulge), his analysis was confirmed.

The Germans were becoming more amenable, but not only because of their desperate military situation. In the autumn of 1944 the Swedes stopped all shipping contacts with Germany, whether with Swedish or German ships, and the Germans feared a Swedish military intervention, especially after Finland signed an armistice with the Soviets on September 19.

Toward the end of 1944, Swedish efforts on behalf of Scandinavians in Germany began to concentrate on Himmler, probably because of the growing inefficiency of the Foreign Office and the decline of its power and the concomitant rise of Himmler's influence. There had been contacts with the SS before—through Kersten, who, as we have seen, used his influence over Himmler to free the seven Warsaw Swedes, four of whom had been sentenced to death for spying. Through Kersten again, the Swedish government acquainted Himmler with their requests regarding internees. Building on this contact, the Swedish ambassador in Germany, Arvid Richert, met Schellenberg on November 15. Schellenberg agreed to fulfill Swedish wishes to a large extent, again provided there was no publicity. The contacts had to remain secret from Kaltenbrunner and Hitler.

The Swedes were aware of Himmler's tentative attempts to create a climate for peace negotiations with the West.[11] In connection with these, Jakob Wallenberg, the Swedish banker and a relative of Raoul Wallenberg's, was asked by his German friends whether Himmler might negotiate a peace with the Western Allies; Wallenberg's answer was negative, but that, of course, would not deter Himmler (if he knew of it). Richert was informed of these attempts through a letter from his Foreign Office (November 27). The Swedes thought—not unlike Dogwood in Istanbul—that the Allies should at least pretend that they were interested in such negotiations, because they might lead to an attempt by Himmler to seize power from Hitler. The practical result was that fifty Norwegians, fifty Danes, and the three remaining Warsaw Swedes were released to Sweden in December.

The Russian offensive in mid-January 1945 changed the military situation completely. Western Poland was liberated, and the Soviets conquered east German territories; in the south the Russians advanced up to the Oder river, only a short distance from Berlin. Work from the Swedish embassy became difficult because of the constant air attacks on the German capital and the growing disorganization. The embassy undertook no further steps, nor did the SS initiate any further talks.

On February 7 the Norwegian ambassador in Stockholm, Niels C. Ditleff, submitted another memorandum to the Swedes, returning to his previous suggestion of sending a Swedish rescue mission to Germany. Crucial for the Swedish decision to act was the appearance, on February 9, in the *Svenska Dagbladet*, of a news item reporting the success of Musy in liberating 1,200 Jews from Theresienstadt—the same item that aroused Hitler's ire and caused him to forbid any further release of Jews. After reading the news, Ditleff turned to the Swedish Foreign Minister, Christian Günther, and repeated his request. Günther's response was immediate and positive: Bernadotte would be sent to Germany. The same evening, Richert was asked to find out whether Himmler would receive Bernadotte for a talk regarding Scandinavian internees. The Swedes were also active via Kersten, who had spoken to Himmler several times in December regarding the problem of the Scandinavian internees. Kersten was also the one who announced Bernadotte's visit in a telephone conversation with Himmler, at Günther's request. But the Swedes went one better: Richert was instructed (February 10) to tell the Germans that Sweden was prepared to receive all the Jews in concentration camps, especially those in Theresienstadt and Bergen-Belsen.[12] We shall return to this intervention momentarily. On February 16, Bernadotte arrived in Germany.

Bernadotte's contacts in Germany were made not only with Himmler but also with Ribbentrop, Kaltenbrunner, and Schellenberg—the Swedes could not afford to have internal German squabbles endanger their goals. Himmler agreed to concentrate the Scandinavians in the Neuengamme camp in Hamburg and to release mothers with children, old people, and the sick. Bernadotte planned to return to Germany in two weeks' time. A later attempt to reach the West through Bernadotte was almost certainly already in Himmler's mind during these first talks. If so, the thank-you note that King Gustaf sent to Himmler through Schellenberg must have strengthened Himmler's readiness to cooperate.

Bernadotte's expedition went under the banner of the Swedish Red Cross; in fact, it was organized by the Swedish state and its army. The Swedish count visited Berlin again between March 6 and 8, when he also intervened on behalf of interned Scandinavian Jews, who would be transported to Neuengamme along with the Danes and Norwegians. Like Bernadotte, Kersten was also asked by the Swedes to go to Berlin and strengthen Himmler's resolve to abide by his promises.

The Swedish expedition was organized quickly enough—by March 13 seventy-five vehicles and 250 men were near Hamburg, prepared to evacuate the Scandinavians and hoping that the Allies, who were informed of the mission, would not attack them from the air. By April all the Scandinavians had been transported to Neuengamme.[13] But the Swedish government was not satisfied with this achievement; it wanted to transport the Scandinavian internees to Sweden, widen the scope of Bernadotte's mission to include non-Scandinavians as well, and, if this did not clash with his main mission, bring some Jews to Sweden. Bernadotte's instruction was to demand that his mission should aid *all* the inmates of Neuengamme, not only Danes and Norwegians, and, specifically, that 25,000 French women should be put in one camp, Neuengamme or elsewhere, under the protection of the Swedish mission.

This Swedish attempt to rescue Jews was not new—the embassy in Berlin had already asked the German Foreign Office in February to release Jews held at Theresienstadt, Bergen-Belsen, and elsewhere and had declared Swedish readiness to accept them in Sweden. Even more important perhaps, the Swedish government had turned to the papal nuntius and the Swiss to address a joint demarche to the Germans "urging the Germans not to massacre the Jews in concentration camps. . . . As neither Nuncio [nuntius] nor Swiss Minister would co-operate, Swedish government now think it useless" to proceed.[14]

As we have seen, the Swedish government had also intervened very forcefully in the Hungarian situation. The King had written his letter to Horthy, two special envoys—Waldemar Langlet and Raoul Wallenberg—had been sent there, and the Swedish embassy had been engaged in protecting Jews in the Hungarian capital from the spring of 1944 on. These interventions were made, in part, at the urging of Hillel Storch, a Latvian Jewish refugee who had become a representative of the World Jewish Congress (and who was opposed to Rabbi Marcus Ehrenpreis, head of the Jewish community in Sweden, who also spoke in the name of the congress). Storch had been in touch with that interesting personality, Edgar Klaus, the Latvian Jew who had been an agent of the Abwehr and who had then been taken over by the SD. It seems that Klaus had informed Storch as early as the summer of 1944 that the Germans were going to release the Kasztner train internees from Bergen-Belsen. On February 8, 1945, Klaus asked Storch to intervene with the Swedes and make sure that Sweden was prepared to take in the Jewish internees. Storch went to the government and received a positive reply, on the eleventh. What he did not know was that the government had instructed Richert a day before to intervene with the Germans in that spirit. On the nineteenth, Richert fulfilled his instructions and told the Nazis that Sweden would be willing to accept Jewish refugees.

Storch's activity involved another Abwehr agent, who presumably now worked for Schellenberg: Werner G. Boening, a friend of Peter Bruno Kleist's, whom we have met already.[15] It looks again as though Schellenberg was pushing the Jewish line in his attempts to extricate his chief and Germany at the last moment. We can see proof in a Klaus letter to Storch on February 25. There Klaus reported that his friend Kleist had intervened in Berlin in favor of Jews, but unfortunately "Jewish circles in Switzerland had also taken certain steps, as a result of which the release of Jews was held up, and Dr. Kleist's mission was made more difficult." In other words, Schellenberg was fighting his war against Becher and Mayer in Sweden through a Jewish agent who was negotiating with a representative of the World Jewish Congress![16]

The radicalization in Swedish attitudes toward the rescue of Jews has to be understood against the background of increasingly intensive Swedish involvement in these matters. After all, the Swedes had saved Danish Jews, had then been involved very deeply indeed in the attempted rescue of Hungarian Jews, and had been increasingly more receptive to Jewish appeals. This aid was undoubtedly due in large measure to real humanitarianism, and it also reflected a desire to gain favor with the Americans, whom the Swedes considered to be very concerned about the Jews.

At the end of February, Kersten met with Storch for the first time, and Storch submitted a plan for action, which he asked Kersten to facilitate by discussing the issues with Himmler. The plan, not surprisingly, had aims similar to those of Mayer and Sternbuch. It provided for food and medicine to be sent to the camps, for the concentration of Jews in a small number of locations, and for large numbers to be sent to Switzerland and Sweden—Sweden was to receive between 5,000 and 10,000.[17] On March 24, Kersten wrote to Storch, saying in Himmler's name that 10,000 Jews could be shipped to Sweden or Switzerland. Storch turned to the Swedish government, which again promised to receive the refugees if they came to Sweden. Himmler, Kersten said, had invited Storch to come to Germany to negotiate with him—the truth probably is that the idea was Kersten's. A letter from Himmler to Kersten (March 15) attached to the note prefigured what Himmler would say to any Jewish representative: that he had always wanted to solve the "Jewish problem" by emigration and now, at last, he had enabled some 2,700 Jews to leave for Switzerland. The folly of war had prevented him from doing so in the immediate past.[18]

On April 2, Bernadotte met with Himmler, and the result of their discussion was that only Scandinavian women and children could be shipped to Sweden; the French women would be allowed to receive 15,000 parcels, but their release was denied. On the way back from the meeting, Schellenberg asked Bernadotte in Himmler's name to see Eisenhower and arrange for an armistice if the situation regarding Hitler changed. Bernadotte replied that he would be prepared to see Eisenhower if Hitler was removed, the Nazi party dissolved, the budding movement to wage a guerrilla war against the Allies dismantled, and the Scandinavian internees shipped to Sweden.[19]

The next meeting between the Swedish count and Himmler took place on April 21. Himmler agreed then to free all the women at Ravensbrück, not only the French. The Neuengamme Scandinavians had been transported into Denmark by the Germans themselves, but they would be permitted to go to Sweden only if Denmark became a theater of war. That, it seemed, had been an instruction from Hitler.

Bernadotte's talk with Himmler on April 21 had been preceded by another meeting, an unprecedented encounter between the chief Nazi murderer and a Jew, Norbert Masur, a Swedish national and a representative of the World Jewish Congress. In the course of that encounter, Himmler agreed to release 1,000 Jewish women, whereas Bernadotte, a few hours afterward, obtained the release of all the Ravensbrück women. More interesting than the practical achievements of the Masur visit, which were very meager, were Himmler's statements to him as Masur and Kersten report them. The reports are more or less the same, but we can perhaps, in this case, rely more on the Masur version.[20]

Himmler said that the Jews were a subversive and foreign element in Germany and had been behind the Spartacist (Communist) uprising of 1918–19.

He had nevertheless tried to solve the problem in a humane way by emigration and had collaborated with American Jewish organizations to solve the problem that way; but the Western countries had refused to accept the Jews. When Germany conquered the East, it came into contact with masses of proletarian Jews, who were diseased, mainly with typhoid. These masses could not be left behind the German lines. He himself had lost thousands of SS men because of the diseased Jews. And, in addition, the Jews had helped the partisans and had shot at German units in the ghetto—a veiled reference to the Warsaw ghetto rebellion. Crematoria had to be built to burn the bodies of all those who had died in epidemics. And now the Allies want to make a hangman's noose for us, he said ("Und daraus will man uns jetzt ein[en] Strick drehen"). We had not wanted a war against Russia, Himmler continued, but when we discovered that the Russians had amassed 20,000 tanks, we had no choice. The war was very cruel, and if the Jewish people suffered in it, so had the German nation.

The concentration camps, Himmler said, had received a bad press because of their name—they should have been called reeducation camps. Not only political prisoners and Jews but also criminal elements were confined there, and as a result, Germany had been practically free of crime after 1941. Treatment in these camps was strict but just. Theresienstadt, for instance, was simply a town where the Jews concentrated there had full autonomy. Transgressions by SS men in the camps had been punished.

Of the Jews remaining under German rule, 450,000 had been left in Budapest to be liberated and 150,000 in Auschwitz. Himmler complained that in Bergen-Belsen the Allies had photographed guards, who had been tied up, together with bodies of recently deceased prisoners, while at Buchenwald they had set a hospital afire and then taken pictures of inmates who had been killed or burnt in the process, and now they were making horror stories out of all that. He, Himmler, had never received any thanks for handing over these camps to the Allies without fighting. No one, Himmler complained, had been a target for such calumnies as he had.

What is interesting about this collection of rather silly lies is their startling resemblance to the arguments presented forty and fifty years later by those who denied that the Holocaust had ever happened. In fact, the denial of the Holocaust, one of the most vicious products of postwar Nazism and antisemitism in the democratic countries, started right then and there. Himmler, during the last days of the worst and most criminal regime that had ever disfigured the face of the earth, was trying to defend it; he apparently wanted to ensure that the ideas of death and destruction that it represented would continue to poison humanity. This hope is apparently the reason why he talked as though preserving the Reich secret—the murder of millions of Jews—was still necessary. The 150,000 who, he claimed, had been left in Auschwitz (only a few thousand sick people had in fact been left behind) and the 450,000 in Budapest (ultimately some 144,000 reportedly survived) later became, in the neo-Nazi legend, the millions who disappeared into Soviet or Soviet-held territory.

Himmler could still afford to speak like that with a Jew who, he must have realized, had received all the information that was available at the time. He knew that he still controlled the fate of the remaining hundreds of thousands of Jews, who were in the clutches of his murderous gangs. Giving the representative of the all-powerful "International Jewry" less than he gave Bernadotte a short while later must have been a reflection of his unchanged fear and hatred of the real enemy of Nazism, the Jews.

One day after this peculiar meeting, on April 22, Hitler decided to stay in Berlin, which was under attack by Soviet ground forces. Himmler concluded from the decision that Hitler had removed himself from the German people, and he now saw himself free to act as he wished to save Germany from chaos. He thought that his SS was the only Central European element that could ensure an orderly transition to a new political reality and wanted to offer the Anglo-Americans an alliance against communism. On the night of April 23 he told Bernadotte that the latter could take with him everything he could, including the Scandinavians. In return, Bernadotte agreed to transmit to the Swedish government Himmler's request to have the Swedes arrange a meeting between himself and Eisenhower to discuss a German capitulation on the Western front. The Swedes and the Allies refused, of course. In the meantime, the Swedish mission, now reinforced by Danes, were feverishly active; in all, the Swedes shipped some 21,000 persons to Sweden; probably 6,500 or so were Jews.[21] On May 8 the war ended.

After the war Kersten and Bernadotte fought bitterly over the question of who had facilitated the release of Nazi prisoners, especially Jews. With the support of the World Jewish Congress and of a special committee nominated by the Dutch Foreign Ministry, Kersten claimed that Himmler's order to hand over all the camps to the Allies and avoid their destruction (March 3, 1945) was his achievement.[22] He also claimed to have saved 63,000 Jewish lives and to have been, generally speaking, the main factor in moving Himmler to change his policies in the last stages of the war. We may well doubt these claims. But equally, we may wonder at Bernadotte's total silence regarding Kersten's role in the negotiations. What is clear is that Kersten was a moderating influence in Himmler's court, that the alliance between Kersten and Schellenberg saved many lives, and that Kersten smoothed the way for Bernadotte's talks with the SS chief. But it was not Kersten who could have led Himmler to a last, desperate attempt to negotiate with the West; only Bernadotte could have done that, so the partial and halting concessions were wrung from a hesitant Himmler by the Swedes, although the way had been prepared by the continuous impact of the Finnish–German masseur.

During those last hectic few weeks before the final German collapse, there were quite a number of initiatives to prevent the wholesale death of camp inmates and slave laborers, though not, as we shall soon see, the deaths of those who had been taken out of the camps on marches. Thus, Carl J. Burckhardt, now president of the International Red Cross, went to see Himmler. Actually, he saw Kaltenbrunner, on March 12–14. He came back with some of the concessions that Himmler had promised Bernadotte in relation to the Scandinavians: Red Cross personnel could, with certain restrictions, feed and treat internees; women, children, and the elderly would be exchanged and shipped out, presumably through Switzerland; and internees would be regrouped by nationality.[23]

Kasztner and Becher, too, were active in those last weeks. Becher reports that on April 5, Himmler discussed with him the fate of the camps "threatened" by the Allied forces and offered to make him responsible for all the camps ("Reichskommissar für sämtliche KZ [*Konzentrationslager*—concentration camp]," according to Kasztner). He would start by inspecting Bergen-Belsen. Becher himself says that he asked for time to consider the offer; after all, he said, he had never had anything to do with concentration camps—his training at Dachau and Oranienburg seems to have been the victim of failing memory. In the end, apparently at Kasztner's insistence, Becher agreed to take on the task (April 14). Even earlier, however, using Himmler's instructions as his authority and accompanied by Kasztner, Becher induced the German commanders to hand over the camp to the advancing British without a fight, thus probably saving the lives of the internees (April 11–12). This did not, of course, save the lives of the multitudes who were already too ill and starved to survive.[24]

Becher, with Kasztner constantly at his side, moved to Neuengamme, where others, apart from the Scandinavians, were being held, including Jews. He claims to have obtained Himmler's agreement that they stay put, rather than be taken on another death march. On April 14, as we have seen, Himmler nominated Becher to supervise the handing-over of the camps at Flossenbürg, Dachau (in Bavaria), Mauthausen (in Austria), and Theresienstadt (in Bohemia). Himmler withdrew this concession the next day after a row with Hitler; the Führer had heard of the surrender of Buchenwald to the Americans with all the inmates in the camp (actually, a large proportion had been "evacuated" to go on a death march). Hitler's intention was clear: not to leave any enemy of the Reich alive in the hands of the Allies, and all camp inmates were, by definition, Reich enemies. As Becher reports it, Himmler now reserved for himself the right of a final decision in each case. Becher did not manage to have Flossenbürg handed over to the Allies, but he claims to have prevented the mass murder of the Mauthausen inmates in specially dyna-mited caves through his intervention with Kaltenbrunner. Others, especially International Red Cross representatives, also claim to have prevented this massacre. Becher says that he also intervened at Dachau—but the U.S. troops were more effective in their liberation of the camp than the SS Obersturmbannführer.[25] In addition, Becher received permission to liber-ate 400 Jews from Bratislava, and Kasztner had gone there (March 31), but it was too late. All he achieved was the rescue of twenty-eight persons (among them Rabbi Weissmandel), and he added twenty-two more from Vienna. He brought these people to Switzerland with the help of Krumey, Becher's colleague.[26]

Becher acted in those days like a convinced Nazi who saw the Third Reich crumbling around him and was trying to maintain his own position by saving lives. His real attitude and inner convictions—if we can talk about convic-tions in relation to Becher—can be gauged from a comment that Moshe Schweiger reports that he made after Schweiger released him from Maut-hausen. Speaking of Himmler, Becher supposedly said, "When you finally make your personal acquaintance with the Reichsführer, you will see what a wonderful person he is."[27]

At the trial in Israel in 1954–55, the main accusation leveled against Kaszt-ner was that he had given Becher a commendation for having rescued Jews, which had helped Becher escape from prosecution at Allied hands. Kasztner made his recommendation at a time when he knew—and indeed wrote—that Becher had extorted money from Jews, though he could not have known the background of his Nazi protector. But to understand why Kasztner helped a Nazi officer escape justice, we must put matters in perspective: Kasztner helped others besides Becher; he was willing to certify to the humanity of SS Gen. Hans Jüttner, he was willing to help Wisliceny, and he wrote letters whitewashing Krumey (February 5, 1947) and Kettlitz (October 13, 1947). From a perusal of these letters and testimonies about Kasztner, the picture emerges of an ambitious and courageous man who wanted to tell the truth about people who had helped him. Becher had undoubtedly been instrumental in the rescue of Jews in the last stages of the war, and if his help was accompanied by a continued loyalty to the murderous anti-Jewish Nazi creed and by despicable extortions, that made no difference. As far as Kaszt-ner was concerned, Becher had saved lives, and Kasztner said as much. By 1954 he must have realized the monumental mistake he had made, and he tried to hide it and lied about it—in vain. The poisoned atmosphere around Kasztner, which led to his murder, was in great part due to the help he had given a Nazi.

Hitler committed suicide; the war ended; and Himmler, who tried to pass through British lines on his way into Germany from Denmark, where he had been staying until then, was recognized. On May 23 he committed suicide, too. About 5.8 million Jews had died in the Holocaust. All the attempts at rescuing them, including the negotiations that have been the subject of this book, had resulted in only very partial and marginal successes. As I said at the outset, this is the story of what might have been, not of what was. But— might the negotiations have worked? Why didn't they?

Epilogue

The accepted interpretation of Nazi antisemitism and the evolving anti-Jewish policy of the regime has been confirmed in our study. So has the policy of the "Final Solution": the Nazi elite's decision to murder all Jews wherever they could reach them was implemented with thoroughness and conviction. But exceptions were granted during the war if tactical advantages could be gained by keeping some Jews alive or by letting some Jews escape to the free or neutral world. There was, as has been argued already, no inherent contradiction between the two policies, one representing the main strategic line of Nazi thinking, and the other a tactical, secondary one. The Nazis expected to win the war, and if they did, they would finally "solve" the "Jewish question" by total annihilation; any Jews who might escape momentarily would in the end be caught and killed.

These considerations became very important later in the war, when the German prospect of victory receded. The primary Nazi objective then became to rescue Nazi Germany from stalemate or worse. If Germany lost the war, the Nazi project of annihilating all the Jews of the world would not be achieved in any case. To win the war and prevent the ultimate survival of the Jews, tactical retreats were justified, Jews could be released, if strategic goods or, better still, diplomatic contacts with the West could be established—contacts that might lead to a separate peace and, it was hoped, German-Western collaboration in a war against the Soviets. Himmler's tentative steps did not contradict the "Final Solution" but made it possible to carry it out in the changed circumstances of a war that was going badly.

We have reviewed one very important aspect of the Holocaust that has largely been ignored: the "Final Solution" policy did not constitute a complete break with the emigration-expulsion policy preceding it. Both policies were based on the same principle, enunciated by Hitler as early as 1919: to "remove [*entfernen*]" the Jews altogether. In prewar Germany, emigration suited the circumstances best, and when that was neither speedy enough or complete enough, expulsion—

preferably to some "primitive" place, uninhabited by true Nordic Aryans, the Soviet Union or Madagascar—was the answer. When expulsion did not work, either, and the prospect of controlling Europe and, through Europe, the world arose in late 1940 and early 1941, the murder policy was decided on, quite logically, on the basis of Nazi ideology. All these policies had the same aim: removal. When, during the course of the war, questions were raised about the wisdom of implementing the murder policy down to the last Jew, especially after the first German defeats, the former policy of emigration-expulsion was strongly enough imprinted in memory to be reverted to on occasion. Both, then, can be seen in the development of Nazi policies: the continuity—that is, the persistence of the idea of emigration and expulsion—and the break, that is, the decision to mass-murder the Jews.

Why should it have been Himmler, the arch-murderer himself, who was the central figure in these tentative attempts? Several reasons come to mind. Himmler was a convinced, ideological Nazi, with a fervent desire to see the victory of National Socialism. On the one hand, this meant, prior to the war, that the German body politic had to be cleansed of the Jewish Satan, and in the conditions then prevailing the most effective means to do so was emigration and, later, expulsion. On the other hand, with the weakening of Germany's position, the desire to make an approach through the Jews to powers controlled by the Jews must have been very strong for a Nazi trying to rescue Nazism. After all, the Jews, in Himmler's mind, ruled the world of the enemy, and it was only logical to try that approach, though other roads could be traveled as well. In the middle period, at the time of the great Nazi victories, thoughts of negotiations were superfluous.

We can see three phases in Himmler's attitudes and policies: the prewar phase, the 1940–42 phase, and the phase of German decline, from the latter part of 1942 to 1945. In the first two, Himmler was in perfect accord with his Führer; in the third, he increasingly recognized the dangers that Nazism was facing and developed a different attitude from that of Hitler. Fearful of the dictator, to whom he had sworn loyalty and allegiance, he continued to carry out the murder policy with all his might and power, but at the same time he hesitatingly established an alternative general policy for Nazi Germany, which would have also meant a temporary cessation of the mass murders. But Himmler was not just afraid of Hitler—he believed in him; and his recognition that his idol's policies were leading Germany into disaster created an insoluble inner conflict.

As we have seen, Himmler did not—perhaps could not—free himself from the Hitler influence. He was, however, fully conscious of the power that he himself possessed. His organization was the only one in the Reich that could effectively execute a volte-face of the kind we have been discussing here—even before July 20, 1944, and most certainly after that date. He was constantly weighing the decision of whether to use his power, and in the end he chose not to. But apart from Hitler himself, Himmler was the obvious person to try to change the course that Nazi Germany had embarked on.

What of Hitler? Did the dictator also have moments when he weighed options? Probably not. Unless we discover new material, we cannot answer that question positively.

The means that Himmler employed to try out different options were based on the work done by his rival, the Abwehr. The fate of the Jews was linked, among other things, to the attempt by the conservative opposition to assassinate or topple the dictator. The Abwehr leaders, with their efforts to reach the West and gain its support in their endeavor to change the regime in the midst of the war, were an integral part of the plot. Had Hitler been assassinated in 1943 or 1944, hundreds of thousands of Jews—if not more—would have been saved, so pivotal was his input in the Holocaust policy. Himmler played with the idea of letting the opposition try its hand, in the expectation of taking over in case of success and rooting the opposition out in case of failure. If Himmler, rather than the generals, had taken over from Hitler, would the Holocaust policy have continued? There is no way to answer such a hypothetical question.

What emerges from our discussion is that Himmler carefully followed the Abwehr attempts to establish a dialogue with the West. He did so partly through aristocrats who had Western connections from before the war, such as Adam von Trott zu Solz, Gisevius, Moltke, and lesser figures; and partly through low-grade, mainly Jewish, contacts, of whom Klaus, Laufer, and Grosz were typical. The most important places where both types of contacts were tried were Bern, Stockholm, and Istanbul. By the end of 1943, Himmler's SS, in the person of its intelligence chief, Schellenberg, was ready to destroy the Abwehr, inherit its contacts, and do in effect what the Abwehr had tried to do—prepare the ground for a separate peace with the West, hoping that either Hitler would somehow disappear or else would himself recognize the necessity for Nazi Germany to seek a separate peace if it wanted to survive. In this quest, Himmler was probably influenced by the supposed historical precedent of Friedrich II's last-minute rescue in 1762–63, when dissension between his enemies, caused by the death of the Russian Empress, saved him from destruction.

Once the Abwehr was gone, as a direct result of the defections in Istanbul in February 1944, Himmler was left with only the low-grade contacts. Those in the aristocratic underground were not cooperating with him, nor could he cooperate with them without admitting that he was accessory to their plot against the Führer. After July 20 their lives were forfeit in any case. There remained Klaus, Laufer, and Grosz, and it was through these shady, underworld figures—who perfectly matched Himmler's own stereotypes of

Jews—that Schellenberg and Himmler tried to reach the Western powers. They were willing to pay a price, if and when such contacts led to results. What was that putative price?

When we consider this crucial question, we have to remember that Himmler, that cautious, circumspect mass murderer, did everything he could to protect himself—against Hitler, against hard-liners like Bormann, Kaltenbrunner, and Müller, against Ribbentrop and others. His coup was obtaining Hitler's agreement in December 1942 to sell Jews for hard currency and, by implication, for real advantages to the Reich. His remark to Becher in Salzburg in July 1944 was typical: We shall see what we keep of the promises we make. Which promises were kept depended on the pressure he was under and on the advantages that the Reich and Nazism would gain. But what he actually conceded indicates what he might have conceded under different circumstances: he let the Kasztner train go through, and he ordered a stop to the preparations for deporting the Budapest Jews to Auschwitz. We need not consider, in this connection, the release of the Weiss family of industrialists from Hungary, because the reasons were purely economic, though it, too, suggests that the "Final Solution" was final in its general conception, not in its tactical ups and downs; and we need not consider his willingness to hand over some of the camps at the very end, because then he felt the knife against his throat. But the conclusion must be, Yes, Himmler was willing to pay a price in terms of Jewish lives—as low as possible, to be sure, and depending on what he would have received in return. From the SS leader's point of view, some Jewish lives, maybe thousands, maybe tens of thousands, maybe hundreds of thousands, might have been saved, it seems, in order for Nazism to survive.[1]

But—the Jews were in no position to give Himmler what he wanted. Only the West could do that, because it was fighting not just for political interests but also for a democratic world. Victory would put an end to the attempt of Nazism and fascism to turn the globe into a hell. Roosevelt and Churchill, and the people they represented, undoubtedly believed in that mission, which included the very central idea of liberating and helping the nations crushed under the boot of the Nazis. The Soviets could not have cared less about such concerns, because their ideological and political agendas were different. But the Western Allies made some crucial decisions that militated against any yielding to the possible blandishments of a Himmler, even if yielding did not detract them from their aim of defeating Germany.

The pivotal importance of the Soviet Union in the fight against Nazi Germany was the main buttress of the Allies' firm stand. The German Army was defeated in Russia and by the Red Army—of that there can be hardly any doubt. The invasion of France on D Day, June 6, 1944, was an important contribution to the final victory, but not the decisive factor. Without the

Soviets, without their terrible suffering and their indescribable bravery, the war might have lasted for years longer and perhaps not been won at all. The Western leaders knew the odds, and the last thing they wanted was to endanger their delicate relations with their Soviet allies by negotiating with the chief murderer of the Nazi regime—especially about Jews, the problematic and unpopular minority. At Casablanca in February 1943 the Allies' policy was announced in the form of a demand for unconditional German surrender. Not to the West alone were the Germans to surrender, but to all Allies. A corollary was the refusal to negotiate anything except surrender; there would be no ransom payments and no population exchanges except in the strictly military sphere or under the Red Cross conventions.

In January 1944 the Western Allied Chiefs of Staff made a decision that had nothing to do with Jews or their rescue: they would not use military means for such civilian aims as rescue or aid. Any Jewish proposal to use the air force or other military units to prevent the Nazis from continuing their murders was thus going to meet objections from the military. Their task, as they had been specifically told, was to disregard all other considerations and concentrate solely on the achievement of victory. The politicians enunciated this "victory first" principle time and time again: Jews, and other victims of Nazism, could be saved only by an Allied victory. Until then, any other policy was self-defeating, because it would simply ensure that the Nazi rule in Europe continued longer than it had to.

A contradiction was inherent in the Allies' stance. They were fighting, among other things, for the liberation of the civilian populations in Europe from the Nazi oppression. Logically, rescue plans that did not hinder the successful pursuit of war should have become a priority. Negotiating to gain time, exerting pressure on the Red Cross to intervene on behalf of inmates of concentration camps and then providing the wherewithal to do this effectively, and promising the neutrals early on that any refugees reaching their borders would not become a burden on the local economy—such tactics did not contradict the military effort. Bombing railways or installations where people were gassed, and aiding Jewish underground fighters on the same scale as non-Jewish fighters—such moves would have been very much in the interest of a successful prosecution of the war. The distribution of leaflets declaring that the bombing was a retaliation for the Nazi murder of civilians, including Jews specifically, would hardly have prolonged the war. The Allies went much further in their refusal to help Jews than even their stated policies, in themselves erroneous and contradictory, required. They contravened their own war aims and left a permanent black mark on their record.

We have seen that there was a very basic reason for the Allied stance, even in cases where Allied leaders—Churchill comes to mind—were sympathetic to Jewish concerns. The Allies never really understood the Nazi policy against the Jews. They did not take Nazi writings and propaganda at face value. They thought that Nazi antisemitism was an instrument to gain power and hold it and failed to realize that for the Nazis, antisemitism was not a tool but an aim. An imbalance was thus created: the Nazis saw the Jews as their main enemies, the enemies who stood behind and controlled all their other enemies; the Allies did not realize, perhaps could not realize, that this purely illusory demonization of a powerless and helpless minority into a global threat was meant seriously. For them the Jews were just a nuisance, and for the British in particular they were a menace to national interests in Palestine and the Middle East. History took revenge: the British lost not just Palestine but their Empire. They would have lost it anyway, but the war undoubtedly accelerated the process.

We must conclude that the Allies would not have received large numbers of Jews if Himmler had offered them. Nor would they pay for Jews whom they did not want, least of all by acceding to any demands by a Himmler. They would not have minded if the International Red Cross protected the Jews in the camps but, as has been pointed out already, would not intervene with the Red Cross to achieve this care—partly no doubt because they were afraid that diverting Red Cross attention to the Jews might affect Red Cross care for their own soldiers in captivity. The Red Cross, on its part, was a cautious, timid organization that needed to be pressured to engage in new ventures, such as protecting civilians in Nazi camps.

A colleague of mine, Shlomo Aharonson, in a book written at the same time as I wrote this one, uses the imagery of a multiple trap to describe the situation of the Jews in World War II. The term appears to me to be very useful: the Jews were indeed trapped between the reluctance of the Allies to help, the determination of the Nazis to murder them, and their own powerlessness. Their powerlessness was the crucial element. Anyone reading the documents on Jews produced by the ministries of the Western Allies cannot escape the conclusion that the Jews were at best a pathetic nuisance in the eyes of the Allies. Individual Jews were in positions of some importance in Allied leadership groups; such individuals were mostly reluctant to identify with the Jewish people's tragedy and were of no help—with a few exceptions, the chief one being the U.S. Secretary of the Treasury, Henry Morgenthau, Jr. The Jews of the United States could not very well oppose Roosevelt, who was conducting the war against the enemies of the Jews; the Palestine Jewish leadership could not very well oppose the British, who were saving Palestine from Nazi occupation. The Zionist right-wing opposition, the Irgun Tzvai Leumi, declared war against the British in January 1944, thus in effect fighting on the side of the Nazis against one of the powers fighting the worst enemy the Jews ever had. The war of the Irgun was, to be sure, the result of

Jewish despair at the lack of succor given by the Allies to the Jews in Europe—and was in itself a symptom of the Jews' powerlessness.

Part of the trap in which the Jewish leaders in the free world found themselves consisted of the impossibility of engaging in direct negotiations with the Germans in the face of an Allied determination not to permit them to do so. Various critics have suggested that the Jews should have approached the Germans regardless. As we have seen, they occasionally considered that option; but there were two decisive arguments against such a course. First, if they had sent a Menachem Bader to the Nazis, he would have had nothing to offer. The Jews had neither goods nor diplomatic leverage with the Allies. And second, any such action would have spoiled the last chance that the Allies really would try to help the Jews, as the WRB did in the end.

The massive social trauma that overcame the Jewish people after the war was not made any easier by their realization that the Allies had not done much to save the Jews from the clutches of the Nazis. Faced with the destruction of European Jewry and the revelations about the inaction of the Allies, many Jews wallowed in self-pity and exaggerated anti-Allied or, more generally, anti-Gentile accusations. But the Allies, after all, did save the remnants of European Jewry and prevented the total destruction of the Jewish people. They did help occasionally. The WRB tried its best—too late, but it tried. The neutrals, including the Vatican, forcefully intervened in Hungary. American agencies helped the thousands of Jews who found their way to the Iberian Peninsula. Public declarations were made against the Nazi murder of Jews. And even in Palestine the British authorities admitted thousands of Jews, however reluctantly. In the lands of the Holocaust, Denmark, Bulgaria, and Italy were examples of nations who refused to collaborate with the Nazis in annihilating their Jews. Overwhelming majorities of Norwegians, Dutch, Belgians, French, and Serbs did likewise. Minorities among the other nationalities made their best efforts to help at great sacrifice to themselves. Not everyone acted against the Jews.

The wrath and frustration of the Jewish people finally turned against itself. Ever since the Holocaust, an increasing number of books and articles have accused the Jewish wartime leadership of failing to rescue, of negotiating with the enemy, of pandering to hostile "Allies." The Nazis murdered the Jews— everyone knows that. The Allies did little to help. But who was *really* responsible? In accordance with "good" Jewish tradition, many Jewish historians, writers, and journalists blamed Chaim Weizmann, Stephen Wise, David Ben-Gurion, Nahum Goldman, Yitzhak Grünbaum, Moshe Shertok, and all the rest of the Jews who tried to rescue their fellows. They were responsible because they had failed. This suicidal tendency in historiography is typical of a frustrated public refusing to recognize its essential helplessness in the face of overwhelming force. This tendency is especially pronounced because the situation has changed since the war with the establishment of the State of Israel; now, paradoxically, a much smaller number of Jews wield more, though still not very impressive, power, just like so many other small nations or peoples. Why did Joel Brand fail? We can almost hear the argument that the Israeli Air Force should have dropped him behind German lines. Anachronistic solutions are offered to the problem of rescuing millions of people being murdered by an implacable enemy.

But rescue *was* tried. Prior to the war, it took the form of emigrating Jews from the German sphere of influence, so that a peculiar coinciding of Nazi and Jewish interests took place. The Nazis wanted to expel, the Jews wanted to rescue—not from a Holocaust of which they did not and could not have known, but from a hostile regime. During the war, with no realistic options for rescue by resistance or by flight, the only way out seemed to be negotiating with the murderers. Himmler's concerns led him down a converging path, as we have seen.

The Jewish individuals who opened the door to negotiation took tremendous risks, personal and communal. In the end, our conclusion must be that they did the right thing, took the only possible way to save lives. Contrary to all logic, some lives were saved. After the war those of the negotiators who survived were reviled, accused, attacked, even murdered, along with the leaders who understood, more or less, what the negotiators hoped to accomplish and helped them. The one exception was Weissmandel, a central figure in these attempts, but he was not reviled because he joined with the accusers in cursing the "establishment" leadership. It is, we might conclude, a thankless job to be a leader of Jews.

The Jewish heroes were no knights in shining armor. Weissmandel was a fanatic, ultraorthodox opponent of Zionism; Brand was an adventurer, a drinker, and a person whose devotion to the truth was not the most prominent mark of his character; Kasztner was an ambitious, overweening, and authoritarian personality, guilty of rescuing Nazis from postwar justice to satisfy his sense of honor and power; Biss was engaged on that same, pathetic mission to save the reputation of a Nazi humanitarian extortioner, Kurt Becher; Mayer was a pedantic philanthropist—and so on. Yet heroes they all are. Their attempts to save Jews involved tremendous self-sacrifice, courage, and devotion. The Jewish people did not erect statues or name squares for them, or include them as role models in the history books for their young. Gizi Fleischmann, Michael Dov Weissmandel, Andrej Steiner, Oskar Neumann, Otto Komoly, Reszoe Kasztner, Andreas Biss, Joel Brand, and Hansi Brand inside the Reich and Saly Mayer, Isaac and Rachel (Recha) Sternbuch, Menachem Bader, Wenja Pomeranz, Joseph Schwartz, and that fascinating character Alfred Schwarz ("Dogwood") outside the Reich—all deserve such recognition. So do the Zionist youth movement leaders in Slovakia and Hungary: Rafi Friedel (Benshalom), Moshe Pil (Alpan), Efra Teichmann (Agmon), Zvi and Neska Goldfarb, Peretz Revesz, and the others. They did not like each other at all. Kasztner despised Mayer, Mayer thought Kasztner was a thief, Biss hated Brand, and Weissmandel distrusted all Zionists. But those are human foibles. They remind us that our heroes were ordinary humans, perhaps more gifted with insight and courage than the rest of us; they did the correct thing at the right time. Given the circumstances, they could not fully succeed. That they did in part is a wonderment. In any case, they should be judged, not by their success or failure, but by the answer to a basic moral question: Did they try? And try they did.

Notes

1
Deliverance Through Property Transfer

1 See Hans Mommsen, *Die Realisierung des Utopischen: Die "Endlösung der Judenfrage" im Dritten Reich*, in *Geschichte und Gesellschaft*, 1983, vol. 9, 3:381–420; Christopher R. Browning, *Fateful Months*, Holmes and Meier, New York, 1991, passim; Martin Broszat, *Hitler and the Genesis of the Final Solution*, Yad Vashem Studies, vol. 13., 1979, pp. 73–126; Richard Breitman, *The Architect of Genocide*, Knopf, New York, 1991, passim.

2 See Uriel Tal, *Germans and Jews in the Second Reich*, Cornell University Press, Ithaca, New York, 1975.

3 On the discussion as to what extent Nazism is a product of what is called modernism, cf. Zygmunt Bauman, *Modernity and the Holocaust*, Cornell University Press, Ithaca, New York, 1988; Jeffrey Herf, *Reactionary Modernism: Technology, Culture and Politics in Weimar and the Third Reich*, Cambridge University Press, New York, 1984; and others. There were undoubtedly modernistic elements in Nazism, but attempts to present it as though it had little if any deep connections with historically developed social and ideologic structures seem to me to be erroneous.

4 In fact, the Palestine Yishuv was to grow to 549,000 souls in 1945. Between 1933 and 1941, some 230,000 Jews came to Palestine, 55,000 of whom came from Germany (or 24 percent). Of these, again, 12,000 came "illegally," without British permits.

5 Yad Vashem Archive (YV), JM/2375, File 1.

6 Ibid.

7 Central Zionist Archive (CZA) S25/9706, Letter to Hoofien, July 27, 1933.

8 *Akten zur deutschen auswärtigen Politik, 1918–1945*, Serie E, Band 5, Göttingen, 1977, pp. 793–95.

9 Avraham Barkai, *Hakalkalah Hanatzit* (Hebrew), Sifriat Poalim, Tel Aviv, 1986, pp. 142 ff.; and Table 3.

10 Bundesarchiv, Koblenz (BA) R2, Folder 1, pp. 166 ff.

11 CZA/S7/9706.

12 CZA/S7/323(3), Folder 5.

13 CZA/S7/86, Folder 5.

14 CZA/S7/350, Folder 5.

15 BA/R2/4380, Folder 1; CZA/S7/85/Folder 2; Yoav Gelber, *Hamediniut Hatzionit Veheskem Haha'avarah*, in Yalkut Moreshet 18, 1974, pp. 35 ff.

16 CZA/S7/232(4), Folder 5 2. A similar argument appears in a report by a Gestapo contact, a Dr. Reichert, who visited Palestine (March 30, 1935), in Eliahu Ben-Elissar, *Kesher Hahashmadah*, Idanim, Jerusalem, 1978, pp. 84 ff.

17 Ernst Marcus, *The German Foreign Office and the Palestine Question in the Period 1933–1939*, in Yad Vashem Studies, vol. 2, Jerusalem, 1958, pp. 181 ff.

18 Christopher Browning, *Referat Deutschland: Jewish Policy and the German Foreign Office (1933–1940)*, in Yad Vashem Studies, vol. 12 (1977), pp. 43 ff.; Francis Nicosia, *The Third Reich and the Palestine Question*, University of Texas, Austin, 1985, p. 126; CZA/S7/85 (1), File 2, Ernst Marcus report, February 14, 1934.

19 Werner Feilchenfeld, Dolf Michaelis, and Ludwig Pinner, *Haha'avarah-Transfer nach Palästina*, Mohr, Tübingen, 1972, p. 69.

20 Gelber, op. cit., pp. 62 ff.

21 BA/R7/3532, Folder 1.

22 Gelber, op. cit., p. 68.

23 Feilchenfeld et al., op. cit., pp. 52 ff. The forbidden goods constituted what were known as the negative lists.

24 David Israeli, *Hareich Hagermani Ve'eretz Israel*, Ramat Gan, 1974, pp. 296 ff.; BA R2/43–46, F4380–1061 IA,1, Sitzungsvermerk, 12/17/35; CZA/S25/9810, Folder 2.

25 CZA/S35/9755, Folder 2; S25/9810.

26 Yehuda Bauer, *My Brother's Keeper*, Jewish Publication Society, Philadelphia, 1974, pp. 153 ff.

27 CZA/S7/350, Folder 2, Margolis report to JA, April 15, 1936. The amounts transferred for Zionist institutions were now radically reduced at German insistence.

28 YV/JM/2224 (4).

29 BA/Chef AO/86/Folder 3; Ben-Elissar, op. cit., p. 25.

30 BA/R18/5524, Folder 3.

31 Browning, op. cit., pp. 47 ff.; BA/R43/11/142/a, Bülow-Schwandte's memo of June 22, 1937.

32 YV/JM/2224 (3), Folder 3.

33 BA/R58/956, Folder 3; *Die jüdische Emigration aus Deutschland, 1933–1941: Die Geschichte einer Austreibung*, exhibition catalog, Judaica, Frankfurt am Main, 1985, p. 215.

34 YV/JM/2224 (4).

35 CZA/S7/464.

36 CZA/S7/464 (2), Folder 4.

37 CZA/S7/677 (1), Folder 4.

38 YV/JM/2224 (1); *Documents on German Foreign Policy* (*DGFP*), Series D (Washington, 1953), vol. 5, p. 754; cf. also Feilchenfeld et al., op. cit., pp. 31–33; BA 33/206, Untermöhle memo, December 27, 1937; BA 971/23, meeting at the RWM, January 22, 1938; BA 11/40, discussions at the AA, September 12 and 22, 1937.

39 CZA/S7/4695, signed by Werner Senator and Eliezer Kaplan; CZA/S7/677, Folder 4, Feilchenfeld's reports of May 12 and 17, 1938.

40 *DGFP*, Series D, vol. 4, no. 271, and ibid., vol. 5, nos. 640, 641.

41 International Military Tribunal, Nuremberg (IMT), German, vol. 23, PA-3358, pp. 237 f.

42 See my article *Who Was Responsible and When? Some Well-Known Documents Revisited*, in Holocaust and Genocide Studies, 1991, vol. 6, 2:129–50.

43 The sums are certainly impressive, and they undoubtedly helped in the upbuilding of a Jewish Palestine, but they most certainly do not justify the argument of Edwin Black in his sensationalist best-seller, *The Transfer Agreement*, Macmillan, New York, 1984, that Ha'avarah built the infrastructure for the State of Israel.

2
Failure of a Last-Minute Rescue Attempt

1 According to JDC files, 1,200 settlers and refugees were admitted to the Dominican Republic. JDC, Agro-Joint, DORSA, File 33, 1939–1943, Statistical Information, end 1942.

2 IMT, PS-1816.

3 A fictionalized version of the event is told by Hans Habe in his book *The Mission*, Coward-McCann, New York, 1966 (the original appeared in German in 1965). Habe interviewed Neumann at Evian and wrote up the story in the *Prager Tagblatt*, the (Jewish-owned) liberal Prague daily, also on July 12. The story in the book, Habe says, is based

on fact, though Neumann's personal life is fictionalized. The story has been researched by Edith Stern of Vienna, and I am grateful to her for the details. Neumann escaped from Vienna in 1939 and died in the United States in the same year. As far as I know, he did not leave behind any documentation. Dieter Wisliceny, who is discussed below, declared in his Bratislava prison on November 18, 1946, that Neumann had been sent abroad—he does not say by whom—to learn about the possibility of emigrating Jews and to acquire foreign currency. IFZ/Fa/164.

4 Michael Mashberg, *America and the Refugee Crisis*, M.A. Thesis, City University, New York, 1970; JDC, 9–27, esp. N. Katz to Baerwald, 8/9/38; David S. Wyman, *Paper Walls*, Amherst, Massachusetts, 1968, pp. 53–56; Raul Hilberg, *The Destruction of the European Jews*, Holmes and Meier, New York, 1985, p. 143; *DGFP*, Series D, vol. 5, pp. 753–67, 780; *Foreign Relations of the United States* (*FRUS*), Government Printing Office, Washington, D.C., 1938, vol. 1, pp. 871–74, and 1939, vol. 2, pp. 77–87.

5 PS-1816: To get rid of the Jews "only costs the currency that each Jew received . . . in order to get the Jews out, there would have to be an emigration action in the rest of the Reich [apart from Austria], lasting at least eight to ten years. We don't get out more than 10,000 Jews yearly."

6 *The Holocaust:* Documents, ed. John Mendelsohn, Garland Press, New York, 1982, vol. 6, pp. 17–18 (Weizsäcker note of 12/20/38) and 20 (Weizsäcker note of 1/4/39).

7 *New York Times*, 2/14/39.

8 JDC, R46, January 1939 reports.

9 An interesting and shady character by the name of Hugo Rothenberg (1882–1948) claims to have encouraged Wohlthat and others in their negotiations. Rothenberg came from Bad Kreuznach in Germany and was engaged first in shipping and then in the leather business, which brought him to Denmark, where he was during World War I. Goering, who was a pilot of an airline in which he was a partner, had an air accident in Denmark in 1919, and Rothenberg took care of him, restoring him to health. A grateful Goering promised never to forget. In 1938, Rothenberg saw Goering at a Hamlet performance in Copenhagen and asked him for help in taking his three sisters from Bad Kreuznach to Denmark. Goering was as good as his word and, in addition, gave Rothenberg a passport without the "J" (*Judes* or Jew) mark; he apparently saw Rothenberg a number of times in 1938–40. Rothenberg traveled the continent freely, until early 1942 or so, and was in touch with the JDC, apparently transferring some money for it to Nazi-occupied Europe. Gerhard Riegner, the World Jewish Congress representative in Geneva, remembers that Rothenberg visited him in early 1942 and brought him some information about Jews in Nazi Europe. Rothenberg apparently also managed to get out of Germany the family of a central member of the German Jewish leadership (Paul Meyerheim). By 1943 Rothenberg had fled to Sweden, where he introduced Goering's stepson to an American intelligence operative. But the British Intelligence Service saw in him a German agent, and indeed it is highly probable that Rothenberg was, in Nazi eyes, a temporarily useful tool to gather information about Jewish affairs and organizations. For our purposes he seems irrelevant, appearances to the contrary notwithstanding (Bernd Bluednikow, *Som om de ster ikke eksisterede*, Samleren, Kjoebenhavn, 1991, passim). Another, similar case was that of David Glick, an American Jewish lawyer, who was sent by the JDC to Germany in 1936 and who entered into contacts with the SS to facilitate Jewish emigration; he was seen by Heinrich Himmler, Reinhard Heydrich, and Werner Best—to the horror of Rabbi Leo Baeck and Otto Hirsch, heads of the RV. His activities were supported by the U.S. diplomatic mission in Germany. In 1937 he traveled throughout Germany and visited local Jewish leaders. He helped some people to reach Latin American countries. He also, it seems, got some inmates out of Dachau. Again, negotiations are not the issue but, rather, an individual who tried to get people out and was apparently used by the SS to push for more Jewish emigration. David Glick, "Some Were Rescued," *Harvard Law School Bulletin*, December 1960, pp. 6–9. Other, similar efforts were made; for

example, Daniel Wolff, a wealthy man who helped Jews to emigrate financially, went to London in November 1938, to talk with Rublee. Such people of commendable intentions will justly be remembered by those whom they helped, but they did not influence the larger picture.

10 Norman H. Baynes, *Speeches of Adolf Hitler, April, 1922–August, 1939,* Oxford University Press, London, 1942, vol. 1, pp. 737–41.

11 Bauer, op. cit., p. 260.

12 Baynes, op. cit., vol. 1, pp. 737–41.

13 IMT, NG-2586-A.

14 *Akten zur deutschen auswärtigen Politik, 1918–1945,* series D (1937–45), vol. 5, Baden-Baden, 1953, pp. 780–85.

15 JDC Archive, 9–27; and JDC Executive Committee meeting, 6/16/39. The participants were Lewis L. Strauss, Henry Ittleson, Albert D. Lasker, Harold Linder, Robert Szold, Stephen S. Wise, and Joseph C. Hyman.

16 Bauer, op. cit., p. 277.

17 Bauer, op. cit., p. 281.

18 JDC, Administrative Committee, 6/26/39.

19 JDC, 6/7/39 memo by J. C. Hyman.

20 Lord Winterton read out the communiqué at a meeting of the IGCR, 7/19/39.

21 "Since the beginning of the French Revolution the world has been drifting with increasing speed towards a new conflict, whose most extreme solution is Bolshevism, but whose content and aim is only the removal of those strata of society which gave the leadership to humanity up to the present, and their replacement by International Jewry." Hitler's memo on the Four-Year Plan, August 1936, *Akten,* series E, vol. 5, pp. 793–95.

3
Enemies with a Common Interest

1 This account, and much of the following, is based on Dalia Ofer, *Escaping the Holocaust,* New York, 1990. Ben-Gurion, 11/11/38, is quoted in ibid., p. 18.

2 Ehud Avriel, *Open the Gates,* New York, 1975, pp. 39–59; K. J. Ball-Kaduri, *Ha'aliyah habilti-hukit miGermania Hanatzit,* in Yalkut Moreshet, no. 8, 1968, p. 131.

3 Ofer, op. cit., p. 14; Bauer, op. cit., p. 61.

4 Herbert Rosenkranz, *Verfolgung und Selbstbehauptung. Die Juden Österreichs, 1938–1945,* Herold, Munich, 1978, pp. 37, 48, 87, 110. Lange later participated in the Wannsee conference as a commander of murder squads in the Baltic region.

5 William R. Perl, *The Four-Front War,* Crown, New York, 1978, pp. 41–43; Ball-Kaduri, p. 132.

6 Ofer, p. 73; Avriel, pp. 70–72; Ball-Kaduri, p. 132.

7 Ofer, pp. 77–78.

8 Heinz Hoehne, *The Order of the Death's Head,* Secker and Warburg, London, 1969, p. 347.

9 The riparian states were Yugoslavia, Bulgaria, and Romania. The British Foreign Office files contain large amounts of correspondence showing the British pressure on these countries and on Italy and Greece.

10 By this time Eichmann was the *Referent,* or responsible official, for Jewish matters in the Geheime Staatspolizei (Gestapo), or Political Police, which itself was part of the Sicherheitspolizei (SIPO), or Security Police, now united with the Sicherheitsdienst (SD) under the command of Reinhard Heydrich. The head of the Gestapo and Eichmann's superior, under Heydrich, was Heinrich Müller. The SIPO and the SD together were a *Hauptamt,* or chief office—part of the SS structure.

11 Francis Nicosia, *The Third Reich and the Palestine Question,* University of Texas Press, Austin, 1985, p. 160. The speech is dated 2/11/39.

12 Steven Bowman, at the University of Cincinnati, has alerted me to the fact that negotiations took place in the summer of 1939 between representatives of the Greek Foreign and Economic Ministries, and the SD—Herbert Hagen and Theodor Dannecker—regarding support of the Greek dictatorship (under Metaxas) for "illegal" Jewish immigration to Palestine in return for promises of German military technological help to Greece. Apparently, an interim agreement was reached by July 6, 1939, but the outbreak of war prevented any further developments. Bowman cites correspondence in the Centre Juif de Documentation Contemporaine, CCXXXIV-8, to that effect.

13 Ofer, op. cit., p. 101; Ball-Kaduri, op. cit., p. 131.

14 Ofer, op. cit., pp. 101–2; Nicosia, op. cit., p. 161; Ruth Zariz, *The Rescue of German Jews Through Emigration* (in Hebrew), Ph.D. thesis, Hebrew University, Jerusalem, 1986, pp. 255–58.

15 See Ofer, pp. 105–27, for the whole Storfer episode. Storfer is also mentioned in many other sources, and I have reached some general conclusions from as many as possible.

16 Avriel, op. cit., p. 73.

17 Ofer, op. cit., pp. 107 ff.

18 Perl, op. cit., pp. 271–340.

19 See the 1994 book by Dalia Ofer and Hannah Weiner, *Parashat Kladovo Sabac* (in Hebrew), on the Kladovo episode, published by the Aliyah Beth Project at Tel Aviv University.

20 Ofer, op. cit., pp. 53 ff.

21 Perl, op. cit., p. 293.

22 NG-2586-G, Wannsee Protocol, 1/20/42.

4
The Road to the "Final Solution"

1 See Christopher R. Browning, *Fateful Months,* Holmes and Meier, New York, 1985; Richard Breitman, *The Architect of Genocide,* Knopf, New York, 1991; Eberhard Jaeckel, *Hitler's Weltanschauung: A Blueprint for Power,* Wesleyan University Press, Middletown, Connecticut, 1972; Yisrael Gutman, ed., *Encyclopedia of the Holocaust,* Macmillan, New York, 1990, s.v. "Final Solution"; Helmut Krausnick and Hans-Heinrich Wilhelm, *Truppe des Weltanschauungskrieges,* DVA, Stuttgart, 1981; Leni Yahil, *The Holocaust,* Oxford University Press, New York, 1990.

2 Eichmann Trial Documents, 06-983.

3 IMT/PS-3363.

4 On September 29, Alfred Rosenberg wrote in his diary Hitler's remark that day that "all of Jewry (also from the Reich) as well as other unreliable elements will be settled between the Vistula and the Bug." See Hans-Günther Seraphim, ed., *Das Politische Tagebuch Alfred Rosenbergs,* Göttingen, 1956, p. 81, quoted in Browning, op. cit., p. 502. The two Hitler statements do not contradict each other: the Jews would be concentrated in the Lublin region and then expelled to the Soviet Union.

5 Seev Goshen, Eichmann und die Nisko-Aktion im Oktober, 1939, Vierteljahreshefte für Zeitgeschichte (*VJHFZG*), 1981, 1:74–96; Christopher R. Browning, *Nazi Resettlement Policy and the Search for a Solution to the Jewish Question, 1939–1941,* in German Studies Review, Fall 1986, vol. 9, 3:497–519.

6 See my *Who Was Responsible and When? Some Well-Known Documents Revisited,* in Holocaust and Genocide Studies, 1991, vol. 6, 2:129–50; the reference here is to Himmler's memo of May 25, 1940, IMT/NO-1880.

7 See Leni Yahil, *Madagascar: Phantom of a Solution to the Jewish Question,* in Bela Vago and George L. Mosse, eds., *Jews and Non-Jews in Eastern Europe, 1918–1945,* John Wiley and Sons, New York, 1974, pp. 314–34; Christopher R. Browning, *The Final*

Solution and the German Foreign Office, Holmes and Meier, New York, 1978, pp. 35–43.

8 See n. 1.

9 Andreas Hillgruber, *Die Endlösung und das deutsche Ostimperium als Kernstück des rassenideologischen Programms des Nationalsozialismus, VJHFZG*, 1972, 2:133–53.

10 Breitman, op. cit., pp. 150–52, 247.

11 Bauer, *Who Was Responsible and When?*

5
"Willy"

1 Michael Dov Ber Weissmandel, *Min Hametzar*, New York, Emunah Press, 1960. Weissmandel died in 1957, and the book was apparently edited and in part supplemented and altered by his relatives and students for ideological reasons.

2 There were 136,737 Jews in prewar Slovakia, but in 1938 the Czechoslovak Republic had to give up large parts of southern Slovakia to Hungary, and close to 40,000 Jews lived there. A few thousand more managed to emigrate or move to Hungary before the end of 1940. See Gila Fatran, *Ha'im Ma'avak al Hissardut?* Moreshet, Tel Aviv, 1992, p. 15. Fatran's Ph.D. thesis and the resulting book are an important source for the Slovak sections of this work. I am grateful to Gila Fatran for permission to draw freely on her book.

3 Some of the main Zionist figures in the Working Group (the clandestine Jewish leadership group discussed below), such as Gizi Fleischmann and Oskar Neumann, did not speak Slovak or spoke it poorly.

4 Fatran, op. cit., pp. 18–28. ŽÚÚ was founded in November 1938 and ceased operating in September 1940, but from early 1940 on, it was no longer an effective organization.

5 The SS, as mentioned already, was divided into a number of Hauptämter (chief offices). Since September 1939, one of these had been the Reichssicherheitshauptamt, or RSHA (Central Reich Security Office), headed by Reinhard Heydrich, which combined most of the police functions under that one roof. Department IV of the RSHA was the Gestapo, headed by Heinrich Müller. Adolf Eichmann was the department expert on Jews and administrative head (*Referent*) for the Jewish section.

6 Institut für Zeitgeschichte, Munich (IFZ), MA 1300/4, T175—Roll 1288, frames 0385–87.

7 Morávek's letter to Tuka is in Tragedia slovenských Židov, exhibition catalog, Bratislava, 1949, p. 11.

8 YV, M-5/137, Onl'ud 17/46, Vašek indictment, p. 13. See also Mach's contribution to the debate at the third meeting of the Political Assembly, 3/26/42, YV-M-5/49, p. 5; trial of Koso, Onl'ud 60/46/11, YV/M-5/148, p. 10.

9 Ladislav Lipscher, *Die Juden im Slowakischen Staat*, Oldenbourg, Munich, 1980, p. 99.

10 Lipscher, op. cit., p. 100.

11 YV, Eichmann trial, 06–899, Wisliceny's testimony. Essentially the same material is repeated in his testimony at the trial of Anton Vašek, YV/Onl'ud 17/46, pp. 131 ff.

12 Wisliceny statement to Michael Geroe, Bratislava, 5/6/46, Eichmann Trial, T899; and IFZ, Wisliceny testimonies. "Eichmann hat damals den Antrag auf Übernahme Familienangehöriger zurückgewiesen, da er angeblich für sie keine Möglichkeit der Einquartierung, bzw. Unterbringung hatte. Das habe ich dann Koso mitgeteilt" (testimonies, p. 2).

13 Lipscher, op. cit., pp. 100–105; Koso trial, Onl'ud 60/46/11, YV/M-5/148, p. 10.

14 Eichmann first demanded RM 300, in his talk with Ziman (see below). Later, he increased the price, because he said he needed to pay for the settlement of the Jews in Poland.

15 Eichmann trial, 06–835. The RM 500 per deported Jew worked out at RM 45 million for the 90,000 Slovak Jews, which was about 80 percent of all the taxes the Slovaks squeezed from them annually. From a cynically economic point of view, the Slovaks did not gain anything.

16 Ibid.

17 IMT, NG-2586-J; YV-M-5/18 a (12). See also Livia Rothkirchen, *Churban Yahadut Slovakia*, Yad Vashem, Jerusalem, 1961, pp. 70–71. On April 29, Vašek expressed the hope that *all* the Jews would be deported by August ("dass bis Ende August die Aktion der restlosen Judenaussiedlung aus der Slowakei beendet sein dürfte"). YV/M-S/33, *Amtsvermerk* of a meeting of Vašek with two Nazi representatives.

18 YV/Onl'ud 17/46, p. 228, testimony of Ladislav Unger, with Wisliceny's admission. In other testimonies, at Nuremberg (11/29/46, Eichmann Trial, 06–584, p. 6) and in Onl'ud 17/46, p. 134, Wisliceny says that he had visited the concentration camp of Sosnowice in the autumn of 1941 together with a Slovak mission that included Koso. Koso had returned from that visit convinced that the Jews could hardly survive under such conditions. But Koso did not necessarily, therefore, "know" that all the Jews were being killed in Poland.

19 BA/NS 19, Berlin Gestapo III B 1 g of 4/10/42, by Viktor Nageler.

20 IFZ, Roll 514, frames 0794–96, MA 558.3/25/42, report to the SD in Vienna, III B. The signature is illegible.

21 YV-M-5/46(3), and M-5/136, p. 188; Lipscher, op. cit., p. 123. The response of the Interior Ministry was to interrogate some of those who signed the petitions to find out how they knew of the impending deportations. Burzio sent a message to the Vatican on March 9 telling of the Slovak decision to deport all the Jews. John F. Morley, *Vatican Diplomacy and the Jews During the Holocaust, 1939–1943*, Ktav, New York, 1980, pp. 71–101.

22 Karol Sidor was bribed with 30,000 Slovak crowns to take the two memoranda to the Vatican. Weissmandel, op. cit., pp. 19–27.

23 IFZ, MA 558, T175-Roll 514, frames 0794–96. Report to Vienna SD-Leitabschnitt, III B, 3/25/42, p. 1. On the Vatican policy toward the Jews in Slovakia, see Morley, op. cit.

24 Morley, op. cit., p. 85.

25 YV/Eichmann Trial document 06–29, p. 4; Wisliceny testimony at Nuremberg, 1/3/46 (IMG, Vol. IV, German, pp. 393–413).

26 Wisliceny testimony at Nuremberg, 1/3/46; and 06–899, Wisliceny testimony of 5/6/46, pp. 6–7. Especially important is the summary of a meeting between (apparently) Eichmann ("emissary of Heinrich Himmler [*s poverencom Heinricha Himmlera*]") and Tuka on April 10, YV/M-5–49/7, containing the Nazis' promise to treat the Jews "as humanely as possible [*tak humanne ako len je možne*])."

27 A German intelligence report relates an incident of April 26, 1942, when a crowd of Slovaks came to the concentration camp at Žilina and "began to curse the fact that the Jews were being concentrated [there] and deported. It almost came to a real demonstration. The [Hlinka] Guards, who were to have guarded the Jews, did not know what to do with the mob and asked the military to intervene. However, the military command refused to intervene. In the end, the military called in the Žilina State Police, who reestablished order." IFZ, MA 650/1, T175–517, German intelligence report, April 1942.

28 Hochberg was born in 1911 in Raab, Hungary, and educated in Vienna and Prague.

29 John S. Conway, *Frühe Augenzeugenberichte aus Auschwitz — Glaubwürdigkeit und Wirkungsgeschichte*, *VJHFZG*, 1979, 2:260–84; Conway, *Der Holocaust in Ungarn — Neue Kontroversen und Überlegungen*, *VJHFZG*, 1984, 2:179–212; and Rudolf Vrba and Alan Bestic, *I Cannot Forget*, Grove Press, New York, 1964. I am grateful to Gila Fatran for her research on a reply to Conway's articles, which is used in what follows here.

30 Conway erroneously assumes that the ÚŽ was set up just then for the purpose of deporting Jews. It had been set up in September 1940.

31 Dionys (Daniel) Lenard had a sister, Rachel Anshel, now (1992) living in Kfar Shmariyahu in Israel but who was then in Sweden, to whom he wrote on August 11, 1944 (the letter is in the possession of Gila Fatran). In it he relates his deportation in March and his sojourn there in the Lublin area until his flight in June, or even July. Parts of his later, lengthy testimony, which repeats in detail what happened to him, is quoted in Livia Rothkirchen, *Churban Yahadut Slovakia*, document 76. In a recent public lecture in Israel, Rothkirchen even claimed that the Lenard testimony did not reach ÚŽ hands until the end of 1942.

32 YV/Onl'ud 17/46, p. 192.

33 Yehuda Bauer, *American Jewry and the Holocaust*, Wayne State University Press, Detroit, 1981, p. 188.

34 YV/Onl'ud 17/46, p. 125.

35 Interview with Ervin Steiner, April 1965, by Erich Kulka, in E. Kulka's private collection, Jerusalem (available through the Institute of Contemporary Jewry, Hebrew University).

36 In fact, Slovak Jews showed considerable initiative in obtaining information from Poland. Local communities and even individuals organized the receipt of information, whether through non-Jews or through contacts with escapees from Poland. See the testimony of Kalman Rubin, YV-Bet Volhyn, 3415/220. The Conway-Vrba argument rests, inter alia, on the assumption that unless the ÚŽ told people generally, they would not know. This, demonstrably, was not the case.

Vrba implies that the ÚŽ was universally hated. If so, why does he believe that any information that the ÚŽ disseminated would have been believed? The truth of the matter is that a group of activists within the ÚŽ disseminated whatever information the organization had, and they were not the only source.

37 Bauer, *American Jewry and the Holocaust*, p. 363.

38 Oskar Neumann, *Im Schatten des Todes*, Olamenu, Tel Aviv, 1956, p. 95. See also Yaakov Ronen's (Benito) letter to G. Fatran, 2/20/85 (in her private possession), in which he tells the story of his own trip to Prešov in northern Slovakia. He stopped in all the communities on his way and informed the leaders, who reacted with despair, and thought that they had no chance to flee. When he reached Prešov, he could not even persuade his own sister and his former schoolmates to run. They thought that they could survive forced labor in Poland—no one was yet talking about mass murder.

39 Vašek trial, YV/Onl'ud 17/46, Vašek testimony, pp. 7, 14–15, 25, 26, and Kováč testimony, p. 66.

40 Conway, *Holocaust in Ungarn*, p. 194.

41 Fleischmann was a first cousin of Rabbi Ungar's (her father was the brother of Ungar's mother), and Weissmandel had married Ungar's daughter.

42 Weissmandel, op. cit., pp. 48 ff. The other accounts put the deliberations first, the approach to Hochberg later. Aron Grünhut, an Orthodox businessman, reports that the deportations were stopped by a telephone conversation between Wisliceny and Eichmann, after which Wisliceny is reported to have said "Sie haben ein Sauglück, Eichmann ist einverstanden." See Aron Grünhut, *Katastrophenzeit des slowakischen Judentums*, Selbstverlag, Tel Aviv, 1972, p. 80. From what we know of the contacts between Wisliceny and Eichmann, it would make sense to place this phone conversation in December, when Wisliceny reports that Eichmann expressed a "desinteressement" in deportations at that time (see below). However, Grünhut is not a reliable witness; he was a member of Hochberg's group of traitors.

43 See my books *My Brother's Keeper*, JPS, Philadelphia, 1974; and *American Jewry and the Holocaust*, Wayne State University Press, Detroit, 1981.

44 The JDC, in its apologetic publications after the war, referred to $64 million that had been "appropriated" to relieve Jewish suffering between 1939 and 1945. The figure has misled many commentators; it refers to the overall sum collected throughout the war years, but different sums were collected in different years. In 1942 and 1943 the amounts of $6.3 million and $8.4 million, respectively, were "appropriated" for all purposes worldwide. The JDC was unable to raise more, though it tried. But none of this money could have been transmitted to Mayer between April 1942 and September 1943; and the appropriations sitting for him in New York ($610,000 in 1942 and $940,000 in 1943) did not help him.

45 Mayer was both observant and non-Zionist, although he maintained a friendship with the young Zionist Schwalb.

46 Steiner testimony to Avraham Fuchs (in A. Fuchs's possession), 4/27/86, Answers to Questions, p. 1.

47 Steiner originally did not remember any sum being paid in the summer, but in a later testimony (to A. Fuchs, 4/27/86) he remembers a payment of $50,000. Neumann and Frieder talk of $40,000, Kováč of $50,000.

48 JDC Archive, SM-64.

49 Riegner's cable (August 8, 1942), based on information that he received indirectly from Eduard Schulte, a German industrialist, speaks of a German plan to murder three–four million Jews in the East (Poland and occupied Russia) through the use of Prussic acid (Zyklon B, the gas used at Auschwitz, was the commercial name of this gas). In other words, Riegner is talking, in August 1942, of a *future* plan, when the "Final Solution" had already been in full operation for thirteen months and a majority of the Jews who died in the Holocaust were already dead. At the behest of Paul Guggenheim of Geneva, Riegner put a disclaimer into his cable, saying that he was not certain of the information he was transmitting, although his source had usually been reliable. With such a disclaimer, the cable was hardly proof of what in fact was going on. See Walter Laqueur and Richard Breitman, *Breaking the Silence,* Simon and Schuster, New York, 1986. Saly Mayer became fully aware of the mass murder from a Jewish official at the Polish consulate in Switzerland by the name of Kühn, a member of Agudat Israel, who informed Mayer of the mass killings on August 15.

50 Andrej Steiner, letter to JDC, 12/29/47, JDC-Givat Joint Archives, Geneva Records, Box 14B/C-36.038, p. 7: "Ein Grossteil unserer Arbeitsgruppe hielt ihn für undurchführbar und zu unreell, als dass sie viel Energie hätten zu seiner Verwirklichung verwenden wollen."

51 See Abraham Fuchs, *Karati Ve'ein Oneh* (2nd ed.), Pear, Jerusalem, 1984, p. 232 (English translation: *The Unheeded Cry,* Mesorah, Brooklyn, 1986), quoting a letter of Weissmandel's dated November 5, 1942, from Lohamei Getaot Archive, Z/3036/SL/108.

52 Protocol of the interrogation of Hochberg by the Slovak Police, 12/12/42, from the Archive of the Federal Ministry of the Interior of Czechoslovakia. The document was given to me by Gila Fatran.

53 JDC-Givat Joint Archives, Geneva Records, Box 14B/C-36.038, p. 6a.

54 Tuvia Friling, *Ben Gurion and the Holocaust,* Hebrew University, Ph.D. thesis, 1990, p. 114.

55 Fleischmann's letter is in SM-64, JDC Archive; Weissmandel's is reproduced in Weissmandel, op. cit., pp. 67–69.

56 Bauer, *American Jewry and the Holocaust,* p. 371.

57 JDC, SM-64.

58 JDC, SM-8.

59 Dobkin, the JA Executive member who interviewed the arrivals, told his colleagues that when he expressed disbelief in what he was hearing from a woman witness, she slapped his face hard. That apparently helped him overcome his doubts. Yigal Lossin, *Pillar of Fire,* Zionist Organisation, Educational Centre, Jerusalem, 1984.

60 See Moshe Shoenfeld, *The Holocaust Victims Accuse,* Neturei Karta, Brooklyn, 1977; Shlomo Giora, *Ot Kayin,* Shocken, Jerusalem, 1983; and Tom Segev, *The Seventh Million,* Hill and Wang, New York, 1993—the last for a very cleverly written "liberal" historical revisionist thesis. The general tendency has been criticized expertly in Dina Porat, *The Blue and Yellow Star of David*, Harvard University Press, Cambridge, 1990; and in Friling, op. cit., passim.

61 Shlomo Aronson, *Hitler's Judenpolitik, die Alliierten und die Juden, VJHFZG*, 1984, 1:29–65.

62 IFZ, Himmler's speeches, p. 41.

63 This is one of many places where the top Nazi leadership identified the war against the Soviet Union as the war against the Jews. In Himmler's terminology, clearly, "Judentum" and "Asiatentum" are expressions of the same racial denotation. As Andreas Hillgruber has shown in his *VJHFZG* article of 1972, the top Nazi leadership saw the Soviet Union as a Jewish-dominated state with a Jewish ideology. Hillgruber, op. cit. Arno J. Mayer's neo-Marxist argument in his *Why Did the Heavens Not Darken?* (Pantheon, New York, 1990)—that the primary motivation of the Nazis was anti-Marxist and that the "Judaeocide," as he calls the Holocaust, stemmed from that motivation— is a total misconception. It is shared by Ernst Nolte in his contributions to the German *Historikerstreit* literature. Mayer ignored primary sources in writing his footnote-less book.

64 Jan Karski, *The Secret State*, Houghton and Mifflin, Boston, 1944, passim.

65 Friling, op. cit., p. 115.

66 Friling, op. cit., p. 116.

67 Moreshet Archive, 1.712, Bader's draft of his memo to Roncalli of 1/20/42, and his letters of March 10 and April 25, 1943.

68 Friling, op. cit., p. 119.

69 John F. Morley, op. cit., pp. 243–47; Weissmandel, op. cit., pp. 23–26.

70 Fleischmann wrote on March 5, 1943, that Willy had visited Bratislava and had promised that the Jews of Saloniki would not be deported. The "problem" would be solved by labor camps in Greece. Wisliceny was in touch with Rabbi Koretz (the head of the Judenrat of Saloniki) and was very satisfied with these contacts. Moreshet Archive, 1.18.10.

71 Fleischmann to Mayer, 5/9/43, Moreshet Archive D.1.467.2

72 Fleischmann to Mayer, letter of 5/11/43, Moreshet Archive D.1.467.2.

73 SM-64, Fleischmann letters of May 11 and June 1; Moreshet Archive, Fleischmann letter of May 7, D.1.1263; Weissmandel, op. cit., p. 162. Steiner says the sum was to have been $150,000 (December 29, 1947, JDC-Givat Joint Archives, Geneva Records, Box 14B/C-36.038).

74 SM-8.

75 Fleischmann letter to Mayer, 6/18/43, Moreshet Archive, D.1.1810.

76 Mayer letter of 7/13/43 to Istanbul, Moreshet Archive, D.1.1263; and Fleischmann letter of 7/17/43 to Mayer, CZA S26/1190.

77 CZA/S26/1190; and JDC-SM; Friling, op. cit., p. 122. The total sent from Palestine to Slovakia in 1943–44 came to £100,000, or about $400,000.

78 The amounts of $25,000, $31,000, and $75,000 were sent from Istanbul in March, April, and June, for a total of $131,000; their receipt was acknowledged from Bratislava on September 9. JDC/SM-65; Akiva Nir, *Va'adat Hahatzalah beKushta—Hakesher Im Slovakia (Ha'avarat Ksafim leSlovakia—1943–1944)*, Seminar Paper, Institute of Contemporary Jewry, 1989. Mayer sent two sums in August (on the 5th and 13th)— SFR 70,000 and SFR 90,000, respectively—and SFR 70,000 on September 22, for a total of SFR 230,000, or $53,600.

79 Eichmann Trial, T/281, depositions of Steiner, Neumann, and Kováč, 2/12/46, in Bratislava, with a handwritten confirmation of the contents by Wisliceny.

80 Eichmann was indeed responsible "only" for deportations *to* Poland, not for the death camps there. But he initiated the murders with the gassings in Auschwitz, according to Rudolf Hoess, the Auschwitz commander, in his postwar testimonies.

81 See Fleischmann's letter to Istanbul, 5/7/43, above, in n. 73 (Moreshet Archive).

82 Fatran, op. cit., pp. 192–96 and elsewhere. But she understands the Jews who were misled by the clever Nazi in the tragic circumstances of 1942–44.

83 SM-65, July 28, 1943.

6
What Really Did Happen in Slovakia?

1 See Akiva Nir, *Va'adat Hahatzalah beKushta — Hakesher im Slovakia,* M.A. diss., Institute of Contemporary Jewry, 1989; Nir bases himself partly on Fatran, op. cit., passim.

2 In Onl'ud 17/46, July 1946, he says that it was after eight days.

3 In other testimony, at Nuremberg, 11/29/45, 06–584, p. 6 (para. 13), and in Onl'ud 17/46, p. 134, he relates the story of his visit to Sosnowice ghetto and the nearby slave labor camp at Gross-Strelitz.

4 06–899, p. 9, repeated in most of Wisliceny's other testimonies.

5 06–1423, p. 22.

6 Onl'ud 17/46, p. 223; Lipscher, op. cit., p. 135.

7 Onl'ud 17/46, p. 146; IFZ, Fa 164; Eichmann Trial, 06–856, pp. 10 ff.; Centre de Documentation Juif Contemporaine, Paris, 88–67, p. 15. The September date is also confirmed by Andrej Steiner in his testimony of 12/29/47, JDC-Givat Joint Archives, Geneva Records, Box 14B/C-36.038. In another statement (n.d., probably 1946, *Der sogenannte Europa-Plan,* also in JDC-Givat Joint Archives) Steiner says that "Hochberg really went to Wysliceni, on our behalf, in September 1942 in order to tell him about the fate of the Jews in Poland."

8 Onl'ud 17/46, p. 146: "v oktobri mi Hochberg odovzdal 20.000 dollarov [in October Hochberg gave me $20,000]."

9 Ibid., p. 16.

10 Eichmann Trial, 06–856; YV/Nuremberg pretrial interrogations, 11/15/45 interrogation of Wisliceny by Col. Smith W. Brookhart, p. 13.

11 Wisliceny's version is confirmed by Steiner: Givat Joint Archives, Geneva Records, Box 14B/C-36.038, p. 6a.

12 Steiner testimonies, JDC-Givat Joint Archives.

13 Ibid.

14 Wisliceny also claims that in Berlin he managed to convince his superiors to establish an exchange camp for Jews who were to be released for ransom and that Bergen-Belsen was later established as a result of this initiative. Wisliceny then managed to send his group of privileged Greek Jews there—the rest he shipped off to be murdered in Poland. Wisliceny even claims that the special status of Theresienstadt as a privileged ghetto was due to his intervention. Neither claim is very convincing.

15 YV/M-20/93.

16 Fleischmann letter of 7/13/43, Moreshet Archive, D.1.1263.

17 NG-4407; NG-4553.

18 Lipscher, op. cit., p. 130.

19 Onl'ud 60/46/11, testimony of Izidor Koso, 8/18/46. In October 1943, Zofia Koso was promised SFR 50,000 to place her son in a school in Switzerland, and she went there to arrange it. The slip of paper that Gizi Fleischmann gave her to present in Switzerland so that she could get the money was found on her by German guards at the border, and she was arrested, then freed through her husband's intervention. Gizi Fleischmann was arrested and spent months in jail after that incident.

20 SM-64, letter to Alfred Silberschein in Geneva.

21 Steiner interview with Avraham Fuchs, 4/27/86 (MS in Fuchs's possession), p. 4. Tibor Kováč mentions that Wisliceny received $50,000 in a number of payments ("*v splatkách*"), Onl'ud, 60/46/11.

22 Steiner says as much; see his interview with Fuchs, 4/27/86, pp. 12–13 ("he [Wisliceny] was only a secondary guy in stopping the deportations. The main people with whom we negotiated and convinced were the Slovaks").

23 IFZ, Fa 164, Wisliceny testimony of 11/18/45, p. 16: "Im November kam dann Himmler's Bescheid dass ich die $20.000 an das WVHA der SS abliefern sollte und dass ich die jüdischen Vertreter anhören sollte."

24 Eichmann Trial, 06–281.

25 JDC Archive in Jerusalem, G.J.7/Geneva/Box 144B/C-36.038, Steiner deposition on the *Kinderaktion*, n.d. [1946].

26 Wisliceny, in a way, is an enigma. There can hardly be any doubt that he was a convinced Nazi, though his 1937 memorandum points to his ability to see the Jewish "problem" as being solved by emigration to a Jewish homeland. Apart from the songs of praise that Steiner, Weissmandel, and Fleischmann all sang for him, we have only one piece of concrete evidence about his real views at the time: a memo from the German embassy in Slovakia dated July 27, 1944, in which Wisliceny is quoted as saying that the application of one Dr. Anna Machálek, who claimed she was an Aryan, should be judicially checked, because it was clear to him that the "Jewess Machálek" simply wanted to avoid danger; and he implied strongly that this should be prevented (NA/T120/4662).

7
Himmler's Indecision, 1942–1943

1 *The Memoirs of Doctor Felix Kersten*, ed. Herma Biffault, Doubleday, Garden City, New York, 1947; *Totenkopf und Treue*, Hamburg, 1952; *The Kersten Memoirs*, with an introduction by Hugh R. Trevor-Roper, Macmillan, New York, 1957 (London, 1956).

2 His chief defender, Dutch Professor N. W. Posthumus of Leyden, suggested him for a Nobel Peace Prize in November 1952, but the nomination was refused. A Dutch governmental investigation committee presented the Dutch parliament with a very sympathetic report on Kersten (1/12/50), IFZ F44/7. Louis de Jong, the great Dutch historian, in a devastating critique (*Hat Felix Kersten das Niederländische Volk gerettet?*, in *Zwei Legenden aus dem Dritten Reich*, by Hans-Heinrich Wilhelm and Luis de Jong, Schriftenreihe der Vierteljahreshefte für Zeitgeschichte, no. 28, Stuttgart, 1974, pp. 77–142), shows that Kersten's story that he had saved the Dutch people from forcible deportation to the East in the spring of 1941 was his own invention. Ibid., p. 138.

3 See Ulrich von Hassel, *The Ulrich von Hassel Diaries*, Doubleday, Garden City, New York, 1947, pp. 233–47.

4 BA/Bestand Alg. Schumacher 240 I. "Ich habe den Führer wegen der Loslösung von Juden gegen Devisen gefragt. Er hat mir Vollmacht gegeben, derartige Fälle zu genehmigen, wenn sie wirklich im namhaften Umfang Devisen von auswärts hereinbringen." Prior to this, Himmler's view on ransom had been negative.

5 Ruth Zariz, op. cit., passim.

6 Eichmann Trial, 06–1164: "Ich ordne an, dass von den jetzt in Frankreich noch vorhandenen Juden, ebenso von den ungarischen und rumänischen Juden alle diejenigen, die einflussreiche Verwandte in Amerika haben, in einem Sonderlager zusammenzufassen sind. Dort sollen sie zwar arbeiten, jedoch unter Bedingungen, dass sie gesund sind und am Leben bleiben. Diese Art von Juden sind für uns wertvolle Geiseln. Ich stelle mir hierunter eine Zahl von rund 10.000 vor."

7 NA/T 120/2720, E421784–7, E420788–9, 8/9/43, 8/12/43.

8 NA/Donovan Papers, Roll 28/2/5/44, for Hewitt's OSS status. Kersten did his best to free seven Swedish businessmen, directors of a Swedish match company, who had been caught in Warsaw and sentenced to death for spying. After difficult negotiations and despite Hitler's own intervention at one point to kill them, Kersten managed to pry them loose; the last three were brought back to Sweden in December 1944. The seven were saved to a large degree by Kersten's efforts (cf. Kersten, *Totenkopf und Treue*, p. 407)—there is no disagreement about that. He may well have been motivated by a wish to become persona grata in Sweden, in case things became unpleasant for him in Germany, but a humanitarian motive certainly cannot be ruled out.

9 IFZ-F44/3, Hewitt statement of May 1953; see also Schellenberg, "Final Report," 9/30/46, p. 59. Schellenberg's statement that he was not sent by Himmler is in NA/RG 226/Entry 123, INF-27, 8/6/45, as is Hewitt's letter to Himmler, 10/24/43; see also NA/Donovan Files, Roll 28, Donovan to the President, 3/20/44.

10 IFZ, F44/4, Kersten's Notizen, 12/4/43. "Denn der Führer hat es im Jahr 1941 in Breslau angeordnet, dass die Juden vernichtet werden sollen." In *Totenkopf und Treue* Kersten puts Himmler's statement under the date of November 11, 1943 (p. 149). He also says that as a result of the Allied landings in North Africa (November 8, 1942) Hitler ordered a more radical policy against the Jews on November 10 (p. 200). In earlier entries in what purportedly is Kersten's diary the murder of the Jews is explicitly mentioned. Under December 12, 1940 (as early as that? the date seems doubtful), he writes that Himmler said that "we must eradicate [*ausradieren*] the Jews; that is the wish of the Führer." On April 18, 1941, Himmler is supposed to have said that "by the end of the war the Jews have to be eliminated [*ausgerottet*]. That is the clear desire of the Führer." On the day that Germany declared war on the United States—December 8, 1941—Himmler is supposed to have declared, "America is being ruled by the Jews. And our only demand at the peace negotiations will be: the handing over of the Jews to Germany."

11 Swiss Press (e.g. *Eidgenosse, Neue Züricher Zeitung, Volksstimme*), 3/9/46, 12/27/47 (*Volk und Armee*), etc. Passages from Schellenberg's testimonies were quoted in the papers telling the story of his meetings with Masson and Guisan from his perspective. Heinz Hoehne, *Krieg im Dunkeln*, Bertelsmann, Munich, 1985, pp. 415–18.

12 Schellenberg's report of June 9, 1945, in Hillel Storch's Archive, Stockholm (I am grateful to Dov Dinur for letting me have a copy); *Volksstimme* and *Volkszeitung* (Swiss newspapers), 3/9/46; *Volk und Armee* (Swiss newspaper), 12/27/47; Eggen interrogation, March 1946, NA, T120; Schellenberg interrogation—final report, 9/30/46, NA, T120.

13 NA/R 226/ Schellenberg Interrogation, 9/15, 9/21/45, p. 8: "Hero and Leander contacts in Lisbon, where Hero was the American Military Attaché, and Leander his assistant Demarest. This contact was maintained from early 1943 till the end of the war, with decreasing importance in the latter part. . . . Hero and Leander discussed a compromise peace with Schellenberg's men." These contacts probably were the regular attempts from the American side to penetrate into German intelligence sources, but they fit into the picture of Schellenberg trying to prepare separate peace options for Himmler.

14 See his statement of 1/13/47, NA/M 1019/Roll 63, fr. 298. He repeats that story in almost all his numerous testimonies.

15 For example, NA, M-1270, Roll 18, Interrogation of Schellenberg, 11/13/45.

16 Heinz Hoehne, *The Order of the Death's Head*, Secker and Warburg, London, 1969, pp. 483–539. The picture that Hoehne presents is very detailed and relies on a large number of sources. He accepts Schellenberg's stories without too much criticism, and he relies on some hearsay, along with a number of much better sources. In my opinion, his analysis, while correct in a general manner, presents the collusion between the SS and the opposition in a much too decisive manner. He argues that the Americans were willing to negotiate with the SS on a separate peace, both in Lisbon and in Bern (Allan Dulles). This way of putting it is much too simplistic. Many of the people in charge of OSS, in the field as well as in Washington, thought the German opposition should be supported somehow, but they were wary of separate peace proposals. The U.S. government policy was, of course, radically opposed to any such overtures.

17 See Yaakov Tsur testimony, Oral History Center, ICJ, Jerusalem. The head of Mono-spol was an Austrian by the name of Zehatko. Tsur's father, Alfred Zierer, was an employee of the Monospol company and traveled widely in Greece, Turkey, and else-where to effectuate the deals. He visited Istanbul in November 1941 with a certain Dr. Reimann, who remained there. Zierer, according to his son Tsur, went there about every three months. His last visit was in 1943, and he returned to Prague in June. After the April 1943 arrests (see below), he was no longer protected, and was sent to Theresien-stadt and very soon thereafter to Auschwitz. Tsur says very clearly that his father told him, before they were deported to Auschwitz, that Jews were being gassed there with Prussic acid (Zyklon B was the commercial name of the same substance). See Tsur's tes-timony at the Oral Documentation Center, ICJ, 1988; see also *Peulot Hatzala BeKushta, 1940–1944*, a symposium at Kibbutz Lohamey Hageta'ot, 12/16/68, Yad Vashem, Jerusalem, 1969, pp. 48–51. On the whole affair see also Hoehne, op. cit., pp. 483–85.

18 Huppenkothen testimonies at YV, Nuremberg pretrial interrogations, 1/29/48, 9/2/47, 12/2/47. Heinz Hoehne, *Canaris*, Doubleday, New York, 1979, pp. 499–529; Peter Hoffmann, *The History of the German Resistance*, MIT Press, Cambridge, 1977, pp. 293–95.

19 The Depositenkasse affair was brought up after the war by the British in a trial of Roeder. The material is at the IFZ, MB-6(1), Strafverfahren gegen Dr. Manfred Roeder, LG-Lüneburg, Anz. Nr. 1787/55, Bd. XV, IJS 16/49. See also Hup-penkothen's interrogations at Nuremberg.

20 Huppenkothen, interrogations; Hoehne, *Canaris*, op cit., p. 508.

21 This interpretation is disputed by Erwin Lahousen—NA/E 190/Box 365/File 5, n.d.—who claims that Himmler wanted to trap Canaris but was prevented from doing so by Keitel, who thought a trial might compromise his own position. This statement, however, contradicts all the other testimonies and is not based on firsthand knowledge. Hoehne, in his *Canaris* book, says that Himmler's motive in not pursuing the Roeder line of investigation was his tremendous respect for Canaris. This sounds a bit far-fetched, nor is it in character for the sly *Reichsführer*. See also *Der Spiegel*, no. 25/1969, for Hoehne's article on the case.

22 Romedio Galeazzo Graf von Thun-Hohenstein, *Der Verschwörer: General Oster und die Militäropposition*, Siedler, Berlin, 1982.

23 Eberhard Bethge, *Dietrich Bonhoeffer*, Kaiser, Munich, 1969, pp. 838–41.

24 YV, section of the Righteous. I am grateful to Mordechai Paldiel for letting me look at these documents. Among the fourteen were Julius Fliess, with his wife and his daugh-ter; Friedrich Arnold, with his wife and two sons; Ilse Rennefeld, her non-Jewish hus-band, and two daughters; Annemarie Conzen; and Charlotte Friedenthal, who actu-ally was the fifteenth, but because she came a few days after the group had formed and was a Protestant functionary, the others did not include her among their number. She left for Switzerland on September 4, the others on September 23, 1942. Dohnanyi also smuggled three people, Walter Kranz, his Jewish wife, and the Jewish mother of Wal-ter Kobold, into Turkey in 1942. See BA/Militärarchiv (Freiburg) MSg 2/120.

25 Lahousen testimony, in NA/E 190/Box 365/File 6, n.d.

26 Freiburg Military Archive, MSg 2/120, Arnold memoranda, October 1946 and April 1972.

27 Kersten, *Totenkopf und Treue*, pp. 280 ff.; BA/R58/1028, for a letter of Heydrich of January 16, 1942, in which some of the tensions within the RSHA in this matter become clearer. Heydrich refers there to his letter of February 7, 1941, in which he instructed the Gestapo to reject courteously, but decisively, any intervention by Langbehn regarding RSHA prisoners. In his letter a year later, Heydrich reverses himself, explic-itly in accordance with Himmler's wishes: "In the meantime, the Reichsführer SS and Chief of the German Police has entrusted the lawyer Dr. Langbehn with certain special tasks." However, in case Langbehn intervened, Heydrich's approval would have to be obtained.

28 Hoehne, *Order of the Death's Head,* pp. 515–16; Schellenberg's statement "Did Himmler Know of the 20th of July?" U.S. Military History Institute, Carlisle Barracks (MHI), Donovan Papers, Box 87B, Folder: Schellenberg.

29 IFZ Zs317/6863/84, Bundesarchiv letter to the IFZ of 4/23/53, which records the statement by Popitz's son, who says that the discussions were prepared by Langbehn and Karl Wolff, Himmler's main aide, and states, "Popitz gave Himmler the names of the conspirators a long time before 7/20 [1944]. Himmler is said not to have made any use of this information, and had tried to hold a protective hand over Popitz long after July 20 . . . Himmler apparently thought to have an alibi in Popitz for the time after the collapse of the Third Reich." No less interesting is an IFZ note attached to the file, which records the response of Wolff, an intimate of Himmler's; he says, "Himmler's attitude presaged the Bernadotte affair of 1945, because after July 20 he felt the need to ensure his position, because he had hesitated and had played along with the conspirators," but, the note adds, "he [Wolff] does not like to talk about this and asks that we do not quote him."

30 Peter Hoffmann, op. cit., p. 225. The other emissary of the conspirators in Switzerland was Adam von Trott zu Solz.

31 Hoehne, *Order of the Death's Head,* pp. 519–20.

32 MHI, Donovan Papers: "Did Himmler Know of the 20th of July?"

33 Hoehne, *Order of the Death's Head,* p. 538, and the sources cited there.

34 MHI, Box 125B, Folder: OSS Chronological File to the State Department, July–October 1944, Donovan memo, 7/22/44.

35 At the Swiss Foreign Ministry, these matters were handled by Philippe Aubert de la Rue. For the International Red Cross, Prince Johann Schwarzenberg dealt with Jewish matters, and after him Paul Kuehne. The senior liaison between the two was Edouard de Haller, federal delegate for international aid societies.

36 NA/T120/4202/E422447–8/Wagner to Müller (Gestapo), 7/13/43, and other correspondence, on the same Roll in T120.

37 NA/T120/4202/K207714–5/ Von Thadden memo, 5/21/43.

38 NA/T120/4202/E422480, 3/29/44.

39 See n. 35 above.

40 Miroslav Kárný, *Svědectví z Osvětimí,* in Tvorba, 14/1989.

41 NA/T120/4202/E422405/Killinger to the German Foreign Office, 4/30/43. These attempts by neutrals and satellites and some of the Allied powers to save small groups of Jews were reflected in another development. The Romanians and the Abwehr launched a trial balloon in November 1942: the idea of emigrating 70,000 Jews from Transnistria to Palestine. The Romanians argued that Hitler himself had given his approval to the emigration of these Jews at a meeting with Marshal Ion Antonescu, but the Germans denied that. The plan created a great stir in the West, and to this day there are pointless accusations leveled against the Jewish leaders, who actually reacted forcefully to support this very peculiar initiative. By the time the proposal reached the West, the German embassy in Bucharest had quashed the whole idea, in January 1943. It is highly doubtful whether the Romanian (and Abwehr) initiative belongs to our discussion, because there is no evidence that Himmler took it at all seriously. The only connection appears to be that at the end of 1942 and in early 1943 such schemes were discussed by some of the Nazi satellites and possibly by some Abwehr individuals, but we do not even know, in this particular case, whether there was indeed any senior Abwehr support for it. NA/T120/4202/E422360, Swedish embassy to the German Foreign Office, 7/7/43.

42 October 4, 1943, IMT/PS-1919.

43 Hans-Georg Gadamer, *Wahrheit und Methode,* Mohr, Tübingen, 1965.

44 IFZ/F37/3, Speech in memory of Heydrich after his assassination by Czech agents parachuted in from Britain.

45 Ibid., speech at the Haus der Flieger, 6/9/42.

46 Ibid., speech to the leadership corps of *Das Reich* Waffen SS division, 6/19/42 ("Mit all diesem Kram überfeinter, zivilisierter Dekadenz zog das gesammte deutsche Volk auch in diesen Ostfeldzug").

8
Dogwood's Chains

1 One problem was that an SI branch was not set up in Istanbul until December 1943, under Major Wickham. The Dogwood chain was set up half a year prior to that, which meant that proper intelligence supervision of the Dogwood chain was lacking from the very beginning. NA/RG 226/E 148/Box 33/Folder 435, "Notes for the History of SI, Istanbul," n.d., signature illegible.
2 Barry Rubin, *Istanbul Intrigues,* McGraw-Hill, New York, 1989, p. 169.
3 Interview of Alfred Schwarz with Barry Rubin and Yehuda Bauer, 1987, in B. Rubin's possession.
4 NA/Record Group 84, Istanbul Consulate, 1944, vol. 17, 820.02, Report no. 234, Source: Dogwood; NA/Donovan Files, Roll 68. See also Hoffmann, op. cit., p. 226; Michael Balfour, *Helmuth von Moltke,* Macmillan, London, 1972, pp. 273–77; Jürgen Heidekind and Christof Mauch, *Das Herman-Dossier, VJHFZG,* 1992, 4:567–623.
5 NA/RG 226/E 88/Box 420/Wash–Commo–R&C–324–Istanbul, August '43 to March '44, Dogwood Report, 10/27/43.
6 Rubin, op. cit., pp. 174–75.
7 NA/Suitland, Istanbul Consulate, 10/20/44, letter of Schwarz to the U.S. ambassador, which includes McVicker's comments of 10/24.
8 Rubin, op. cit., 175–77; NA/Donovan Files, Roll 68, passim.
9 NA/RG 226/E 190/Box 72/File 14.
10 Ingeborg Fleischhauer, *Die Chance des Sonderfriedens,* Siedler, Berlin, 1986.
11 NA/E 190/Box 309/Folders 247, 249.3/10/44, 4/17 Maddox (London) to Macfarland, and other similar material there.
12 Rubin, op. cit., p. 194; NA/RG 226/E 88/Box 420/Wash–Commo–R&C–324/Istanbul, History of the OSS in Istanbul, pp. 120 ff.
13 According to GR material, 110063, HSSPF Hungary report of 4/3/44, Messner was arrested on March 31.
14 Archiv des Österreichischen Widerstandes, Vienna, files 113, 4722, 12048, 8378, et al.; personal information from Dr. Helen Legradi, 1987.
15 NA/RG 226, E 154/Box 35/File 522, Toulmin to Joyce, 7/30/44.
16 NA/E 190/Box 76, British SIS (ISLD) information, 5/23/44; NA/RG 226/WASH-SECT-R&C-97-Folder 6, 5/1/44–7/31/44, cable of OSS Washington to Busby, Istanbul, 6/26/44; NA/RG 226/E 121/Box 12, cable of 6/26/44. In his testimony at the Eichmann trial, protocol, p. 896, Brand says that Laufer was a converted Jew, then contradicts himself by saying: "I think his wife or his grandmother were converted Jews." Rubin, op. cit., pp. 192–97. Rubin quotes one source that said that Laufer was "half"-Jewish. All the other sources that we have say he was Jewish on both sides.
17 NA/E 120/Box 20, CIC analysis of the Brand-Grosz mission, n.d., but most probably late June 1944.
18 Schwarz told this story in his postwar interview, but he also told it to an OSS investigator at the time (probably in early June 1944): "He [Laufer] has proposed using a Jewish refugee deal, in which refugees in Central Europe would be exchanged for either material or money, but this scheme has apparently never been more than a wild dream." NA/RG 226/E 148/Box 34.
19 Letter of Andreas Biss to me, 10/16/87; and my interview with Alfred Schwarz in Jerusalem, 2/22/88.

20 PRO/FO 371/42811/WR 422/9/G, interrogation of Grosz by Lt. N. J. Strachan, SIME.

21 Randolph L. Braham, *Politics of Genocide,* New York, 1981, vol. 2, p. 944; NA/RG 226/E 88/Box 420/ Wash-Commo-R&C-324-Istanbul, August '43–March '44, Cereus Report, 10/26/43; Grosz interrogation. Also Bauer, op. cit., pp. 113–17.

22 Earle was an eccentric character; among his exploits were talks with Canaris in Istanbul in January 1943 and with Leverkühn in April. It is not known what exactly was discussed. Nothing resulted from these contacts.

23 The most successful German agent of the OSS had only marginal contacts with the conservative conspiracy. Through a Jewish businessman by the name of Kocherthaler, who had fled Germany in the early 1930s, Allen Dulles established contact with a German diplomat, Fritz Kolbe, who served as the *Referent* of the ambassador for special assignments (*zur besonderer Verfügung*), Karl Ritter. Ritter was Ribbentrop's hatchet man; all the cables from German diplomats all over the world passed through his hands, and he sifted them for Ribbentrop. Ritter—and Kolbe, of course—also read all the conversations of German Foreign Office officials in Berlin with foreign diplomats and German agencies. In 1943, Kolbe visited Bern and, through Kocherthaler, met with Dulles. Visiting Switzerland every three months on the average, but also sending in the material in various ways, Kolbe provided not only a full account of what the German Foreign Office was up to but also details about industrial plants and other targets for bombing attacks. Kolbe organized a group that he called the Inner Circle, twenty to twenty-five people from the military, the industrial world, and the Foreign Office, who were in touch with the July 20 people; but Kolbe said that he never believed in the success of the plot. The Kolbe Circle held, and was never discovered by the Nazis. Kolbe's motives were a deep hostility to Nazism and a conviction that only the defeat of Germany could lead to the abolition of the regime. We could assume that another motive was his Catholicism and his deep friendship with Prelate Schreiber, abbot of the Ottobeuern monastery in Bavaria. Interview with Kolbe, 9/26/45, IF/MA/300/2.

   Gisevius's efforts were paralleled by those of Adam von Trott zu Solz, emissary of Moltke's Kreisau Circle. Both of them maintained their contacts via Gero von Schulze-Gaevernitz, a "half-Jew" with a German aristocratic father from a well-known liberal family in Freiburg; Schulze-Gaevernitz had become a U.S. citizen in 1936, and served as Dulles's expert on German affairs at the OSS mission in Bern. Like Dogwood, Dulles and Schulze-Gaevernitz tried to persuade their government to take the Breakers, as they called the German conspirators, seriously. Despite Donovan's sympathy for that approach, the administration resolutely refused; cf. Jürgen Heidekind, *Gero von Schulze-Gaevernitz*, in Michael Bosch and Wolfgang Niess, eds., *Der Widerstand im deutschen Südwesten, 1933-1945*, Kohlhammer, Stuttgart, 1985.

24 Rubin, op. cit., pp. 227–29; NA/Donovan–Washington Center files, Roll 165, 2/15/44, Macfarland to Washington; the German material on this can be found in NA/T120/Rolls 360, 395, 400.

25 NA/T120/1757/E025155/7/18/44, Wagner memo on information from Kaltenbrunner.

26 GR/AA/487/45—11–345–7, 5/13/44, for the arrest of the Budapest Abwehr people for reasons of corruption (because they had transmitted Zionist funds and had taken rake-offs): "unter den Festgenommenen befindet sich der Hauptagent Dr. Rudolf Gerhard Schmied, der Halbjude Josef Winninger und ein Rudolf Schwarz. Die Namen sind Decknamen." See also E 422117/8, 7/1/44, interrogation of Wehner-Popescu.

27 He had the military rank of *Oberstleutnant.*

28 Moyzisch could not be accepted into the SS although he was an SD operative, not because of his Jewish-sounding family name, but because his mother was an illegitimate child, and her father was unknown. Berlin Document Center (BDC)-Moyzisch file.

29 NA/T120/688/311771/Lisbon to Berlin, 2/11/44.
30 NA/RG 226/E 190/Box 176, X-2, March 12, 1944, interrogation of Karl von Kleczkowski.
31 Rubin, op. cit., pp. 143–45.
32 NA/RG 226/110895, n.d.
33 See Gyula Kadar, *A Ludvikatol Sopronköhidaig,* Magreta, Budapest, 1978, passim. I am grateful to Kalman Keri in Budapest, who in June 1987 gave me some private information about Hatz which he asked me not to record on tape. Colonel Keri was Kadar's adjutant and a personal friend of Hatz's.
34 Letter of Ferenc Bagyoni to Saly Mayer, 7/8/47, in my possession.
35 Rubin, op. cit., p. 187.
36 NA/RG/E 88/Box 420/Wash-Commo-R&C-324-Istanbul, August '43 to March '44, 10/4/43, Dogwood report.
37 NA/T120/4355/E421958/ Veesenmayer to Ritter, 4/18/44.
38 The SS were aware of the idea of handing over Hungarian airfields to the Allies if they came through Yugoslavia. See NA/T 120, Kienast memo, 12/28/43.
39 NA/RG 226/E 154/Box 32/File 481, Donovan memo to the Chiefs of Staff, 11/20/43.
40 NA/Macfarland to Donovan, 12/26/43, Shlomo material.
41 MHI, Donovan Papers, Boston Series, vol. 15.1, Box 79B, "The Hatz Case."
42 Ibid.
43 See Macfarland to Toulmin, 1/19/44, NA/RG 226/E 148/Box 34/Folder 446 (Gyorgy Ranki published the documents, partly in Hungarian translation, in *A Wilhelmstrasse es Magyarorszag,* Budapest, 1968, pp. 383–85, 755–58); MHI, Donovan Papers, Special OSS Reports, Box 86, 1/4/44.
44 NA/RG 226/E 88/Box 495/Wash-Commo-R&C-381–382, Minutes of Secret Meeting held on January 22, 1944.
45 *Akten zur deutschen Auswärtigen Politik, 1918–1945,* Serie E: 1941–1945, Band VII, Göttingen, 1979, doc. 197.
46 NA/RG 226/E 134/Box 298, Macfarland letter to Donovan, 2/5/44.
47 NA/E 190/Box 71/File 11, n.d., memo signed by Macfarland.
48 NA/R 226/E 148/ Box 34, Knickerbocker report, 7/31/44.
49 GR material, 110300–1, 5/5/44, HSSPF report of 5/4.
50 NA/820.02 Hungary, Burton Y. Berry report, 6/18/44. Hatz said that he had been released because Grosz could not tell the Germans anything about Hatz's involvement in the Sparrow mission (see below) and because of Horthy's intervention, which led to his appointment as the aide-de-camp of the chief of the General Staff. He also promised to report for duty on the Eastern Front. His veracity can be demonstrated by his statement to the Americans that until his departure from Budapest on June 8, no Hungarian Jews had been deported, only non-Hungarian citizens. Berry believed Hatz, not the Jews.
51 JDC/SM Hungary, Bagyoni letter to Mayer, 7/8/47. The story is based, among other things, on Zoltan Makra, *Honvedelmi Miniszterek Szolgalataban 1940–1944,* privately published, Munich, 1986. I am grateful to Zvi Erez and Zeev Taub for making translations of relevant passages for me. See p. 81 for Beckerle's cable of February 1, 1944.
52 On the Sparrow mission see Rubin, op. cit.; and NA/Donovan Files, Roll 7.
53 Fritz (František) Laufer was born in Prague in 1900. By 1938 he was living in Prague with his third wife, a convert from Judaism to Christianity; he was probably a waiter. Like Grosz, he was also a petty criminal, and in 1940 he was hauled before a Prague court for fraud. That apparently made him a convenient tool for the Abwehr. His Abwehr superior was Capt. Erich Klausnitzer, a German from Sudetenland (German-speaking area of prewar Czechoslovakia). He was sent to Zagreb and Belgrade and then to Istanbul on Abwehr missions, but he also "worked" in Prague. He insinuated himself into the Czech resistance movement against the Germans, which he then betrayed.

In early 1944 Klausnitzer sent him to Budapest. At the end of the war he returned to Prague, but Klausnitzer caught up with him—obviously, Laufer knew too much. Laufer and his wife were arrested on April 15, 1945, at Klausnitzer's instigation and executed the same day. Archive of the Czech Ministry of the Interior, AMV.325-10-2. I am grateful to Pavel Škorpil for this information.

54 NA/RG 226/E148/Box 34, for Reports Officer Harry R. Harper's judgment of the reasons for Dogwood's "failure." One of the interesting sidelights is that Harper still thought Iris was worth contacting. There is no date on Harper's report, but it seems to have been written in mid-June 1944.

55 Macfarland to Shepardson, chief SI officer in Washington, 6/10/44, in NA/RG 226/E 148/Box 33/Folder 437.

56 NA/E 154/Box 33/File 509, 9/25/44 Cairo conference with Coleman.

57 NA/E 154/Box 33/File 510, 2/16/45, Aldrich to O'Gara; Wisner to Shepardson, 8/8/44, NA/RG 226/E 148/Box 33/Folder 439.

58 In Sweden, at exactly the same time as the Brand-Grosz mission developed, Peter Bruno Kleist, another SS man who appears to have been taken over from the Abwehr, who was then apparently one of Schellenberg's men, proposed a ransom scheme for 2,000 Jews from Latvia, for $2 million, later changed to 2 million Swedish kroner, which would be used to buy materials for humanitarian aid for Germany (see above). Then Kleist said that no money was actually needed. The OSS in Sweden thought that this proposal could have been "a last minute effort to purchase good will in the US and Sweden." Kleist asked for refugee status because he was of Jewish ancestry but reappeared in Sweden in 1945, again representing the SS. WRB, Johnson to Washington, 6/28/44, no. 2362.

9
Satan and the Soul—Hungary, 1944

1 The argument is usually understood in terms of a "charge," but what is so negative about someone showing economic initiative?

2 Randolph L. Braham, *The Kamenets Podolsk and Delvidek Massacres: Prelude to the Holocaust in Hungary,* Yad Vashem Studies, 1973, vol. 9, pp. 133–56.

3 Randolph L. Braham, *Politics of Genocide,* Columbia University Press, New York, 1981, p. 231.

4 Randolph L. Braham, *The Destruction of Hungarian Jewry,* World Federation of Hungarian Jews, New York, 1963, vol. 1, pp. 86, 87, 89, 95, 151.

5 According to OSS reports in MHI, Box 90C, there were 822,000 licensed radios in Hungary in March 1943, of which 88 percent were capable of picking up broadcasts from abroad. According to a Hungarian government survey during that month, 43.7 percent of listeners listened to foreign broadcasts.

6 Robert Major, *The Holocaust in Hungary,* in Jewish Currents, December 1965. Another interesting source is the story of a young girl of Anne Frank's age, Eva Heymann, written by her mother. She is said to have known that Poland meant death and that the Jews were being deported to Poland. *The Diary of Eva Heymann,* Shapolsky, New York, 1988.

7 Kasztner letter to Istanbul, 7/31/44, in Ludwig Kastner Archive, YV/048/88.

8 See my *Holocaust in Historical Perspective,* Seattle, 1978, pp. 94–155.

9 Joel Brand, *Beshlichut Nidonim Lamavet,* Ayanot, Tel Aviv, 1956, p. 54.

10 Avriel of Mossad presents Schulz as a friend of the Jews; see Avriel, op. cit., pp. 161–65.

11 Sandor Szenes, *Befejezetlen mult: Keresztenyek es zsidok, sorsak* (Unfinished past: Christians and Jews, destinies), Budapest, 1986, passim. On May 27 another two Auschwitz inmates, Czeslaw Mordowicz and Arnost Rosin, fled from the camp, reached Slovakia, and integrated their report into that of their two predecessors.

12 The WRB was set up by President Roosevelt on January 22, 1944, as a result of pressure

within the administration and in Congress. It was composed, in theory, of the Secretaries of Defense, State, and Treasury and was mandated to rescue people whose lives were threatened by the Nazis and their allies. In practice, most of the WRB efforts were devoted to the rescue of Jews. See David S. Wyman, *The Abandonment of the Jews*, Pantheon, New York, 1984.

13 Zoltan Mor, *Die Juden Ungarns*, MS, pp. 292–306. There were twelve emissaries to the provinces. Seven of them can be identified by name: Esther Schechter, Haim Fetman, Hava Bermat, Miklos Gottesmann, Anna Czech, Efra Teichmann (Agmon), and Neska Goldfarb.

14 Randolph L. Braham (in *The Politics of Genocide*) and others have pointed out that while the Catholic church in Hungary in effect supported the deportation of the Jews to their deaths, the papal nuntius, Angelo Rotta, protested the anti-Jewish policy of the government as early as April 27, 1944, to Deputy Foreign Minister Michael Arnothy-Jungerth, saying that Hungary, which had prided itself in being a Christian nation, was now pursuing a road that went against the Christian message. Some Catholic prelates, such as Aron Marton, archbishop of Cluj (Koloszvar); Baron Vilmos Apor, bishop of Gyor; Gyula Czapik of Eger; Endre Havas of Csanad; and Ferenc Virag of Pest opposed church policy and the deportations.

15 Lohamei Gettaot Archive, letter from Brand, 1/3/44.

16 I am grateful to Randolph L. Braham for bringing to my knowledge the unreliability of Carmilly's testimony.

17 John Mendelsohn, ed. *The Holocaust, Selected Documents in Eighteen Volumes*, New York, 1982, vol. 15, p. 29.

18 The arms were 150 pistols, forty grenades, three rifles, and two machine guns, of which one was serviceable. PRO/FO 371/42811/WR 324/3/48, Brand interrogation in June 1944.

19 This episode is mentioned in a number of sources. Less-known is the conspirators' plan to arm the Jewish labor battalions on the eve of the planned Horthy announcement that Hungary was leaving its alliance with Germany (October 15, 1944).

20 Szilagyi still represented the Hashomer Hatzair movement, but by that time he had been read out of it. See Avihu Ronen, *Hashomer Hatzair BeHungaria, 1944,* Tel Aviv, MS, 1994.

21 Brand, in his interrogation, says the meeting took place on March 29; in his talk with the emissaries in Istanbul (MA/D.1.721) he says the date was the twenty-second. In his talk with Shertok at Aleppo it became the twenty-fourth. In his final report Kasztner says the meeting happened on April 5. Landau, op. cit., pp. 70–72. In his letter to Istanbul on July 31, 1944 (Ludwig Kastner Archive, YV/048/88), the date is April 3. If Wisliceny was approached by Freudiger two days after the German occupation of Budapest and immediately afterward by Kasztner, it does not sound convincing that Kasztner should have waited for almost two weeks before meeting with Wisliceny. The April dates may also refer to a second, less important meeting with Wisliceny. The most likely date is March 22–24. But the question of exact dates is difficult to resolve in many more instances in this affair.

22 Ernest Landau, ed., *Der Kastnerbericht*, Kindler, Munich, 1961, pp. 71–78; Brand, op. cit., pp. 61–66; Randolph L. Braham, *The Destruction of Hungarian Jewry, a Documentary Record*, vol. 2., pp. 922–28.

23 Friling, op. cit., p. 285; Shertok's talk with Brand in Aleppo, 6/11/44, of which there are several versions (see below).

24 MA/D.1.721.

25 Again, Brand and Kasztner are unsure of the dates. In his report in Istanbul, Brand says that the meeting happened on April 2. The third meeting took place on April 9, and the fourth a few days later.

26 The names of the Abwehr group were pseudonyms in most cases. The real names are not known.

27 John Mendelsohn, op. cit., p. 17.
28 Brand testimony, Eichmann Trial (Eduyot B, p. 876); Brand interrogation, PRO/FO 371/42811/WR 422/9/6, p. 18, where he says that the first meeting with Eichmann took place on the sixteenth. In his later testimonies it is the twenty-fifth.
29 Landau, *Kastnerbericht*, p. 89.
30 John Mendelsohn, op. cit., pp. 64 ff.
31 Brand interrogation, p. 20; and Mendelsohn, op. cit., pp. 156–57 (Hirschmann's account of his meeting with Brand). Brand contradicts himself regarding the dates. In this interrogation (p. 18) he says that the first meeting took place on April 16, and the second on April 25 (his birthday). Veesenmayer later denied that he had participated in the meetings.
32 Brand interrogation, pp. 23–24. Other, much larger figures are mentioned by Brand on other occasions, but they are as unreliable as the sum mentioned here.
33 Brand's interrogation, p. 25.
34 Kasztner says the last but one Brand-Eichmann meeting took place two days before he, Kasztner, was arrested. That occurred on May 10, hence our assumption that the meeting took place on May 8.
35 Bauer, *Holocaust in Historical Perspective*, pp. 112–13.
36 Mendelsohn, op. cit., p. 172.
37 Brand interrogation, p. 27.
38 Brand testimony, Eichmann Trial (Eduyot B, pp. 876–77); Becher testimony, Nuremberg, no. 929, 7/7/47, pp. 5–10.
39 There appear to have been four meetings between Brand and Eichmann—see Mendelsohn, op. cit., p. 158; and Hirschmann's interview with Brand—and the exact dates and sequences are not completely clear. As time went on, they must have become somewhat hazy in Brand's memory, and tended to become combined.
40 Kasztner, quoted in Kurt Emenegger, *Reichsführer's Gehorsamster Becher*, a series of investigative articles in *Sie und Er*, 1962–63; the quotation appears in the issue of January 17, 1963: "Zwischen den einzelnen SS-Stellen war das Zusammenspiel musterhaft: das Judenkommando vernichtete, der Wirtschaftsstab kassierte."
41 German microfilms in Budapest, Historical Institute, private collection of the late Gyorgy Ranki (GR material), E 422117–8, Report of the HSSPF, Hungary (Winkelmann), 7/1/44. Wehner was arrested in November 1943 on the Bulgarian-Turkish border as he was on the point of fleeing to Turkey. He was brought to Budapest by the Hungarian G-2 and interned at the Kistarcsa camp. He was freed by a ruse of his friend Winninger and escaped on May 26, but was caught by the SD in June. From this report it could be inferred that Schmidt's real name was Korda.
42 Brand interrogation, pp. 21–23.
43 Bela Vago, *Intelligence Aspects of the Joel Brand Mission*, in Yad Vashem Studies, vol. 10, pp. 120–21; Brand, *Beshlichut Nidonim Lamavet*, pp. 81–84; interrogation of Bandi Grosz, PRO-FO/371/42811/WR422/9/G.
44 Brand interrogation, p. 27.
45 Grosz interrogation. In addition, Grosz also told his interrogator that Clages had "said that they had only *asked* Brand if he would be able to order war material and he had immediately said he could. They had reported this to Berlin and received instructions that Brand must be sent on a mission." P. 36.
46 Eichmann trial, protocol, Brand testimony, p. 897.
47 Grosz interrogation, p. 37. Laufer even had Grosz deliver a letter to Dogwood (Schwarz) in Istanbul suggesting that he, Laufer, should go to Switzerland to negotiate with Allied representatives. NA/Donovan Files, Roll 179, Macfarland to Washington, 5/28/44 (NA/R 226/WASH-SECT-R&C-97, Folder 6).
48 Braham, *Politics of Genocide*, vol. 2, p. 630.
49 Mendelsohn, op. cit., p. 52; Becher testimony at Nuremberg, YV/3/2/48.

50 Dov Dinur, Introduction, *Dokh Kasztner* (in Hebrew), Private publication, Tel Aviv, 1981, p. 21.

51 WRB, Box 70, no. 274, 6/28/44.

10
The Mission to Istanbul

1 Brand interrogation, PRO/FO 371/42811/WR324/3148, p. 29.

2 The Hungarian firm, Antalya Transportgesellschaft, was chaired by Mehmed Sipahioglu, who was reputedly pro-Jewish. The contact had been established by Ludwig Kastner (no relation to Reszoe Kasztner), a Slovak Jewish refugee and a representative of Agudat Israel in Turkey. It was he who secured a visa for Grosz. YV/048/88, 8/1/44, *Allgemeiner Bericht an Agudas Israel*.

3 Mendelsohn, op. cit., p. 66.

4 Tuvia Friling, *Ben Gurion and the Holocaust*, Hebrew University, 1990, Ph.D. thesis, p. 276.

5 Friling, op. cit., pp. 275–76.

6 Mendelsohn, op. cit., pp. 96–97.

7 Friling, op. cit., p. 280.

8 Yehuda Bauer, *The Holocaust in Historical Perspective*, University of Washington Press, Seattle, 1978, pp. 118–21.

9 CZA/Z4/6/27/44, Shertok report.

10 MA/D.1.714 Bader-Wenja, 5/27/44: "I have not said a word yet [in the letter] about Joel's behavior when it finally became clear to him that there is no way out [of being sent back to Hungary]. There are no words to describe his courage and calm and the friendly look when we parted."

11 Grosz interrogation, PRO/FO 371/42811/WR 422/9/G; NA/RG 226/Box 32/5/21/44 Macfarland to Shepardson.

12 The document did not reach Budapest until July 10. Kasztner letter of 7/31/44, L. Kastner Archive, YV/048/88.

13 Bauer, op. cit., pp. 122–23. In his Cairo interrogation Brand again reiterated that he had not wanted to return to Hungary at that point (p. 30).

14 MA/D.1.720, 6/10/44, Bader-Wenja (Venia Pomeranz).

15 Amos Elon, *Timetable*, Doubleday, New York, 1980, pp. 150–73; WRB, Box 7, Ira Hirschmann's interview with Brand, October 7, 1944. Brand and Bader both thought that if Brand returned to Hungary, he would be killed because the SS would have wanted to hide the fact of its separate peace feelers. Brand therefore asked Bader for cyanide to avoid being tortured and left his last will with him. Ariel Hurwitz, "Shlichuto shel Menachem Bader umagaei Hashomer Hatzair im Yahadut Eiropa hakvushah" in Yalkut Moreshet, no. 35, April 1983, pp. 153–202. Elon knew better. He had been given the relevant documents, but he distorted the picture in order to vilify the JA leaders.

16 Mendelsohn, op. cit., p. 100.

17 All this stands in stark contradiction to the tales spread by Tamir and later detractors of the wartime Zionist leadership, such as Tom Segev, and in recent publications by ultraorthodox anti-Zionist writers.

18 Friling, op. cit., p. 281.

19 Mendelsohn, op. cit., p. 117; Bauer, op. cit., pp. 125–26.

20 Mendelsohn, op. cit., pp. 100–110.

21 Bauer, op. cit., pp. 131–32; PRO/CAB 95/15/JR(44)/13.

22 Mendelsohn, op. cit., pp. 92–95.

23 U.S. State Department, *Foreign Relations of the United States*, Washington, 1944, vol. 2, p. 1062.

24 Goldman was a nonvoting member of the JA Executive and a central figure in the World Jewish Congress (WJC); he had moved to the United States from Switzerland in 1940.
25 Mendelsohn, op. cit., p. 98.
26 Mendelsohn, op. cit., pp. 203–4, 205. Ben Gurion and Shertok erred when they assumed that the WRB had a formal mandate to negotiate with the enemy. The mandate was implied, and any inquiry in Washington had to elicit the response that the WRB was not allowed to engage in direct talks with enemy nationals.
27 Mendelsohn, op. cit., pp. 116, 124.
28 For Shertok's account see *Ma'ariv*, 6/6/1954.
29 Friling, p. 287, Brand at Aleppo.
30 Mendelsohn, op. cit., p. 16.
31 Mendelsohn, op. cit., pp. 17, 19.
32 The history of Seredi's interventions has been dealt with by others; see Randolph L. Braham, *Politics of Genocide*. On April 23, 1944, Seredi intervened with the government and demanded the exclusion of converts to Catholicism from anti-Jewish regulations, their freedom from the authority of the Judenräte, and permission for them not to wear the yellow badge of Jews. In addition, priests of Jewish extraction and old and sick converts should be permitted to keep domestic servants. On May 10, Rotta demanded that Seredi turn to the Catholic public to oppose the anti-Jewish actions, but Seredi did not answer until June 8, and then he said that with government censorship being what it was, arousing the Catholic public was useless.
33 PRO/FO 371/42809,p. 115.
34 Mendelsohn, op. cit., p. 138.
35 Friling, op. cit., p. 288.
36 Friling, op. cit., p. 291.
37 Mendelsohn, op. cit., p. 164: "Schroeder is Laufer, the leading Gestapo agent in Hungary." This is also confirmed in Kasztner's letter to Schwalb, 7/15/44, in the Schwalb materials, Labor Archive, Tel Aviv; and in Brand's testimony at the Eichmann trial, protocol, pp. 878–79.
38 At yet another special meeting of the JA Executive on June 24, Shertok was given the leeway to decide when he would return. The purpose was, among other things, to make sure that he utilized every opportunity to push for the implementation of Brand's mission's goals.
39 PRO/CAB 95/15/JR(44)/15, Eden memo, 6/26/44.
40 Mendelsohn, op. cit., pp. 145–47.
41 NA/840.48 Refugees, Pehle to Morgenthau, 6/19/44.
42 WRB, Box 70, June 19, 1944.
43 PRO/CAB 95/15/JR (44) 15, June 29, 1944.
44 PRO/FO 371/42807/WR 49/3/48, 6/28/44.
45 Bauer, *Holocaust in Historical Perspective*, pp. 137–38; Friling, op. cit., p. 296.
46 WRB, Box 34(188), cable 4295 from Harrison, Berne.
47 PRO/FO 371/42897/WR 48/3/48, from Victor Mallet in Stockholm. The message from Sweden came one day after the Eden-Weizmann-Shertok meeting, and a minute on the report read: "It is difficult to see what can be done by those who, like ourselves, would do anything in our power to stop it."
48 PRO/FO 371/42807/WR 75/3/48.
49 PRO/FO 371/42808/WR169/3/48—Cabinet Conclusions 85(44), 7/3/44. Other comments were made. When the World Jewish Congress office in London suggested that a public declaration be issued by the West and by the Pope, an official minuted: "Why are we the tools of these people? Why should the Pope condemn the murder of Hungarian Jews before he condemns use of flying bombs against this country?" Ibid., 42807/WR 28/3/48, 6/26/44.
50 Bauer, op. cit., p. 140; PRO/FO 371/42897/WR 34/3/48.

51 PRO/FO 371/42807/WR 170/3/48.

52 Friling, op. cit., p. 300.

53 Friling, op. cit., pp. 299–307.

54 Mendelsohn, op. cit., pp. 186–89, 195–99.

55 WRB, Box 70(433), cable 1641 to Moscow.

56 Mendelsohn, op. cit., p. 134.

57 PRO/CAB/JR (44) 19, 7/12/44.

58 NA/RG 226/E 120/Box 20, CIC Report, n.d. "The fact that Gross [*sic*] was to keep his mission secret from Brandt [*sic*] in Turkey, that both were to contact separate sources . . . is inconsistent with the plan for them to approach identical sources (Joint [JDC]) in Switzerland or Lisbon. This highlights the personality of Schwarz, or his importance in German estimation, as the ideal intermediary. Schwarz—[is he] a possible Jewish Agency agent? . . . Any arrangement with the enemy for the rescue of the remaining Jews in Europe could hardly be expected to be discriminated against by the Zionists on security grounds." Similarly colored anti-Jewish reports were occasionally filed by the OSS as well. A report on an interview with a recent arrival in Istanbul in June 1944 approvingly mentions the "fact" that "all these reports" about deportations are wrong—the implication being that they are the result of Jewish propaganda. NA/RG 226/87437. Sometimes these anti-Zionist rantings came from the Washington OSS headquarters and had a comic ring to them. When Bagyoni arrived in Stockholm, and Bader sent a cable to the WJC representatives there to consult with him, the OSS became very alarmed, because Bader had asked to "consult with [Bagyoni] concerning one Ezra Hager. . . . Use extreme caution, group dangerous." Ezra Hager was the Zionist code for rescue of Jews in Hungary. OSS to Macfarland, NA/R226/E088/Box 609.

59 Mendelsohn, op. cit., pp. 234–35; MA/D.1.713,722; Ben-Gurion Archive (BG), Sdeh Boker, Bader letter of 6/10/44. Bader thought that the Nazis, or perhaps even the Jews, wanted to have a hostage in Budapest in case Brand and Grosz did not return.

60 Kasztner trial, Bader testimony, p. 539, Israel State Archive. This statement stands in some contradiction to Bader's report at the time (MA/D.1.746), quoting Stiller: "The Special Department of the Foreign Office in Berlin has told us by cable to assist you in a journey to Berlin. Our courier aircraft has been waiting for you since yesterday. They are expecting you tonight in Berlin." There was no "special department" at the German Foreign Office dealing with such negotiations. The date of the meeting was either July 8 or 11. See also Hurwitz, op. cit.

61 Mendelsohn, op. cit., p. 200; Moreshet Archive, D.1.713, 1.721,1.746; PRO/FO 371/42807/WR 102/3/48; WRB, Box 70, for more material on this. See also Menachem Bader, *Shlichuyot Atzuvot*, Sifriat Poalim, Merchavia, 1954, pp. 110–13.

62 Friling, op. cit., pp. 299 ff.; Bader, testimony at the Kasztner trial, pp. 539–40. In a recent article (Istanbul, Yuni 1944, in Iyunim bitkumat Yisrael 4, June 1994), Friling quotes NA, RG 226, E 120, Memos of 6/22/44 and 8/27/44, as well as other NA material, to show that during Hirschmann and Shertok's visit to Cairo around June 22, a meeting or meetings took place between Hirschmann, Shertok, Joseph J. Schwartz, and S. Pinkney Tuck, an American diplomat. The purpose was for the JDC to set up a fund in Switzerland to pay ransom to the Germans if the need arose. Tuck apparently was friendly to the idea, provided it could be dressed up as money donated by neutrals. The JA and the JDC were obviously thinking in terms of an action that would be independent of the Western Allies—but with tacit American support. For reasons we do not know, nothing came of this initiative.

63 WRB, Box 70 (69), 7/13/44.

64 PRO/CAB/JR(44) third meeting, 7/13/44; Emerson, head of the IGCR, volunteered the observation that the Jews had suggested negotiations via the Swiss because they thought the United States would take into account the Jewish vote in New York and would agree to such a proposal.

65 MA/D.1.723.

66 Mendelsohn, op. cit., pp. 207–8.

67 NA/T120/4203/E025305/Ribbentrop to Veesenmayer, 7/20/44; reply of Veesenmayer, 7/22: "Die Angelegenheit erfolgte auf geheimen Auftrag des Reichsführers SS. Gesandtschaftsrat Grell mitteilte mir heute, dass er gehört habe, dass die Verhandlungen gut ständen, dass die Reutermeldung vermutlich nur erfolgen würde, um die Angelegenheit gegenüber den Russen zu tarnen, in Wirklichkeit aber sei man seitens der Westmächte bereit, auf ein solches Geschäft einzugehen."

68 Interestingly, Schellenberg in testimony to the British denies any knowledge of the Brand mission. Either he was lying or else Clages was in direct touch with Himmler's office. See NA/RG 226/E 123/Bern SI-INT-71–75, 6/27–7/12/45, p. 24.

69 Mendelsohn, op. cit., p. 214.

70 Kollek to Bader, 1/18/55, Israel Prime Minister archive, 009/657.

71 *Zionist Review*, 9/22/44, quoted in Bauer, *Holocaust in Historical Perspective*, pp. 28–29.

11
The Bridge at Saint Margarethen

1 WRB, McClelland's report to Washington, 8/11/44.

2 Labor Archive (Archion Ha'avoda—AA), Tel Aviv, Schwalb Archive, Kasztner-Nathan, 7/12/44.

3 Hansi Brand testimony, Eichmann trial (Eduyot B, p. 914). See also Israel Szabo's testimony. Szabo was a leader of the Maccabi Hatzair youth movement, and he advised all his comrades to avoid the train. It was a trap, and they would all end up in Auschwitz, he warned. Dov Dinur, op. cit., p. 20.

4 Dov Dinur, op. cit., p. 17, citing Krausz's letter to Geneva.

5 Randolph L. Braham, *The Politics of Genocide*, Columbia University Press, New York, 1981, p. 953.

6 Kasztner, in his testimony at Nuremberg (7/18/47, YV, Interrogations), implied that Becher might have agreed to less, but that Himmler demanded $1,000. He claims to have seen a Himmler letter to that effect.

7 Kurt Emenegger, *Reichsführers gehorsamster Becher*, in *Sie und Er*, Zurich, 1/17/63.

8 Braham, op. cit., pp. 954–55.

9 Dov Dinur, op. cit., p. 25.

10 This and the following paragraphs lean heavily on Emenegger, *Sie und Er*, 1/31/63, 2/7/63, 2/14/63, 2/21/63, and the documentation referred to therein.

11 IFZ Eichmann-Vernehmungen, Kurt Becher, 6/20–21/61, pp. 7 ff.

12 Emenegger, op. cit., 2/21/63.

13 Ribbentrop was furious: the SS had not only pulled off a coup but had smuggled Jews out of Germany without the knowledge of its Foreign Office. An investigation revealed that the visas and other documents enabling the Weiss group to escape had been forged by the SS. Ribbentrop was powerless to move, because his Führer supported Himmler over the Weiss affair. NA/T 120/4203/K209194–7; 1757/ E 025085–96; 3237/ E54883032; and other documents on these rolls.

14 NA/T120/1757/E025079/ 7/19/44, Ribbentrop to Veesenmayer, quoting Hitler ("Der Führer hat daraufhin entschieden").

15 Emenegger, op. cit., 2/14/63.

16 NA/T120/1757/E025093–6/Veesenmayer-Ribbentrop, 7/9/44.

17 Emenegger, op. cit., 1/17/63.

18 Emenegger, op. cit., 1/17/63. Emenegger mentions people like Martin Sternberg and Vera Gulyas, owners of large fashion stores, who gave their property to Becher in return for protection.

19 Braham, op. cit., p. 957.

20 Paul L. Rose, *Joel Brand's "Interim Agreement" and the Course of Nazi-Jewish Negotiations, 1944–1945,* in The Historical Journal (Britain), 34/4 (1991) pp. 909–29.
21 Dov Dinur, op. cit., p. 23.
22 Some tractors (not trucks) were delivered with Mayer's funds (see below). By the way, McClelland was not a Quaker, as has so commonly been assumed; his wife, Marjorie, was. McClelland was born in Palo Alto, California, in 1914.
23 Emenegger, op. cit., 4/18/63, p. 21.
24 Emenegger, op. cit., 4/18/63, pp. 85, 87.
25 Emenegger, op. cit., 4/18/63.
26 Berlin Documentation Center (BDC), Kurt A. Becher. Becher received the Iron Cross Ist Class and the Iron Cross IInd Class, both in 1941, and the "German Cross in Gold [Deutsches Kreuz in Gold]" at an undetermined date.
27 Emenegger, op. cit., 4/25/63. Cf. Karla Müller-Tupath, *Reichsführers gehorsamster Becher,* Konkret, Fulda, 1982, passim.
28 Emenegger, op. cit., 4/25/63, pp. 85, 87.
29 He became a member of the Haus Seefahrt guild in 1966 and participated in the festive dinner in early 1967 (*Weser Kurier,* 2/11/67). His rehabilitation was smoothed by a large gift to the guild.
30 See Henry Feingold, *Politics of Rescue,* Rutgers University Press, New Brunswick, New Jersey, 1970, p. 267.
31 Attempts by representatives of some of the neutrals, such as the Portuguese, to bring out small numbers of Jews had been made before July. NA/T 120/4355/E 422022.
32 NA/T120/4203/E420969, Ribbentrop to Veesenmayer, 7/7/44.
33 T120/1757/E025088–9/Veesenmayer-Ribbentrop, 7/9/44.
34 NA/T120/4355/E422224–5/Ribbentrop to Veesenmayer, 7/10/44.
35 NA/T120/4355/E421778–9/Veesenmayer-Foreign Office, 7/25/44. The permission that the Swiss were seeking for Jews with Palestine papers to leave Hungary was dependent "von der deutscherseits gestellten Bedingung der Judenevakuierung Budapests."
36 IMT/NG Eichmann to RSHA, 7/24/44 1806, and T120/4355/E421778–80/ Veesenmayer-Foreign Office, 7/25/44.
37 NA/T120/4203/K209321–2/ memo (*Vermerk*) of 8/4/44.
38 NA/T120/1757/E025082–4/Ribbentrop to Veesenmayer, 7/17/44. The language, incidentally, shows again that Hitler was personally and directly involved in such a relatively minor matter as the permission for small numbers of Jews leaving Nazi Europe at a time when the Germans were threatened with the loss of France.
39 NA/T120/4355/E422278–9/8/14/44, Veesenmayer-Foreign Office; GR/AA/E 422226.
40 NA/T120/4255/K214066/8/19/44, Grell to Foreign Office.
41 NA/T120/4355/E422180/Veesenmayer-Wagner, 8/24/44.
42 NA/T120/4355/E422181/Veesenmayer-Ribbentrop, 8/25/44.
43 NA/T120/4355/E422128–9/7/8/44, Winkelmann-Ritter. The report was submitted to Hitler, who apparently read all such reports, and he ordered parachutists to be shot; the order did not pertain to the Palestinians, but to another group of four British parachutists.
44 The documents are now in Israel. I am very grateful to Dov Dinur for making copies of them available to me, with Hebrew translations from the original Hungarian. The meetings were with Becher on July 15, 1944, with Eichmann, Veesenmayer, Becher, Krumey, and Grüson on August 12, and with Wisliceny on August 18.
45 Zvi Singer's article in *Yediot Acharonot,* 11/18/1988.
46 From a document now in Israel; see n. 44.
47 Andreas Biss, *Der Stopp der Endlösung,* Seewald Verlag, Stuttgart, 1976.
48 WRB, McClelland to Washington, 8/1/44, no. 4197.
49 JDC, SM-9, August 1 conversation with Lisbon.
50 JDC/SM-17, 6/15/45 report by Wyler-Schmidt.

51 WRB/8/21/44, no. 2867.
52 JDC/SM-13; Braham, *Destruction of Hungarian Jewry*, 2:635–637, 481. Becher testimony, YV/9104, p. xiv. Becher sent off his cable from Budapest at 6:10 P.M. on the twenty-fifth. While the problem remains, one has to consider also the unlikelihood of Becher waiting for four days before sending off his report to Himmler, and returning to Budapest before he did that, even if he must have argued with Kasztner what he should report. It may not be impossible that Becher had a telephone conversation with his chief, and then sent a written report. Werner Grothman, Himmler's adjutant, explicitly says that Becher's report caused Himmler's order—in his signed testimony at Nuremberg, 1/4/47.

12
The Swiss Talks and the Budapest Tragedy

1 IMT-NG 2234, Veesenmayer to Ritter and Ribbentrop, April 3, 1944.
2 GR/AA/E 487148–9: "und soweit sie zugelassen wird, von einer wertvollen Gegenleistung abhängig zu machen." See also ibid., E 422315, von Thadden to the Swiss legation in Berlin, 9/5/44.
3 The Hilfsverein für jüdische Flüchtlinge im Ausland was established in Switzerland in 1938. Isaac Sternbuch's wife, Rachel (Recha), who was the most active member of the group, was the daughter of Rabbi Rottenberg of Antwerp.
4 *Sie und Er,* 9/14/61–11/9/61, a series of articles by Truempy.
5 Ibid., photocopy of the document printed on 10/5/61.
6 JDC/SM-39.
7 JDC/SM-13, SM-17.
8 Biss, op. cit., p. 175.
9 Landau, *Kastnerbericht,* p. 187; JDC/SM-13, notebook.
10 JDC/SM-13, notebook.
11 Alain Dieckhoff, *Une Action de Sauvetage des Juifs Européens en 1944–1945: L'"Affaire Musy,"* in *Revue d'Histoire Moderne et Contemporaine,* 1989, 2:287–303.
12 JDC/SM-21, Musy report, n.d.; WRB, 7/31/45, McClelland's final report. According to Becher (YV/Nuremberg testimonies, no. 2710-c, 1/22/48), Himmler thought Musy was an old fool because he had offered the Nazis pharmaceutical products, whereas Himmler wanted trucks. See also Dieckhoff, op. cit., p. 291, who reports that Musy said of Himmler, "Il m'ecouta attentivement et fit effort pour comprendre mon point de vue, fort eloigne du sien."
13 IFZ, 48a, 11/18/44, Musy to Himmler.
14 WRB/10/14/44, Olsen to Washington, no. 4187, and 10/18/44, no. 279.
15 JDC/SM-14,17; Landau, op. cit., p. 208.
16 JDC/SM-17; Landau, op. cit., pp. 211–17.
17 WRB/11/21/44, no. 3932.
18 WRB/11/28/44, no. 4014 to McClelland; 12/9/44, no. 8045, McClelland to WRB.
19 Landau, op. cit., p. 235.
20 JDC/SM-39, 11/30/44: "Man könne ihm, B.[echer], keine Märchen erzählen."
21 Swiss National Archive, Berne, 2200/Berlin 3/Klasseur 3, 1bis-A18.5, 11/27/44, Heinz Vischer (Berlin embassy) to Berne: "Dass der RsF [Reichsführer, i.e., Himmler] zur Überzeugung gelangt sei, dass ein Austausch ungarischer Juden gegen Waren wenig Aussicht auf Erfolg hat, da die Alliierten ihre Güter doch schlussendlich nicht zum Export in das Reich freigeben werden. Es sei deshalb der Plan aufgetaucht, die ungarische Judenschaft gegen Deutsche in alliierter Hand auszutauschen, vornehmlich gegen die zahlenmässig starke deutsche Volksgruppe in Rumänien."
22 JDC/SM-21(2); WRB/12/13/44, McClelland-Washington, no. 8118.
23 WRB/12/19/44, to McClelland, no. 4273, and the reply from McClelland of 12/28;

WRB/1/6/45, to McClelland, no. 102; *Foreign Relations of the United States,* Government Printing Office, Washington, D.C., 1945, vol. 2, p. 1121.

24 "Und geben uns zu einer solchen Unanständigkeit, diesem armen, von den Juden gequälten Volk neue Juden hinzuschicken, nicht her." IFZ, 48a, Himmler material, 1/18/45 (*Zu Meinen Akten*).

25 WRB/1/25/45,1/28/45,2/8/45 from McClelland to Washington, Nos. 424, 605, 881; Franz Goering testimony, Schellenberg Documents, Box 87B, MHI.

26 YV/0–51/DN-39/2119: "Wer ist derjenige mit dem die amerikanische Regierung wirklich in Verbindung ist. Ist es ein Rabbiner-Jude oder ist es die Jioint?" See also IFZ, 48a. Dieckhoff, op. cit., p. 291, summarizes Musy's other achievements, in addition to those mentioned already: the release, at the end of February, of sixty-one Hungarian Jews and, in April, of the relatives of some of the rabbis associated with the VH. A similar effort was made—we do not know by which SS faction—via a group of Dutch Jews in Switzerland, apparently in mid-February, who were offered 1,500 Dutch Jewish internees at Theresienstadt and Bergen-Belsen for SFR 1,000 per head, or SFR 2.5 million. The Dutch government-in-exile turned to the British, and they refused to support this ransom scheme. PRO/FO 371/51112/XL/A014758, pp. 90–98.

27 Becher, YV/Nuremberg testimonies, no. 2710-c, 1/22/48. Schellenberg's many testimonies are full of invective against Becher.

28 Landau, op. cit., p. 291; JDC/SM-17. The Red Cross was now amenable to accommodating Jewish demands. Carl J. Burckhardt went to see Himmler, and the Red Cross sent emissaries to Bratislava (George Dunant) and Vienna (Lutz Thudicum), who, with JDC funds, were instrumental in saving Jewish lives in both places.

29 British officials talked about July 18, because that was the date on which the British received the offer.

30 NA/T120/3237/E548787–8, Veesenmayer to Berlin, 11/21/44. Hoess was in charge on the Austrian border, and he refused to take any more Jews over forty or any more women. Szalasi's government decided to stop marching women and to transport them only by train. Because no trains were available, the deportation of women ceased.

31 In a testimony (YV/9104, 1945, p. xvii), Becher claims that he received an order from Himmler to stop the marches.

32 Robert Rozett, *The Protected Children's Houses: Rescue in Budapest, 1944–1945,* paper for the Institute of Contemporary Jewry, Hebrew University, 1981; Rozett, *Jewish and Hungarian Resistance in Hungary,* Yad Vashem Studies, 1989, vol. 19, pp. 269–88.

33 Eichmann Trial, 1053, Biss letter to Mayer, 7/6/45.

34 Eichmann Trial, testimonies 06, Becher testimony, 6/20–21/61, p. 22.

35 IFZ, Michael Salamon letter to Lutz, 4/15/47.

13
The Final Months

1 Gyula von Szilvay, *Die nationalsozialistische Verschwörung und Aggression,* MS at the IFZ/Fb 109/2, IV Teil.

2 NA/R226/79428, 6/30/45.

3 These Jews were Julius Ecker, Georg Kramer, Alexander Mandel, Nicholas Weiss, Lilian Braun, Martin Sternberg and his wife, Ignaz Auspitz, and Irene Wiesner. Emenegger, op. cit., 1/10/63.

4 Becher's postwar testimony to the Hungarians includes a lengthy and detailed description of how he had all along defended the interests of Hungary in protecting the evacuated industries from greedy German officials. He had seen himself as the *Treuhand* (administrator) of the Manfred Weiss works and other industries and all he wanted was

to return all the property to Hungary after the war. Becher surely must be one of the most selfless and upright Nazis of the period. See his interrogation, 12/11/45, Magyar Allamrendörseg Budapesti Fökapitanysaganak Politikai Rendeszeti Osztalya (Political Department of the Hungarian State Police in Budapest), no. 21588. I am grateful to Hava Baruch for her translation of the document.

5 Yahil, op. cit., pp. 646–48.

6 YV/Nuremberg testimony 929, of Becher, 7/7/47, pp. 19–22. Kasztner had Becher agree with his statement that General Pfeffer-Willenbruch in Budapest had cabled Himmler, asking him what to do with the Budapest Jews. Becher intervened, on January 9, 1945, and Himmler sent a cable to Hungary. Since the city was liberated in January–February, the date is rather late in any case.

7 On April 10, 1945, when Schellenberg lunched with Kaltenbrunner, the latter reportedly quoted Hitler: "Besides, there is the general directive of Hitler . . . that all camps should be evacuated and especially Jews should be regarded as hostages." NA/M1270/Roll 17, Schellenberg testimony, 11/13/45. See also YV/Werner Grothman testimony at Nuremberg, 1/4/47: "Hitler [hat] darauf bestanden dass kein aussländischer Häftling lebend in die Hände des Feindes fallen darf."

8 See PRO/FO371/51114/XC/AO14652, Board of Deputies of British Jews to Paul Mason at the Foreign Office, saying that there was a report that the Germans were transporting large numbers of Polish Jews as they were retreating.

9 Yahil, op. cit., pp. 539–42, 651; Yehuda Bauer, *The Death Marches, January–May, 1945*, in Michael R. Marrus, ed., *The Nazi Holocaust*, Meckler, Westport, 1989, vol. 9, pp. 491–511; Shmuel Krakowski, *The Death Marches During the Evacuation of the Camps*, in ibid., pp. 476–90.

10 The Swedish side of the story is in large part based on the official Swedish account of 1956 of these negotiations, in its German translation: *Vorspiel und Verhandlungen zu der schwedischen Hilfsexpedition nach Deutschland, 1945*, IFZ/F 44/7; and on Steven Koblik, *The Stones Cry Out*, Holocaust Library, New York, 1988.

11 Gerhard Ritter, *Carl Goerdeler und die deutsche Widerstandsbewegung*, DVA, Stuttgart, 1964, p. 420.

12 Koblik, op. cit., p. 125.

13 For the details of the Swedish efforts and the negotiations with Germany, see Koblik, op. cit.

14 PRO/FO 371/5113/XC/A014652, Mallet to London, 2/8/45.

15 Material from Hillel Storch's Archive, copies in Dov Dinur's possession. I am grateful to Dov Dinur for giving me permission to use this material. See also IFZ/Zs/1624; Peter Kleist, *Zwischen Hitler und Stalin, 1939–1945*, Athenäum, Bonn, 1950; Kleist, *Die europäische Tragödie*, Schütz, Göttingen, 1961.

16 Dinur material, Storch archive.

17 Koblik, op. cit., p. 128.

18 PRO/FO 371/14978/WO 208/685A, Stockholm to FO, 3/27/45; WRB/4/3/45, Olsen to Washington, no. 5356. Koblik (op. cit., p. 131), quoting a Storch letter to Adler-Rudel of March 27, says the offer came on March 21 and that the 10,000 were offered to Sweden only.

19 IFZ/F44/7, p. 30.

20 Norbert Masur, *Yehudi Mesocheach im Himmler*, Israeli-Swedish Friendship Society, Tel Aviv, 1985. This is a translation of Masur's account in Swedish (*En Jude Talar Med Himmler*), written in 1945. See also WRB/4/25/45/from Olsen, no. 1547.

21 Koblik, op. cit., p. 138.

22 Report of the Committee (A. M. Snouck Hurgronje, Prof. A. J. C. Rueter, and C. J. van Schelle), 1/12/50, IFZ F44/7.

23 PRO/FO 371/51987/XC/014652, Berne no. 30, reported from Washington, 3/13/45.

24 Kasztner letter of 4/11/45 to Mayer, Dinur material, copy in my possession.

25 All the preceding statements by Becher are contained in his 1945 testimony at Nuremberg, YV/9104.

26 Dinur's material; and Landau, op. cit.

27 "Wenn Sie erst den Reichsführer persönlich kennenlernen werden, werden Sie sehen, was für ein wunderbarer Mensch er ist." Emenegger, op. cit., 1/10/63.

Epilogue

1 Richard Breitman and Shlomo Aronson, *The End of the "Final Solution"? Nazi Plans to Ransom Jews in 1944,* in Central European History, 25/2, 1993, pp. 177–203, have reached similar conclusions and have been working on parallel materials. I am grateful to both for their comments and critiques. I do not share all their conclusions, as will be evident if their article and this present work are compared. However, the differences are minor.

Bibliography

Archival Sources

I have been fortunate to have access to the following archives—occasional materials from other archives are mentioned in the notes—and have used the abbreviations indicated.

BA Bundesarchiv, Koblenz, and Bundesarchiv, Bonn (the Foreign Ministry part of the BA)
BDC Berlin Documentation Center
BG Ben Gurion Archives, Sdeh Boker, Israel
CZA Central Zionist Archives, Jerusalem
　　　Eidgenössisches Bundesarchiv, Bern
IFZ Institut für Zeitgeschichte, Munich
JDC American Jewish Joint Distribution Committee Archives, New York, Geneva, and Jerusalem
MA Moreshet Archives, Giv'at Haviva, Israel
MHI Military Historical Institute (U.S.), Carlisle, Pennsylvania
NA National Archives (Military Archives), Washington, D.C.
PRO Public Records Office, London
SM Saly Mayer Files, JDC
WRB War Refugee Board Archive, Roosevelt Archives, Hyde Park, New York
YV Yad Vashem Archives, Jerusalem

When using Nuremberg Trial documents, I used the customary abbreviations, usually IMT, followed by the codes NG, NO, PA, PS, and so forth. When using documents from the Eichmann trial, I used the customary T designations or the investigation (06) numbering.

Books

Akten zur deutschen Auswärtigen Politik, 1918–1945, Serie D, Baden-Baden, 1953; Serie E, Göttingen, 1979.
Avriel, Ehud, *Open the Gates*, Atheneum, New York, 1975.
Balfour, Michael, *Helmuth von Moltke*, Macmillan, London, 1972.
Barkai, Avraham, *Hakalkalah Hanatzit*, Sifriat Poalim, Tel Aviv, 1986.
Bauer, Yehuda, *American Jewry and the Holocaust*, Wayne State University Press, Detroit, 1981.
———, *From Diplomacy to Resistance*, Jewish Publication Society, Philadelphia, 1970.
———, *My Brother's Keeper*, Jewish Publication Society, Philadelphia, 1973.
———, *The Holocaust in Historical Perspective*, Washington University Press, Seattle, 1978.
Bauman, Zygmunt, *Modernity and the Holocaust*, Cornell University Press, Ithaca, New York, 1988.
Baynes, Norman H., *Speeches of Adolf Hitler, April 1922–August, 1939*, Oxford University Press, London, 1942.

Ben-Elissar, Eliahu, *Kesher Hahashmadah,* Idanim, Jerusalem, 1978.

Bethge, Eberhard, *Dietrich Bonhoeffer,* Kaiser, Munich, 1969.

Biffault, Herma, *The Memoirs of Doctor Felix Kersten,* Doubleday, New York, 1947.

Biss, Andreas, *Der Stopp der Endlösung,* Seewald, Stuttgart, 1976.

Black, Edwin, *The Transfer Agreement,* Macmillan, New York, 1984.

Braham, Randolph L., *The Destruction of Hungarian Jewry, a Documentary Record,* World Federation of Hungarian Jews, New York, 1963.

———, *The Politics of Genocide,* Columbia University Press, New York, 1981.

Brand, Joel, *Beshlichut Nidonim Lemavet,* Ayanot, Tel Aviv, 1956.

Breitman, Richard, *The Architect of Genocide,* Knopf, New York, 1991.

Browning, Christopher R., *Fateful Months,* Holmes and Meier, New York, 1985.

———, *The Final Solution and the German Foreign Office,* Holmes and Meier, New York, 1978.

Cohen, Michael J., *Palestine to Israel: From Mandate to Independence,* Cass, London, 1988.

Dinur, Dov, *Dokh Kastner,* Hotzaah Atzmit, Tel Aviv, 1981.

Documents on German Foreign Policy, Series D, Government Printing Office, Washington, D.C., 1949–83.

Eduyot Bemishpat Eichmann, Ayanot, Tel Aviv, 1965.

Elon, Amos, *Timetable,* Doubleday, New York, 1980.

Fatran, Gila, *Ha'im Ma'avak al Hissardut?* Moreshet, Tel Aviv, 1992.

Feilchenfeld, Werner, et al., *Haha'avarah-Transfer nach Palästina,* Mohr, Tübingen, 1972.

Feingold, Henry L., *Politics of Rescue,* Rutgers University Press, New Brunswick, N.J., 1970.

Fischer, Wolfram, *Deutsche Wirtschaftspolitik, 1918–1945,* Peters, Lüneburg, 1961.

Fleischhauer, Ingeborg, *Die Chance des Sonderfriedens,* Siedler, Berlin, 1986.

Foreign Relations of the United States, 1938, 1939, Government Printing Office, Washington, D.C., 1944.

Friling, Tuvia, *Ben Gurion Vehasho'ah,* Ph.D. dissertation, Hebrew University, Jerusalem, 1990.

Fuchs, Avraham, *The Unheeded Cry,* Mesorah, Brooklyn, 1986.

Gadamer, Hans Georg, *Wahrheit und Methode,* Mohr, Tübingen, 1965.

Giora, Shlomo, *Ot Kayin,* Schocken, Jerusalem, 1983.

Gruenhut, Aron, *Katastrophenzeit des slowakischen Judentums,* Selbstverlag, Tel Aviv, 1972.

Gutman, Yisrael, ed., *Encyclopedia of the Holocaust,* Macmillan, New York, 1990.

Habe, Hans, *The Mission,* Coward-McCann, New York, 1966.

Hassel, Ulrich von, *The Ulrich von Hassel Diaries,* Doubleday, New York, 1947.

Herf, Jeffrey, *Reactionary Modernism,* Cambridge University Press, New York, 1984.

Hilberg, Raul, *The Destruction of the European Jews,* Holmes and Meier, New York, 1985.

Hoehne, Heinz, *Canaris,* Doubleday, New York, 1979.

———, *Krieg im Dunkeln,* Bertelsmann, Munich, 1985.

———, *The Order of the Death's Head,* Secker and Warburg, London, 1964.

Hoffmann, Peter, *The History of the German Resistance,* MIT Press, Cambridge, 1977.

Israeli, David, *Hareich Hagermani Ve'eretz Yisrael,* Ramat Gan, 1974.

Jaeckel, Eberhard, *Hitler's Weltanschauung, a Blueprint for Power,* Wesleyan University Press, Middleton, Conn.

Kadar, Guyla, *A Ludvikatol Sopronköhidaig,* Magveto, Budapest, 1978.

Karski, Jan, *The Secret State,* Houghton and Mifflin, Boston, 1944.

Kersten, Felix, *The Kersten Memoirs,* Macmillan, New York, 1957.

———, *Totenkopf und Treue,* Hamburg, 1952.

Kleist, Peter B., *Zwischen Hitler und Stalin,* Atheneum, Bonn, 1950.

Koblik, Steven, *The Stones Cry Out,* Holocaust Library, New York, 1988.

Krausnick, Helmut, and Hans-Heinrich Wilhelm, *Truppe des Weltanschauungskrieges,* DVA, Stuttgart, 1981.

Landau, Ernest, ed., *Der Kastnerbericht,* Kindler, Munich, 1961.

Laqueur, Walter, and Breitman, Richard, *Breaking the Silence,* Simon and Schuster, New York, 1986.

Lossin, Yigal, *Pillar of Fire,* Zionist Organisation, Jerusalem, 1984.

Makra, Zoltan, *Honvedelmi Miniszterek Szolgalataban, 1940–1944,* Privately published, Munich, 1986.

Masur, Norbert, *Yehudi Mesocheach im Himmler,* Israeli-Swedish Friendship Society, Tel Aviv, 1985.

Mayer, Arno J., *Why Did the Heavens Not Darken?* Pantheon, New York, 1990.

Mendelsohn, John, ed., *The Holocaust: Selected Documents in Eighteen Volumes,* Garland, New York, 1982.

Morley, John F., *Vatican Diplomacy and the Jews During the Holocaust, 1939–1943,* Ktav, New York, 1980.

Neumann, Oskar, *Im Schatten des Todes,* Olamenu, Tel Aviv, 1956.

Nicosia, Francis, *The Third Reich and the Palestine Question,* University of Texas Press, Austin, 1985.

Ofer, Dalia, *Escaping the Holocaust,* Oxford University Press, New York, 1990.

Ofer, Dalia, and Weiner, Hannah, *Parashat Kladovo-Sabac,* Tel Aviv University, 1994. (Forthcoming.)

Perl, William R., *The Four-Front War,* Crown, New York, 1979.

Petzina, Dietmar, et al., *Sozialgeschichtliches Arbeitsbuch, III, 1914–1945,* Beck, Munich, 1978.

Peulot Hatzalah beKushta, 1940–1944, Yad Vashem, Jerusalem, 1969.

Porat, Dina, *The Blue and the Yellow Star of David,* Harvard University Press, Cambridge, 1990.

Ranki, Gyorgy, ed., *A Wilhelmstrasse es Magyarorszag,* Kossuth, Budapest, 1986.

Ritter, Gerhard, *Carl Goerdeler und die deutsche Widerstandsbewegung,* DVA, Stuttgart, 1964.

Rosenkranz, Herbert, *Verfolgung und Selbstbehauptung: Die Juden in Österreich, 1938–1945,* Herold, Vienna, 1978.

Rothkirchen, Livia, *Churban Yahadut Slovakia,* Yad Vashem, Jerusalem, 1961.

Rubin, Barry, *Istanbul Intrigues,* McGraw-Hill, New York, 1989.

Segev, Tom, *The Seventh Million,* Hill and Wang, New York, 1993.

Seraphim, Hans-Günther, *Das politische Tagebuch Alfred Rosenbergs,* Göttingen, 1956.

Shoenfeld, Moshe, *The Holocaust Victims Accuse,* Neturei Karta of U.S.A., Brooklyn, 1977.

Tal, Uriel, *Germans and Jews in the Second Reich,* Cornell University Press, Ithaca, N.Y., 1975.

Thun-Hohenstein, Romedio Galeazzo, Graf von, *Der Verschwörer: General Oster und die Militärpolitik,* Siedler, Berlin, 1982.

Tragedia slovenských Židov, exhibition catalog, Bratislava, 1949.

Vrba, Rudolf, and Bestic, Alan, *I Cannot Forget,* Grove Press, New York, 1964.

Weissmandel, Michael Dov, *Min Hametzar,* Emunah, New York, 1960.

Wyman, David S., *Paper Walls,* University of Massachusetts Press, Amherst, 1968.

————, *The Abandonment of the Jews,* Pantheon, New York, 1984.

Yahil, Leni, *The Holocaust,* Oxford University Press, New York, 1990.

Zariz, Ruth, *Hatzalat Yehudim Germanim al-yedei Hagirah, 1938–1944,* Ph.D. dissertation, Hebrew University, Jerusalem, 1986.

Zweig, Ronald W., *Britain and Palestine During the Second World War,* Boydell, London, 1986.

Articles and Chapters in Books

Aronson, Shlomo, *Hitler's Judenpolitik, die Alliierten, und die Juden,* in Vierteljahreshefte für Zeitgeschichte, 1984, vol. 1, pp. 29–65.

Ball-Kaduri, Kurt J., *Ha'aliyah habilti-chukit miGermania Hanatzit,* in Yalkut Moreshet no. 8, 1968, pp. 127–44.

Barkai, Avraham, *German Interests in the Haavarah-Transfer Agreement,* in Leo Baeck Institute Year Book no. 25, Mohr, Tübingen, 1990, pp. 245–56.

Bauer, Yehuda, *The Death Marches, January–May, 1945,* in Michael Marrus, ed., *The Nazi Holocaust,* Meckler, Westport, 1989, vol. 9, pp. 491–511.

———, *Who Was Responsible and When?* in Holocaust and Genocide Studies, 1991, vol. 6, 2:129–50.

Braham, Randolph L., *The Kamenets Podolsk and Delvidek Massacres: Prelude to the Holocaust in Hungary,* in Yad Vashem Studies, no. 9, 1973, pp. 133–56.

Breitman, Richard, and Aronson, Shlomo, *The End of the "Final Solution"? Nazi Plans to Ransom Jews in 1944,* in Central European History, 1993, vol. 25, 2:177–203.

Broszat, Martin, *Hitler and the Genesis of the "Final Solution,"* in Yad Vashem Studies, no. 13, 1979, pp. 73–126.

Browning, Christopher R., *Referat Deutschland: Jewish Policy and the German Foreign Office (1933–1940),* in Yad Vashem Studies, no. 12, 1977.

———, *Nazi Resettlement Policies and the Search for a Solution to the Jewish Question, 1939–1941,* in German Studies Review, 1986, vol. 9, 3:497–519.

Conway, John S., *Frühe Augenzeugenberichte aus Auschwitz: Glaubwürdigkeit und Wirkungsgeschichte,* in Vierteljahreshefte für Zeitgeschichte, 1979, vol. 2, pp. 260–84.

———, *Der Holocaust in Ungarn: Neue Kontroversen und Überlegungen,* Vierteljahreshefte für Zeitgeschichte, 1984, vol. 2, pp. 179–212.

Dieckhoff, Alain, *Une Action de Sauvetage des Juifs Européens en 1944–1945: L'"Affaire Musy",* in Revue d'Histoire Moderne et Contemporaine, 1989, vol. 2, pp. 287–303.

Emenegger, Kurt, *Reichsführer's Gehorsamster Becher,* in Sie und Er, Zurich, 1962–63.

Gelber, Yoav, *Hamediniut Hatzionit Veheskem Haha'avarah,* in Yalkut Moreshet no. 18, 1974, pp. 23–100.

Goshen, Seev, *Eichmann und die Nisko-Aktion im Oktober, 1939,* in Vierteljahreshefte für Zeitgeschichte, 1981, vol. 1, pp. 74–96.

Heidekind, Jürgen, *Gero von Schulze Gaevernitz,* in Michael Bosch and Wolfgang Niess, eds., *Der Widerstand im deutschen Südwesten, 1933–1945,* Kohlhammer, Stuttgart, 1985.

Heidekind, Jürgen, and Mauch, Christof, *Das Hermann-Dossier,* Vierteljahreshefte für Zeitgeschichte, 1992, vol. 4, pp. 567–623.

Hillgruber, Andreas, *Die Endlösung und das deutsche Ostimperium als Kernstück des rassenideologischen Programms des Nationalsozialismus,* in Vierteljahreshefte für Zeitgeschichte, 1972, vol. 2, pp. 133–53.

Hurewitz, Ariel, *Shlichuto shel Menachem Bader umaga'ei Hashomer Hatzair im Yahadut Eiropa hakvushah,* in Yalkut Moreshet no. 35, 1983, pp. 176–92.

Jong, Louis de, *Hat Felix Kersten das niederländische Volk gerettet?* in Hans-Heinrich Wilhelm and Louis de Jong, eds., *Zwei Legenden aus dem Dritten Reich,* Schriftenreihe der Vierteljahreshefte für Zeitgeschichte, no. 28, DVA, Stuttgart, 1974.

Kárný, Miroslav, *Svědectví z Osvětími,* in Tvorba, 1989, vol. 14.

Kleist, Peter, *Die europäische Tragödie,* Schütz, Göttingen, 1961.

Krakowski, Shmuel, *The Death Marches During the Evacuation of the Camps,* in Michael Marrus, ed., *The Nazi Holocaust,* Meckler, Westport, 1989, vol. 9, pp. 476–90.

Major, Robert, *The Holocaust in Hungary,* in Jewish Currents, vol. 12, December 1965.

Marcus, Ernst, *The German Foreign Office and the Palestine Question in the Period 1933–1939,* in Yad Vashem Studies, no. 2, 1958, pp. 179–204.

Mommsen, Hans, *Die Realisierung des Utopischen: Die "Endlösung der Judenfrage" im Dritten Reich,* in Geschichte und Gesellschaft, 1983, vol. 9, 3:381–420.

Nir, Akiva, *Vaadat Hahatzalah beKushta: Hakesher im Slovakia,* Seminar Paper, Institute of Contemporary Jewry, Hebrew University, 1989.

Rose, Paul L., *Joel Brand's "Interim Agreement" and the Course of Nazi-Jewish Negotiations, 1944–1945*, in Historical Journal (U.K.), 1991, vol. 34, 4:909–29.

Rozett, Robert, *The Protected Children's Houses: Rescue in Budapest, 1944–1945*, Paper, Institute of Contemporary Jewry, Hebrew University, 1981.

————, *Jewish and Hungarian Resistance in Hungary*, in Yad Vashem Studies, no. 19, 1989, pp. 269–81.

Truempy, Carl, *Rettungsversuche*, in Sie und Er, Zurich, September–November 1961.

Vago, Bela, *Intelligence Aspects of the Joel Brand Mission*, in Yad Vashem Studies, no. 10, 1974, pp. 111–28.

Yahil, Leni, *Madagascar: Phantom of a Solution to the "Jewish Question,"* in Bela Vago and George L. Mosse, eds., *Jews and Non-Jews in Eastern Europe, 1918–1945*, Wiley and Sons, New York, 1974.

Index

Abwehr: Budapest Ast, 129–30, 133, 153; contacts with Jews, 125–26, 162–66; Hitler assassination plot, 107–12; Istanbul Ast, 132–33; and Nazi policies toward Jews, 254; Vienna Ast, 129

Agami, Moshe, 46

Aharonson, Shlomo, 257

Aid and Rescue Committee, Budapest, 152–53, 158, 160–62

Aid Organization for Jewish Refugees Abroad (HIJEF), Zurich, 222–23

Aldrich, Harry S., 142

Aliyah Beth. *See* Immigration to Palestine, illegal

Allgemeine Treuhandstelle für Auswanderung (Altreu), 24

Allied powers: death marches and, 241; Istanbul mission and, 173–77, 183–84, 185–90, 191–93; Jewish persecution and, 60–61, 256–58; knowledge about Auschwitz, 187; Nazi contacts with, 104–7, 109, 166–71; peace negotiations with Hungary, 134–40

Alpan, Moshe, 237

American Jewish Congress: and economic boycott of Germany, 11

American Jewish Joint Distribution Committee (JDC): and illegal immigration to Palestine, 50–51; income figures, 40; and Jewish emigration from Nazi Germany, 39–41; Slovak Jews and, 76, 88, 90

Arlosoroff, Haim, 10

Arndt, Walter, 122, 129

Arnold, Friedrich W., 109

Aronson, Shlomo, 82

Auschwitz concentration and death camp, 66, 67; Allied powers' knowledge about, 187; bombing of railways leading to, 182, 187; deportations, 114, 156; dismantling of gas chambers, Himmler's order for, 229; Eichmann's offer to liberate Jews from, 164–65; evacuation of inmates, 241

Austria, resistance groups in, 127–28

Averbuch, Moshe. *See* Agami, Moshe

Avigur, Shaul, 45, 180

Avriel, Ehud, 46, 51–52, 129, 130, 174–75

Bader, Menachem: and Europa Plan, 84, 85, 89, 90; and Istanbul mission, 173–76, 190–91

Baerwald, Paul, 40, 41

Bagyoni, Ferenc, 135, 137, 139–40, 190

Baky, Laszlo, 154

Balko, Jan, 67

Banyai, Mihaly, 223

Bardossy, Laszlo, 148

Barlas, Chaim, 84, 172, 173, 174

Becher, Kurt A.: as commissioner of concentration camps, 249–50; as evacuation chief in Hungary, 239–40; and Himmler, 209–12, 250; intervention on behalf of Budapest Jews, 236–37; and Kasztner, 216–18; as member of Kommandostab Reichsführer SS, 208–9; and Nazi negotiations in Switzerland, 220–21, 224, 226, 227–31; and negotiations with Hungarian Jews, 164, 165, 167, 198–99; personal life, 207; in Poland, 207; postwar career, 212; professional training, 206–7; and SS control of Weiss industrial concern, 201–4

Beckerle, Josef, 137, 138, 139, 141
Ben Gurion, David: on illegal immigration
    to Palestine, 45; and rescue of European
    Jews, 82–85, 89, 173–74, 179–80,
    183–84, 190, 191, 194–95
Benshalom, Raffi, 232, 237
Bergen-Belsen concentration camp, 104,
    199, 247
Berger, Gottlob, 228
Bergson group, 184
Bernadotte, Folke, 242–44, 246, 248
Betar movement, 44
Billitz, Wilhelm, 203, 204, 205
Bismarck, Gottfried von, 111
Biss, Andreas, 198, 205, 206, 218, 224, 236
Blum, Josef, 70, 72
Boening, Werner G., 245
Bonhoeffer, Dietrich, 108, 109, 126
Born, Friedrich, 236, 237
Boycott: economic boycott of Germany,
    11–16, 18, 19; Jewish businesses in
    Germany, 11–12
Brand, Hansi (Hartmann), 152, 197, 198
Brand, Joel, 130, 152; and Hungarian Aid
    and Rescue Committee, 152–53, 154,
    159; and Istanbul mission, 162–78,
    180–81, 183, 194
Breitmann, Richard, 59
Britain: Guiana project, 41; Istanbul mission
    and, 173–77, 178–81; policy on immi-
    gration to Palestine, 40–41; policy on
    settlement projects, 41; White Paper on
    Palestine, 40, 84. See also Allied powers;
    Secret Intelligence Service, British
Buchenwald concentration camp, 247, 249
Budapest: Abwehrstelle in, 129–30, 133,
    153; Aid and Rescue Committee,
    152–53, 158, 160–62; children's homes
    in, 235–36; foreign protection of Jews,
    232; Judenrat, 155, 156–57
Bulgaria, 185, 186
Burckhardt, Carl J., 83, 249
Burzio, Giuseppe, 67, 68, 69, 86, 97

Canaris, Wilhelm, 107–9, 132, 133, 138, 141
Carol II, King of Romania, 47

Ceipek, Ferdinand, 51–52
Central Economic Office (ÚHÚ), Slovakian,
    64, 67
Central Office for Jewish Emigration,
    Berlin, 49
Central Office for Jewish Emigration,
    Vienna, 48
Central Union of German Citizens of the
    Jewish Faith (CV), 7
Chelmno death camp, 66
Children: Bialystok children's transport to
    Theresienstadt, 113–14; children's
    homes in Budapest, 235–36; Feldscher
    proposals for emigration of, 113; negoti-
    ations on rescue of, 99–100
Chorin, Ferenc, 201–4
Churchill, Winston, 136, 182, 187, 192
Ciano, Galeazzo, 72
Clages, Gerhard, 154, 164, 166, 198, 228, 233
Cluj, 159–60, 197–98, 199–200
Cohen, Sam, 9–10, 15
Coleman, Archibald, 122, 138, 142
Concentration camps: Himmler on,
    247; during last weeks of World
    War II, 249–50. See also under specific
    names
Confessing Church, 6
Confino, Baruch, 47
Conway, John S., 70–71, 73
Counterintelligence Corps of U.S. Army
    (CIC), 239–40
Csatay, Lajos, 135
Currency payments to emigrants, 16
Currency reserves, in Germany, 13–16

Dachau concentration camp, 250
Danielsson, Carl I., 232
Danube River, 48
David, Leo, 15
Death marches, 241
Deportations: Europa Plan and, 79–90; to
    France, 58; from Greece, 87; from
    Hungary, 148–49, 155–58, 181–83,
    212–15, 227; Madagascar solution,
    57–58; to Poland, 53, 57, 70–90;
    reasons for cessation, 96–101; from

Slovakia, 65–73; Vatican and, 68–69, 72, 85, 86
Depositenkasse affair, 107–8, 126
Deutsche Christen, 6
Deutsche Donau-Schiffahrtgesellschaft (DDSG), 48
Deutscher Freiheitsbund (DFB), 125
Ditleff, Niels C., 243
Dobkin, Eliyahu, 191
Dogwood. *See* Schwartz, Alfred
Döhle, Walter, 24
Dohnanyi, Hans von, 108, 109, 126
Dominican Republic, 31
Donovan, William Joseph ("Wild Bill"), 112, 120, 124, 125
Duke, Florimond, 140
Dulles, Allen W., 106, 111, 121, 128, 132

Earle, George, 131
Edelstein, Jacob, 74
Eden, Anthony, 185–88
Eggen, Hans W., 105–6
Ehrenpreis, Rabbi Marcus, 245
Eichmann, Adolf, 26; deportation policies, 66, 69, 92–93, 100, 149, 212–14, 233; Feldscher proposals and, 113; and Himmler, 237; and illegal immigration to Palestine, 47–54, 88; and negotiations with Hungarian Jews, 163–70, 196, 197, 198; offer to liberate Jews from Auschwitz, 164–65
Elias, Joszef, 157
Elon, Amos, 176
Emenegger, Kurt, 205, 209–11
Emerson, Herbert, 34
Emigration of Jews: from Germany, 23–24, 25; Hitler's policy on, 26–28; from Hungary, 158. *See also* Transfer of property
Emniyet, Turkey, 121
Endre, Laszlo, 154
Europa Plan to stop deportations to Poland, 79–101
Evian conference, 30–32

Fatran, Gila, 89, 97
Fay-Halasz, Gedeon von, 149

Fegelein, Hermann, 207, 208, 209
Feldscher, Anton, 113
Fellgiebel, Erich, 111, 112
Fiala, Friedrich, 93, 128
"Final Solution": Poznan speech by Himmler and, 115–17; tactical approach to, 59–60
Fischböck, Hans, 33
Fleischmann, Gizi, 70, 71, 74, 78, 79, 81, 87–89, 96, 98, 101
Flesch, Hermann, 47
Fliess, Julius, 109
Flossenbürg concentration camp, 249
Foreign Currency Office, German: and transfer of property, 20, 22
Foreign currency payments to emigrants, 16
Foreign Office. *See* German Foreign Office
France, deportations to, 58
Frank, Hans, 53, 57
Frankel, Eugen, 153
Freudiger, Fülop von, 154–55, 197, 199, 206
Freund, Hans, 133
Friedel, Raffi. *See* Benshalom, Raffi
Friedenthal, Charlotte, 109
Frieder, Rabbi Armin, 74, 79
Fuchs, Abraham, 79
Funk, Ilsebill, 207

Gancwajch, Abraham, 70
Generalgouvernement, in Poland, 55–56
German Foreign Office: Jewish capital transfers and, 9–11, 19; memorandum on Jewish policy, 38–39; views on illegal immigration to Palestine, 49
Germany: boycott of Jewish businesses, 11–12; Central Office for Jewish Emigration, 38; currency reserves, 13–16; economic boycott of, 11–16; economic conditions in *1930*s, 12–16; emigration from, 23–24, 25; foreign currency payments to emigrants, 16; exports in, 12–13; and illegal immigration to Palestine, 47–54; Ministry of Economic Affairs, 10, 19; policies toward Jews, 5–7, 34–37, 252–53;

Germany (*continued*)
  radicalization of Jewish policy, 34–37;
  trust fund for Jewish emigration, 33–34;
  unemployment, 12–13; Zionists in, 7–8
Gibson, Harold, 122, 174
Ginsburg, Pino, 49
Gisevius, Hans-Bernd, 132, 254
Goebbels, Josef, 46
Goerdeler, Carl, 112
Goering, Hermann, 33, 36–37, 38
Goldberger, Leo, 202
Goldfarb, Zvi, 237
Goldman, Nahum, 179–80
Goldstein, Franz, 215–16
Golomb, Eliyahu, 45
Greece, deportations from, 87
Grell, Theodor Horst, 154, 193, 214
Grobba, Fritz, 25
Grosz, Bandi, 130–32, 135, 136, 141; and
  Istanbul mission, 143–44, 153, 164,
  166, 169–73, 175–78, 183, 194
Grünbaum, Yitzhak, 82, 84, 173, 174, 184
Grünwald, Malkiel, 3, 145
Grüson, Max, 223–24
Guisan, Henri, 106
Günter, Christian, 243
Gustav V, King of Sweden, 182, 244, 245

Ha'avarah. *See* Transfer of property
Hadari, Ze'ev, 84, 89, 90, 173
Haganah, and illegal immigration to
  Palestine, 45
Hagen, Herbert, 25–26, 48
Halevy, Benyamin, 145
Hall, George, 187
Haller, Paul, 47
Hamburger, Wilhelm, 133
Hanfstängl, Erna, 111
Hansen, Georg, 112, 133
Harriman, Averell, 189
Hartenstein, Hans, 15–16, 20
Haster, Wilhelm, 223
Hatz de Hatzsegy, Otto, 135–41
Hechalutz, 45
Henderson, Ian L., 188

Hentig, Otto von, 19, 25, 27
Herzl, Theodor, 152
Hess, Rudolf, 23
Heszlenyi, Joszef, 149
Hewitt, Abram Stevens, 104–5
Heydrich, Reinhard, 33, 49, 54, 55–56
Himmler, Heinrich: contact with Allied
  powers, 104–7, 166, 243, 248; and
  deportation of Hungarian Jews, 149,
  200, 212–13, 217–18, 221; and Europa
  Plan negotiations, 100–101; knowledge
  of Abwehr contacts with Jews, 126,
  164–66; knowledge of Hitler's assassination plot, 107–12; and negotiations
  with Hungarian Jews, 164–70, 193–94;
  order for dismantling gas chambers at
  Auschwitz, 229; and Eichmann, 237;
  personality, 102, 117–19; policies
  toward Jews, 57, 83, 92–93, 103–4,
  246–48, 253–55; Poznan speech,
  115–17; and SS control of Weiss industrial concern, 202–4; suicide, 250–51;
  and Swedish intervention with Nazis on
  behalf of Scandinavian detainees in
  Germany, 242–44, 246; and Swiss
  negotiations, 225, 228–31
Hindenburg, Paul von, 5
Hirsch, Aryeh, 159
Hirsch, Otto, 23
Hirschmann, Ira A., 164, 165, 173, 177,
  184–85, 189
Hitler, Adolf: assassination plot, 107–12;
  sees Bolshevism as "International
  Jewish Conspiracy," 58–59; hands-on
  policy on Jews, 37, 204, 213–14; and
  occupation of Hungary, 153–54; plans
  for World War II, 37–38, 42–43; policy
  on emigration to Palestine, 26–28; rise
  to power, 5; speech of January *30, 1939,*
  35–36; and trust fund for Jewish
  emigration, 33–34; views on physical
  destruction of Jews, 57
Hlinka, Andrej, 62–63
Hlinka Guard, 62–63, 69
Hoare, Sir Samuel, 106

Hochberg, Karel, 70, 73–75, 80, 91, 93–94, 96, 108
Hoess, Rudolf, 156, 167, 233
Hohenlohe, Prince Max-Egon von, 111
Hollischer, Franz, 127
Holocaust: denial of, 247–48; information about, in Hungary, 150–51, 157
Höpfner, Alexander von, 49–50
Horthy, Miklos, 135, 140, 141, 147, 153–54, 157, 182, 212, 214, 233
Horthy, Miklos, Jr., 138
Hull, Cordell, 189, 190, 224
Hungary: Abwehrstelle in Budapest, 129–30, 133; antisemitism, 147; border crossing into Romania, 159–60; deportation of Jews, 148–49, 155–58, 181–83, 212–15, 227; emigration of Jews, 158; flight of Slovak Jews to, 73–74; German occupation of, 153–55; knowledge of Holocaust in, 150–51, 157; Jewish community, 146–47; Jewish forced labor at Austrian border, 233–34; Kasztner train, 197–200; Nazi evacuation from, 239–40; negotiations with Nazis, 162–71; Palestinian Jewish parachutists in, 215–16; peace negotiations with Allied powers, 134–40; Polish Jewish refugees in, 150; resistance movement, 160–61; Slovak Jewish refugees in, 150; SS control of Weiss industrial concern, 201–4; Zionist movement in, 151–52, 158–60, 234–35, 237. *See also* Budapest
Hunsche, Otto, 163
Huppenkothen, Walter, 108
Husseini, Hajj Amin al-, 88, 100, 186

Ickrath, Heinz, 107
Immigration to Palestine, illegal, 44–47
Intergovernmental Committee on Refugees (IGCR), 31, 32–33
International Red Cross (IRC), 83, 94, 227, 230, 232, 236, 249, 257
Intria, 17

Irgun Tsvai Leumi, 257–58
Istanbul: Abwehrstelle in, 132–33; British Secret Intelligence Service in, 122; Office of Strategic Services (U.S.) in, 121–44; Palestine Jewish delegation, 81–82, 84–85
Istanbul mission: Allied powers and, 173–77, 183–93; background information, 163–71; Britain and, 173–81; Soviet Union and, 180, 189, 193; United States and, 177–82
Ittleson, Henry, 40

Jabotinsky, Vladimir Ze'ev, 17, 47
Jäger, Maximilian, 231
Jagow, Dietrich von, 149
Jaross, Andor, 154
Jeckeln, Franz, 148
Jewish Agency for Palestine (JA), 7; and rescue of European Jews, 82–85, 88, 90, 173–74, 176, 179–80, 183–84, 190–91; views on illegal immigration to Palestine, 45–46
Jewish Center (ÚŽ), in Slovakia, 64, 70–73
Jewish Councils, in Poland, 56
Jewish Distribution Committee. *See* American Jewish Joint Distribution Committee
Jewish Labor Party (Mapai), 45
Jong, Louis de, 102
Judenrat, Budapest, 155, 156–57
Junger, Ladislav, 67
Jüttner, Hans, 233–34

Kaas, Ludwig, 107
Kadar, Gyula, 137, 138, 139
Kallay, Miklos, 134, 149
Kaltenbrunner, Ernst, 200, 201
Kamenets Podolskiy, 148, 150
Kanal, Yitzhak, 159
Kaplan, Eliezer, 82, 85, 190
Kapp, Nelly, 133
Karski, Jan, 83
Karthaus, Wolfgang, 46

Karváš, Imrich, 86, 97
Kasztner, Israel, 151–52; and Aid and
  Rescue Committee, 158, 160, 183; and
  Kurt Becher, 216–18; Judenrat in
  Budapest and, 155; libel suit in Israel,
  145, 159; and negotiations with Abwehr,
  162–63, 165, 190, 193, 196–201, 205–6,
  212, 215, 224, 226–28; Palestinian
  Jewish parachutists and, 215–16; and
  rescue of Bratislava Jews, 250
Kasztner train, 197–200
Katz, Nathan, 32
Katzki, Herbert, 81
Katznelson, Berl, 45, 46
Keitel, Wilhelm, 108
Kelemen, Ferenc, 201
Keller, Otto, 127
Keresztes-Fischer, Ferenc, 148–49
Kersten, Felix, 102–5, 106, 110, 112, 242,
  243, 245–46, 248
Kertesz, Miklos, 235
Kettlitz, Herbert, 224, 226, 227, 229
Kibbutz Meuchad Federation, 44
Kirk, Alexander C., 123–24
Klatt, Richard [Fritz Kauders], 125,
  131–32
Klaus, Edgar Josef, 125, 143, 245
Klausnitzer, Erich, 129, 162, 166
Kleczkowski, Karl von, 133
Kleist, Peter Bruno, 168, 225, 245
Klinger, Hayka, 160
Knatchbull-Hugessen, Sir Hugh, 134
Kollek, Teddy, 46, 129, 130, 136, 194
Komoly, Otto, 152–53, 155, 162, 163, 198,
  232, 240
Konrad, Franz, 207, 209
Kornfeld, Moricz, 201, 202, 203
Koso, Isidor, 65–66, 75, 97
Kováč, Tibor, 74, 79
Kövess, Lothar, 136–140
Krausz, Moshe, 153, 158, 162, 198, 213,
  231–32
Kreisau Circle, 109
Krell, Erich, 229
Krem, Joszef, 152

Kristallnacht, 35
Krosigk, Lutz Schwerin von, 5
Krumey, Hermann, 163, 190, 250
Kullmann, Gustav, 184
Kun, Bela, 147

Lada-Mocarski, Vala, 138
Lakatos, Geza, 212, 233
Landauer, Georg, 17, 24, 26
Langbehn, Carl, 110
Lange, Rudolf, 47
Langlet, Waldemar, 232, 245
Laufer, Fritz, 128–30, 139–40, 141, 143,
  166, 185, 217
Law, Richard, 187
League of Nations, 31
Leb, Zsigmond, 198
Legradi, Thomas, 127, 128
Leibowitz, Bela, 76, 78
Lenard, Dionys, 71
Leverkühn, Paul, 123, 124, 132, 133, 134
Lichtheim, Richard, 85
Link, Gyula, 197, 205
Lipsky, Luis, 17, 39
Lischka, Kurt, 50
Lublin, deportations to, 57
Ludin, Hans, 67, 68, 96–97
Lutz, Charles, 158, 162, 231, 234, 235,
  237

McClelland, Roswell D., 182, 206, 218,
  221, 225–227, 230
MacDonald, Malcolm, 41
Macfarland, Lanning, 121, 137, 138, 141,
  142, 175
MacMichael, Harold, 174, 175, 177, 183, 184
McVicker, Charles P., Jr., 124
Madagascar solution, 57–58
Maier, Heinrich, 127, 128
Majdanek concentration camp, 69
Malcolm, Neil, 31
Mandler, Robert, 51
Mann, Thomas, 151
Manteuffel, Baron von, 129
Mapai, 45

Maregna-Radwitz, Rudolf von, 129
Masson, Roger, 105–6
Masur, Norbert, 246
Maunsell, R. G., 174, 185
Mauthner, Hans von, 201
Mayer, Arno J., 83
Mayer, Saly, 76–78, 81, 87–89, 164, 193, 206, 218–31
Meir, Joszef, 235
Meirov, Shaul. *See* Avigur, Shaul
Merkly, Anton von, 131
Messner, Franz Josef, 127–28, 140
Ministry of Economic Affairs, German, 10, 19
Moffat, Pierrepont, 40
Moltke, Helmut von, 109, 110, 123–24, 126–27, 254
Monus, Illes, 152
Morávek, Augustín, 64, 65, 91
Morde, Theodore, 125
Morgenthau, Henry, Jr., 186, 257
Morrison, Herbert, 188
Moses, Siegfried, 17
Mossad Le'Aliyah B, 45–54. *See also* Immigration to Palestine, illegal
Moyne, Lord, 183, 185
Moyzisch, Ludwig, 133, 134
Müller, Heinrich, 49, 108
Müller, Josef (Sepp), 107
Musy, Jean-Marie, 225, 230, 243

Naday, Istvan, 134
Nazi Party: Organization Abroad, 25; policies toward Jews, 5–6, 34–37, 252–53; race war against Jews, 83
Neuengamme concentration camp, 244, 246, 249
Neumann, Heinrich, 32
Neumann, Oskar, 70, 73, 74, 79
Neurath, Baron Konstantin von, 5, 19, 25
Nisko, deportations to, 57
Nussbacher, Joel, 215–16

Offenbach, Sandor, 197
Office of Strategic Services (OSS), U.S.,
112, 120; Istanbul branch, 121–44; Sparrow mission to Hungary, 140
Olsen, Iver, 168
Oster, Hans, 108–9

Palestine: exports to, 21–22; illegal immigration to, 44–45; Nazis oppose immigration to, 113; White Paper on, 40, 84. *See also* Transfer of property
Palestine Jewish delegation, in Istanbul, 81–82, 84–85
Palestine Trust Company, 10, 18
Papen, Franz von, 125, 133–34
Pappenheim, Isidor, 64
Pappenheim, Moritz, 51
Pechy, Thomas de, 239
Pehle, John W., 186, 189, 190
Perl, Willi, 46, 47, 51, 53–54
Perlasca, Jorge, 236, 237
Peters, Margot, 207
Petö, Ernö 157
Platen, Hermine von, 207
Poland: deportation of Jews to, 53, 57; establishment of Jewish Councils, 56; Europa Plan to stop deportations to, 79–90; Generalgouvernement, 55–56
Pomeranz, Wenja. *See* Hadari, Ze'ev
Popescu, Eric. *See* Wehner, Erich
Popitz, Johannes, 111
Property, transfer of. *See* Transfer of property
Proskauer, Joseph, 40

Raffay, Sandor, 157
Ravasz, Laszlo, 157
Ravensbrück concentration camp, 246
Red Cross: International Red Cross (IRC), 83, 94, 227, 230, 232, 236, 249, 257; Swedish Red Cross, 232, 242, 243–44, 246, 248
Reichsvereiningung der Juden in Deutschland (RVE), 49–50, 53
Reichsvertretung der Juden in Deutschland (RV), 23
Remenyi-Schneller, Lajos, 157

Rescue Committee of [Orthodox] Rabbis (VH), 223, 225, 227
Resnik, Reuben B., 177
Revesz, Perets, 159
Ribbentrop, Joachim von, 33, 113, 141, 192, 193, 212–13, 222
Richert, Arvid, 243, 245
Ridiger, Franz Josef, 122, 127, 130
Riegner, Gerhart, 79
Roeder, Manfred, 108
Romania, 47, 185, 186; border crossing by Hungarian Jews, 159–60; Transylvanian Jews, 228
Roncalli, Angelo, 85
Roosevelt, Franklin Delano, 30, 39–40, 42, 179, 181, 184, 191
Rose, Paul L., 206
Rosenberg, Alfred, 27
Rosenberg, Walter. See Vrba, Rudolf
Rosenman, Samuel I., 40
Rothmund, Heinrich, 219–20
Rotta, Angelo, 157, 181–82, 237
Rubinfeld, Leo, 223
Rublee, George, 31, 32–34, 37–39
Rustow, Alexander, 122, 123, 125

Salonika, deportations from, 87
Sauckel, Fritz, 155
Schacht, Hjalmar, 13–14, 20, 32–34, 37–39
Schellenberg, Walter, 104–7, 110–12, 231, 245, 254
Schind, Ze'ev, 89
Schmidhuber, Wilhelm, 107
Schmidt, Josef, 163
Schmidt, Kurt, 18
Scholz, Rudi, 129, 154
Schwalb, Nathan, 76, 77, 80, 81, 85
Schwartz, Alfred, 121–31, 134–44, 175
Schwartz, Joseph J., 76, 81, 183, 190, 218, 229–30
Schwarz, Heinrich, 64, 70
Schweiger, Moshe, 160, 161, 239, 250
Schweizerischer Israelitischer Gemeindebund (SIG), 76
Sebestyen, Arpad, 70, 73

Secret Intelligence Middle East (SIME), 177
Secret Intelligence Service, British (SIS, MI6): Istanbul branch, 122, 129, 173; Palestinian Jewish parachutists and, 215–16; Secret Intelligence Middle East, 177
Senator, Werner, 18, 26
Seredi, Justinian, 157, 182
Seyss-Inquart, Artur, 32
Sharett, Moshe, 45, 82, 218; and Istanbul mission, 173–75, 177, 180–81, 183–84, 187–88, 191
Shertok, Moshe. See Sharett, Moshe
Silberschein, Alfred, 81, 84
Silver, Rabbi Abba Hillel, 46
Simmonds, Anthony, 190
Sivak, Jozef, 86, 97
Slovakia: Central Economic Office, 64; deportations from, 65–73; flight of Slovak Jews to Hungary, 73–74; history of, 62–63; Hlinka Guard, 62–63, 69; Jewish Center, 64, 70–73; Jewish community, 63–64; statehood, 63; Working Group, 74–75, 79–101; Židovská Ústredná Úradovna, 64
Slovak People's Party, 62–63
Smend, Maria, 207
Smuts, Jan, 123
Sofia, 131–32
Sokal, Helene, 127, 128
Sonderegger, Franz Xavier, 108
Soos, Geza, 157
Soviet Union: and defeat of Nazi Germany, 255–56; German decision to attack, 58–59; Istanbul mission and, 180, 189, 193
Sparrow mission to Hungary, 140
Springmann, Samuel, 152–53, 197
Squire, Leslie A., 177–78
Squire, Paul C., 83
SS: control of Weiss industrial concern, 201–4; and illegal immigration to Palestine, 47–54; Security Service (SD), 133, 141. See also Eichmann, Adolf; Himmler, Heinrich

Steed, Wickham, 192
Steiger, Alois, 236–37
Steiger, Eduard von, 229
Steiner, Andrej E., 71, 74, 77–80, 91,
    94–95, 98, 99–100
Steiner, Ervin, 71
Steinhardt, Laurence A., 124, 173, 174, 189
Stern, Samu, 148, 155
Stern, Solomon, 75
Sternbuch, Elias, 222
Sternbuch, Isaac, 206, 222–23, 225, 227,
    230–31
Sternbuch, Rachel, 222
Stettinius, Edward R., Jr., 179
Storch, Hillel, 245–46
Storfer, Berthold, 50–51, 52–53
Strauss, Lewis L., 40
Stroock, Sol, 40
Stuckart, Wilhelm, 25
Sweden: and rescue of Jews, 244–48;
    Scandinavian detainees in Germany,
    241–43
Swedish Red Cross, 232, 242–44, 246,
    248
Switzerland: Aid Organization for Jewish
    Refugees Abroad, 222–23; monetary
    help to Slovak Jews, 76–81; Nazi
    contacts with, 105–6, 218–21, 222–31;
    Schweizerischer Israelitischer
    Gemeindebund, 76, 219
Szalasi, Ferenc, 148, 227, 233
Szekely, Maria, 157
Szenes, Hanna, 215–16
Szent-Györgyi, Albert, 134
Szilagyi, Ernst, 153, 162, 198
Szilvay, Gyula von, 239
Szlachta, Margit, 150
Szombathelyi, Ferenc, 135, 137
Sztojay, Döme, 154, 204, 212

Tabenkin, Yitzhak, 44
Tamir, Shmuel, 3, 145
Taylor, Myron C., 30, 32, 40
Teichmann, Efra, 232, 236, 237
Teitelbaum, Rabbi Joel, 199, 223

Tennenbaum, Joseph, 41
Theresienstadt: Bialystok children's trans-
    port to, 113–14; deportations to
    Auschwitz, 114; transport of Jews to
    Switzerland, 230
Thiele, Fritz, 111, 112
Thompson, Dorothy, 123
Tindall, Richard G., 124
Tiso, Jozef, 63, 67–68, 69
Toulmin, John E., 121, 129
Transfer of property: anti-German
    boycott and, 19; capital transfers, 9–11,
    23–24; foreign currency payments to
    emigrants, 16; German attitudes
    toward, 27–29; and German Foreign
    Currency Office, 20, 22; and German
    Foreign Office, 9–11; losses on, 20–21;
    Nazi motives in agreeing to, 18–22;
    Nazi Party Organization Abroad and,
    25; opposition to, 25–26; proponents'
    arguments for, 17–18
Transylvanian Jews, 228
Trott zu Solz, Adam von, 254
Truempy, Carl, 223, 229
Trujillo, Rafael J., 31
Tuka, Vojtěch, 63, 65, 67–68, 86, 92,
    96–97
Tutvölgyi, Albert, 239

Überall, Ehud. See Avriel, Ehud
Ujszaszy, Istvan, 135, 140
Unemployment, in Germany, 12–13
Ungar, Lilly, 216
Ungar, Rabbi Shmuel David Halevi, 64
Union of Swiss Jewish Communities
    (SIG), 219
United States: Counterintelligence Corps
    of U.S. Army, 239–40; Istanbul mission
    and, 177–82; as organizers of Evian
    conference, 30–31; Rescue Committee
    of [Orthodox] Rabbis, 223, 225, 227; and
    Swiss negotiations with Nazis, 226–27;
    War Refugee Board, 157, 163, 168, 178,
    182, 184–86, 230. See also Allied powers;
    Office of Strategic Services, U.S.

Untermeyer, Louis, 11
U7 (Unternehmen 7, or V7) project,
    109–10
Ústredna Židov. *See* Jewish Center, in
    Slovakia
Uzgorod, 159

Vaada. *See* Aid and Rescue Committee,
    Budapest
Vali, Ferenc, 134
Varga, Imre, 161
Varga-Karady, Katalina, 137
Vašek, Anton, 75, 97
Vatican: deportations from Hungary and,
    181–82; deportations from Slovakia
    and, 68–69, 72, 85, 86
Veesenmayer, Edmund, 154, 164, 165, 167,
    182, 192–93, 213–14, 221, 222
Veress, Laszlo, 134
Vermehren, Erich, 132–33
Vermehren-Plattenberg, Mrs., 132–33
Vienna: Abwehrstelle, 129; Central Office
    for Jewish Emigration, 48
Vojtaššák, Jan, 67
Vrba, Rudolf, 70, 72, 156–57
Vyshinski, Andrei, 180

Wagner, Otto, 137, 138, 139, 140
Walker, Archibald, 136, 141–42
Wallenberg, Jakob, 112, 243
Wallenberg, Raoul, 214, 232, 234, 237, 245
Wannsee conference, 66
Warburg, Felix, 23, 24
Warburg, Max, 23–24
War Refugee Board (WRB), 157, 163, 168,
    178, 182, 184–86, 220, 230
Wehner, Erich, 130, 131, 165
Weil, Shraga, 234
Weinberger, Rabbi Moshe, 159–60,
    199–200
Weiss, Dov, 237
Weiss, Edith, 154–55
Weiss, Manfred, 201
Weissmandel, Rabbi Michael Dov Ber, 64,

70, 250; on bombing of railways to
    concentration camps, 182; on cessation
    of deportations from Slovakia, 98–99;
    on negotiations in Slovakia, 62, 74–75,
    77–81, 84, 86, 89; view on Dieter
    Wisliceny, 100–101
Weizmann, Chaim, 17, 45, 82, 179, 187
Weizsäcker, Ernst von, 25, 33
Welles, Sumner, 40
Wetzler, Alfred, 70, 156–57
Whittall, Arthur, 174
Wilbrandt, Hans, 122, 123
Williams, Lansing, 122, 129
Winkelmann, Otto, 154, 164, 165
Winninger, Josi, 130, 131, 153, 154, 165
Wise, Rabbi Stephen S., 11, 17, 39, 41
Wisliceny, Dieter, 62, 65; and deportation
    of Hungarian Jews, 149, 154–55, 197;
    and deportations from Salonika, 87;
    Europa Plan negotiations, 99–100;
    negotiations in Slovakia, 65–67, 76, 78,
    79–81, 87–101
Wisner, Frank G., 142, 143
Wohlthat, Helmut, 22–23, 34
Wolff, Heinrich, 9–10, 17
Working Group, Slovakia, 74–75, 79–101
World Zionist movement, 7
Wulff, Wilhelm, 106
Wurst, Timotheus, 24–25
Wyler-Schmidt, Marcus, 224, 226

Zaslani, Reuven, 185
Zaugg, Ernest, 210
Židovská Ústredná Úradovna pre krajinu
    Slovenska (ŽÚÚ), 64
Zierer, Alfred, 125
Zimmels, Max, 49
Zionist movement: German Zionists, 7–8;
    Haganah, 45; in Hungary, 151–52; poli-
    cies in *1933,* 8–9; revisionist movement,
    45–54; view on illegal immigration to
    Palestine, 44–45; World Zionist move-
    ment, 7; youth movements in Hungary,
    158–61, 234–35, 237